# FAMILY IN TRANSITION

# FAMILY
# IN TRANSITION

## A Study of
## 300 Yugoslav Villages

VERA St. ERLICH

PRINCETON UNIVERSITY PRESS

PRINCETON, NEW JERSEY

1966

Previously published as
*Porodica u Transformaciji*
by Naprijed, Zagreb, Yugoslavia,
1964

Printed in the United States of America
by Princeton University Press, Princeton, New Jersey

# PREFACE

░░░░░░░░░░░░░░░░░░░░░░░░░░░░░░░░░░░░░░░░░░░░░░░░░░░░░░░░░░

## Story of a Survey

░░░░░░░░░░░░░░░░░░░░░░░░░░░░░░░░░░░░░░░░░░░░░░░░░░░░░░░░░░

IT BEGAN in Zagreb in 1937, when a group of student friends suggested that I write for the Yugoslav press a series of articles on the position of Moslem women. The students were bitter about the "enslavement" of their sisters who had been married in traditional manner. I was not very enthusiastic about attacking the women's veil or the lattice window, but I was willing to study and report on Bosnian family life. It was the end of the spring-summer term, and we drew up a questionnaire which the students took home with them during their summer vacation. It was to be a small research effort into the domestic way of life of the Bosnian Moslem.

During this same summer I gave a series of lectures on psychology in a teacher seminar. Teachers had come from all parts of Yugoslavia to a mountain resort. When they heard of my plan to study the Bosnian family, they at once wanted to know: Why only the Bosnian Moslems? In their own Serbia, Montenegro, Macedonia, there still existed bride purchase, bride abduction. . . . "Come along to our parts too, and make an inquiry," they said, "we will help you." Alas, I told them, I had no funds for such an undertaking! But they insisted that all I needed to supply was paper and postage stamps; they would provide the rest. "We will prepare for you a list of a thousand teachers, the outstanding ones from all provinces, and country doctors too. Come on, make your inquiry!"

During the summer school I discussed the problems of their home districts with these teachers, and we tried out various questionnaires till I had worked out a satisfactory form. They, for their part, obtained membership lists from their official organizations, and from these they selected the most suitable village teachers in every part of the country. In Yugoslavia, most teachers are men, thus the majority of those I polled were men. I sent out one thousand questionnaires, each containing a hundred and thirty questions on fourteen pages. To each set I attached three blank sheets.

When the reports began to come in, I realized the enthusiasm with which the work had been taken up. I received back a third of my questionnaires, and of these 305 were usable, most of them painstakingly filled in. One could not help but feel that these teachers

v

228137

eagerly welcomed the initiative for such an undertaking. They had assembled information tirelessly, made trips into the surrounding countryside, reported at length on particular questions, described typical peasants of their areas, and pointed out peculiarities of their districts.

The actual replies to my questions were only part of the material I received from my interviewers. One youth wrote from a remote mountain village: "Are you mad? Why not put in at least ten more sheets?" Clearly, there was not a scrap of paper to be had in his back-of-beyond place, yet he was full of impatience to tell me all about what he considered fascinating conditions. Indeed, most of my young helpers were equally enthusiastic.

Many of these students and teachers—there were doctors and priests among them—lived in remote villages where they were the only educated persons. They felt that they were storing up treasures before it was too late. They were anxious to record their knowledge of old ideas and traditional attitudes before they all were lost. Already Nazis were on the march. How long would it be before Yugoslavia was attacked—and then who could tell who or what would survive? The shadows cast by the war were dark indeed.

Together with many answers came invitations to visit their localities. "I will be your guide through the Shumadia, the heart of Serbia; nobody knows every house as I do. My father still lives here, and he fought against the Turks." "Come to Herzegovina to see me," wrote another, "I am a doctor in the most out-of-the-way Moslem settlements. This is where you can see archaic family life!" "Come to me," ran another letter, "I am a magistrate near Sarajevo, I can show you every village in these parts and also gypsy settlements." And so on. The University of Belgrade sent for me, and I had to accompany their ethnologists and sociologists on their expeditions. This resulted in an engagement for a series of lectures at Belgrade University, where I reported the preliminary results of my inquiry.

All this time, the menace of German invasion hung over us. There is a fairy tale by the Grimm brothers in which a princess is making shirts for her brothers, who have all been turned into swans by a witch. The shirts must be ready on a certain day, and when they are put on the swans, these will turn back into men. The princess stitches day and night, to get her shirts finished, but she cannot complete the last sleeve. When the swans fly past and she throws the shirts over them, they all turn into complete men except the youngest, who retains a wing in place of one of his arms. During two drawn-out years I had the increasing feeling that I had to hurry, to get my shirts ready, or I might not succeed at all, and my swans would stay bewitched and fly away from me. I feared that I would never be able to digest all the mass of material; yet I had to extract its essence. Quicker, ever quicker! I worked at breathless speed!

I felt I was trying to race an oncoming flood. The Nazis marched into Vienna. They marched into Prague. There were already Nazi units on the Yugoslav frontier. The pressure was rising. Police and government were riddled with fifth columnists. Whoever was not in the service of Germany had become suspect. I was among the many to have my premises searched by the police. My enormous mail-bag had aroused suspicion. Who knew what lay behind it? But we still had "connections," and they succeeded in preventing my arrest and ensuring that my research material was not touched.

But my tension grew with the mountain of questionnaires and reports that accumulated in my home. I tried to devise a statistical method for handling the data, but that was possible only so long as I had my questionnaires with me, and I was afraid that this would not be long. My tension was increased by the excited letters my interviewers sent me daily. Their feverish mood came from a keen awareness that they too had a short time remaining to collect data on the old ways of life. Their excitement was heightened by the great impoverishment of the countryside and the terrible living conditions of the women.

The economic depression which hit Yugoslavia in 1930 was still pressing hard on Yugoslav country folk in 1937. As Nazi pressure increased, political factors deteriorated more and more. Many of my teachers expected and suggested steps I might take to help "the countryside." The excitement of the teachers made it increasingly hard for me to remain objective. The partisan tone of their descriptions, which began to assume almost a fictional coloring, constituted a genuine obstacle to my work. To master the excess of material and the emotional nature of the reports I had to find some sort of key to bring them all down to an objective common denominator. Months went by while I worked this out, then assembled and analyzed my matter, drew graphs, and calculated percentages.

Then came April 1941, and the Nazis invaded Yugoslavia. The German invasion, complete with Gestapo, ended everything. Desperately I was working on my last sleeve. I now concealed the questionnaires in the house of a neighbor, but I did not let out of my sight the extracts I had made. I continued to work on my tables of statistical results, always keeping handy the colored pencils for my graphs. But at last the Gestapo caught up with me. Two of their men came "to call." It was night, and I was alone in the large house. The rest of the family was no longer there. But I found myself absolutely calm, and I actually succeeded in persuading these agents that what I was handling were statistics on venereal diseases, a piece of work for the Institute of Hygiene, which "everybody" knew about. Wonder of wonders, they swallowed this and left me, saying they would "call again." Another chance to finish the last sleeve.

But after that visit I had to move. I left our home, my beloved native city, Zagreb, and my native land. A paid adventurer smuggled me through the enemy lines to Dalmatia, then occupied by Italians. My guide got me through. Few succeeded, but I was one of the lucky ones.

At that time Germans were not in control of the Adriatic coast. Before I left, I had packed my material and most important notes in a large suitcase which I handed over to some Croatian naval officers. My native Croatia was now a German vassal state, and Yugoslav naval officers of Croatian origin were—at least in name—German "allies." Among them were some old friends whom I trusted to keep my suitcase for me. Some weeks later, it was again in my possession. The officers had taken it across a frontier guarded by German, Croatian, and Italian troops. The naval boys brought it to me at Split, the capital of Dalmatia. With broad grins they saluted and were gone!

In the "Fortress of Europe," there was the silence of the grave. Only in this small region under Italian command could one breathe—cautiously. Dalmatia, with its cities and former republics for centuries connected with the Republic of Venice, has a character of its own. Here, in the attics of the patrician houses, I discovered old books and papers; so during this forced stay I set about collecting further material. I also filled pages of my notebooks in the markets and the fishermen's harbor.

In the autumn of 1943, Mussolini's empire collapsed, after the Allies had invaded southern Italy. The Italian occupation forces in the Balkans disintegrated. Now the Nazis occupied northern Italy and the whole of the Balkan peninsula. When they came up against Split, the Partisans at first tried to defend the city. There followed three weeks of Stuka bombardment. When at last the Germans came in, a third of the population left the city to avoid them, and withdrew into the rocky mountains of the *Karst* and on the islands, farther south.

In the battle, our house had been hit and burned to the ground. Also destroyed was the place where I had intended to hide my valise. But in good time I had taken to the streets of Split, dragging my famous suitcase with me, looking for shelter. No sooner had I found one than here too German troops marched in. Trapped again, I did not leave this shelter for a month; but when I did venture out of the house a miracle happened: I ran smack into the very man who, two years earlier, had smuggled me from Zagreb to Split. Once again he had planned an escape route and, together with his bride, he helped me to get out of the town. It was she who carried my valise through the German lines. All I carried was a string bag with bottles of milk. This girl, however, seemed on excellent terms with all soldiery, and thus I reached the guerilla territory in the woods outside Split.

There followed months of wandering through the wild mountains, with the Germans driving us—fighting Partisans and refugees— farther and farther south. Some of us escaped in small boats through waters infested with swift German patrol boats. I held on to my suitcase. In moments of acute danger, I held it overboard, ready to drop it into the water.

Thus, at Christmas 1943, I reached the island of Vis, a Yugoslav island near the coast of southern Italy. The Germans frequently bombed this outpost, but it remained the one Dalmatian island which they never captured. Vis became the headquarters of the Partisans, and Churchill sent a military mission to this island. All civilians were now evacuated, and only fighting personnel were allowed to remain. A small vessel built to take 300 carried 1,500 civilians to the liberated part of southern Italy. But nobody was allowed to take any luggage, and there could be no thought of taking the heavy suitcase full of documents. I concealed my treasure in a wine-cellar, in the care of a woman friend who was to stay behind.

We crossed the remaining part of the Adriatic. During our two-day voyage, Stukas bombarded us, but, though boats in front and behind us were sunk, we got through! Southern Italy had been liberated. One could breathe again. Yes, but what about my research material back in that cellar on Vis? What if the Yugoslav headquarters were transferred to southern Italy and the island left to the Germans? That had been the fate of all other islands. Or what if somebody stumbled on my suitcase? We were at a critical point of the war. Nobody was likely to believe that all this was only scientific notes about the domestic way of life of peasant folk. A thousand sheets of text complete with maps and tables or figures? It would certainly provoke suspicion! I mentioned the matter to Partisans and British officers, going back to Vis, but they would not think of taking even a letter either way—they were not going to risk a firing squad! Partisan courts were not given to dilly-dallying. Nobody would waste time investigating the truth of such a fantastic story.

Then came the first UNRRA mission, flown in from Cairo. Among the UNRRA people was a marvelous Canadian girl, a social welfare worker who knew little of war or spy mania and seemed never to have heard of such things as courts martial. She listened to my tale of woe and promised to bring me back my suitcase. She was going across to Vis anyway, she said. For her it was as simple as that! And so it was. Three weeks later, there among her smart luggage, was my battered suitcase, and not one scrap of my precious papers missing, either. When I flung my arms round her neck, she was actually surprised. What was there so wonderful about bringing someone her suitcase?

For a year, Bari, where I was staying, served as a base from which a break-through northward was prepared, and the Germans took care to bombard us. All day long there were crowds of soldiers and civilians staring at the beflagged maps in the window of the British Information Office. Those little flags never seemed to move. In North Africa the Germans were falling back as they did in the East. But nothing changed on the Italian front. Meanwhile, however, I was able to go on completing my material. For south Italy was full of Yugoslav peasants—fighters and refugees. Cross-examining them was a sort of check on my earlier researches. Were these folk going to behave abroad, in wartime, as my studies showed? Would they remain true to the styles I had found when they were still welded in the framework of the family?

The war was still not over when a doctor friend of mine drove through Yugoslavia from Split to Belgrade. When he came back his words were: "The whole way through I did not see a single house in a single village with its roof on." Only when I heard that did I realize what it was that I had brought out of the war. It was the last picture of a foundering ship; the last record of the patriarchal social system which was about to crumble. After four years of enemy occupation and resistance warfare, there could now be left only fragmentary traces of the patriarchal life.

I now realized that the tense excitement I had shared with my team in those days on the eve of war had been a foreboding of what was fated to happen. However we succeeded in saving a great part of our material, and, through a series of miracles, I had been able to take it with me. But most of those who had provided me with my answers had given their lives in resistance fighting. To all those dear friends who thus in the eleventh hour helped me to prepare these records of the age in which we had lived, an age fated to vanish—to them, to those who perished and those who survived, I dedicate this book.

# ACKNOWLEDGMENTS

Many persons from two continents were in some way responsible for my undertaking and completing this study.

The first stimulation came from three Bosnian students: Muralem Ljubović, Sulejman Azabagić, and Muhamed Dusinović (now all professional men in Bosnia) with their passionate request that I begin the struggle for the emancipation of the Moslem women. Soon teachers from various regions joined them and persuaded me to embrace the whole country in my investigation. They became my indefatigable investigators. The teachers were organized by Dragutin Franković and the late Franjo Marinić. A young student, Maya Schwarz, accompanied me during my field work as devoted friend and assistant (she is now a noted architect, Mrs. Henry Gottlieb, in Denver, Colorado).

From the beginning, I received strong support from Dr. Rudolf Bićanić, then connected with the Peasant Party, now Professor of Zagreb University. He offered me data, figures, and maps, and his own ample experience. His revealing interpretation, full of humor, of my first statistical tables induced me to carry on with statistical work. Professor Bogdan Teodorović offered me in a most helpful way much material on health statistics.

The Law Faculty of Belgrade University gave me further support. Their Dean, the late Professor Gjorgje Tasić (killed by the occupation forces), invited me to Belgrade to present the first reports of my survey at the University. Assistant Svetislav Božović-Čabo organized excursions into the Serbian countryside, and he has been an ardent supporter of my survey ever since. The young Professor Jovan Gjorgević was also very helpful, as were three other prominent professors, from each of whom I learned a great deal: Professor Slobodan Jovanović, Serbian history; Professor Dragoljub Jovanović, rural sociology and a thorough knowledge of all aspects of Serbian peasant life; Professor Sreten Vukosavljević, ethnology. When Sreten spoke to the peasants on our excursions, he was for me the living example of patriarchal authority with the democratic element in it.

In the Shumadia area of Serbia, Mrs. Bulka Josifović was my leader, in Herzegovina, Dr. Lovro Dojmi di Delupis of Mostar. Dr. Isak Samokovlija in Sarajevo opened my eyes to the nervous disposition of the Bosnian peasant; Dr. Mićo Branisavljević of Jajce told me about the problems of maternity; Judge Samuel Kamhi discussed with me the law problems, and he also let me hear the beautiful folk songs of Bosnia. In the mountains around Sarajevo, Ilija Grbić (killed in the resistance fighting) and his wife Vukica, both young teachers in the village of Romania Mountain, were my hosts. All the warmth and affection of Bosnians were mirrored in the peasants' eyes when I came with their beloved teachers to visit their homes.

In the dark days of refugee life in Dalmatia, my friend Dr. Filip Reiner encouraged me to carry on with my work until the day he was captured.

I was introduced to statistical work by Professor Maria Jahoda of Vienna, today in London, formerly Director of the Institute for Human Relations at the New York University and author of a well known textbook on social research. A few days before the "Anschluss" in 1938, and her own emigration, she gave me precious advice and recommended a statistician to work with me. Later on, in the United States, Professor Jahoda offered me help and constructive criticism. The friend she sent to me was Dr. Theo Neumann of Vienna, who came to Zagreb to work with me on the survey material for many months. His zeal and devotion for this work helped me to overcome my fatigue from endless counting without machine. Without Dr. Neumann, I would not have been able to complete the tables in the shadow of the threatening German attack, and I could never make this up since the original questionnaires were lost during the German occupation.

I had no opportunity to thank the two young Naval officers who risked carrying my material through guarded frontiers. Only recently did I discover their names: Jan Žižkov and Velimir Škorpik; but I could not find them. I have been able, however, to thank Mr. Mate Crnić and Mara Crnić, who had hidden part of my material for years and kept it under the most difficult circumstances. My gratitude extends also to Mr. Josef Fischer, who performed what was almost a miracle in saving my material in a dangerous moment. Thanks to Dr. Iruda Borković and Mrs. Vera Miše-Gavella for keeping my material in the darkest war days.

When I came back to Yugoslavia after nearly twenty years, I found a great interest in and assistance with the rescued material. Dr. Ljuba Vuković of Belgrade watched in a most devoted way over the manuscript. Dr. Milenko S. Filipović, professor of ethnology at Sarajevo and Belgrade, gave me the most cordial advice, offered his constructive criticism, and recommended the study for publication. Professor Rudi Supek, Zagreb University, made successful efforts for publication of the study, as did Mrs. Nada Sremec and Mrs. Anica Magašić.

Their attitude toward this study made it possible to publish the book in Yugoslavia in memory of the many collaborators who were killed in the Resistance.

When I arrived in the United States, two old friends, Mr. Alfred Bondy and Mr. Paul Neuberger, helped me actively, enabling me to prepare reports and applications to scholarly foundations for assistance to complete the work. It was a long time before I obtained help, as I had to apply to forty-three foundations before I received a favorable answer.

My project was accepted by the Wenner-Gren Foundation for Anthropological Research. Its director, Dr. Paul Fejos, provided me with a considerable grant, which made it possible to devote myself to research and writing. Dr. Fejos' and the foundation's generosity was great indeed, even greater since I had no American degrees nor recommendations. Although my presentation of the project was by no means in perfect English, Dr. Fejos evaluated my material as precious and considered the potential contribution of my study as high for anthropology in general. I received an unconditional grant. Dr. Fejos' authority has been also of great help for my academic career.

At the University of California in Berkeley, two famous anthropologists received me with open arms: The late Professors A. L. Kroeber and Robert H. Lowie. Besides teaching at the Slavic Language Department, I became a research fellow at the Department of Anthropology and had the privilege of discussing in detail my material with both professors; I am unable to express my gratitude to these generous scholars. Also their younger colleagues were helpful to me, Professors George Foster, David Mandelbaum, and sociologist Wolfram Eberhard. Mr. Max Knight, editor of the California University Press, was my untiring tutor in organizing the material. Professor Irwin T. Sanders, New York, read my book in the Serbo-Croatian edition, evaluated and reviewed it, and helped me greatly in my efforts to prepare an American edition, as did Professor Reuben Hill of Minnesota in a most kind and generous way.

If this book contributes somehow to the understanding of man, much of the merit goes to the many unselfish persons who helped me to collect, save, present, and publish the survey material.

### ABOUT THE TRANSLATION

The late Alec Brown translated half of this study; that is Chapters II, III, IV, V, VI, VIII, X, and XI; I translated the other half.

Mr. Brown, a well-known British author and translator, was an expert in Serbo-Croatian and knew the Yugoslav country intimately. His study *Yugoslav Land and Landscape*, published by Elek Books (London and New York, 1954), can be considered one of the best books on the subject. A distinguished graduate of St. John's College Cambridge, Alec Brown was a Slavonic scholar, with many translations from Serbian and Russian, as well as from French and German, to his credit. He was decorated in 1931 by the Yugoslav Government for his archaeological researches in that country. In the United States, several of his books were published in the inter-war years, including *Beethoven Deaf and other Poems* (Dial Press) and *Daughters of Albion* (Doubleday, Doran and Company).

### ABOUT THE PICTURES

The photographs included in this book show people from different regions, with the bearing, gestures, and costumes of the patriarchal era. The pictures are documents of a bygone time, since these costumes and also partly the expressions of the people have disappeared to a great extent in most parts of Yugoslavia. Like the reports of my interviewers, the pictures caught their subjects at the very last moment, before the storms of history spoiled their style. Their beauty, grown through centuries, disappeared in a few years under the blows of enemy occupation and fighting during the Second World War and the onrush of the machine era.

Acknowledgement is made to the following for the use of copyrighted photographs: to Mr. Toso Davac, Zagreb, for Nos. 1, 2, 3, 8, 9, 10, 13, 14, 15, 16, 18, 19, 20, 22, 23, 24, 27, 27; to Mr. Mladen Grčević, Zagreb, for Nos. 6, 12, 17, 21, 25, 28, 30, 31, 32.

# CONTENTS

xvii

# LIST OF ILLUSTRATIONS

# FAMILY IN TRANSITION

# NOTE ON PRONUNCIATION

C is always read and pronounced as *ts* in bi*ts,* ge*ts.*

Č and Ć are pronounced like *ch* in child, with a slight difference in the pronunciation between them.

Š is pronounced as *sh* in ship.

Ž is pronounced as in pleasure.

Dj and Dž (with a slight difference between them) are pronounced as *j* in just.

j is always pronounced as *y* in yet.

Other letters are pronounced approximately as in English.

# Introduction

## *Problems and Goals*

WHEN I began this survey in 1937, my object was to study relations in the Yugoslav family and the changes which showed themselves so dramatically during the interwar period when the whole complex of traditional customs, normed attitudes, and automatic reactions began to disintegrate at a quick pace. Though at that time the patriarchal regime was still intact in part of the country, over large areas it was only a memory, although a very lively one, since the older generation had grown up within its framework. My attempt to discover the reasons for the great changes was facilitated by the fact that the entire life of the villages was still going on, on the more or less even basis of a subsistence economy. I searched for historical reasons for the great differences among the various regions, inquiring especially into the impact of cultural influence from outside. The adjustment of the social pattern to the penetrating money economy came to be central to my study.

My point of departure was more socio-psychological than ethnological. I concentrated on problems of authority, conflicts, rivalries, love and hate, groupings, rank and position in the family, as well as on the process of transformation of all family relations. As I felt that the ethnological data had already been studied thoroughly and a very considerable literature on them published in Serbo-Croatian, I devoted less care to traditional customs and folklore.

When I finished the survey in 1941, the world collapsed—for Europe, for the Yugoslav villages, and for me personally. The rescued survey material became historical documents, irretrievable indices of a perished world. I myself, thrown out of my home and my native land, spent nearly twenty years in different countries. This catastrophe, however, gave new possibilities for comparison as well as a new background for the old material.

I had the opportunity to deal with people in refugee camps, catapulted from their burned villages, isolated from their families, and evacuated to foreign lands. As a social worker, I was in charge of thousands of young people who had survived German concentration camps, many of whom were the only ones left from big families or even entire towns. I observed how they gradually came back to life as they attempted to found new families, and how they built up

3

family affections from scratch, showing the irresistible need for family living with or without an interrupted condition.

In sharp contrast to these scenes, I saw two settings with stable and warm family relations on traditional lines and with strong emotional coloring: Italy and Mexico. There the friction between the sexes seemed small and the conflicts between generations still smaller, as if these countries had remained untouched by the historical storms of our time.

I learned to know the most highly urbanized and industrialized country—the United States, connected and adjusted to a machine-science society with family relations very different from those in the Slavic South or in the Romance countries. My American experience gave a new perspective to some of my first findings. I found many tendencies, only surmised in the Yugoslav villages, developed to an extreme in the form of "ideal types" in the United States.

A quarter of a century between the beginning and the completion of this study, and experience in several settings, have changed somewhat its accent, without changing its objective and goals.

The Yugoslav rural family on the eve of the Second World War, and the changes that were taking place in it, remained the primary task; general conclusions drawn from this material came second. The Yugoslav family became in a certain sense an example for the demonstration of certain general themes and theories. Elements which are common to all people and not only to those of rural Yugoslavia came into the focus of my research, for example the complementary play of individualistic and collectivistic tendencies, the readiness for adjustment as well as for resistance, the longing for security as well as for independence, the general need for family living, and the riddle of culture contact.

# CHAPTER I

## Historical Background

YUGOSLAVIA presents many riddles to the observer—its wavering between East and West being probably the most intriguing one.

Anyone who visited Yugoslavia between the two wars would remember its contrasts and its quality of oscillation; it was East and West; simultaneously traditional and modern. The northern cities reminded one of the Habsburg Monarchy; Bosnia, however, was definitely Oriental. On the Adriatic littoral, San Marco's winged lion recalled memories of the Venetian Republic and the songs of Italy. In the Dinaric Alps near the coast, one might have imagined oneself among the knights and crusaders in the Middle East: People spoke of Sultan Murat as though he had just invaded Europe and endangered Christendom.

The country was backward and progressive, and both to an extreme extent. One could travel from Paris to Constantinople across Yugoslavia on the fashionable Orient Express. But by getting off at a Yugoslav station and walking a few hours into the Bosnian mountains, one would find oneself in a remote archaic epoch, where burdens were carried on the backs of pack animals or people. The markets looked like Indian markets in Latin America, with peasants standing or squatting before baskets full of colorful fruits, vegetables, and poultry. They were clad in handwoven embroidered costumes and sandals. However, in conversation with peasants, let us say, from the Shumadia district of Serbia, one would hear sharp and independent comments on world politics.

In intimate and family relationships the contrasts were equally great. Love relations were based on deep passion. Suicide and death because of the loss of a loved one and a "broken heart" were not rare among peasants. South Slav love songs were unequalled in beauty. Yet the ascetic trend, too, was stronger here than elsewhere: During the resistance fighting in the Second World War, the Partisans punished love affairs by death.

For an understanding of any aspect of Yugoslav life, one needs some knowledge of historical background; without it, many phenomena cannot be understood at all. This is true of the Yugoslav resistance to occupation, or Tito's break with Stalin, as well as of relationships within the family. The goals which guided these people, the values which determined their behavior have a political-historical mark.

The main reason for this may be geographical as the country is located on the Balkan peninsula at the gate of Asia. The peninsula is a bridge between Europe and Asia with many roads leading to it and through it. The Balkans are unprotected, there is no impediment to entering them, no mountain barrier separates them from the continent such as exists in the north of the other south European peninsulas. The Balkans are linked so intimately to the continent by the Danube and its tributaries that Yugoslavia might be considered as part of Central Europe, or else Hungary as a part of the Balkans. The gentle Adriatic with its many islands creates a close connection with the West.

This position has tempted many powers to invade and attempt to seize the Balkans. Such attempts to conquer or win over the South Slavs are by no means new. Soon after their arrival in the Balkans (in the sixth and seventh centuries), they found themselves between the eastern and the western church centers of the disintegrating Roman Empire. There were always several neighbors claiming the Balkans, and every power had to fight rivals. Yet the fights seldom brought decisive victories, the frontier between great powers and spheres of influence ran mostly across the middle of the peninsula.

These many temptations, threats, and invasions had a curious result: The South Slavs were never compelled to submit unconditionally to a given situation; they never had to conform to a penetrating force. There were always other alternatives; it was always possible to resist and become the ally of another power. Always they could—and therefore had to—make far-reaching political decisions. This caused the political element in the culture to become dominant, much more important than such others as economics. The historical or political element has dominated all areas of life, including family relations. It is also the reason that I have devoted more space to the historical background than may seem warranted at first glance.

### Five Hundred Years of Ottoman Empire

When the Slavs migrating to the South reached the Balkan Peninsula, they had penetrated to the core of European culture and civilization, to Byzantium, the East-Roman Empire. Only when the Byzantine Empire was weakened did the South Slavs attempt to establish their own states. Croats and Bulgarians, Serbs and Bosnians

The Balkans between the two World Wars

founded more or less independent states, which grew rapidly but were quickly supplanted by others. In the fourteenth century, a Serbian prince succeeded in building up the Serbian state to a great power, of which Macedonia was the center, and became Emperor as Czar Dushan. The glory of this period, sung in many folk epics, was never forgotten. After Dushan's death, his empire disintegrated into several princedoms, only loosely connected.

At that time the Ottomans[1] had begun their victorious drive toward the west. Their founders were shepherds of the Arabic desert, well organized and modest as to their personal needs, with the outstanding discipline and intelligence of many nomads. During the

[1] The Ottoman Empire (called after its founder, Sultan Osman) included many nations. The most influential one was Turkey. During the existence of the Empire, the names "Turks" and "Ottomans" were used interchangeably, but the state was mostly called "Ottoman Empire" or "Osman Empire."

Middle Ages, several nomadic peoples from the steppes had invaded Europe and had proved invincible wherever they attacked sedentary populations. The Ottomans, too, had overcome all resistance in Asia. In the fourteenth century, when they reached the Balkan Peninsula and won their first battle, the Serbian princes united in order to resist. A decisive battle was fought on Kosovo Plain in 1389. The Serbs were defeated, their commander King Lazar fell, as did most of the other princes and knights. Sultan Murad was also killed. The surviving Serbian princes became Turkish vassals and disappeared a few decades later. In this period the Turks conquered Constantinople, the Croatian territories, and Hungary. They advanced to Vienna, where the wave was broken in the early sixteenth century. Parts of Central Europe became Turkish for one and a half centuries, but the Balkans remained under the Turkish rule for half a millennium.

While all other nomadic peoples had disappeared or were absorbed by the sedentary populations after one generation, the Ottomans, with their unique organization, remained for many centuries. This is probably due to the fact that desert nomads had penetrated to the heart of European culture. The Ottoman striking force and gift for organization blended with Byzantine order, law, technique, and culture, resulting in the creation of the great Ottoman Empire of the early period. The state was a Utopia, an idea consistently reiterated. It was of such perfection that it fascinated the Europeans and easily absorbed the conquered nations. Even the Balkan Slavs did not rise to resistance until much later.

The system was built up in the tradition and in accordance with the experience of desert shepherds (as Toynbee formulates it). The hierarchy was a steep structure, the Sultan being military commander, head of the church, and unlimited lord over life and death. The people were looked upon as cattle, and called *raya*, meaning cattle. Cattle and raya had to deliver products, but otherwise were left alone, and no attempts were made to change or reform them. Only if they broke loose or revolted, would they be killed. The raya were kept in check by a special caste comparable to watchdogs. The officers and functionaries of the state were not free men, but the Sultan's slaves.

The South Slavs (except the Islamized ones) became a homogeneous people, since the nobility disappeared and the priests became peasant-like. The peasants were in a much better position than those in the European feudal system. They were not obliged to perform personal services. They had only to deliver part of their agricultural yields to the Moslem lords, and only the *Spahis* had the obligation for military service (as cavalry). In Austria this system was considered so favorable for the peasantry that special privileges were established for the Austrian frontier soldiers in order to give them living conditions similar to those enjoyed by the peasants on the other side of the Turkish frontier.

All Ottoman state officers were slaves, according to the principle that children and men do well only when they are completely dependent on their educators and commanders. No free Moslem could become an officer, and sons of officers were equally excluded. Only drafted Christian children, prisoners of war, and kidnapped slaves could become civil servants. They were taken to Constantinople and thoroughly trained in schools and military institutes. The most gifted ones went to academies or were made pages in the Serail, the Sultan's residence. After completing their studies, they were sent to high administrative positions. Many military commanders and *vezirs*—chief ministers—were Balkan Slavs, and the best troops of the Empire, the Janissaries, were drafted Christian boys from the Balkans. Their position and the name of the slaves—*kul*—was an honor, as they were "in His Majesty's service."

In this system, one democratic principle had become evident: Only the individual qualities counted, regardless of the national, religious, racial, or class background of the boys. This was the extreme opposite of the contemporary European notion of social strata. But the success of the system in the Ottoman Empire was so obvious that European observers considered it a miracle. These slaves had unlimited opportunities, yet they were completely exposed to the will of the Sultan. Since they were considered to be something like watchdogs, any moment could bring them the death sentence; every failure, the slightest suspicion could cost them their heads. Their power and glory stood always under the shadow of fear.

The leading goal of the Ottoman state was missionary: The world had to be conquered for Islam. Accordingly, officers had to be Moslems, and the students and cadets were Islamized; as they stood under the suggestion of the power of Islam, they did it voluntarily. The raya, however, were left undisturbed in their customs and their religion. Every national or religious community—*Millet*—was represented by its priests. The state was a supra-national compound of many nationalities and religions.

The Ottoman system made one fateful mistake: It did not take human nature into account. Officers would not accept the verdict to be poisoned like watchdogs with real resignation; nor in the long run would the raya accept, without resistance, their position and their lowly name. From the start many institutions carried the germ of the ultimate fall of the state.

One example of this disregard of human nature was the children's levy, known as the "tax in blood." Every fourth year the sons of the Balkan raya were drafted. The strongest, most handsome and gifted boys, ranging in age from nine to twelve, were taken from their parents and included in the Sultan's slave household. These children had excellent opportunities for career, so good, in fact, that some Moslem parents cheated to have their sons included. Nevertheless, this tax in blood was one reason for the unreconcilable hatred of the South Slavs against the state. Although this institution was abandoned at the end of the seventeenth century, the South Slavs could never forget it, and nowadays one can still hear talk about it as the height of brutality.

The whole system was inflexible and not suited to reforms. After about two hundred fifty years of unparalleled rise, the gradual decline of the Empire began, lasting for about an equally long period. Starting with the second defeat of the Turks before Vienna at the end of the seventeenth century, the military advantages of the European countries became evident. The formerly progressive Turkish organization had become backward. The military failures had a reciprocal effect on the decline of the administration. The defeats meant burdens on the treasury; corruption and disorder spread. The whole system of the Sultan's slaves became undermined: The officers succeeded in having their sons and grandsons accepted for state service. The Spahis, who had received their estates as feudal tenure for military service, succeeded in establishing the heredity of these estates. The Janissaries deteriorated to privileged bands, to which membership could be bought. *Bakshish*—tip and bribe—became part of the system. Injustice and insecurity became general. Nothing remained of the brilliant organization which had ruled over large parts of three continents. The raya, exposed to violence, became enemies of the state.

Migrations within the state, which had started shortly after the Ottoman invasion, acquired political features partly hostile to the state. From the central regions and the major military roads, many peasants had migrated to more sheltered regions. This was a selective process, as the belligerent elements moved to the impassable mountains in order to be far from the reach of the Turkish lords, more peaceful elements or those friendly to the Turks migrated to the valleys, where life was easier. In the Dinaric Alps near the Adriatic, the attitude of the people became more and more unyielding. Bands of *hayduks* gathered, attacking and robbing the Turks.

In the course of the wars between the Ottoman and the Austrian Empires, another migratory movement developed—that toward Austria. Whenever the Austrian armies penetrated the Balkans, the raya collaborated with them; when the armies retreated, a large part of the population joined them to escape from the Turkish revenge. In 1698, when Austria withdrew her occupation army from Macedonia, 40,000 families, led by the Orthodox Patriarch, joined the army and went to Austria. They were resettled at the Austrian southern border as had been many other waves of refugees before and after this event.

The defeat on the Kosovo Plain became a legend which nurtured the idea of revenge. The names of the heroes of Kosovo lived on in the daily talk of the people. The goal of the men became to fight for the "venerable cross and the golden freedom." The epics of the death of the Serbian princes acquired religious features and received the support of the Orthodox Church. The day of the catastrophe of Kosovo, the St. Vitus' Day—*Vidovdan*—became a day of remembrance.

The Orthodox Church had become the intermediary between the Balkan Slavs and the European powers. In many places the priests were the only literate people. Also, the defense of Christendom was the only legitimate motive for asking assistance from European powers, as the national idea was not yet acknowledged. When Russia became the protector of the Balkan Slavs in the eighteenth century, it was believed that Russia helped her smaller brothers because she belonged to the Orthodox Church. Only later did the national motive appear, and national aims were frankly pursued.

The great antagonist of the Ottoman Empire was Austria. In the heart of Europe, the Habsburgs had organized the struggle against the Turks. Before Vienna, two waves of Turkish attacks were broken. It was here that the Turks had to resign their hope of conquering the whole world. Austria's large South Slav population was incessantly engaged in the struggle against the Turks.

In the eighteenth century, the central Ottoman power was weakened so much that the Balkan regions were ruled by usurpers and bandits who made cities and roads insecure and refused to obey the Sultan. The Janissaries, formerly the best Turkish infantry, by then was a band of gangsters and robbers which several times threatened even Constantinople. Sultan Selim attempted to establish law and security, proclaimed reforms, and tried to get rid of the Janissaries. The leaders of the Janissaries, called *Dahis*, were especially aggressive in the Belgrade Pashaluk. The Pasha of Belgrade, in order to enable the Serbs to defend themselves against the Janissaries, distributed arms. This action had fateful consequences. The Serbs used the arms as it suited their own needs and desires.

Serbia, for centuries a battlefield between the fighting Empires, became depopulated. Then in relatively calm periods of the eighteenth and nineteenth centuries a large immigration began into this scarcely populated region. Most of the immigrants were belligerent people, determined to revenge Kosovo. A forest district—Shumadia— not too far from the Austrian border, not too near the great military roads, became the center of resistance. For a long time the administration there was almost completely in the hands of village headmen—the *knez'*—and Turks were found only in the cities. When in 1804 the Dahis started a massacre among the village knez', the people revolted. Led by Kara-George, the Serbs defeated the Janissaries and declared their independence from the Ottoman Empire.

When Napoleon attacked Russia, Serbian independence suffered some setbacks, but in 1815 a second revolt flared up. In the subsequent years, the link with the Ottoman Empire became increasingly looser until the last Turkish garrisons left in 1867. In the beginning of the seventies, in connection with the upheaval in Herzegovina (another South Slav region under Turkish rule), war broke out against the Turks. Russia helped the Balkan Slavs, and Bulgaria was freed by the Russians. Serbia, however, gained little, and did not reach its goal of acquiring Bosnia and Herzegovina. The European powers, anxious to keep an equilibrium, did not want Russia to become too strong with the support of all the newly liberated Balkan Slavs. An international conference was called—the Berlin Congress of 1878—to solve the "Oriental question." According to its decisions, the Balkan states became sovereign, but Bosnia and Herzegovina became Austrian provinces, and were occupied by the Austrian army.

The national ambitions of the Balkan Slavs grew stronger. In 1912 the Balkan War broke out. Serbia, Montenegro, Bulgaria, and Greece allied to fight against the Turks, and the war ended in total Turkish defeat. Immediately following, war broke out between two of the allies: Serbia and Bulgaria, who fought over the division of the newly won Macedonia. Serbia won and received nearly the whole of northern Macedonia. Southern Macedonia, with Salonika, became Greek.

Turkey retained only a small territory in Europe including Constantinople and the Dardanelles. This was the end of the Ottoman era and of Turkish rule in the Balkans. The Ottoman state, which had once stormed over Europe like a young giant, perished as the "sick man on the Bosporus," the "giant with the feet of clay."

Many South Slav features still reflected Oriental influence. Among the consequences of the decline of Ottoman rule were economic backwardness, the low standard of living, and a conservatism which served as a brake on technical progress. But, in the calm of the villages, a folk culture of extraordinary beauty had grown up, and even the Oriental philosophy of life was embraced by the peasants.

A set of very different features, characteristic of the freedom-loving highlanders, was also a consequence of the long Turkish domination of the Balkans. These features by themselves are by no means Oriental, but they emerged under the Ottoman system and the position of the raya in it, which was felt as a provocation. The resistance of the South Slavs had produced a democratic spirit and political experience within the declining Ottoman state. (Both these styles of life which developed under Oriental influence are discussed in detail in the chapter "The Riddle of Culture Contact.")

## Five Hundred Years of Habsburg Monarchy

Long before the Ottomans attacked Europe, the Habsburgs had been one of Europe's leading dynasties, and most western countries belonged to their crown in different periods. (One Habsburg king could say that in his kingdom the sun never set.) It was through resistance to Ottoman aggression that Austria itself, located in the heart of the continent, became a great power. The Habsburgs organized the fighting against the Turks, uniting the Danube area for defense. The two waves of Ottoman advance which were broken before Vienna destroyed Turkish hopes of conquering the world for Islam.

When in 1526 the Turks pushed up to the center of Europe, Ferdinand of Habsburg was chosen as King of Hungary and Croatia, or rather of the remnants of these countries which had not been conquered. Great parts of them had fallen to the Turks and remained for one hundred fifty years under Turkish rule. The Ottoman Empire had become the neighbor of Austria and threatened

13

its borders for centuries. For half a millennium Austria kept the lead in the fighting.

While one-half of the South Slavs came under Turkish domination and after that lived inside the Ottoman Empire (or in permanent resistance fighting against it), the other half became Austrian. From this time, two very different cultures—the Oriental and the Central European—influenced the South Slavs. Both empires were among the greatest powers of their time, and some elements were common to both: The imperial claim, the stability of the state for half a millennium, and the unceasing fight against each other. But the principles and practices of these two rival states were entirely different, and thus the South Slavs on both sides of the frontier came under very distinct cultural influences. The resulting contrasts were much greater than any common trends.

The fundamental principle of the Habsburg state was contrary to the Ottoman one. The Ottoman state was based on the right of conquest: All territories were conquered in religious wars. The Sultan, at the same time Kalif and Allah's substitute on earth, was lord over life and death; the people were without power. Absolute obedience to the Sultan was the supreme law. The result was either a fatalistic and passive attitude among the raya or else the other extreme, daring and death-defying rebellion.

Austria was founded under different circumstances—she was born "under another constellation." In the course of time the Habsburgs acquired lands by means of inheritance, dowry, treaties, and election. Consequently every part of the Austrian Empire had a particular position within the state. Every region, every province had different claims, different guaranteed rights for which they fought within a constitutional framework. Relativity had been raised to a principle; the right to struggle for one's position was basically never denied. In Croatia too, the Habsburgs had become rulers by election. After Hungary and Croatia were defeated by the Turks in the decisive battle of Mohacz in 1526, the Austrian emperor was elected as their king. Large parts of Hungary and Croatia, however, remained Turkish for one hundred fifty years.

Over the Austrian border, wave after wave of refugees from the Turkish territories streamed in, carrying with them their hatred of the Turks, their fighting spirit, and the Kosovo tradition. With a special statute, the Austrian border area was organized as a military frontier—the Military March—against the Ottoman neighbor. It included a big part of Croatia. In the Military March, everything stood under military command; men, women, and children were military personnel. The "frontier men," not having feudal status, were under the direct jurisdiction of the Emperor. They appreciated these privileges and were loyal to their adopted state. Although the Austrian command was strictly authoritarian, the refugees had no conflict with it, and became, despite—or because of—their fighting spirit, the best Austrian soldiers. Many Austrian commanders-in-chief and many generals, even as late as the First World War, had been peasant sons from the Military March. This area remained under the special statute until the end of the nineteenth century, until the occupation of Bosnia.

The Austrian rule of five hundred years was interrupted only for a short time by Napoleon's creation, the Illyrian Kingdom, including all Austrian (and Venetian) regions with South Slav populations. After Napoleon's fall, Dalmatia at the Adriatic, which formerly had been under Venetian domination, became Austrian too. Stimulated by Napoleon, a South Slav national movement developed in Croatia and Dalmatia. Its goals were not revolutionary, however, like those of the Serbian freedom fighters but rather cultural. Only very slowly and gradually the national ideals of Croats and Serbs came closer to each other, and a mutual contact was established.

The Austrian occupation of Bosnia-Herzegovina in 1878 was a terrible blow to Serbia, which had claimed these provinces. When Austria finally annexed the provinces in 1908, a war with Serbia seemed imminent. The South Slavs in the Monarchy sympathized with free Serbia and began to identify their own goals with those of their "Serbian brothers."

In Central Europe, nationalism became irresistible. Most active among the Austrian Slavs were the Czechs under the leadership of Thomas G. Masaryk. The Italians had an *Irredenta* movement longing to be incorporated into Italy, and the Hungarians claimed still more autonomy than they already possessed within the Monarchy. Like the discontented raya, people first struggled only for greater independence from the Austrian central power without planning to blow up the Empire. Yet fate did not favor such a solution: Crown Prince Rudolf and Archduke Franz Ferdinand, who might have helped a federal Austria to come true, were given no opportunity; old Franz Joseph remained Emperor for sixty-eight years, and both heirs to the throne died before he did.

The hostility to the state of the various peoples within the Austrian Empire grew stronger. Nationalistic feelings became extreme, bitter struggles developed over language trifles such as the name of a railway station, a military command, or the lettering on a postage stamp. In reality, the pressure inside the Austro-Hungarian Monarchy was not especially strong if compared to later developments in Central Europe. Austria was economically and technically progressive, with a law-abiding bureaucracy, with an administration unmatched in that part of the world. But the people did not judge these matters dispassionately, and many felt imprisoned. At least a considerable part of the students and the intelligentsia of the Slav regions felt this way.

In June 1914, maneuvers were held in Bosnia. The Archduke Franz Ferdinand visited Sarajevo on "Vidovdan," the St. Vitus' Day, the mourning feast commemorating the battle of Kosovo. The Serbian nationalistic youth considered this visit and the whole maneuvers as a provocation, and their answer was his assassination; the Austrian heir to the throne and his wife were shot. As Austria supposed that the assassination had been prepared in Serbia, it declared war on Serbia. The First World War began.

After four and a half years, the Central Powers including Austria were defeated by the Allies. The South Slavs from the Monarchy had fought as Austrian soldiers but, toward the end of the war, deserted in masses to the forests. In London a South Slav committee had prepared the foundation of a new state. When defeated Austria fell to pieces in October 1918, the Austrian South Slav regions united with Serbia and Montenegro into a common state.

Austria had grown in the struggle against the Turks. Her raison d'être had been unification of Central Europe in order to defend Europe against Ottoman aggression. This goal was reached after centuries of struggle. When, however, in these fights the young South Slav peoples grew strong and wrecked the Ottoman Empire, the hour of death had arrived also for its antagonist—the Austrian Empire. For more than five hundred years, the two empires had lived as hostile neighbors; almost to the end they had fought each other, and they died at the same hour, both by the hand of their own children.

Yet, just as their births, their deaths too were different. While the Ottoman Empire lost one province after another and, in a long-lasting disintegrating illness, became the caricature of its own former greatness, Austria perished apparently in full health, with a perfect administration and nearly unbroken military power. The same Slav peoples, in some cases the same persons, destroyed the Turkish as well as the Austrian Empire. In both cases, Slav nationalism triumphed over a multinational state.

Like the South Slavs in the Ottoman Empire, those in the Habsburg Empire had acquired distinct features. While the absolute demands in the Ottoman state drove the Slavs to rebellion, in Austria, due to its flexible constitution, they were brought to conformity. Here the centers of the state were located in economically more highly developed regions than the areas where the South Slavs lived. Therefore, in Austria, everything coming from the state was technically, scientifically, and administratively progressive. People belonged to a stabilized great power with legal security and good administration, and this was the background for life also for the peasantry—including family relations. Austrian order and authority were the reasons that aggressive trends were pushed into the background, at least for the time being.

Like most great cultures, the Austrian had grown out of a fusion of different elements (German, Hungarian, Italian, Rumanian, and Slav peoples all contributed to the making of their empire). Out of all these components a whole developed in which the parts blended perfectly as in a chemical compound.

The specific style of life that grew up in the Austrian Empire lasted much longer than the state under which it had arisen. People from what were once Austrian regions still reveal their extraction in innumerable details, in bearing, attitude, and speech habits, as people from other Yugoslav regions with a different cultural heritage sense keenly.

Notes from my diary of 1940 from Bosnia show how people remembered Austria twenty-two years after its death: "From all talks with the peasants, a nostalgia for old times can be heard. It is strange that the Moslems, the Catholics, and the Orthodox speak in just the same way, constantly comparing the present with the old Austrian days. I heard the same words repeated in peasant homes and backyards, at the markets, around the courtrooms and hospitals in Banjaluka, Jajce, Visoko, the villages on Romania Mountain. How much easier it was to live before—how everything was according to rule—how wonderful it would be if things would be done as before and not forever left pending. My companions with whom I visited the villages were silent. How could they oppose this reasoning when it was they who had undermined old Austria. But when we were alone my friends, considering taxes, legal courts, schooling, actions taken against malaria and for the maintenance of the roads, the tobacco monopoly, would admit to me '. . . unfortunately it is not being done right. People would be happy, believe us, happy and satisfied if the administration were just and in order, even if there were not more bread to eat. . . .' "

## The First Twenty-Two Years of Yugoslavia

With the creation of the Yugoslav state, East and West met. Eastern and Western influences were revealed by the religious affiliations of the people.[2] The Serbian-Orthodox part of the population (48.5 per cent of the total) and the Moslems (11.5 per cent) belonged to Eastern faiths. Western influence was shown in the Roman Catholic Church (37.25 per cent of the population).

The South Slavs with the Austrian imprint were markedly different from those who formerly had been Turkish raya, but they were also different from the Dinaric freedom fighters. These three elements were united in the Yugoslav state and made life in the first era a difficult problem after centuries of estrangement. Contrary to the hopes and desires of the founders and of the people themselves, the beginning of common life was very difficult. The divisive tendencies seemed to grow stronger than the unifying ones, and the regional peculiarities, developed under Eastern and Western influences, seemed to become even more extreme than before. The process of meeting, mixing, amalgamation, and "acculturation" was stormy to the point of explosion.

The unification operated in a certain sense like the contact of different cultures. In some regions, it affected the people as an invading foreign culture would have. The new state influenced their lives through military service, police force, taxation and courts, state monopolies and agrarian reform, relief funds for "passive areas" and political parties in a manner which was completely strange to many of them.

The specific qualities of the new state were derived from those of the various regions; these emerging qualities, in turn, influenced the historical regions in a reciprocal process. The result was more and different than the sum of regional qualities. Some qualities were nullified, others strengthened one another, while some qualities emerged as dominant in the whole compound, the Yugoslav state.

The first common quality which emerged was friction and disappointment with each other. In this atmosphere even the question of

---

[2] These and all other figures are from the 1931 Census, which served as a basis for my survey.

18

nationality became a problem, although all South Slavs have one ethnic foundation and the language differences are smaller than differences between dialects of other peoples. A peculiar detail sharpened the contrasts, namely the lack of a traditional common name. The names of Serbs, Croats, etc., recalled proud memories; the name "Yugoslavs" or "Jugoslavs," however, is an artifact[3] meaning South Slavs, as "jug" means south.[4] For the sake of the new name no one wished to relegate his historical name to second place. The Italians, or the Germans, who had united into national states fifty years earlier, had not only regional names but also a common name from time immemorial, and therefore their common nationality was never questioned. Here, however, in fraternal struggles the first thought was that of parting.

The most important cause of discord and unhappiness was the weakness of the Yugoslav state administration, which was generally felt to be a failure. Although many of the leading statesmen had fought for unification and started to work with great enthusiasm, the sad truth became apparent very soon: The administration everywhere dropped to a level lower than it had been before the war. The different traditions did not blend, rather they made each other ineffective.

It seemed as if the merits of each former routine of administration were erased in the new state, and only their shortcomings remained. Little was left from the efficient Austrian administration, of the Serbian and Montenegrin democratic ways. The heroic tradition, especially, seemed unsuited to a new, bigger state, composed of different elements. In the central offices, nepotism and corruption developed, and people began to fear state offices and officers. Unscrupulous businessmen and corrupt bureaucrats divided funds and bribes, causing the standard of living to drop lower and lower. Ordinary citizens and honest administrators were impotent against the cliques of profiteers. Moreover, the fights among the cliques looked dangerously like fights among the Yugoslav peoples themselves.

Administrative practices had developed from old Serbian procedure. But in Serbia before the First World War weaknesses in organization were counterbalanced by patriarchal dignity and responsibility. The distances in the country were small; everything

[3] It is for purely political reasons that the Bulgars are not called Yugoslavs as they, too, are South Slavs.

[4] During her first years the new state was called SHS, state of Serbs, Croats (Hrvati), and Slovenes; it was not officially renamed Yugoslavia until 1929.

could be settled personally; paper work was unimportant. In the unified state, this way of familistic dealing had unfortunate results. For every application, for the smallest official decision, people had to travel to Belgrade, the capital, or else entrust the business to an "interventionist." Every movement seemed braked, to linger and loiter, to remain forever pending. The Serbian peasants, who were the bearers of the state idea and of the tradition of freedom, were unable to overcome these difficulties.

The money economy too developed under unfortunate conditions. Serbia as a state was built through revolutionary action; gradual evolution was virtually unknown. State institutions did not become more flexible in connection with a money economy as in other countries; when the world-wide depression hit, they were completely helpless.

Many measures seemed to be ill-fated, causing setbacks and unforeseen reactions, as for instance the policy of the state monopolies. The idea was that the state monopolies would cover a great part of the state expenses and that direct taxes could be held low. But this policy caused a further lowering of the standard of living, as nearly everything the peasants bought were items of state monopoly. Salt, tobacco, matches, and kerosene for lamps were monopoly articles; coffee and sugar also stood under monopoly tax. The price of sugar was the highest in Europe, four times as high as in England. Those peasants who produced tobacco were the sworn enemies of the monopoly administration because of the low prices they received for their products. They sold the larger part of their tobacco crop illegally, which resulted in endless fights with the armed police.

Agrarian reform was a similar case. The division of the great estates was intended to help the peasants with little or no land. But the reform did not bring much success—few were contented and many were embittered. The new owners were not able to use the land successfully as they lacked the capital to buy equipment and livestock. The land was often parceled out according to political judgments (and prejudices) to the disadvantage of the Moslem population. The impoverishment of Bosnia was caused partly by the peculiar way the agrarian reform was carried through.

Poverty in the countryside was the other main cause of unhappiness. At the time of this survey, the whole of life was overshadowed by the *kriza*, the depression. The economic world crisis hit Yugoslavia in 1931, before she had even reached her twelfth birthday, preventing any consolidation and economic growth. Agrarian products could not be sold, the peasants lost all credit. In many parts of the country, especially in the Karst areas, where only tobacco and wine were produced, starvation lasted for years. The peasants had no money at all; many could not even buy salt, but "salted" with ash. In every single region people were worse off than in "peace time," as the prewar period was nostalgically called.

This decline was, however, blamed not so much on the world-wide depression as on the administration and bureaucracy, for it was obvious that the administration was completely unable to parry the blows. In all regions, one could hear people sigh: "If only the administration were orderly, decent, speedy, as it was in peace time, it would not be so hard to bear poverty!"

This stormy period of twenty-two and a half years left its mark on the people, and the generation which grew up in the interwar period carries the visible stamp of the first Yugoslav era just as clearly as did the generation which had grown up in Austria or in the Ottoman Empire. The youth acquired the belief that dissatisfaction was the unchangeable fate of humans, and impotence toward a country's administration and economy was inborn in man.

The consequences of living in a common state were entirely unexpected; no one could have foreseen the difficulties which would arise. Nor could anyone have predicted that reactions in the various regions would become so different, and that the divisive forces in public life would become so strong. Least of all could anyone have known that qualities would develop below the surface which would come to the fore only later, under the pressure of an enemy occupation, and which would testify in favor of this much-blamed first Yugoslav era.

The German occupation and the fighting against it showed that a certain amount of fusion had taken place, although this did not become visible before the Second World War. It seems that in spite of everything the heroic component became dominant, as the resistance during the war showed.

A little scene which a foreign traveler experienced, on the very day when the period we are dealing with finished, is not untypical. The scene was described to me by the well-known Austrian poet and playwright Franz Theodor Csokor. Csokor was in Yugoslavia when the Germans invaded the country. Fleeing with many others toward the Adriatic coast, he entered an inn at the roadside to rest. There he noticed a young Yugoslav army officer sitting exhausted and desperate at a table and murmuring over and over again: "If we had only given supreme command to Miloš Obilić instead of to Vuk Branković, this could never have happened!" Csokor, who only understood a little of the language, was most curious to know whether the officer was talking about cabinet ministers and officers of the general staff or about Belgrade politicians, and asked him. It took Csokor a long time to understand that the officer was talking about the heroes of the Kosovo battle, who to him were not dead at all in that spring of 1941.

## Some Statistical Data

About fourteen million people lived in this country of about the size of Great Britain; the great majority of them were peasants who lived in the villages where they had been born. The two million strong national minorities (mostly Albanians, Hungarians, and Germans) were also peasants, settled for generations. Yugoslavia had the highest percentage of agrarian population in Europe: According to Yugoslav statistics, based on occupational distribution, 76.5 per cent were peasants. According to League of Nations statistics, based on size of residence, 83 per cent lived in rural communities. For comparison, the number of peasants according to the latter definition were for Italy 44 per cent, Czechoslovakia 33 per cent, Switzerland 22 per cent, England 5 per cent.[5]

Production as well as export was that of a peasant country. The main products of the country were corn and wheat, flax, wine, plums, and tobacco. Exports were lumber, corn, plums, hemp, tobacco, pork, poultry, eggs, fish, leather (and copper). Forests were of great importance, as they covered nearly one-third of the land. Cattle breeding was equally important; there were nine million sheep, two million goats, four million cattle, three million swine, and one and a quarter million horses, practically all owned by peasants. Sheep and goats were concentrated in the mountain areas and provided the highlanders with food and clothing. Industry was insignificant.

There were 347 administrative districts plus 72 urban communities.

## Historical Regions within Yugoslavia

The eight regions which were united in 1918 remained of paramount importance for moulding the life of the people through all the interwar period. Especially in the rural areas, the newly founded state of Yugoslavia often seemed less real than did the historical

[5] Dudley Kirk, *Europe's Population in the Interwar Years*, League of Nations, 1946.

The Austro-Hungarian
frontiers - - - - - -

The Yugoslav frontiers as
drawn in 1918 ——————

The Balkans and the Austro-Hungarian Monarchy in 1914

regions with their traditional ways of life, standards, and relationships.

Of these regions, the following had formerly belonged to Austria:

*Slovenia,* an Alpine region, until the unification closely linked with the Austrian half of the Monarchy. It had a highly developed economy and school system, as the area had been removed from the fate and the fights of the Balkans. Slovenian is a South Slav language, long acknowledged, having a rich literature. Religion, Catholic.

*Voyvodina* in the Danube basin, belonging to the Hungarian half of the Monarchy. It possessed a fertile plain, Serbian Orthodox population, and large Hungarian and German minority groups.

23

*Croatia and Slavonia,* partly fertile land with dense population, partly Dinaric Alps. Belonging to the Hungarian half of the Monarchy, they never lost their autonomy and independent political life. The Military March had, to a great part, a Serbian Orthodox population. Language, Serbo-Croatian. Religion, in the majority Catholic.

*Dalmatia,* at the Adriatic coast, pure rocky Karst. Peasants here were engaged in fishing and seafaring. The area had belonged for centuries to the Venetian Republic and had a progressive economy. It was also linked with the West through numerous emigrants overseas. Language, Serbo-Croatian. Religion, Catholic.

*Bosnia and Herzegovina,* combining Eastern and Western influences, belonged to Austria for forty years after the Turkish epoch. Its rich land was covered with forests. Influential were feudal traditions and strong Oriental ties. Language, Serbo-Croatian. Religion, Orthodox, Moslem, and Catholic.

Three regions that were united into Yugoslavia had never belonged to Austria. The first two were dominated by resistance fighting against the Turkish rule and had won their independence, the third was dominated by the Turks:

*Serbia,* a region of fertile, rolling hills, an immigration area for the past two centuries. At the time of unification, it was a kingdom under the rule of the Karageorgevich dynasty. The Serbian king became king of Yugoslavia, Belgrade its capital. Language, Serbo-Croatian. Religion, Eastern Orthodox.

*Montenegro,* the "Black Mountains," a region of bare Karst rocks and high mountains. It was a kingdom under the dynasty of Petrovich-Nyegosh. The Montenegrins were the core of resistance fighting of the Serbs against the Turks. Language, Serbo-Croatian. Religion, Eastern Orthodox.

*Macedonia,* a land of an old sedentary population, vestiges of Byzantine culture and long-lasting Turkish rule. A strong Moslem minority, mostly Albanians, dominated. Language of the majority, Macedonian—at time of the survey considered a Serbo-Croatian dialect, today acknowledged as separate language. Religion of the majority, Eastern Orthodox.

Together with Macedonia the areas Sanjak, Metohia, and Kosovo, between Serbia and Montenegro, had been freed from Turkey 1912-1913.[6]

6 For reviewing the historical background of the various regions see chapter "The Yugoslav Regions," where it is presented in detail.

The historical regions of Yugoslavia

The historical regions within Yugoslavia remained decisive for every aspect of life, despite the fact that officially they were non-existent. They were merely historical relics, having ceased to be administrative units. In 1929 the government had divided the country into nine areas, called *banovinas*, different from the traditional regions. This was done in order to weaken separatist tendencies and to promote unification. This goal, however, was never reached. Regional characteristics could not be eliminated, and the inner cohesion of each region became even stronger. After the Second World War, the historical regions became the federal republics of postwar Yugoslavia. The regional divisions I have employed here are very similar to today's official ones. The fact that people lived primarily in regional traditions compelled me to do my research work along these lines, and to look for a method of presenting material which would take this reality into account.

## Research Method Based on History

The key for studying norms and changes in the South Slav family was a comparison between villages. I had chosen villages as smallest unit, and not families or individuals, mainly because it was impossible to find large numbers of investigators to whom the peasants would reliably confide their intimate problems. To get information about villages as a whole, however, was quite possible. The opportunity of examining hundreds of villages in all parts of the country with the help of people born in them or living in them for many years was a unique piece of good fortune.

While there was not much difficulty in collecting abundant material, the problem of how to deal with it was not so easily solved. A statistical method had to be found, as it was hardly possible to examine, interpret and present 305 sets of answers without statistical treatment. An additional reason for using statistics was the emotional nature of the replies. There was the danger of getting lost in touching details, and of becoming influenced by the attitude of the investigators, which was often far from objective.

The first question was how to group the villages for comparison. I tried several principles for grouping them; for instance, according to their economy or their distance from traffic or city centers. Yet all results were unrevealing, unsatisfactory, or even apparently false. It turned out that the historical-political moment or the regional style was so decisive for every aspect of life that it could not be ignored. I had to give up—at least for the moment—my attempts to find an alternative to the regional principle for the statistical treatment.

This was necessary although I ran into a troublesome technical obstacle as at the time of the survey the administrative units were banovinas: Over-all figures for the historical regions did not exist. If I needed some demographic data, from Bosnia for instance, I had to apply to three different statistical offices in three different towns, to collect the data for my villages, as this region was split between three banovinas. Although I could never entirely overcome this technical obstacle, there was no other way. Not taking into account the regional division meant a failure in bringing about anything of research value.

26

The behavior of people was conditioned to a high degree by the particular quality of life in any separate region of Yugoslavia, and this regional coloring was apparent in every single questionnaire. The regional style was so powerful in the villages that it even colored the manner of the expression of the reporter, so that merely from these shades of style one could guess the origin of any set of answers. (I frequently extracted answers the content of which contained no specific regional details and translated them for my Viennese statistical collaborator who did not understand Serbo-Croatian. In most cases he was able to recognize the origin of the reports merely from the style in which they were written, a further evidence for the decisive significance of the regional factor.)

When it was decided to group the villages according to historical regions, a second question arose: In what sequence were the regions to be listed so they would most faithfully represent reality, and thus avoid statistical tables presenting data without inner link and meaning. I found that here again I had to apply the historical principle, and I established a hypothesis about the historical sequence of the regions.

The fact that the historical or time element stood out clearly in every questionnaire and in every set of answers helped me to find this hypothesis. Each set came either from an old-world or a modern setting. Place of origin and stage of development were immediately apparent. For instance, a study of the replies left one with the inescapable impression that in Macedonian family life one was in a sense witnessing the past of family life in other regions. Bosnia seemed rather more recent, Serbia and Croatia more recent still. Each region set off the past of the other. In many districts millennial customs and standards seemed to have remained unchanged, whereas in others they had come to resemble those of the West European environment. The old Slav customs and standards of relationships were also apparently transformed to varying degrees in the various regions. The temporal succession was, as it were, shown on a background screen of spatial distribution. It was not far from this realization to the idea of making the various regions symbols of periods of time, and to compare regions in order to compare historical phases. Therefore, in order to obtain a scale I endeavored to classify my regions according to their degrees of development.

To achieve this arrangement it was, of course, necessary to specify the degree of "seniority of development." The seniority of any village was, however, easily recognizable to anyone reading the replies to the questionnaire. Nevertheless, to arrange the regions in a definite order, it was essential to have a definition and some system of marking off one from another. One had to decide exactly what one meant by "old-style" or "old." Was it ancient culture, economic backwardness, or a conservative attitude? Was "up-to-date" or "modern" identical with economically progressive, or with chaotic conditions, or with the great changes that had occurred in recent years?

As "old-style," I decided to mark those regions in which family relationships were consolidated on a traditional basis, where men's attitudes in various situations of daily life were clearly defined, and where people accepted such rules as eternal laws. Despite variations, many features were common in the patriarchal regions. I therefore treated the patriarchal setting as being a unitary stage of development, to be contrasted with various stages of change. These were the regions which I have marked as "old-style" or "patriarchal," using these adjectives as synonymous.

"Old-style" means backward in a very specific and restricted sense, and has no derogatory meaning, for the patriarchal regions are mostly regions of earlier high culture. For a long time they had been in the economic, technical, and artistic forefront, and only later was their manner of living petrified under the conservative influence of the decay of the Ottoman Empire. They may be compared to two regions, in one of which we have technical leadership, in the other a technical lag. An example would be Paris, which, with its first electric subways, was for a time the most advanced city in the field of transport. When, however, other cities constructed subways (partly modeled after the one in Paris), each successive system was better and more "up-to-date." The old "Metro," with its bad ventilation, seems old-fashioned today, and the city of Paris is now backward in the field of transport. However, Paris is quite capable of once again assuming first place. Indeed its earlier technical success in more than one sense gives it an advantage. Likewise with the "old-style" regions in Yugoslavia: Once progressive, they still have their potential, and are not behind the others in any disparaging sense.

As "up-to-date" or "modern," I classified regions in which patriarchal modes of life were destroyed under the influence of economic and political changes. In many districts, this took place at great speed, and family life was reduced to an anarchic state. Here men were guided much more strongly by their individual leanings and aims than in the patriarchal regions, and friction with other members of the family became much more frequent. For this reason, all replies from such villages bear the mark of an atmosphere of conflict. These regions were therefore marked as in a state of "abrupt transformation," or as "modern."

There are, however, regions in which economic changes took place gradually, in the course of several generations. These are the districts through which pass great lines of communications, particularly those along the Adriatic coast, which at an early stage came under the influence of more progressive, Western economic life and administration. Here people adjusted to new conditions without losing their balance, and conflict played a lesser part. Family life is almost as stable as in the patriarchal world. These regions adopted new relationships at a relatively early date and, in a sense, have been modern for a long time. The social climate is both old-style and modern. They are regions with continuous development, a new equilibrium, and, despite the conservative element in them, are classified as the "most modern." The coast region here occupies the most advanced position.

To obtain a more reliable definition of the priority of the various regions, I endeavored to find objective indices. One proved to be the emancipation from Turkish rule, which occurred at varying times in the various regions. Since the conditions of life in the Ottoman Empire clearly had a conservative effect on all relationships, including those within the family, the regions which were longer under Turkish domination retained more indices of conservatism than those liberated earlier. The regions which were not liberated till 1912 were more old-style than those which broke away as early as the seventeenth century. Arranged according to this criterion, I established the following sequence of regions:

1. *Macedonian Albanian villages.* That is of the Albanian minority villages in Macedonia. A few villages in neighboring regions (such as in the Sanjak, Metohia, and Kosovo) are counted in with the Macedonian. The majority are Moslem. This region remained under Ottoman rule till 1912.

2. *Macedonian Christian villages.* The corresponding Christian villages of Macedonia. They are exclusively Orthodox.

3. *Bosnian Moslem villages.* Villages of Moslem faith in Bosnia and Herzegovina, to which are added those with mixed Moslem Christian population. This region was Turkish till 1878 and 1908, respectively.

4. *Bosnian Christian villages.* Orthodox and Catholic villages in Bosnia and Herzegovina.

5. *Serbian villages.* Those of the Serbia prior to the Balkan wars (pre-1912). Here emancipation began in 1806 and was completed in 1867.

6. *Croatian villages.* Those in Croatia, including Slavonia and Dalmatia, within the pre-1918 boundaries, with the exception of the coastal villages. The larger part of this area was never under Turkish rule, the remainder was freed from Turkish rule at the end of the seventeenth century.

7. *The Littoral or Coast Region.* Villages of the Adriatic coast within three miles (five kilometers) of the sea. This region includes the northern coast, formerly a district under Croatian rule, and the southern, or Dalmatian, coast. In this narrow zone, only the villages (but not the cities) belonged to the Ottoman Empire.

The inquiry was confined to regions in which Serbo-Croatian was at the time the official language, and Slovenia was not included. Montenegro and the Voivodina were only partially included in my statistics because I had not enough replies to the questionnaire from these regions.

The classification of the regions according to their liberation date from the Turkish rule coincides with the general impression of the prevalence of old style or new elements given by the reports, and with my direct observations. The regions, listed according to their seniority, follow this scale:

Littoral

Croatia

Serbia

Bosnia Ch.

Bosnia Mo.

Macedonia Ch.

Macedonia Al.

The sequence of regions for the statistical tables established according to the principle of seniority proved most helpful in further research. Many conclusions of this study became possible only with the help of the hypothesis about the time element in the regions, or the historical meaning, or regional characteristics.

At the end of the study, under the heading "The Methods Applied," a detailed discussion is given about my experience with the statistical method and techniques. Discussed there are matters such as the collection of data, the decision to take the village as a unit, the reliability of the reporters, and the statistical procedure adopted.

# CHAPTER II.

## The Patriarchal Regime

IT IS not necessary to excavate in order to dig out patriarchal vestiges in the Slavic South. This regime does not belong to the distant past, but to yesterday, to the period of my survey. It looms also in the present. One can hear echoes of it even today and even in the cities of the most progressive region—the Adriatic coast—where people ask "Whom do you belong to?" (A čiji si ti?) when a younger person appears in a gathering. The wording of the question expresses the supposition that this boy or girl must be a member of a certain (and to all, known) extended family or clan. Single, "unattached" persons, severed from kin, seem to be unknown.

The mood of the people and their affection for the extended family in the time of the integral patriarchal order is shown in the following folk poem:

> On the farther bank of Sava river
> Three young maidens dance the kolo,
> In the chain is pretty Mara,
> And this is what that maiden says:
> Is there any of my kinsmen
> To take my message to my mother
> Never to give my sister's hand
> To any man who lives alone,
> But to marry her as I was,
> Where the company's big as here,
> With mother and with father-in-law,
> With brother and with sister-in-law
> Where husband has many sisters.
> When I go to see my mother
> Mother-in-law makes me a cake,
> Daughters-in-law prepare my satchel,
> Sisters-in-law deck me with beads,
> Make me feel queen of the world,
> See me gladly on my passage.
> When we reach the village outskirts
> Hang my satchel on my shoulder,
> While I stand with satchel ready,
> Cluster loving all around me,

Sending greetings to my mother,
Then upon my tender cheeks
Young wives, young girls plant their kisses
And, returning to the homestead,
Lingering eyes watch me depart.

*from Croatia*

## The Extended Family Zadruga

In the shelter of two great empires in the course of half a millennium there grew in the countryside a complex of traditional ways
of living, a body of custom which had deep roots in the distant past
of the Balkan and Slavic peoples. The patriarchal way of living was
a whole with its parts closely interconnected, and for centuries it
resisted all historical transformation.

At the center of the patriarchal regime was the extended family,
called *zadruga*, a specialty of the Slavic South. In its framework the
conjugal family had its place, and the whole subsistence economy
developed inside it. The zadruga was to be found in all Yugoslav
regions, except Slovenia; and there were zadrugas also in some parts
of Bulgaria. The zadruga has been largely known in sociological
and anthropological literature under its original name. In English
writings, other terms are also used, such as joint family, multiple
family, communal joint family. The word zadruga in Serbo-Croatian
means simply association or community.

During the survey, in many regions the zadruga was still intact,
in other parts it was in different stages of disintegration. But a few
decades earlier it had been the standard everywhere, and the individual peasant holding was definitely in the minority. In every
region the zadruga was remembered and always mentioned as a
standard of comparison for changed relationships, as the older generation had everywhere grown up in its fold.

The basic principle of the zadruga was that the male members
never leave the common home. Sons and their descendants remain
within it, and only the daughters leave it on marriage to become
members of the zadrugas of their husbands. The zadruga was gov-
erned by a hierarchical system, every member having a definite rank
within it. Rank was determined by age and sex, the sex criterion
being stronger than the age criterion; all males were superior to any
of the womenfolk, particularly in regions with a fighting tradition.

At the top of the hierarchy was the *domaćin* (from *dom*, home)
or *starešina* (from *stari*, the old one, senior), who represented the

zadruga in dealings with the authorities, bought and sold for the community, arranged the marriages of children and grandchildren, organized the economy, and in every respect was the final arbiter. But though in some parts the elder was unconditionally obeyed and shown regal honors, he was nowhere the absolute master over family or property, but rather enjoyed the position of representative or embodiment of the zadruga membership. All married men had the right to participate in decisions, and the elder took counsel with them. He might even be removed if he proved incapable or unworthy, though this very rarely took place. Frequently, he recommended his successor and this was as a rule respected by the members after his death. In many districts the new head was in principle elected, if the old head did not designate one. But often enough such an election was merely formal. There was one district in which, having reached agreement, it was customary of the members of the zadruga to pronounce the formula: "We are not going to impose a new law on an old land," and then proceed to elect their senior.

The head of a zadruga had much less authority than the head of a small peasant family who in law was the sole proprietor of the land holding. Sanders remarks that, in the Bulgarian zadruga also, the senior man takes notice of the other members, whereas the father of a small family assumes and feels his authority to be given by God, and behaves accordingly, allowing no criticism.[1] A zadruga head was expected to show a certain degree of severity and to maintain discipline but on no account to act arbitrarily or dictatorially.

An illustration of the democratic element in zadruga organization is given by Krauss,[2] who quotes typical remarks made by young peasants in Herzegovina during Turkish times. When peasant sons pressed their father to break up their zadruga and the father refused, they used to say to him: "We are not on the coast, in Dalmatia, where the father is everything and the children nothing." They were alluding to Austrian law in neighboring Dalmatia, which was known to them. They found its provisions about the individual ownership of landed property unjust. According to customary zadruga law, all men had rights on the holding, as well as in a decision to break it up. The right of the father was more restricted by patriarchal custom than by modern civil codes.

As a rule, the *domaćica*, or female head of the home, was the

[1] Irwin T. Sanders, *Balkan Village*, University of Kentucky Press, 1949, p. 66.
[2] Friedrich S. Krauss, *Sitte und Brauch der Südslaven*, Wien, 1885.

domaćin's wife. She administered domestic matters, was hostess to visitors, and assisted the girls to prepare their trousseaus. All the other wives, and unmarried girls, had precisely specified tasks in kitchen, household work, and economy. A young wife entering a zadruga, was known as the *mlada* (the word means "the young one" but also has the connotation of bride) and enjoyed a special position. In her first year she was not given a place in the *rota* of work, or rather, she had the task of becoming liked by her new family and thereby acquiring its trust. The children too all had their tasks, principally stockminding. They were considered to belong not only to their parents but also to the commune as a whole. If any mother was widowed and wished to remarry, it was only with great difficulty that she was allowed to take her children out of the commune.

In the zadruga, apart from clothing and small objects, there was no private property. Money was administered by the head, or else by another of the men to whom buying and selling had been assigned. There is, admittedly, a later stage of development in which the private sector was considerably enlarged. The daughters-in-law brought dowries and employed any revenue from these funds for themselves and their children, but such private property proved to be in contradiction with the communal principle, and wherever a daughter-in-law brought in any dowry in the form of immovable estate or livestock, the zadruga rapidly decayed, as people developed their own individual economic interests.

There were some variations of zadruga rules according to whether regions formerly belonged to Austria, to Turkey, or were in the Dinaric Alps.

In the regions which belonged to Austria, the zadruga set-up was particularly well developed. These were in the main lowland districts, in which agriculture takes precedence over stock-raising, and particularly over sheep-rearing. In these regions, there was more democracy than in others, the women had more rights. In some districts, the zadruga head enjoyed his authority only on an annual basis, not for life. There is a Slavonian proverb (Slavonia is part of Croatia) which runs: "All power is temporary, only God's is eternal, and zadruga authority goes in turns."

The feudal system of Austria favored the zadruga, and this was further fostered by the statutes governing the Military March. In this area it was forbidden to break up a zadruga without the special assent of the military command. The zadruga was looked upon more or less as a military unit, and hence was subject to military discipline.

The zadruga system was well suited to army purposes, for it was only with zadruga farm economy that a large proportion of the menfolk could be maintained under arms without agriculture suffering.

Even in the period when the feudal system and the Military March no longer existed, Austrian civil law supported the zadruga and laid down the lines of its development. Since Austria was a state based on a written code, everything was much more clearly defined and less mobile than elsewhere, with only unwritten custom law and observance to govern affairs. In some Austrian districts, the local authority elected the new zadruga head when the old one died, though this usually followed consultation with village headmen and the members of the zadruga concerned.

In Moslem districts, the zadruga never flourished as it did in other areas. The intimacy of the married couple and the apartness of the wife are important Moslem principles, and these did not quite fit into the zadruga institution. In the whole region once Turkish, including Serbia, the zadruga developed more independently than in the Austrian region, as it was not tied up by codifices. Since the relationships of peasants in the Ottoman Empire were not regulated by written law, zadrugas could at a certain moment break up easily, and therefore their integration was accompanied by less hostility and resentment than in the Austrian provinces.

In the Dinaric districts, with their fighting tradition, the Illyric past, and a pastoral economy, life was centered on the tribal set-up. The zadruga was not the central point even of economic life. Here there were no large peasant holdings with gardens, orchards, vineyards, and arable fields grouped around the buildings as in the lowlands. The houses were built of and on rocks, with only a few small fields and cultivable dales (*dolinice*, little valleys) scattered around among the rocks. The maintenance of the family and any prosperity was based on flocks of sheep, and these were pastured on common pasture-lands.

The tribal system was particularly developed among the Montenegrins (as also among the Albanians of Albania), and there are traces of this in Herzegovina and in southern Dalmatia. The various tribes were established each on its own territory, generally a closed valley cut off from the surrounding country by mountains. The tribes (*pleme*, plural *plemena*) varied greatly in size; one of 4,000 "guns," that is to say 4,000 adult males, was a powerful tribe.

The tribes consisted of several clans or brother-groupings. All members of such a *bratstvo* (from *brat*, brother) held that they were descended from a single ancestor so that they were all brothers and sisters. These groupings were exogamous. Pastures on the mountains belonged to these clans. Since the greater part of the peasants spent the summer months with the livestock up in the mountains, zadrugas lost some of the significance they had had in the lowlands. However, the zadruga hierarchy was here a steeply graded system with enormous differences in the rank and rights of the various members, and zadruga discipline was severe in spite of the fact that tribe and clan were so important.

Within tribe and clan there were close-knit solidarity and unity. The fighting tradition was strong, the interest in economics and farming insignificant. (The tribal system and ways of life will be discussed in detail in the chapters "Culture Contact" and "Yugoslav Regions.")

Regarding problems of family relationships, the stage of break-up of the zadruga, that is, whether it was intact, half-way toward dissolution, or completely dissolved, seems to be of greater importance than the particular form of the zadruga set-up. For this reason, in the present study, I shall treat all forms of zadruga life as a whole and will regard the traditional way of living, patriarchal system, and zadruga set-up as identical, using the terms interchangeably.

### Preservation of the Zadruga

The zadrugas began to break up in every region at different points of time and at different speeds. Parallel to the disintegration of the zadrugas, the concept of the zadruga itself was gradually changing. Therefore it was necessary to get clear what in every area was considered to be a zadruga. Answers to the question in the questionnaire "Who as a rule is included in a household?" were divided in four groups.

Into the first group fall villages in which the majority lived in the old-patterned large zadrugas. Married sons and their families stuck together even when the father died. Other relations frequently lived too in the zadrugas according to old zadruga customs. Some answers from these villages are:

> Families are often large and include more distant relations. Even today there are some quite large zadrugas. Latterly splitting-up has become more frequent.

> It is very rare for sons to split the community while the father is still living. There are only two cases in this village.

> (*Macedonia, Žegligovo district*)

The second group embraces villages in which, in the majority of families, the married sons stayed with their parents till the father died, then as a rule split up, or those in which they all stuck together till all the sons were married. For example:

> Division is rare before the father's death. As a rule they split up immediately after this. Regarding division, it is the father and the law that govern. If the father does not leave one child a larger portion, the property is divided into equal portions. If a household does split up while the father is alive, this is usually due to dispute caused by the father or mother making one son the favorite. Cases of litigation are rather rare. (*Orthodox village, Stolac district, Herzegovina*)

Into the third group fall villages with transitional forms, where the married sons customarily stayed with the parents for a certain time, as, for instance, while their own children were still small, or while there were still few children, but later divided the property. In such villages, as a rule, there were also small families with individual economies. For example:

> When a son has grown-up children with whom he will be able to establish a separate home and get on, he splits off from his father and bothers. (*Orthodox village, Sanski Most district, Bosnia*)

The fourth group consists of villages in which small, independent families were in the majority. Here the parents lived together with their unmarried children. This group includes also families in which, in addition to the unmarried children, there might also live a married son or daughter, with their families. There was sometimes also some other relative without family. For example:

> In the main parents and children live together. A son separates from his father when he marries. There are no households with a large number of persons in them, at most ten in the whole village. There are no zadrugas.

> In most instances sons separate from their fathers during his lifetime. A son builds a small house for himself and then separates. I know a father whose son separated from him with only one acre of land, the father having seven acres and six more unmarried sons.
>
> (*Kordun area, Dvor na Uni district, Croatia*)

Graph 1 clearly shows how the first two types of zadruga prevail in the "old-world" regions, but are rapidly disappearing in the face of "modern" forms. One can clearly see the great gap between Macedonia, which till quite recently was under Turkey, and all other districts, that is to say, even Bosnia, which was separated from Turkey a generation earlier, when it came under Western influence.

37

Graph 1. Who as a rule is included in a household

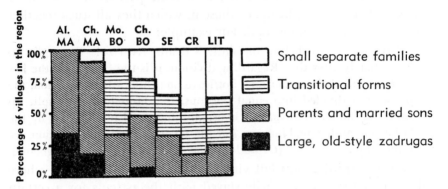

Small separate families

Transitional forms

Parents and married sons

Large, old-style zadrugas

Graph 2 shows all villages in which there were still any of the large, old-style zadrugas, without regard to whether such zadrugas constituted the larger part of the village or not.

Graph 2. Large, old-style zadrugas

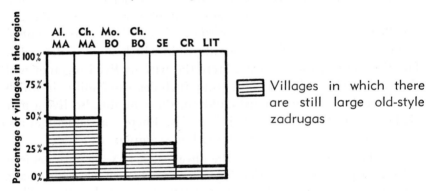

Villages in which there are still large old-style zadrugas

This graph presents a very simple picture: In Macedonia we have a large block of preserved zadruga life, with lesser blocks in Christian Bosnia and in Serbia. If we omit Moslem Bosnia, Yugoslavia as a whole is seen to fall into three stages. The intermediate stage is interesting because, though Bosnia and Serbia were emancipated from the patriarchal system under differing historical conditions, these regions nevertheless reveal similar stages of abandonment of the zadruga way of life. (Serbia in fact freed itself from Turkey at a much earlier date, whereas Bosnia earlier came under the influence of a Western country and more advanced economy.)

In the lowest grade are Croatia and the Littoral, regions which in the main were never under the Ottoman Empire, or, only for a short period. To some extent this graph corrects the picture given by the first, for, in that, Croatia and the Littoral are shown to have some villages counted as zadruga villages, whereas closer examination shows that they do not show true zadruga life, or at least, have not maintained the zadruga tradition.

A series of typical replies from the various regions may illustrate the picture. Among the Albanians, all villages fall into the first groups of zadruga organization:

> Sons do not separate from their father while he is alive. Such division is regarded as shameful in the extreme.  (*Andrijevica district*)

> Usually father and sons live together in the family. After the father's death, the sons continue their joint life, till such time as they accumulate sufficient for each to set up his own home and each has built his own dwelling. Then they divide up.

> There are cases of division immediately after the father's death. There have been and still are zadrugas in which only brothers are the members, since more distant relations, and also brothers as they marry and get children, have split off. Sons never split off from the father, whether they are married or not.  (*Struga district*)

In the Orthodox villages of Macedonia the conditions were the same as among the Albanians. From the answers given, we see that they considered the old-style, large zadrugas as the norm and considered a household in which only the married sons lived to be a small family.

> Only married sons live in a family.  (*Žegligovo district*)

> Sons do not split away from their father, that is held to be sinful and shameful.  (*Morihovo district*)

> Frequently in one family, blood brothers and male cousins on the father's side live all together in one household. Before the war,[3] "in Turkish days," there were zadrugas with from 15 to 20 members. However, now there are large zadrugas but principally with 10 to 15 members. Sons rarely split from their father.
> (*St. Nikola Ovče Polje district*)

> There used to be zadrugas. Averaging 25-40 members. Latterly they keep splitting up. Before the war there were zadrugas with 90-100 members. Sons never split from their father. There was only one instance. That was a great scandal, in the end father and sons made it up again and they still live together.  (*Nerodimlje district*)

In Moslem Bosnia we find the different types of zadruga, but not the old-style, large zadruga.

[3] References to "the war" are always to the First World War of 1914-1918, preceded in some parts by the Balkan wars of 1912-1913.

There are cases of married sons and more distant relations living together, and some of the opposite case. There never were zadrugas. Married sons rarely split off while their father is alive. (*Tuzla district*)

There used to be zadrugas. After the war they mostly split up. Now there are no large ones. Husband, wife, and children live together. Wherever there are a number of sons in a family, as soon as they marry, they separate from their father while he is living, leaving him as a rule with the eldest son in the old home.       (*Rogatica district*)

In the Christian parts of Bosnia there were rather more villages with the old, large zadrugas than in the Moslem parts. From the three following answers we see the gradual process of departure from the old large zadruga:

Families include both married sons and more distant relations, sometimes to the fifth degree. There are still zadrugas today, most households are zadrugas. Large zadrugas (of 50 members) began to break up just before the war. In the surrounding villages there are today some with about fifty members. (*Orthodox village, Jajce district*)

A family embraces only married brothers with their father. Before the war, zadruga life existed but since the war a splitting has begun owing to a weakening of authority.       (*Tuzla district*)

Before the war there were more zadrugas. They even held out after the war, till the crisis,[4] whereas more recently a zadruga here has been a rarity. Latterly zadruga intolerance has become still greater. As a rule the zadruga is put up with while the father is still alive, division immediately follows.       (*Sarajevo district*)

Serbia had gone a step farther from the zadruga than had Bosnia.

A son lives with his father solely from regard for public opinion; apart from this there is great intolerance between them. (*Niš district*)

Till five or six years ago,[5] there were very large zadrugas, with from 30 to 40, even 45 members, but in later years division has come in very swiftly. Father and mother live in community with their children, their married sons, and grandchildren. Latterly, if there are a number of brothers, they split up, and the zadrugas are broken into pieces.

       (*Dobričevo district*)

There are few zadrugas. Remnants drag on. It is as a rule the younger sons and grandchildren who break away. Father and mother and one son remain. Nearly three-quarters of the total population live in small households; it is the most prosperous who live together. What we call

---

[4] By "the crisis" is always meant the economic depression of the thirties.

[5] I.e., until about 1932.

domaćin houses (distinguished households) number between 10 and 20 persons. The larger zadrugas number 15-20 persons.

*(Kosmaj district)*

In Croatia there were even fewer zadrugas than in Serbia; their break-up began somewhat earlier than in Serbia. In Croatia, conditions tend to differ from those in other regions for the reason that here a special zadruga law prohibited division, or rather, permitted it only subject to fairly stringent conditions. For instance, the availability of a certain amount of land was insisted upon, also the consent of all members of the zadruga and so forth. Nevertheless, the tendency toward a splitting-up of the zadrugas did, despite all obstacles, win here. Zadruga members split up "secretly," which, in actual wording, means that they split up, merely avoiding the legal consequences of their new system of ownership of the land. The law proved to be no brake on the force of this process.

In one family live father, mother, and their children. Today only zadrugas with a reduced number of members can still exist. After the war particularly large numbers split up. Previously, it was regarded as shameful to split up, but today it is the usual thing—a need. As soon as the sons have married, they divide the property mutually. The father and mother as a rule go with one of them, though there are cases in which they remain by themselves. It is rare for such a son to split off from the father, but there are even cases of that.

*(Petrinja district)*

There were zadrugas right through till the March was demilitarized (1873 and 1881). Today there is not one zadruga in the true sense. They exist only as far as legal ownership goes, but these constitute only 3 percent. Otherwise, relationships have been completely adapted to the modern spirit.     *(Bjelovar district, former Military March)*

In one house as a rule live parents and their children, the male children remaining on the property, the female when they marry, or later, being bought off with a money payment. In the end, one son only remains on the estate, the others obtaining land shares and a money payment toward a new house. There were a few zadrugas, but even those were wound up either publicly or in private 50 years since.

*(Virovitica district)*

In joint economy live parents, children, and near relatives. There are now no zadrugas. 30-40 years ago there still were. Frequently, sons split off from their father while he is still alive. In such a division, the father decides. It is customary for it to come to litigation, for the father gives the son only the essentials. There are turns of phrase like: "The son would like to cling to platter and wine goblet and make his father

41

eat out of the pig's trow." There is a case of litigation in this village between father and son which has lasted 11 years. (*Varaždin district*)

In this respect, as in many others, the Littoral stands distinct from continental Croatia. Because in our definition of the zadruga we were ruled by the formal aspect, namely, whether or not the married sons remain in joint economy with the father, we obtained as a result a fairly high number of villages in the Littoral that had zadrugas. But close examination established that in many cases one had here common life without true zadruga set-up. Communal life through three generations without the zadruga is to be found in no other district but the Littoral. A greater stability of living conditions in this region made joint living feasible without a strict arrangement.

Zadrugas used to exist. An old woman tells me that her family's zadruga numbered 48 members. They began to split up 50 or 40 years ago." (*Isle of Ugljan*)

Parents and children live in community. The married sons generally split off sooner or later. It is unknown whether there were ever zadrugas. If there were, it must have been a very long time ago. Here the Romance influence is predominant. (*Isle of Rab*)

As we see, the very concept of zadruga changed when life got away from patriarchal relationships. Whereas in old-world surroundings the term zadruga was taken to mean the large old-style zadruga, which in principle never breaks up, in modern regions the zadruga was held to mean merely joint economy of parents and married sons to the death of the father. Whereas in the old-style regions, division of the zadruga was understood in the sense of division among the brothers after the father's death, in modern regions it was taken to mean division while the father was still alive. Both the concept and the very forms of the zadruga were undergoing a process of gradual change.

## Time Element

When money economy infiltrated the countryside at the end of the nineteenth and beginning of the twentieth centuries, the massive structure of zadruga and patriarchal life, which had withstood historical changes for centuries, was shattered. Peasant life was changed objectively as well as subjectively: What had been loved became hateful. What the zadruga had meant for innumerable generations was forgotten.

But people who grew up in zadrugas remember them with affection and nostalgia even today. Within it there was no loneliness and no insecurity nor any arduous struggle for a living. It offered every-body the possibility of maintenance, marriage, and the upbringing of children. It conferred standing and a sense of importance on the individual. Without any particular effort, in due course everybody grew up into the higher rank of its hierarchy. Youth lived a carefree life, able to devote much time to artistic handicrafts, singing, danc-ing, and parties. A relatively affluent mode of living, without great effort or worry and without excessively hard work was known solely in a zadruga. The peasant outside any zadruga was commonly re-garded as a poor man, as witness such familiar turns of speech as "individual farmer—a martyr" and "individual home—empty cave."

Only under special circumstances would a zadruga break up, the reason being usually that it had become too large. Milićević wrote about his zadruga in the beginning of the nineteenth century, when his great-grandfather Milić, then 85, called his children and grandchildren to tell them what he had decided. He said that "the beehive was crowded and it was necessary to fly out." The younger ones thought first that someone had offended the senior and looked around for whom to blame. But the old man said: "No one insulted me, only I myself want to break up. I am most sorry that what was ours, will be ours, yours, theirs. But it is better to do so now than later on." They split up the zadruga; yet the children could not grasp it, and played the whole day in this and that house and remained for the night just where they were. When they were told, "go home now, that is not your home," they used to cry bitterly.[6]

Another example is mentioned by Krauss[7] from the eighteen-seventies. In a zadruga of sixty persons in a Slavonic village, an old woman died as she sat in her usual place behind the warm stove, and nobody noticed her death. She was discovered only a few days later. Count Janković, who was the patron of this village, requested the break-up of the zadruga, as he considered it too big to care properly for all members.

The process of political and economic change which influenced the villages gradually or suddenly will be discussed a little later. As the external changes progressed, the less pleasing aspects of the zadruga way of life became visible, and the members of the zadruga became aware that their freedom was limited by countless rules and by their dependence on the senior members of the zadruga. Dissatis-faction made its appearance, and this proved a personal factor hasten-

[6] Milićević, *Glasnik srpske slovesnosti*, IX, 1857.
[7] Krauss, *Sitte und Brauch der Südslaven*, Vienna, 1885.

ing the process of dissolution. Now the zadruga was no longer capable of resisting the objective circumstances which were already undermining it. Under the influence of historical, political, and economic factors, varying from region to region, the zadruga dissolution began at varying times. During the period of this survey, the process of decay had begun in every region but had advanced differently in the various regions. In some one saw the last stages of the storm which two generations earlier had dealt powerful blows to the great structure of the zadruga. In other regions, most of the zadrugas broke up during the First World War or immediately after it. Whereas in a third group it was only in recent years that the zadruga began to disintegrate, during the depression of the thirties.

The villages of the first group, in which the zadruga began to fall apart before the First World War are, in a certain sense, progressive, in that the influence of the economy with the money nexus began to influence them early. Here are examples from three different regions:

There were zadrugas 50-80 years ago. They split up in the main about 1870. In many cases (60 per cent) the father shared out the estate while alive, but 90 per cent of those could then not agree and shared out the estate [sic]. Today it is the rule for only the family— father, mother and children, to live together.

*(Krapina district, Croatia)*

Here there were many zadrugas, but they began to split up immediately after the occupation of Bosnia (1878), and particularly after the annexation (1908), and further after the war (1918).

*(Čajniče district, Bosnia)*

In one family live only the married sons. The split-up of the zadrugas, which existed to the end of last century, a few up to the war, began at the commencement of this century.

*(Mladenovac district, Serbia)*

In villages in which the zadrugas broke up some decades ago, there were few vestiges of zadruga life.

The second group comprises those villages in which the majority of the zadrugas broke up either during or immediately after the First World War.

The break-up began after the Liberation (1913) for previously the *begs* and *agas*[8] would not permit it. The married sons and their parents live together, and sons rarely break off from the father while he is alive. There were zadrugas in this village till recently.

*(Plevlje district, Sanjak)*

[8] Turkish squires and dignitaries.

1. Bosnian peasant in sheepskin coat      2. Old Moslem from Herzegovina

3. Men from the Dinaric Alps (Dalmatian Hinterland)

4. Bosnian peasants in the fields

5. Man from Bosnia

Before the war there were 80-100 per cent zadrugas with 10-20 members. In the ten years immediately after the war, all the zadrugas split up. Very frequently the sons break off from the father during his lifetime. They usually break off when all the brothers have married.

*(Posavina district, Serbia)*

After the war, all the zadrugas split up. The sons go on living with their father, but after his death they split up.

*(Samobor district, Croatia)*

In villages in which the zadrugas split up during or immediately after the war, there were more vestiges of the zadruga way of life than in the first group.

In the third group, we have villages in which the zadrugas began to break up on a large scale only after 1930, after the commencement of the economic depression. Here we find villages with a well-preserved patriarchal life. These villages, which came into contact with the world market so late, were in a sense backward.

There are no large zadrugas, they kept going till the "crisis," but after 1930 they broke up. The last zadruga numbered 60 members. Today in one household live married sons and father, and they do not break up during his life, for that would be considered most shameful. *(Albanian village, Andrijevica district)*

Before the war, folk lived in zadrugas, but after the war the zadrugas began rapidly to break up, particularly when the economic "crisis" started, and the zadruga members could not prosper as they had done. In one household lives the married son, who rarely breaks away while his father is alive, unless there is friction between father and son or father-in-law and daughter-in-law, or because of disagreement among the brothers. *(Vlasotince district, Serbia)*

In the villages in which the zadrugas broke up last, there was as a rule the most prominent trace of the zadruga way of life.

Graphs 3 and 4 show the three groupings of villages.

This reveals that among the Albanians the zadruga was still not breaking up, while in the Littoral it had ceased to do so, that is to say, what zadrugas did exist have already broken up. In the remaining regions, there was a great measure of decay of the zadruga. In Serbia the process was still in full swing, and was not much less than in the preceding period. In Croatia the process was already tending to slow down. The peak of such activity was in the Christian parts of Bosnia and Herzegovina.

Graph 5 shows that the process had slowed down, or perhaps one should say that in most districts it was completed. It had only begun

Graph 3. Break-up of old-style zadruga

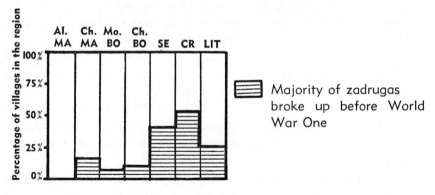

Majority of zadrugas broke up before World War One

Graph 4. Break-up of old-style zadruga

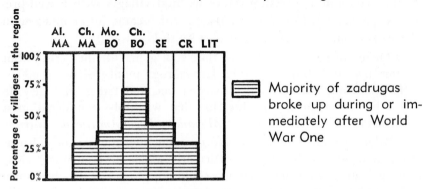

Majority of zadrugas broke up during or immediately after World War One

Graph 5. Break-up of the old zadruga

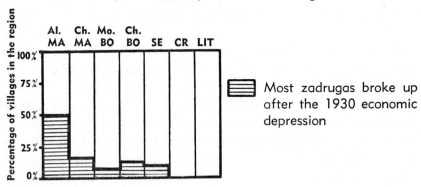

Most zadrugas broke up after the 1930 economic depression

among the Albanians, where it was vigorous. In Croatia and the Littoral, the split-up of the zadrugas was complete. Those zadrugas which had remained in a modified form in Croatia had adapted to economic conditions and exhibited vestigial characteristics of the old-style large zadrugas.

Comparison between these three graphs shows a regular curve of change from modern to old-world regions. Great economic changes attacked each region and brought it into the complex of the modern state and of world economy, at a different period and under different circumstances. Individualism has awakened in men everywhere.

A letter from one of our teachers demonstrates how the various economic factors in the three periods acted on one village and zadruga life in it:

Before the war, a large number of men, particularly married men, went to America, whence they sent large sums of money home to their wives. The wives gave up folk costume and began to deck out their daughters with ready-made garments and thereby trained the girls away from needlework. The folk custom of the "sewing bee" had meant the girls getting together in this house or that, where two rooms were set aside for embroidering on cloth and open work in linen, but now they get together just for parties, to be joined by the lads with *tamburas.*[9] So long as money flowed in from America, they spent freely, even getting into debt at shops and inns (which rapidly sprang up) but when money ceased to pour in, when they felt the burden of debts, there began dissatisfaction in many households and the splitting up of the married sons.

The zadrugas broke up, for after the war the men traded in live-stock—cattle, horses, pigs—and earned big money, and everyone wanted to be his own master and get rich. That commercial prosperity destroyed the zadruga, and with it went influences which utterly transformed the village, so it looked quite different from what it had been before the war.

In particular, the younger generation became dissatisfied. Songs were rarely to be heard, in fact, one could even say they were no longer to be heard at all out at work in the fields, where formerly the air had rung with them in the frequent breaks in work, nor was singing to be heard on Sundays or on holidays, when formerly the young folk had stayed out till early evening dancing the characteristic *Lika kolo,* which now lost its true form. Now it's all mucking about and horse-play, they get tired and go home early. It is a sad thing no longer to see that old-time youthful gaiety, young people are too serious, life has become hard, through greater demands and poor earnings. *In the days of prosperity an economic change took place but there has not yet been any psychological change.* This change was brought about *by the depression* since young folk go off after earnings, which free them from domestic discipline and the authority of their parents.

(*Gračac district, Lika, Croatia*)

[9] Small plucked-string instruments.

47

## Reasons for the Break-up of the Zadruga

The decay of the zadruga in the Slavic South has its parallels in underdeveloped countries on other continents, where traditional socio-economic systems also gave way to money economy and industrialization. Into these countries penetrated the "new economy" and technology from the economically highly developed centers of Europe and America, building up industries, importing capital, and connecting them to the world market. All this first induced and then accelerated the economic development of these areas. In various Yugoslav regions the course of events was similar. It was infrequent that things developed slowly and "organically" without initiative or interference from outside. The peasants considered the innovations introduced into the villages as alien to them, regardless of whether they came from nearby cities, from centers of the state such as Vienna and Budapest, or from abroad. Also the Yugoslav students spoke mostly of "infiltration," "penetration," "irruption," and only seldom of evolution of the subsistence economy toward a money and market economy. They too considered the change primarily the result of "external" influence.

This penetration is illustrated by the development in Croatia, as presented by the Yugoslav economist and sociologist Rudolf Bićanić.[10] Bićanić regards the agrarian world crisis at the end of the past century as the immediate cause of the decline of the zadruga economy in Croatia. This depression lasted from 1873 to 1895 and, during these years, annihilated the zadruga. The crisis was connected with the whole technological and economic development of the world. The establishment of railroad and steamship transportation reduced the costs of transportation to such a level that agricultural products from overseas could be imported to Europe. Larger and larger areas were cultivated in the countries overseas, and production and export of grains increased with great speed. As Bićanić states:

> Thus in the period of railroad construction cheap grain began to come to Europe. The appearance of this grain upon the European market caused a real revolution of prices. At first this was evident in the grain prices, particularly in wheat; later it extended to all agricultural products.

The drop of the price of grain raised the buying power of the urban population, and had disastrous consequences in the villages.

10 Rudolf Bićanić, *Agrarna kriza u Hrvatskoj 1873-1895* (*The Agrarian Crisis in Croatia 1873-1895*), Zagreb, 1937.

"Millions of peasants were proletarianized or emigrated to overseas countries" writes Bićanić. He continues:

> Before the agrarian crisis emigration from Europe amounted on the average to three and a half million persons per year, but during the latter stages of the crisis emigration attained a peak of six to seven million people a year.
>
> . . . The peasant could satisfy his ordinary needs in his own zadruga by old established methods. He was now compelled to sell his products, and later when the zadruga was destroyed, the same forces which had penetrated his economy from the outside compelled him to buy factory goods. The main external forces through which capitalism broke through were: the bureaucratic-capitalistic state, and also the railroads and foreigners, especially foreign capital.

The influence of the state upon the rapid change of the economic and social structure in Croatia was very strong. The general goal was to organize the country on the European model, and the main efforts were to encourage commerce and industry, as it was believed that these meant riches for the country in which they were developed. A prerequisite for this development was a modern government administration, for which taxes in cash were needed. At the end of the last century, which coincides with the first phase of the agrarian crisis, the taxes in Croatia were tripled. "Thus the peasant," Bićanić observes, "in order to have money available for taxes, had to sell more and more of his products. This brought him more and more into contact with money, and with its consequences."

Modern means of transportation—railroads, roads, and ship transport—were expanded in this period and made it possible for large amounts of village products to be brought to market. These goods, which the peasant produced, had become cheaper, and the peasant had to sell greater and greater quantities in order to get the money he needed for taxes, salt, and other fixed expenses.

The cities grew rapidly under the influence of the agrarian crisis and the new enterprises which were established by foreign capital. This capital flowed from countries with a highly developed economy into those with a more backward economy, where the money earned higher interest. Bićanić says: "The pressure of the crisis on the structure of the peasant economy can indirectly be seen in the vast increase of laborers and servants. In ten years their number doubled, and consists now almost exclusively of pauperized peasants, who by the destructive effect of the depression were cast from their homes and forced from the village to the city."

49

This phenomenon known as "flight from the village" now reached large dimensions.

A tension arose between the very flexible prices of agricultural products and the less flexible prices of those goods the peasants buy, up to completely fixed expenses (such as taxes, debts, etc.) which make up the greatest percentage of the cash expenses in the underdeveloped money economy. The price of wheat dropped from 15 forints to 5 forints, and the increased expenditures for taxes, salt, and tobacco had to be paid in cash. During periods of increasing prices and in good years people acquired the habit of buying goods. Merchants brought goods into the village, especially after the railroad made transportation cheaper. When prices dropped, it was difficult to give up this habit. The old customs also could not be maintained since the incomes of the peasant families had been reduced and the cash expenditures had relatively increased.

The debts of the peasants increased rapidly. Tax debts, especially, accumulated. More and more attachments and tax sales occurred; the peasants' holdings were sold more and more frequently; they changed owners, and land began to be handled as an article of commerce.

It is a fact that the greatest population increase in Croatia is recorded in the years 1880-1890 and that most zadruga divisions occurred immediately after this period. The rapid increase of population upon economic foundations that had remained unchanged was bound to lead to severe tensions and to a change of the social organization.

It is clear that with the wheat price at 5 forints the economy could not be carried on as it had been when wheat cost 15 forints. The old customs could not be maintained in the face of expenses and to meet taxes when 234 kilos of wheat was no longer enough but 1,026 had to be found. Small wonder that the zadruga members became dissatisfied and the old order could not be maintained. As long as everything proceeded in the house according to old customs, the zadruga members did not criticize the senior, nor blame him for bad management. But when the price of agrarian products dropped, all needs could no longer be satisfied in the old way. Therefore each individual sought to make life easier for himself by private means, which he obtained through marriage.

Bićanić presents a table showing how many zadruga divisions occurred in individual districts in Croatia in the four five-year periods of the depression. From this may be seen very clearly how the process gripped one district after another, beginning with the wheat regions, which were closely connected with the world economy, and ending in the poor regions in the Dinaric mountains.

What Bićanić showed for the districts of Croatia with a great deal of material and precise figures also happened in the entire South Slav region: One after the other, the regions were penetrated by the world and money economy, which was followed inexorably by the decay of the peasant zadruga.

### Patriarchal System and Poverty

In our material, many descriptions make it evident that, in very poor patriarchal villages, a humane element was often in the foreground. Such atmosphere is in sharp contrast to the atmosphere of cynicism, brutality, and violence evident in some villages in less "backward" settings. The question arises whether there was some connection among the patriarchal regime, poverty, and humane emotions. Are these three phenomena mutually linked, and, if they are, in what way? Two strongly drawn pictures illustrate this triangle. The first is from Bosnia:

A small group of houses on a slope in Central Bosnia. The village lies a full two hours' walk from the highway and the market town, a fact which is, however, of no importance for the inhabitants. There is absolutely no connection between village and markets since the villagers have nothing to sell and buy nothing. The paths which lead to the village are stony and lead over steep mountain ridges. Wagon roads are completely superfluous, since the entire traffic takes place on the backs of small Bosnian pack horses.

Twenty years ago there were 15 families, now there are 25, but there were more people in the 15 families than are now in the 25. The peasants claim that this is so because the life of their fathers was "better and easier." They are all nostalgic for the past which, according to their tales, was carefree and easy.

The main food, which is often the only food, is rye or corn bread, and they do not have enough of this. "We are never full, we are always hungry!" In Ahmed's house there are two windows, each a square foot in size. The two rooms are tiny and there is no furniture, nor is there any in the other houses. They use homewoven carpets as blankets. Only five people in the village can read and write, but the peasants consider this unimportant.

While Mujo is reporting this to me, he weeps. He is forty years old, but looks like an old man. Nobody in the village is older than forty or fifty. Many people die in the spring when food is scarcest. The last time a physician visited them was 23 years ago. The people cure themselves with various herbs and incantations. Many women die in child-birth, which takes place without any help whatsoever, often in the stable, where the umbilical cord is cut with a hoe or a knife.

The situation of the women is much harder than that of the men. Heavy work goes on throughout the year and the women keep at it till the very moment of the birth, after which they immediately get up. The men are aware of the difficult situation of their women and they do not in the least look down on the women nor do they keep them in slavish dependency as is characteristic of many other places. The children start working at five years of age, as soon as they can hold a stick in their hands.

There are almost no family conflicts. Although the zadruga is split up, many of its customs remain: e.g., the common family councils, the protection of the weaker members, and so on.

One can always sense an atmosphere of compassion: the children are brought up with love and not with force. The parents almost never hit them but say: "A soft word will open an iron door."

*(Bosnia, Bugojno district)*

Another example from Macedonia:

The people in this village live in smoke and darkness. A few years ago the Hygienic Institute in Skoplje furnished the peasants with iron bedsteads. But nobody sleeps on them. They have been thrown out or stowed away. An old man said to me: "I think I'd die if I should lie down on a bed."

The house is the most dreadful and miserable thing in their lives. No words can describe the interior of the monstrosity which they call "house." On one side there are oxen, a horse (if they have one), a donkey, tied to the manger. On the other side is the fireplace where the children and the rest of the family crouch near the ashes to keep warm. The smells from the cattle are stifling. The house is always full of smoke. Anyone not born here cannot stand it for a half-hour without getting smarting eyes. There must always be smoke so that cattle and people stay warm. Thus everything in the house is covered with soot. Of course, there is no wooden floor, the earth is simply left as it was.

In this village there are 100 men to 74 women. It is not likely that a man beats his wife; there are 60 married couples and in the course of eight years beatings have occurred only twice. The peasants regard beating as the right of the husband, but do not consider it "nice," since God gives no blessing to such a home.     *(Macedonia, Skoplje district)*

The patriarchal system did not originally develop in regions where people were destitute, but, on the contrary, where they were rather well off. There are many indications of this: The rich and highly developed folklore together with beautifully embroidered costumes and gold ornaments in the previously Austrian areas. Also, in the regions of Oriental influence and in the Dinaric Alps, the people used expensive clothing, silver ornaments, weapons, richly caparisoned horses, and many extravagant ceremonies. It is known that the large zadrugas used to have a high standard of living. Between the two world wars, however, purely patriarchal customs and relationships existed almost exclusively where poverty was prevalent—mostly in villages in unproductive mountain regions, far from the stream of traffic. Hunger and need, always the rule in such regions, were aggravated by the helplessness of the people. Their isolation and their way of life, unchanged for centuries, strengthened their conservatism and prevented an adjustment to new conditions.

In these remote villages, poverty and conservatism formed a vicious circle. For a long time, these villages were not touched by the waves of capitalistic penetration for they had no commercial appeal; their inhabitants had nothing to sell and could buy nothing. Later, the money economy reached these areas with an impact and speed to which these hitherto untouched places could not adjust. The zadrugas fell apart, and there was no compensation for their collapse. The people received no benefits from the changed circumstances such as freedom of movement or the possibility of earning a living. Instead, they sank deeper into the bitterest poverty. They knew no way of acquiring relief; they did not know how to get credit, tax deferment, or help from public funds which were provided for needy areas.

In addition, provisions of a short-sighted government and, frequently, animosity toward certain population groups resulted in complete misery for some villages. At the time of the survey, there were mountain areas where hunger had been endemic for years, for objective and subjective reasons.

At a certain historical moment patriarchal ethics and trust in the decency of others became meaningless as well as dangerous. People's attitudes and reactions, developed under different conditions, were no longer helpful in meeting life's difficulties but on the contrary created additional troubles. The time-honored qualities of faith, honesty, modesty, and openhandedness assumed extreme forms, and seemed to be naïveté or rigid conservatism, and ignorance of the ways of the world. Noble qualities became completely separated from real life. The philosophy of life—equanimity in accepting bad turns of luck and the grateful enjoyment of good turns sent by "destiny"—all this acquired a mark of desperation and defeatism. Here is an example of the extravagance of customs for festivities:

There is much fasting—more than half the year—under the influence of the Orthodox Church, but the saving connected with fasting is completely irrational. The festivities, especially the feast of the Patron-Saint of the home, uses up the entire meat supply of several months. They spent 1,200 to 1,500 dinars on these occasions, which is an enormous sum. The customs connected with burial and the various ceremonies at the grave are just as expensive. People go to the funerals with brandy and big dishes, and again "for the soul" after seven days, after forty days, after half a year and after a year. The conventions are so binding that the individual cannot extricate himself, although at the present time most of these customs are disastrous.

*(Sandjak, Sjenica district)*

An example of extreme generosity connected with personal modesty:

I saw the account book of Huso, a poor servant, in which he had entered all his expenses for years past. He never bought meat and spent insignificant sums for coffee and sugar, but relatively large amounts for chocolate. I asked him how this came about and he replied that he and his wife often went to visit friends and relatives and that he had to bring the children presents. Neither he nor his wife had ever tasted chocolate. *(Moslem village in Bosnia)*

The following little scene shows still more clearly the irrational attitude toward money:

A poor Moslem village laborer whose daily wages were ten dinars, arrives at the village inn in tatters. He orders his favorite song from the singer. While she is singing, he stands at the door and listens . . . gets ecstatic, tosses her his entire day's wages and leaves.

*(Bosnia, Tuzla district)*

The man's gesture and his rags show clearly his loss of social status. His proud conduct is in obvious contrast to his sad and endangered existence. His patriarchal contempt for the newly rich who would "die for a dinar" (*umire za dinar*) takes on tragic overtones since just this dinar might be essential for his subsistence, and thus his contempt for money results only in a deeper and deeper sinking into poverty.

The first waves of money economy which reached these villages, until then untouched, were so unexpected, powerful, and brutal that they sometimes endangered even the lives of the people as in the Bosnian village in Bugojno district reported above. In the first Yugoslav era, the influence of the modern state with its unfavorable political factors and the sudden economic changes connected with the depression meant a heavy pressure for the patriarchal villages in every respect. Although we cannot conclude that the city civilization with its technical progress strangles humane feelings and attitudes, it seemed that when it invaded these regions it provided momentum to an unrestricted individualism and, with it, inconsideration and brutality in the family.

## Subjective Factors

The peasants who lived in the center of the storm were not aware of the factors which were undermining the zadruga, especially those which were pushing them out of it. They may have seen a little more clearly the reasons which drew them out, as these belonged to the category of values and goals. The goal of becoming his own boss, the objective of independence without obligations to kin, have an irresistible power. These goals were so attractive that all considerations of an economic nature lost their importance. Although the peasants might have recognized the burdens of a dwarfed farm, crippled by unfavorable divisions, they closed their eyes to these dangers and overcame great obstacles just to carry through the division of their zadruga. Because before their eyes was the aim—freedom.

Intolerance of the old order was directly connected with that goal. The unwritten law of the zadruga, which limited freedom, seemed insupportable. There was an overwhelming desire among peasant sons to be emancipated from the parental authority of father and older brother, and among young wives to be rid of the mother-in-law. Knowledge of the greater individual freedom which a money economy had brought to young people and women throughout the world reached every village and every home, aroused the desire for freedom, always latent in people and which always begins to stir whenever its realization becomes a possibility.

The following examples show the intolerance and the uncontrolled individualism which inflated the zadrugas almost without distinction of region and area, even penetrating into the gentlest ones. The first report is by one of my interviewers, an old village priest, showing the turmoil in the Croatian zadrugas:

It is of no avail to aged parents to try to maintain authority or order, in the home, by fair means or by force. They are too lenient toward one or two of the children, bring these up badly, and in their old age this takes its revenge on them, when the children grow up and marry. When a son marries, he soon wants to be his own boss, but how can he be if his father is still alive? The young wife eggs her husband on and hell begins. The young wife would like to idle, dress up, be her own mistress, cook for herself, have her own household. The son asks the father for a separate farm for himself, that is, part of the land as his own property. The daughter-in-law would like to manage by herself the cow she got from her own parents. Once she has her own cow and milk, she wants her own pasture, pigs, hens, and so on. Thus the gulf between parents and son is enlarged, and it is rare for the father's authority or filial love to win the day. It was better before the war, for then the young man did not want his girl to bring him two acres and a couple of cows. But now, true, the bride does bring both land and cow, but for this reason she wants to manage them herself. But that again is not sufficient to maintain the young household and they become morose, spiteful, quarrelsome and more or less regularly break up family peace. The married daughters simply hate their parents and the mother secretly robs the household of all she can "so her daughter can be better off." The son looks askance at all this and puts up with it only till he is married, but as soon as this takes place, hell begins. When the parents fall ill or grow old and incapable, in the grip of fate, the son or son-in-law frankly blackmail them.

"If you want me to do your ploughing, give me that meadow or that vineyard or that arable land for myself." This is all round an unhealthy development, but there is nothing to be done. In their old age, the parents have a poor time, living in want, to end up on their backs on a plank bed in a cubby-hole under the stairs or a miserable room without light or air. There are indeed meritorious exceptions, but such exceptions are rare. (*Dugoselo district, Croatia*)

Previously there were zadrugas. They split up before the war. The fault is in the younger generation—the womenfolk cannot agree.

(*Littoral, Isle of Rab*)

There were numerous zadrugas before the war. Now it is frequent for a son to separate from his father, and this is usually done after marriage, the young daughter-in-law wanting to be her own mistress, not under the mother-in-law's commands. (*Županja district, Slavonia*)

It is a regular thing for the zadrugas, even now, to break up through the quarrels of the wives of the brothers in the family. One is a *planinka* (dairy maid) and another complains that she feeds her own children better than the other children in the zadruga, whereupon quarrels arise. When these frequent quarrels get to the stage of blows, the zadruga splits up, and as a rule there is impoverishment.

(*Sjenica district, Sanjak*)

What is it which moves and prompts the peasants especially the girls to avoid the zadruga is shown by Nada Sremec.[11]

. . . To pay the tax, something the household possesses must be turned into money, i.e., sold. Some household goods, or wheat, must be taken to market.

Thus the day came when our peasantry became acquainted with the money relationship, at first in a small way, shyly, but once the peasant had got to know what it meant, it was an end to the old way of life. What is not to be had for money? A gaily colored kerchief, a silk apron, coffee, sugar, alcohol, better tools, and many another thing is to be bought with money, and the whole of life looks different. Money can ease and improve it, so why go on living in a commune? What do we want with zadrugas?

All at once the zadruga seemed an obstacle. Then it appeared unnecessary *to the individual.* A man would begin to think how he himself would manage things. He ceased to belong to the zadruga mentally, and began to view it critically. The zadruga head was now a hated overlord in his eyes, he himself an oppressed person, to whom it would seem as if he worked too hard and others less. He became suspicious and got the notion he could manage better. And finally, there came the desire: let me have a go myself! Be my own boss!

And by now the song the girls sing is:

> I'll find a husband where it's all show,
> I'll be my own mistress from the very word go!
> Not where it's one of three brothers for me,
> Let him be on his own though ever tipsy.

*Slavonia*

Objective considerations of the advantages and the disadvantages of the two systems—individual or zadruga farming—do not play an important part in the zadruga's break-up. As always, on the eve of innovations and turnovers, the people do not confront two comparable issues, that is to say two realities. They contrast rather a well-known reality with their desires, hopes, or delusions. The old reality—that is, the irksome present—is contrasted to plan and project, which in this phase has no blemishes, for the shortcomings of the new system show up only after its realization, and not before.

Only when the zadruga had been broken up could the old and the new regimes be compared on a fair basis. Then it was possible to

[11] Nada Sremec, *Nismo mi krive* (*We Are Not To Blame*), Zagreb, 1940.

collate two experiences, and such judgment might have some objective value. Such an evaluation was given to me by an old Serbian
peasant woman, who had lived a long life in both family regimes.

In the autumn of 1940 I was the guest in a large old peasant home
in the hills of the Shumadia district in Serbia. In this village, the
revolt against the Turks had started 130 years previously. Nana, the
great-grandmother of the tiny children of the household, talked half
the night to me. She was thin, upright, and serious as a Gothic figure
with deportment and gestures full of dignity. Her seventy years were
not apparent although she had borne and reared eight children. With
a soft but deep voice without excitement but in accusation Nana
told me:

Oh, I just don't know how I can stand it if God lets me live
longer. . . .

Formerly we followed beaten paths, broad streets! We kept our health
longer, even though there were so many births . . . worries did not kill
us off! Women stayed young longer. Everything was arranged by the
man, the housefather. Women didn't have so many worries!

Of course, we also had our troubles and tribulations before! Carrying
my child and its cradle on my back and also food for twenty workers in
the fields, with spindle or knitting in my hand, I went into the fields a
few days after childbirth . . . even in the greatest noonday heat. Yet in
the zadruga things were easier. There were five married brothers in our
house. Among us five sisters-in-law each had to take care of the cooking
once every five weeks. For four weeks I was without any cares, only
working in the fields, and rather light work too.

And now? The wife has to take care of everything by herself, the
children, the livestock, the heavy work in the fields, the cooking, the
making of clothes . . . and along with all that there are worries and
troubles! No one spares her, no one respects her, especially if she is an
old woman . . . and never anyone to help her out!

Formerly we wore home-spun clothing and home-made *Opankas* (raw
hide sandals). They were pretty and durable, even if they were an
awful lot of work to make. Now we wear bought fabrics, terribly expensive and not worth anything. Everything rips right away . . . the
children wear factory-made sandals for a week and then new ones have
to be bought!

Formerly women were healthy in spite of the many births! Now they
are ruined because of abortions . . . and because of worries. The
younger people are spoiled, everyone is ailing, stunted. Girls have a
headache all the time. Women age early!

We all used to be afraid of our fathers-in-law and our husbands.

Things are different now. The women are impudent, they argue and protest. There was no contradicting one's father-in-law; younger people stood up when an older person came into the room. That doesn't happen now! There is no love among people, everyone hates everyone else, they are always fighting one another. People persecute each other. . . . Where will it lead? . . . Can you tell me that?!"  (*Serbia*)

# CHAPTER III

# The Status of the Father

THE position of the father of the family is the key to understanding the patriarchal system as a whole, as the term itself indicates. In this system, where the hierarchy is built up according to sex and age, the male principle is more important than that of seniority—all men are higher in rank than the women, especially in the tribal environment. And for the men the sequence of age is decisive. This is mirrored also in the language: *Stariji* in Serbo-Croatian not only means "older" but also indicates superior rank, just as *mladji* means both "younger" and "of lesser rank." We find these words used with reference not to years but to rank in both the army and the civil service.

In this chapter, the position of the father will be discussed, mainly in relation to his sons. The authority and respect he enjoyed, the power he commanded, the responsibility he carried in the patriarchal environment will be compared with his position in a later phase, when he was involved in a defensive struggle to maintain his status.

Two questions will be especially investigated: First, in the patriarchal phase, were the rights of the younger members of the family better protected and the position of the younger people more favorable than in later phases; and second, under what conditions were there peaceful and friendly relationships in the family, and under which ones did conflicts and fights prevail? Or, asked in another way: In the Slavic South, could stable family life be found only where there was a clearly defined authority and strict discipline, or also in settings where there was no steeply built-up hierarchy with the father at the head?

Finally a question of a more theoretical nature will be touched upon, one which has been much discussed in American social-psychological writings. This is the thesis that the autocratic bearing of parents, especially of the father, causes many unfavorable phenomena in attitudes and character of people who were reared in such a setting. Some students assume that the "authoritarian character" is closely connected with nervous disturbances as well as with violence, racial prejudice, and the leaning toward totalitarian regimes. The authoritarian and patriarchal family is put in sharp contrast to the "democratically" organized family. We will see whether the Yugoslav rural family confirms these assumptions and could support this theory.

The survey offers a great deal of material for discussing both concrete and the theoretical questions in connection with the status of the father.

## Attitudes of Sons to the Father

In various Yugoslav regions, we found a whole scale of attitudes of younger people toward older, ranging from ceremonial acts demonstrative of respect and awe to crude, even savage attacks on an aged father. Rights coupled with sanctions in family hierarchy were best to be seen in the attitude of grown-up sons to the father. If sons show the father and domaćin (or head of the zadruga) respect, the patriarchal system was intact; but should the system weaken, the sons were the first to deny the father obedience. Wife, daughters, and younger children offered him respect much longer, being physically weaker and economically dependent. The very essence of the patriarchal system is the obedience and submission of persons with greater physical and economic strength to the one commanding authority which was the usual case of sons and an old father. The acid test of the patriarchal system is—as when the father is old—for there to be obedience and submission of those who have become physically, hence economically the stronger.

The attitudes of grown-up sons to the father fall into three groupings.

First we have villages in which the father was shown awesome respect or at least respect, and courtesy was obligatory.

Before the war, the authority of the father was unimpaired. A younger son, even if married, never dared sit down in his presence or speak without being asked something. Nor did a married son dare smoke or drink in his father's presence, which holds to this day, nor dare he talk to his wife much before him. (*Gornji Polog district, Macedonia*)

Next are the villages in which there was good behavior, yet without particular respect and/or any very marked deference to the father. Here rather a "humane" atmosphere prevailed. There was a tendency to gradation in the respect of older people. For instance, they enjoyed respect when they were "wise," "respected," "capable." Disputes were not serious and were ruled by a sort of equality between father and son.

Here, relations between them sometimes became rather cool when the son married. Such a relationship might arise in two cases, either at the end of the process of break-up of the zadruga, when the storm was over and any disputes forgotten, or where there was a gradual process of adaptation to money economy. Here is an example from a village of the Littoral from which the zadruga vanished long ago:

> Here relations are good and everything flows smoothly. Nobody particularly emphasizes his authority so as to come into conflict with anybody else; the one thing they all know is that they have to work, and the desire to earn is great. As a rule, all the menfolk of a family do not work the same work (farming) where one of them would have to be in command, they usually find employment in timber saw-mills or are in America, so that parental authority or obedience of the children are questions which do not arise at all. The rule hitherto has been for a child of 14-15 years to insist on being sent to America, at his own desire, and thereupon his independent life begins, which he begins to see as early as 13, noticing how independent his friends only a little older are, and knowing that in a year or two he will be so too, so that as it were on account of this he gets a sort of foretaste of independence.
>
> (*Novi district, Littoral*)

The third group comprises villages in which there were frequent serious quarrels and conflicts between sons and fathers, where behavior toward the father was markedly bad, where there were assaults on the father and he was mocked by the sons, or where there was at least an unpleasant attitude, with great lack of sympathy for the father. Such an attitude arose in the stage of transition to the money nexus economy, when individualistic aspirations gained sway and the younger folk called for a break-up of the zadruga. When the older generation, as the conservative element, opposed this, endless conflicts and disputes result. In place of the old order is turmoil and brute force, often indeed without any intermediate stage. Here is an instance from the Military March:

> It is a rare son who respects his father's word; indeed, on the contrary, it often comes to a clash between father and son, quite capable of turning into fighting between them. When through the years the father grows weak, the son as a rule avenges himself for his old father's attacks. The son may then go so far as to beat up his father and by main force compel him to agree to his will; particularly will he force him to do what he as son wants in regard to transfer and division of the land.
>
> (*Slunj district, Kordun, Croatia*)

As might be expected, Graph 6 indicates that profound respect prevailed in Macedonia and Moslem Bosnia. Outstanding too was the high degree of respect in the Littoral, where the authority of the

Graph 6. Attitude of grown-up sons toward the father

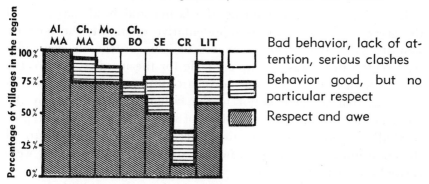

Bad behavior, lack of attention, serious clashes

Behavior good, but no particular respect

Respect and awe

father was based on greater equality of rights between older and younger folk. One lacks here the awe and blind obedience such as there was in the old-style districts, but there were also no serious clashes connected with rapid change.

The general curve of many other of our graphs reappears here. We see this nearly everywhere when we look into relations between members of the family with regard to the existence of conflict or peace. The semicircular line of the curve has the sense of a spiral: The level in a modern region is somewhat different from that in an old-style region. The behavior of individuals as a rule drops from the level of a stable standard to a depth of chaos and struggle, only to rise again to a new level of stable equilibrium. This stage of a new equilibrium, with elements of a settled system of relationships and recognized standards is, despite the appearance of new factors, to a great extent similar to the patriarchal environment.

The peak of disunity was found in various relationships in the Christian villages of Bosnia, in Serbia, and in Croatia. The break-up of the patriarchal system began earlier in Croatia than in Serbia, hence, one might put it, had time to strike more deeply. In the one region, the force of the first shock was already diminishing. In Serbia, on the other hand, we now come upon the first powerful blows at the bastion of patriarchal life, but the waves of this shock had still not taken hold of all villages. Regarding the relationship of sons to father, the peak of disunity is clearly in Croatia. Despite the fact that here the break-up of the zadruga had already gone very far, family life still quivered with excitement in the struggle about how the zadruga is to be divided up.

## Ceremonial Forms of Respect

In a patriarchal environment, the father and head-man enjoyed the greatest respect. He was representative of dignity, he bore responsibility, and he had the power to issue orders. In every old-style region there was a complete code for the manifestation of the father's high rank. There was no relationship so rich in formal elements as that showing honor to the father and head-man by the younger generation. The symbolism of such ceremonial was emphasized all the more in contrast to the technically primitive nature of the environment—as if the crowning and anointing of a king were carried out in a poor cottage.

Common to all districts as one mark of respect to the father was abstinence from all stimulants and erotic enjoyments in his presence. The height of respect rested in the requirement of great solemnity toward the father, together with an attitude of dignity.

A son may not smoke in his father's presence, *be lacking in solemnity, laugh,* stretch, or swear or do anything of that sort, neither in his father's presence or that of any other senior person. Where there is a difference of age of about 10 years, there is general respect toward the older person. (*Albanian village, Struga district, Macedonia*)

A son generally stands, he speaks less, he does not attempt to joke or find any fun in anything. One may only speak *seriously* to one's father. (*Žegligovo district, Macedonia*)

A son may not speak or take a seat in a café if his father is there, and, when there is merrymaking, *should not show his merriment* if in his father's company. He must be quiet and calm.

(*Posavina district, Serbia*)

And a few examples of the prohibition of smoking and drinking in the presence of the father, affecting both young men and even older men:

Children do not smoke or drink coffee. I know a case where a father has three sons. The eldest is 40 and the youngest 32, and though all three *do smoke and drink coffee,* not one has ever done so before his father. (*Catholic village, Brčko district, Bosnia*)

There are cases today of a man of 50-60 not venturing to smoke in the presence of his father of 80. He does not either speak to his wife or call her by name in his father's presence. (*Nerodimlje district, Macedonia*)

A further mark of awe of the father was a restrained form of behavior toward girls, even a demonstrative lack of attention toward one's own wife:

Even a married son dare not smoke in his father's presence, or drink. He may not talk to his wife very much in his presence.

*(Gornji Polog district, Macedonia)*

He may not smoke, may not speak roughly, or swear. Without permission, he may not *sit with his father* or listen to the conversation. He may not *stand* with a girl. *(Orthodox village, Bijeljina district, Bosnia)*

Almost without exception a son may not smoke in his father's presence and often even unmarried men of 20-30 do not smoke in the father's presence out of politeness and respect. Before the war this was much stricter. A son dared not stand with a girl if his father was looking and would very rarely allow himself the liberty of a joke, no matter with whom, if his father was listening. It went to the point of *never giving his wife a pleasant* look if the father was watching, *but had to be completely solemn.* *(Šavnika district, Montenegro)*

The height of concealment of affection from the parents was to be found in Serbia:

A husband *did not look at his wife* in the presence of his parents, nor did a young wife dare hold her child, *or speak a word to her husband.* For that matter, all this is tending to change, though it still holds with most people even today. *(Arilje district, Serbia)*

Younger folk might not talk much in the presence of their seniors. This refers principally to children, but also affects adults:

One may not *talk a lot* in the presence of one's father, or smoke, or loll about, or disagree in any way with what he does.

*(Albanian village, Prespa district, Macedonia)*

Before the war the father's authority was great; in his presence children were *as quiet as little bugs.* After the crisis, and today, children fear their fathers less and are less shy. *(Banja district, Serbia)*

The signs of submission are: The place at table (the younger folk being in the background), not daring to smoke, drink black coffee, or talk, except to answer questions. *(Mostar district, Herzegovina)*

Younger folk stood when the father came into a room and, when out walking with him, kept a few paces behind him.

When a father sits down, his son remains standing. He may not smoke.

*(Moslem village, Galičnik district)*

Children *get up* when the father comes and do not sit down till he does, they do not smoke in his presence, and may not interrupt when he is speaking. The father begins to eat first. Children are much more intimate with their mother. *(Stolac district, Herzegovina)*

In the street one never goes in front of one's father, always behind him. In any gathering, when the father comes in, the children *rise* in respect.

When a father speaks, the children must listen and not contradict him.

*(Albanian village, Andrijevica district)*

A few more answers, typical of the various regions: Macedonia: Here respect for all seniors, even a brother, was typical, and intimate speech was avoided when addressing them:

One kisses the hand of seniors and particularly of senior relations, and makes way for them in every respect. This is immediately obvious in the behavior of younger people toward all seniors. With girls, when dancing the kolo, as a rule it is the senior who leads. The same with the men. So younger folk respect their seniors. A younger sister or brother will not call a senior brother or sister by name, but a sister is called *dada* and a brother *bato*.          *(St. Nikola Ovčepolje district)*

The senior has priority of speech, younger folk must always address seniors by a term of relationship, whether relations or not—such terms as *babo, čičo, dedo* ("father," "senior," or "uncle," "grand-father") .

*(Veles district)*

Reports from Montenegro give us the pure style of patriarchal dignity:

Respect for senior men is one of the basic rules (custom laws) of the *ethic* of these districts, or so it was before the war. Today there has been considerable change, so that this respect has declined. *(Šavnik district)*

Younger people always address seniors *with courtesy* and show signs of respect and rarely oppose the advice of an older man. *(Nikšić district)*

Younger people respect seniors, listen to their counsel. *They are convinced of their knowledge and respect.* If only youth knew, if only old age could.          *(Andrijevica district)*

Here from Moslem Bosnia is a report which indicates the general notion of respect:

Younger people respect the older, and for instance, were anybody to come from another village and *behave badly toward elders*, he would quite simply be beaten up and driven out.          *(Foča district)*

In the Littoral, however, good behavior toward elder people did not include any particular respect, let alone any formal signs of awe. It is rather a friendly attitude which comes out here:

When working together with elder folk, a young man considers that he has the same rights and same duties. It would be difficult to find anybody to take his place. There is no trace of formal gallantry. At the same time, behavior is reasonably good, for instance, most likely a younger man will take the initiative in bidding a senior the time of day when he meets him on the road, though such greeting is not very much the custom.          *(Isle of Ugljan)*

66

Before the war, elder people knew more than the younger, so the younger had more respect. Today the younger people go about the world more and have more knowledge and experience and, though they hear what the elders have to say, have their own opinion. Nevertheless, sons always respect their father, even when he grows old. They rarely attack their parents, and there are only three cases of a share-out during the father's lifetime. *There is no forcing of transfer of property.* Younger people still regularly obey and respect the elder. It is *not seemly to decry* an old man. When older men have their say, they are heard, even if the younger do not agree with them.

(*Biograd on Sea district*)

One of the commonest signs by which younger people show their submission and humility regarding older people is the kissing of the hand.

Children kiss the hand of father, mother, grandfather, grandmother, and elder brothers and sisters.

(*Albanian village, Žegligovo district, Macedonia*)

Children kiss the hand of the father's parents. Respect is expressed by absolute obedience. . . . The father's hand is kissed on various holy days. (*Christian village Žegligovo district, Macedonia*)

Children kiss the hand of all older men and women generally. By "older" is understood those who are married and those over 25-30 years who though not married look more or less serious.

(*Brčko district, Moslem Bosnia*)

Children kiss the hand of father, mother and the grandfather during Bairam (Religious holiday). (*Doboj district, Moslem Bosnia*)

As a rule the hands of parents are kissed, particularly among the Moslems. Among them, kissing elder men is common, even younger men if they are, say, officials, priests, teachers or such.

(*Bosanska Krupa district, Bosnia*)

It depends on the family. Girls kiss the hand of any older man who enters the house. Children kiss the hand of father, mother, grandfather, grandmother and sometimes the father's older brothers or sisters. (*Šavnik district, Montenegro*)

Children kiss the hand of father, mother, grandfather, grandmother, and if in a zadruga, also other relations. (*Arilje district, Serbia*)

Children kiss the hand of grandfather, grandmother, father, mother, uncles and aunts and old men before and after prayers and when they go visiting. (*Azbukovac district, Serbia*)

Children kiss the hand of all older men. (*Moravica district, Serbia*)

67

Children kiss the hand of all married members of the household.

*(Dobričevo district, Serbia)*

In almost all reports from Croatia and the Littoral, one reads "we do not have that custom." The exceptions are a few Dinaric Mountains districts. The following report is typical:

Today there is no kissing of the hand to anybody, though once upon a time, on the parents' request, children did kiss the grandfather's hand. It is training to submissiveness to elders.    *(Knin district, Dalmatia)*

Graph 7 reveals considerable divergence from that of general respect for the father:

### Graph 7. Children kiss hands

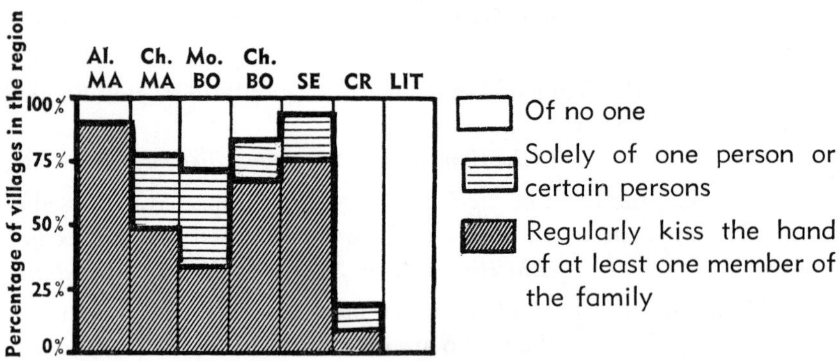

This custom was most widespread among the Albanians and in Serbia. The greatest gap was between Serbia and Croatia, that is, between districts formerly Austrian and those formerly Turkish. It would seem that in this custom the influence of the East was strong, or particularly developed among pastoral folk or people of pastoral origin.

The observance of the custom of showing honor to elders emphasizes the importance of the whole system. Some of these customs, such as kissing the hand, were kept up much longer than real respect of the father and of elder folk, that is to say, longer than absolute obedience and acceptance of orders without resistance. In Serbia, where such a relationship was already undermined, certain external signs of respect, however hollow, still lived on as unconnected observances.

### Abrogation of Respect

The transformation of the zadrugas into individual land holdings, from subsistence economy into money economy, without exception

68

led to abrogation of respect for the father and head-man. There arose not merely lack of respect or indifference on the part of sons, but also ill-treatment and uncouth behavior.

In a report from Montenegro the economic factor is emphasized in the refusal of respect to the father:

> The village was hit by a new wave of scarcity and poverty, and, as a result, the standing of the older people was undermined and hence that of the family. Today more often than ever previously one has children prematurely leaving their parents and not respecting any of the parents' wishes. Connected with the impoverishment of the village and the great indebtedness of the peasants to the mortgage bank, one feels lack of agreement in the domestic life of the peasants more and more. Every day, the standing of the older members of the family sinks to a lower level. This is best seen if one enters peasant homes which are better off (there are very few of these here) and observes that the respect shown the older people is here much greater than in poorer homes.
>
> *(Nikšić district, Montenegro)*

Another report reveals the process of transformation of the zadruga in its early stage:

> Before he gets old the father is as a rule disregarded, not exactly not respected, though there are such cases, but one of the sons, who is "cleverer," takes over headship of the zadruga home. Then it frequently occurs that the father is given no tobacco to smoke, he cannot go out to see other men, or, when he is old, he is even sent up the mountain to mind the livestock. At this moment a zadruga in the village is breaking up at the request of the youngest son, as he is the "most intelligent." The peasants have nothing good to say for such behavior on the part of sons. "Brothers split up, but like men, not Gypsies. Now, just think of it, trying to split a rope in two or share an icon!" Under the influence of our times and this crisis, which has upset people's minds, the old moral way is slowly disappearing. "These young folk have gone to the bad, and that's the truth of it!" cries an old man.
>
> *(Sjenica district, Sanjak)*

The following report typifies Macedonian villages in which the authority of older people was vanishing. Here too the changes were colored by the former gentleness and dignity of the district and passed without internecine conflict:

> Change in the respect of older people is to be seen in the frequent self-willed actions of young men. Yet what are the parents to do? They tuck their tails between their legs and hold their tongues, a sign that the transformation of family life which has taken place is accepted without any active resistance on the part of the older people. In short,

they conclude that all this must be and should be, for "a new age has come in." *(Veles district)*

Here is a rare instance of disrespect for older people in Moslem Bosnia:

When the father grows old, he is often abandoned by the sons, and if he lives with them, they even knock him about, forcing division of the property and its transfer to them. Formerly, the authority of the older people stood higher, whereas today it is only by externals, such as *the moustaches and beard*, that one can tell who is the senior.

*(Moslem village, Bijelina district)*

The following are a few instances of Christian villages of Bosnia, showing all stages from the old-style zadruga way of life to individual money earning, and the consequences of these changes for relationships in the family:

Sons respect the father or nobly "put up with him" till he becomes old beyond work and their children have grown up and loaded them with worries, then the father becomes an illness of which they long to get rid. They force him to divide and legally transfer the property. The old men find this hard to bear, not being like the mothers, their wives, accustomed to always having their hands tied.

*(Orthodox village, Sarajevo district)*

The authority of the father was greater before the war and before the crisis than it is now. Often, when the sons do not agree, the father's requests are met with the roughest opposition and argument. They make fun of his outlook and disobey him, even doing some jobs wrong out of spite and intolerance of his old man's slowness in grasping more up-to-date ways and suchlike. *(Orthodox village, Sarajevo district)*

Before the war, authority was much greater. The clearest picture of the fall in the authority of the father is in the fact that it has become quite common for children to knock their fathers and mothers about. Nor do they need any serious reason of a material nature, as, for instance, legal transfer of the property or suchlike.

*(Orthodox village, Derventa district)*

Relations between father and son in Serbia were less sharply in conflict than in Croatia. In particular, the struggle over the split-up of property did not seem so impassioned as in Croatia. Perhaps one reason for this was that, by Serbian law, a zadruga might be divided up on the demand of merely one member, whereas in Croatia the acceptance of all the zadruga's members was required. Thus, in Serbia a son could often more easily achieve the division of the zadruga than he would be able to in Croatia, where he was obliged by hook or by crook to get the consent of the father and the other zadruga members.

> Grown-up sons have little respect for their father. Those whose fathers have money make an exception. 70 per cent force the father to division and succeed in this. Once upon a time, particularly before the war, younger folk showed more respect, though this was often enough merely formal. Now they only show respect if they depend materially on those they respect. *(Posavina district, Serbia)*

The vestiges of patriarchal respect, which we found more frequently in Serbia than in Croatia, emerge from the following report:

> Young people are insincere toward their elders, they are silent and avoid the company of older people. The result is quarrels, after which agreement is reached. The father is to the sons still something against which they cannot show open opposition. In extreme cases, the son parts from the father. *(Kosmaj district)*

Definite uncouthness is also shown in the following reports. Attention should be paid to the phraseology, which indicates a struggle for prestige, somewhat different from the way the matter is put in Croatia, where one had always a clear-cut case of struggle over the division of a zadruga:

> The father's words are respected, but the son's proposal too is adopted and with respect. A father who has grown old is generally isolated from everything. He is outside any responsibility. What work he does is up to him. He is materially (economically) dependent on his sons, *then has to hold his tongue* and wait for death. There is no fighting. *(Kosmaj district)*

> The father is rarely respected. They usually quarrel, for, subsequent to various changes in production, and with this the outlook of men, the old folk are dissatisfied. The sons, being younger and stronger, often knock them about. *(Kosmaj district)*

> It often happens that in this way sons knock their fathers about and maltreat them until they consent to partition. Bad behavior begins as soon as he is the weaker. They say: "He's old, he's had his time, he'll die tomorrow." *(Kosmaj district)*

In Croatia, the process of break-up of the zadrugas was already complete, but the tendency toward atomization of the peasant holding continued. Every youth when he married wanted to break away, and endless disputes went on. Examples show to what uncouth behavior this conflict can lead.

The younger folk respect their seniors until they themselves are physically and economically the stronger, and it is very rare for respect to continue to the old folk's death.                    (*Varaždin district*)

While the father is physically the stronger, he is the master, otherwise, the children destroy his authority. So long as he can still do some work, he has a say in the house, but the moment he stops bringing anything in, they force him to transfer the property to them. (*Varaždin district*)

If the father is weak and incapacitated, he is in their way. They long for his death, and do not try to hide this from him. They do not respect him, and if he objects, they knock him about. (*Grubišno Polje district*)

Here old men and women are commonly the object of everyday mockery by the young folk. In their intolerance of the old, some go so far as constantly to drive them away and attack them. The old women are still greater victims of the young people. As weaker persons, and women, they are the victims of much more unrestrained demonstration of the young folk's arbitrary will than the old men are. (*Slunj district*)

There is mockery and much criticism, often even knocking about. Old men and women are respected only if they have still not transferred the property, so the younger look to inherit it. If the property has been shared out, they often treat them badly, and fail to give them the promised "maintenance."                    (*Benkovac district*)

A few instances of lack of respect for the father with a less aggressive note:

Sons as a rule respect their fathers. The only pressure brought to bear to get the property made over is the threat of abandoning the old man. It is customary for the parents to manage the property while they are younger. When they grow old, the economy is managed by the sons. Where they have not split up, *this is by agreement*. Against this, sons respect their fathers when grown old, though if they propose something on the farm which in the opinion of the sons is not profitable, they are not listened to. But the old people do not interfere much, they leave everything to the son and say: "As you do, so you shall have," or "The better you look after things, the more you'll have" or something like that.                    (*Garešnica district*)

Before the war, every older man, merely by reason of being older, was the authority. Today that is no more. Today the elder are respected for their age only to a point. Sons wish to attain economic independence as soon as they can. To be set up, married, one's own master, earning for oneself, is the ideal of them all, they want division or transfer of the property, but offer no force if the father is stubborn in not giving way.                    (*Knin district*)

72

While the father can work and manages things sensibly and so long as the sons are not married, the father has the principal say. As soon as the father becomes too enfeebled for work, his authority drops. As soon as the son has married, he makes every effort to take over the farm. The quarrels are frequent, but do not come to blows. The son always wins, but division comes more rarely. One should remember that the authority of a peasant depends on his yield, that is, on his working capabilities. For this reason the aged and weak are always defeated.

*(Novska district)*

On the Littoral, respect for the father was greater than in other Croatian districts, but without any patriarchal element. In this region one clearly discerns a connection between the early economic independence of young men and their independent attitude toward their fathers:

When the father is incapable of work, the property is divided up, and he remains in his house, but takes his meals with the children in turn, week by week. *(Isle of Krk)*

Both before the war and before the crisis, the authority of the father was greater. If today the sons find it impossible to do what their father orders, *they go off to the town* and look for a living there. Great economic changes have totally changed the attitude of children toward their fathers, from whose homes and land they have nothing to expect. When a clash takes place, the children's reactions are more free.

*(Knin district)*

There is no question of the parents' authority. A child goes through the primary school and in due course further adds a trade, and he is independent. He goes to the town to find work. The town and the struggle for a living make him independent. *(Sušak district)*

Other examples reveal a good relationship with parents, that is, with the father, though general respect for the older people had been lost. Such a combination was the opposite of that in districts where there had been great changes in the family, and the struggle against the father was fiercest, whereas unrelated older men were treated with indifference, a better attitude than that toward the father.

A father is obeyed. Physical force is not used. Young people look after their old folk, both equally. Children have no respect for unrelated older people. *(Dalmatian island)*

Children respect their father, but as a rule there is no particular respect of young for old. They behave as if equal and there is no respect for them. *(North Croatian Littoral)*

73

Down the Littoral as a whole, any great conflict between the generations was lacking. In the attitude of sons to the father there was a moderate kind of respect.

It would seem that the struggles about division of the zadruga and family land called out the deepest and most savage of men's passions and gave rise to the employ of brute force between the two male generations in the home. The process of reshaping of the farm economy and break-up of the family hierarchy was often tragic for the old.

## Acquisition of Authority

By what means did the seniors build up and try to maintain their authority? How was a high degree of authority acquired in a patriarchal environment?

In all districts, practically the same means were employed, though with varying success. Many of the interviewers mention economic pressure and physical punishment. Fathers resorted to frightening a son with the threat of expulsion and disinheritance, which was sometimes carried out, or the father might offer him a bait of some kind. In some districts there was also mention of religious or ecclesiastical influence, the threat of Divine punishment. But frequent mention is made of "means" of another kind, such as gentle persuasion, kind treatment, good example, gentleness, not force. Yet if we inquire into those villages in which the father enjoyed the greatest authority, we see that in these no special means whatsoever were used to build up or maintain authority. It was a general influence which "was in the air" that acted on younger people. My reporters often call it "natural authority" or "inborn respect of one's elders." A general climate of established relationships had an unobservable but inevitable influence on children.

A few reports from Macedonia illustrate this effect of a traditional environment:

> Even adult peasants are very highly disciplined in their attitude toward their elders. Consequently, children grow accustomed to this from infancy. Spoilt children do not exist. As for discipline among school children, this is excellent. For instance, in four years I have had no occasion to use a stick even in the mildest way, as both Christian and Moslem children are very obedient. The only means by which such disciplined behavior is to be obtained is *the example of one's seniors.*
> (*Skoplje district*)

> The father's authority is natural, and is not to be shaken. He maintains it in the main by gentle means. In my opinion the father's authority

is maintained mainly by his superiority in experience and relations with others, while the children are cut off from everything and forced to be obedient. *(Skoplje district)*

Parents in the main acquire their authority by gentle means. Here one can also see a church influence, which dates from old times. Their saying is: *sila Boga ne moli*, i.e., force does not pray to God, in other words, force is impotent. *(Djevdjelija district)*

Here it is *customary* for children to obey their parents. And parents use the good opinion and renown of the peasantry as the most efficacious means for maintenance of their position and authority over children. The church influence is of great importance.

*(Gornji Polog district)*

Nor in the villages with a new equilibrium, particularly those of the Littoral, do we find any particular means for the building up of authority; it appeared "naturally":

Nobody consciously brings up. *(Sušak district)*

A kind word from the parents plays an important part in the upbringing of the children of this village. *(Kastav district)*

In an environment where life was changing rapidly, all "inborn" authority vanished. The older folk strove to buttress the crumbling walls of zadruga and patriarchal modes of life, trying so to speak to support them from outside, but it rarely helped. The means which in the previous stage of family life were used with success, for instance, the threat of a beating, or economic pressure, merely excited more vigorous resistance and open conflict. Now parents often tried to apply drastic measures:

Parents exercise their authority in the main by economic pressure and material goods. "If you obey me, I shall buy you what you want" says father or mother to a child on every occasion. This means that material influences have most effect in the formation of the character of the children in the village here. *(Bjelovar district, Croatia)*

The parents exercise their authority physically. By economic pressure. They will not buy a son a suit of clothes, so that often the son has to steal from the father, or in the village (stealing poultry by night). "Are you not afraid of God and ashamed of people for not respecting your elders?" *(Varaždin district, Croatia)*

Most frequently, parents exercise their authority through dependence. The father holds the kitty and buys things for whom he pleases. Whereas, if he is a poor man, no notice whatsoever is taken of him.

*(Bosanski Petrovac district, Bosnia)*

The use of brute force in districts with a fighting tradition is deeply rooted:

> Parents in the main exercise their authority by force, and this means plainly, by beating. This is why it is so frequent for a son to marry as early as he can, to be free from his father's hand.
>
> (*Dvor on the Una district [Kordun] Croatia*)

> According to tradition, the head of the family is respected. Any special means to this end are very rare and unefficacious, if the relationship between parents and children is upset.
>
> (*Croatia, district Vojnić Kordun*)

Educational means of acquiring authority are effective only under certain conditions. So long as the whole environment supported the authority of older people, all means were successful, and often enough they were not even required. On the other hand, in the phase of general abrogation of obedience, even drastic measures were unsuccessful. As soon as the older folk had to have recourse to the use of special repressive measures to support their undermined authority, it was already too late, they were unable to maintain it. It looks as if only that authority is safe which, though it has means for its maintenance at its disposal, never uses them, or but very rarely.

### Punishment of Children

There is much discussion in anthropological literature of a connection between the treatment of children in the family and the character of the people, especially of "primitive," illiterate peoples and tribes. The general supposition is that there is a close relationship between the method of upbringing and the behavior and reactions of the adult. Many illiterate peoples are known who never use force in the upbringing of children, and never strike a child. In none of the Yugoslav regions is there such a negative attitude toward the use of a stick, and nowhere can one find consistent unity of theory and practice in favor of upbringing without punishment. Though there are parents in some districts who look askance at beating children, very few families bring up their children completely without it. In most villages beating is employed, though without severity.

Graph 8 indicates little difference between the regions, and our curve shows only a trace of rise and fall. It is only from the phraseology of the reports that one can judge where there was harsh use of force and where treatment is mild. I made further inquiry into the relationship between theory and practice in corporal punishment

6.  Spinning and fishing at Lake Ohrid, Macedonia

7.  Potter in the Lika area, Croatia

8. Macedonian pastures

9. Shepherds with flutes in Macedonian cabin

Graph 8. Whether parents beat children much

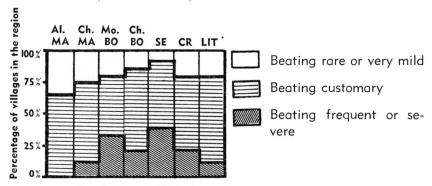

and found that there were only a few instances of agreement, while in some regions there was direct conflict.

Among the Albanians, the following report is typical, showing restraint and dignity, from which one can draw the conclusion that beating was rarely applied:

Children are very rarely beaten. Up to the tenth year it does still happen, but after that, never, particularly not boys. Mild upbringing among older people is considered to be the rule, though this attitude is never revealed to children, but on the contrary, parents are stern in their dealings with children, and all "younger" in rank.

(*Struga district*)

Other reports reveal that among the Albanians a hostile attitude to beating prevailed. Theory and practice here agree, on the principle of *noblesse oblige*.

Reports from Orthodox Macedonia also show gentleness toward children:

As a rule older people and people of calm temperament console children and follow them with blessing and heartache, teaching them humility. (*Žegligovo district*)

People say: As I care for him, he will care for me. (*Skoplje district*)

Thus we observe that, though in Macedonia the old demand of absolute submission of the younger generation was still alive, the stability of the general climate did not allow the application of crude force. Indeed, in this area more in theory favor the use of beating than in fact apply it.

In Montenegro, children were treated with dignity and attention in a patriarchal manner; but there was also an unmistakable combative note leaning toward the use of force:

Girls are struck even up to their twentieth year, and boys up to fifteen, for from that age one has to reckon with the dignity of a youth. In olden days there were soldiers of sixteen, and to strike a soldier would have been the greatest of insults. *(Cetinje district)*

In Moslem Bosnia, we find a fatalistic strain, taking the form of doubt in the value of punishment. Yet the least resistance to the father's authority was treated with great severity. Whether beating became the custom after the first signs of the break-up of the patriarchal way of life or whether it existed previously, we cannot say with certainty.

Parents make use of gentle upbringing, for from fear of God children are not disobedient. Children are brought up godfearing. From infancy their little heads are stuffed with the notion that God will punish them if they are disobedient and children never even think of being disobedient. *(Foča district)*

It is rare to beat children. I have seen cases of parents being most accommodating to children. The proverb says: *"Kind words open even iron doors."* *(Bugojno district)*

They say: "We beat small boys most" and: "A girl feels shame, a boy fear." Children are as a rule beaten up to puberty. It is rarely anybody brings up a child without punishment. Of certain children people think it "born kindly" so it must be "treated kindly." A child defends itself from its mother, less from its father. Then the mother says: "My switch broke." It is rare for a child to attack its parents. This is expressed: "His hand would drop off." Parents beat children when they let the livestock out, for carelessness and disobedience. Where the switch of parent or teacher strikes, they say that *dzhehemen* (hell) will not catch fire. *(Mostar district, Herzegovina)*

Children turn more to the mother. Often enough they do not even dare turn to the father, but the mother then acts as intermediary between children and father. As a rule children are kept severely. There are cases of children not even daring to utter a word in the father's presence. Regarding punishment, they mostly stick to corporal punishment. The peasants do not like gentle upbringing. They want obedience without a word. *(Bosanska Krupa district)*

Children say: "Everyone at home beats us." There is no upbringing without punishment. The belief is that finer upbringing is possible, but not very efficacious with poor people. *(Bugojno district)*

Typical of Moslem Bosnia was the variance between theory and practice. The parents were often in favor of gentle upbringing, but the arduous life in this pauperized district reduced them against their will to harsh measures. The demand for gentleness and fatalism linger on even when the facts of life and a mood of desperation rule them out. Parents would gladly bring up their children "in a nicer way," but "in our poverty that is of no avail."

In the Christian villages of Bosnia, two tendencies commingled. One was Oriental and fatalistic; the other in principle endorsed the application of force.

Some say: "The stick came from Paradise," others that: "He whom God appointed to be good will be good without beating, while even beating won't improve the others." There are families which never punish, and such children are excellent and very obedient to their parents. *(Orthodox village, Sanski Most district)*

The peasantry are in favor of gentle upbringing, and the children are rarely beaten, and that not harshly. Excessive beating is considered mistaken. *(Orthodox village, Bihać district)*

Children are brought up authoritatively. However, where the children are left without the mother, or where some children of the family have died, upbringing is gentle. Gentle upbringing is regarded as weakness, or is called upper-class upbringing.[1] *Children are not beaten.* There may be an isolated case, but even so, punishment is mild, with a switch. The most original and frequent punishment of a child is not to provide it with a new outfit of clothes on a feast day or for it to have to perform some task, instead of playing.

*(Catholic village, Stolac district, Herzegovina)*

From a village many of whose people emigrated to America, a teacher reports as follows:

It is the mother principally who beats the children. Out of the 40 pupils of my class, the mother beats 25, the father 9, while 6 are not beaten at all. About 20 per cent of the families do not beat the children. The notion of gentle upbringing is not shared by everybody, the majority believing that children must be whipped, though the minority, in the main folk with more general understanding, are decidedly against.

*(Stolac district, Herzegovina)*

From Bosnia, on the other hand, there were many reports expressive of the opposite tendency, namely, where parents stood absolutely for beating:

"Swish away, sir, if the bones are mine, the meat's yours." That is invariably what I have been told throughout my career as teacher here. They are critical of my gentle methods, and any failure in school is prescribed to this. *(Derventa district)*

---

[1] The adjective "upper-class" or "pertaining to gentry" is used here in a sense of scorn for those who are not peasants.

In Serbia both theory and practice were in favor of beating. The exceptions were individual families in advanced villages.

Children are frequently beaten. Most often with a belt, rope, or the hand, or punished by pulling the ears, by making them kneel, by turning them outside in the snow in the night and so on. Beating is such an important factor in the education of the younger generation that any failure to have recourse to it gives rise to a fear lest the authority of the head-men should be called into question (for it holds and is maintained by beating). Nowhere else do people call out so much for it. With every visit of parents, there is the same request: "Beat him," "Let him have it!" "Don't spare the rod," "Swish him." Attempts to explain and convince are vain. In the end, the teacher is "going to ruin the children" because he does not beat. "They won't know who's head. The children have nobody to fear." And they are all identical in this request, consistent and stubborn. Women are beaten, children are beaten, even the teachers are beaten—by the children. (*Arilje district*)

The following report reveals that beating resulted not in the obedience of young lads to their parents, but in their coarseness:

They beat girls longer, that is, keep an eye on them, parents beating them till they are married, when the husband takes on. Boys are beaten till their fifteenth year. Boys knock their mothers about as soon as they are over 15. That is common, in self-defense. There is no toleration whatsoever for gentle upbringing, everything being brought back to the justifying phrase: "The stick came out of Paradise." (*Arilje district*)

Nobody brings a child up without punishment. It is unknown. Gentle upbringing is no good. It is condemned. A friendly attitude in school is terrible to them. They say: "Lay on with the stick, they're bad children." Boys are most beaten, girls being obedient (as the weaker). Usually beating goes on to the nineteenth year. When a boy is considered a grown lad, they leave him alone. Larger children resist, even the little ones bite their mothers back (the mothers complain to me). There are even cases of beating a married son and father.

(*Kosmaj district*)

The germ of a new attitude is revealed in the following report:

There are more affluent houses in which the children are hardly ever beaten. In the main, democratically inclined homes. (*Kosmaj district*)

The report from a conservative village in the south of Serbia shows it belongs to a patriarchal environment:

They are right to think about gentle upbringing. It is held to be good and should be applied, but. . . . (*Vlasotince district*)

The wide dissemination of excessive beating in Serbia cannot be solely the effect of a particular historical stage of rapid transformation; there was present in addition a general combative disposition, bound up with the Dinaric tradition and a past full of wars and fighting.

In Croatia too we found much harshness toward children, but rarely quite such unanimity in the demand for the use of corporal punishment as in Serbia. In distinction from the reports from Serbia, the question was put less violently in Croatia:

> The peasantry do not know of gentle upbringing, for life is rigorous, and they too are much beaten by it, nor have they the time for patience to give to gentle upbringing. *(Krapina district)*

> Children are much beaten, by hand, with a switch, a belt, or a horsewhip. Children are also made to kneel on corn or on a plank with sharp projections. 2-3 per cent of families bring children up without punishment. Eighty per cent think that in this way "one gets nowhere." Seventeen per cent think it would be good, but are unable to make the effort to get out of the old way. *(Prelog district)*

> Gentle upbringing is admitted by none, and they are angry with the teachers for beating the children so little nowadays. *(Kutina district)*

Following are two examples from advanced villages with few children. The fact that there are few children in the families involved acts in the direction of diminishing severity:

> Children are almost never beaten. If they are, it is generally the father who punishes. Gentle upbringing is used, most are in favor of this and the village children are very spoilt. *(Kutina district)*

> About 30 per cent apply gentle upbringing, and these families offer the example of the most happy and stable families. The majority are envious of the happiness and peaceful life of these families. It is increasingly realized that the stick does not improve, but, on the contrary, spoils children. The school utilizes every possible occasion to point out to parents that the good example of the parents is the best educational instrument. *(Bjelovar district)*

The above report reveals the influence of a fine woman teacher who has worked in this village for many years. Such cultural influences which profoundly influence family life are exceptional.

> There is no gentle upbringing. In cases of punishment, this is with a switch, "which came from Paradise." Fear (or rather, respect) of the parents is so great that these rarely have occasion to punish children. *(Gospić district)*

The following answer shows a more gentle Bosnian influence:

The children are rarely beaten, efforts are made to influence them by well-chosen words. The children regularly obey their parents, and they tend the livestock, and there is no reason to beat them.

*(Imotski district)*

In the Croatian districts existed all stages between patriarchal fear of savage punishment and gentleness and a civilized bearing that was both old and new style.

In the Littoral, a number of new factors tended to act against the punishment of children: The early independence of children, the slight effort made to maintain authority, and finally a sort of southern habit of shouting and getting excited without result:

It happens that some punish very little, particularly if the children are weakly, or it is an only child. It is principally the mother who beats the children, but also older brothers and sisters. Beating is not severe and parents in the main are tolerant toward their children. Mothers shout at children and curse them more than they beat them. They hold that gentle upbringing makes them badly behaved. All in theory are in favor of severe upbringing with punishment, but in practice parents are tolerant. *(Isle of Ugljan)*

The demand for severity, inherited from older times, was being imperceptibly transformed into a more gentle modern practice:

In matters of punishment, parents make great mistakes. When the father punishes, the mother pets and takes the child's side, or vice versa, and similarly the grandparents disagree with the parents. The mothers beat the most (perhaps being more at home), and they also use the father as a menace. As a rule children are more nagged than beaten. If a child does something wrong, the mother rather takes its part than punishes it. Children are beaten, but one cannot say it is harshly done.

*(Isle of Ugljan)*

Children are left to play together, their relations have no particular method or plan of upbringing, things develop of themselves.

*(Novi district)*

In the Littoral also, severity of punishment was endorsed more in theory than in practice. Teachers asserted that the parents often asked them to beat children, and later attacked the teacher even for using harsh words. A law of severity without any connection with reality provided the general climate.

Upbringing left "to itself" was typical of every environment with stabilized relationships. In regions with rapid changes, sharp conflict developed between the generations, with beating of small children and bitter conflict with the elder ones. But these measures had almost no effect, and were incapable of preserving the father's shaken authority.

Children's reactions to punishment were made the subject of special inquiry. They rarely presented a picture of complete submissiveness or awe, but more often than not resisted. It was only in an environment where authority was so strong that force was scarcely ever used that we find complete submission with no thought of resistance. In such an environment it was only occasionally that young men reacted forcibly to blows:

> Larger boys are not struck, for account is taken of a young man's dignity. It is rare for children to defend themselves, that is to say, to attack their parents, but, though full of shame and revolt, they still bear with the parents' blow without resistance.
>
> *(Cetinje district, Montenegro)*

Statistical study of the question of children's reactions to beating show that there was very little resistance from the children in old-style regions and down the Littoral, while in regions with stormy ferment there was much more resistance. This means that much beating resulted in much resistance, or vice versa. Gentleness or uncouthness in parents are reflected in the children. Some examples from Bosnia:

> Children never dare defend themselves, or raise their hand against their parents. *(Moslem village, Bosanska Krupa district)*
>
> Children as a rule run away in order not to have their ears boxed, and hide till their parents' anger is over. When they grow up, there has been only one example of a son hitting his father. *(Sanski Most district)*
>
> It very often happens that an older boy attacks his mother or father. If not prompted to it, they do not. *(Stolac district)*
>
> Larger children defend themselves, and some, in self-defense, even attack their mothers and refuse to be punished. *(Sarajevo district)*

The reports from Serbia say the same:

> Children do sometimes defend themselves. They attack their parents when their strength is greater than that of the parents.
>
> *(Jablanica district)*

From Croatia:

> They beat boys most. They beat them as long as they think they are the stronger, and the children will get the worst of it.
>
> *(Varaždin district)*
>
> They beat up to fifteen years old, that is to say, boys. Beating anybody after fifteen is said rather to be "fighting it out." The children

defend themselves, and sometimes they attack the parents. Often in such cases it comes to the doctor, police, and court. *(Ivanec district)*

Here is a particularly combative report typical of the Lika; former Military March:

Children defend themselves. They throw stones or throw the furniture about. *(Gospić district)*

In the Littoral, one observes a quite different climate:

Larger children defend themselves and hide, but they never attack their parents. *(Biograd on Sea district)*

Children do defend themselves, but do not attack their parents. When a child leaves school he goes fishing and earns, and on that account does not allow anybody to beat him. *(Isle of Ugljan)*

In all regions where rapid change was evident, one finds the same story of crude force both in the beating of children and in the children's resistance to this. On the other hand, there were vital distinctions between regions with stable conditions. Children's lack of resistance to force took place on a different level in old-style and modern environments. In the first, it was based on the unshaken authority of the older folk, which did not require the application of brute force; in the other it was based on a new distribution of forces and rights, that is, on the relative equality of the younger folk with the older.

Taken as a whole, the data on the punishment of children in the various regions tempt the conclusion that the generally combative disposition of the Southern Slavs was closely connected with the application of force in upbringing. Yet such a conclusion would be premature, indeed mistaken, since it is in disagreement with observations in patriarchal districts. For in patriarchal districts there was less beating of children than anywhere else, yet it is those regions which were the most combative districts, with tribal organization. For this reason the question of any mutual influence of force in upbringing and combative temperament in the adult must be left open.

### Acceptance of Authority

The acceptance of authority by the younger generation varies in the different environments, ranging from blind obedience to the fiercest conflict. The answers given to my question "How does the younger generation take demands and prohibitions of their parents, or their father?" have been classified into three groups. The group of "obedient sons" embraces those villages in which the lads showed no resistance to their father's authority. Though they may have grumbled, they did carry out the father's instructions. If they complained of their parents, it was in secret. The group of "resistance" embraces villages in which the lads behaved with definite disobedience, where the "younger folk did what they like," where boys openly complained of their parents and sought protection. Under the heading "serious clashes," I have grouped villages where the clash between the generations was harsh, with public scandal, fighting, and revenge against the parents' earlier severity. Here we have neglect and ill-treatment of parents and such reactions as emigration abroad through quarrels with the father, or cold-blooded fights necessitating the intervention of the authorities.

Graph 9 reveals a close block of villages with the younger generation resisting authority.

Graph 9. Acceptance of parents' authority

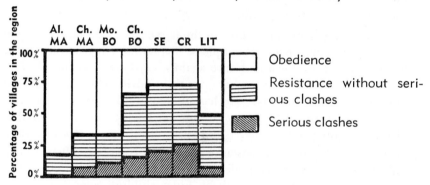

A surprising aspect of this graph is the great number of villages in the Littoral showing resistance. This result arises because the central group was formed to include cases where there were *no serious clashes*, but the father's authority has gone, and children decide for themselves what they will do and pay no heed to the parents' wishes.

In a patriarchal environment the principle was expressed in the words: "U mlađega pogovora nema"—(a person of lower rank has no right to oppose).

Whether such complete submission means that resistance and indignation by the younger generation was not felt at all or whether outward discipline concealed dissatisfaction cannot as a rule be judged. But one thing is surely clear; the all-round pressure of the patriarchal environment as a whole on subjected members of the family did kill resistance.

Nevertheless, nowhere in all our information has it proved possible to find absolute submission. We cannot say whether this is a sign that the patriarchal system was already beginning to relax in all the villages which came into this investigation, or whether it means that, though in the recognized ethic of an intact patriarchal system, there might be a demand for absolute submission, in practice this never occurred.

Before the war there was never grumbling, but the parents' demands were considered sacred. (*Sjenica district, Sanjak*)

They willingly obey their parents. Indignation is never seen.
(*Preševo district, Macedonia*)

Resistance and complaints of any kind against parents are very rare. Parents are as a rule always right. (*Žegligovo district, Macedonia*)

Although there is dissatisfaction among sons, they keep it to themselves, one will grunt out something, complain secretly to his mother or some intimate friend, and that is the end of it. (*Sjenica district, Sanjak*)

Reports from Moslem Bosnia are typical for this region:

The younger generation submits to the parents. It does indeed happen that something or other does not please them, they will grumble a little, but it soon settles down and once again everything is as the old folk want it to be. Often their teacher gives them advice which they take up quite readily, for they say: "He has studied and knows what is best" and very often the old folk too ask him for advice and in this or that give way to the younger folk. (*Foča district*)

Female children show no resistance and do not complain, whereas male children do not readily accept demands or prohibitions. They go away— run off—rather than perform them. Elder children complain openly, but revenge when the parents grow old is not frequent. As a rule they do not oppose a mother's order either openly or secretly.
(*Brčko district*)

In Christian villages of Bosnia there was much more resistance than in the Moslem villages, as may be seen from the graph. However, here too were signs of the old Bosnian gentleness or indifference:

The only truth is that nothing is any more obeyed blindly, that is, accepted, not even from parents, whom they are everywhere taught to obey. But I think there is no unreasoned resistance, even in the youngest. They are more for argument about decisions than their parents were in their time. Where a parent is intelligent and knows this, he obtains good results. I have not heard of any cases of children at war with their parents, or talking outside the home against them, or having revenge on them. (*Sarajevo district*)

Acceptance of parental authority is coupled with resistance. They object openly, and very often it comes to a physical show-down. Before the war, resistance was out of the question. Now if they refuse to satisfy a demand of the son, they are physically attacked.

*(Bosanski Petrovac district)*

In Serbia, we come upon a sharp struggle between the generations. While there was still much traditional respect for the father in the formal sense, from reports on resistance to the father's authority it is clear that the struggle of the generations was in full swing. Here are some extreme expressions of it:

The younger generation accept this while too weak to defend themselves, but as soon as they can do so, the father has to fall back. If they complain, they do so openly. *(Arilje district)*

Authority is accepted with derision and never admitted. Though it may exist in appearance, there is really none, for there is no sincerity between them. Father and son are in a state of incessant and irreconcilable struggle. Where as exception a father does not require any particular show of respect, the relationship is more bearable, more sincere, closer, intimate. Comradely, friendly attitudes on the father's part are unknown and alien to our people. *(Kosmaj district)*

Opposition to the demands of the father are frequent. Complaints against them are still kept within the narrow circle of relations and friends. Open resistance is limited to questions of inheritance. In most cases the life of elderly parents is not at all to be envied. Son or daughter-in-law look after them only so far as they expect something from their estate. *(Morava district)*

In Croatia we find still more villages than in Serbia with serious conflicts, and the struggle is very fierce.

Generally, sons resist their parents' demands. First they complain in secret, then to the town council. In their old age they neglect them.

*(Glina district, Kordun)*

Ten per cent voluntarily submit to their parents' requests and desires, the remainder offer concealed resistance. When the child is about ten years old, this becomes open, and later it comes to blows between them.

*(Prelog district)*

In Slavonia stabilized relationships prevailed, as in the Littoral. The struggles between the generations have already quieted down where they did exist. Here are three typical reports from Slavonia:

Open complaints of young against old are rare. There are conflicts, but the war "chewed up" the old folk too and they abandon their old views more easily. *(Pakrac district)*

87

This report is evidence of mutual giving way by both young and old, whereas the following report emphasizes that recently there had been no changes in the relations between old and young and says that this is the principal reason for the pacific atmosphere in Slavonia.

Quite naturally, if they are young, the sons accept the father's demands and prohibitions without protest, but older children often protest or quite openly do not obey. There is no revenge. This has remained just as it used to be. *(Djakovo district)*

Younger folk accept authority as something which is natural, which must be, which life itself demands. If a father is too harsh, his children still do not take revenge, even when they could. They forgive him.

*(Novska district)*

Whenever the expression "natural" appears in regard to relations in the family, we know we have stabilized, standardized relationships.

In the Littoral, relationships were similar to those of Slavonia. Here, more clearly even than in Slavonia, it is obvious that an important reason for the new equilibrium in the family was that the children acquired economic independence quite early.

Cases of arbitrary demands by parents are rare. Since the sons too earn, the father takes counsel with them. The majority still submit to their parents, a minority resist. It is rare for sons to take revenge from spite against their parents, but the fate of old people is bad, for a bride pays little attention to the old man, and, if he lives with the son, his washing is regularly done by a daughter, even if married.

*(Biograd on Sea district)*

One can see discontent in sons, but they take note of the good intentions of their parents, and give in. They do not complain of their parents. *(Split district)*

As a general rule, parental demands are not taken seriously by the children. They are lighthearted and superficial. Later it all takes a turn for the better. Lack of means drives them early to work, where their hot temperament is soon changed and a disobedient child becomes a serious, hard-working, prized worker. *(Kastav district)*

This report rather suggests the American situation, where earning does a great deal to discipline children and young people generally.

In an old-style environment, where the authority of the father was still of value, the sons did not oppose his orders. In a region of gradual development, the father did not make harsh demands regarding respect for seniority, and for this reason there was no serious opposition from independent sons. In a region where there was

88

stormy ferment, authority was in ruins and the resistance of the young people was strong. This shows an effort by the father to retain his eminent position longer than the sons were willing to recognize it.

### Changes in the Authority of the Father

In all regions—except to some extent the Littoral—the authority of the father had fallen below what it used to be. The formal signs of submission were disappearing, sons were making more independent decisions and adopting a freer attitude. Graph 10 shows these changes.

Graph 10. Changes in the attitude of young lads
to their father and elder men

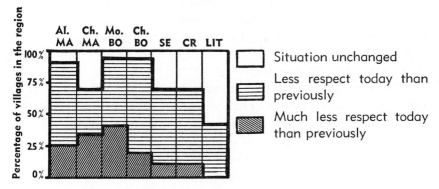

A comparison of this graph with Graph 6, illustrating the attitudes of grown sons to the father, shows the following results.

Among the Albanians there were great changes. With them, it is true, there was still great respect and awe of the father, but until quite recently it had been much greater. The patriarchal ceremonial forms have precisely now begun to decay. A great part of the villages were affected by these changes.

In Orthodox Macedonia too there were many changes, but the situation was not so simple. One-third of the villages were entirely undisturbed, another third were in a state of moderate change, and the remaining third were changing rapidly. In the whole region there were more great changes than in the "modern" parts of the country. The process began later here than elsewhere, and only now was affecting a large part of the villages.

In Bosnia, the trend reached its peak, with its highest point in the Moslem sector, where practically every village was touched by changes regarding the authority of the father. In Moslem Bosnia, the father's authority was undergoing most powerful blows. During the previous twenty years, a complex of many circumstances delivered a shock to the Moslem family, breaking down the old relationships with great force and speed. Though today there is still much respect for older people, everything has changed when compared with former times. As people sing: "Even *Bairams*[2] are not what they once were."

In Serbia and Croatia there were many more villages where no change had occurred. The disruption of the authority of the father was to a great extent complete. The final stages of a great process were now taking place, a process which first affected the grandfathers of the young peasants of today, particularly in Croatian districts.

In the Littoral, in the majority of villages there had been no changes in recent years in the authority of the father. Family relationships were stabilized because changes in the way of life were completed long ago. Judging by the position of the authority of the father in the Littoral, the family was in a better state of equilibrium than that of the old-style regions.

The principal reason that investigators in the old-style regions refer to the most extensive changes from former conditions is that the reporters and those who informed them were mainly young people who had knowledge of only a few years of village life. Thus their answers to the questionnaire referred solely to what to them were recent years. Even older people, when asked about changes in family life, generally thought of the past twenty years, that is, the years since the beginning of the First World War, or else from the economic crisis of 1930, for these two events had a powerful influence on family life. The First World War and the world economic depression were influences which every man in a village noticed. It was particularly the men of the old-style parts who observed the effects, for in such regions there had, since time immemorial, been no comparable changes.

The break-up of an old, deeply rooted system does not take place all at once but, as a rule, in a series of waves connected with great political and economic changes. Historical blows, acting with great force, destroy this or that part of the old edifice of the patriarchal system. In periods of peace this work of disintegration finds its completion. When our investigators speak of great changes in respect for the father in conservative villages, this means that the first blows at the old family order and at the authority of the father had just

2 Moslem feast after annual period of fasting.

reached the district. In regions which had been in a state of ferment for some time, the investigators rarely referred to great changes in respect for the elders, for the reason that neither they nor their informers remembered the high authority for older people which had once existed. For instance, in Croatia and in the Littoral, zadruga life was seriously smitten as far back as at the end of the nineteenth century.

Asked about changes in family life, men mainly recalled the First World War and the depression, though in fact those two events have no longer had much of this position of the father as a sort of chief to destroy, for as far back as men's memory went, the edifice of rigid family hierarchy had been laid in ruins. The zadrugas had long since fallen to pieces.

## Conclusions

The authority and status of the father passed through a whole spectrum, from veneration and royal honors to being completely ignored or even maltreated by his sons. The fierce struggle over the authority of the father offers one of the grimmest pictures in the whole of this study. The breaking down of the authority of the old head of the zadruga sometimes resulted in really hellish scenes. Under the terrible blows of this earthquake, the walls of stable family life shivered and cracked, till in the end the last vestiges crumbled away.

The relation between father and son in the patriarchal environment was very different from what is generally assumed by people not familiar with this set-up. The privileged position of the older people did not permit them injustice or arbitrariness, oppression or exploitation of authority. In the South Slav regions it was precisely in the patriarchal system that the rights of all members of the family found their highest realization. In the patriarchal phase, all rights and obligations were respected; there was consideration toward the weaker individuals, and violence within the family was abhorred. On the other hand, in the stage of the decay of the patriarchal system, the rights of every member of the family became insecure, hence everybody at once fought for more rights. In this stage it is the survival of the fittest—the strongest—that serves as law. The diminution of the father's authority had little advantage for the young ones. Both in law and in actuality, they now had far fewer rights to property than in the old zadruga, for the father became the individual owner of the farm, and the children depended on him in quite a new way.

We can discern certain advantages in the patriarchal regime. Every senior person had already revealed his worth and his ability, for in the zadruga it is only those with skill and experience who enjoyed the honor of being heads. Experience, tribulations, knowledge, and wisdom were recognized, and invested efforts and successful work were rewarded. Another point is that the older folk had fewer personal ambitions than did the younger. Their interest was concentrated not on themselves but on their children and grandchildren, for which reason alone they were able to be more objective than the younger generation, which was closely engaged in the struggle for personal success and self-affirmation. It is a common thing for parents to love their children more than the children love them, so that, if authority is in their hands, they look after the young far better than the young do for the old when the situation is reversed. Besides, the younger generation as it grows up has before it the prospect of advancement and a rise to a position of greater importance; whereas, when the younger generation rules, it has only loss of status to face when it ages.

Although the equality of all members of the family may well be the aim of some societies, the aim is nowhere realized. In some countries the younger generation enjoys a particularly favored position; everything is adapted to the young, and their manner of living is decisive. Although these facts are plain indeed to every observer, the beneficiaries of this system call it democratic and insist that complete equality has been reached. There is, however, a particular dignity in the patriarchal system deriving from the circumstance that theory and practice are in harmony, for the older people have authority not only by right but also for practical reasons. No one who has ever seen the older people of this environment can ever forget their dignity, their sense of responsibility, their noble features and manners. They are far removed indeed from any tyranny or struggle for prestige.

There was nothing in our material to support the hypothesis of a number of social psychologists that the authoritative family harms the development of the young. It is rather the contrary: Peasant sons show inconsiderate attitudes and violence not in the patriarchal phase but in the phase in which the family hierarchy disintegrates. Roughness and brutality cannot be a direct result of an authoritative upbringing, since we know that many generations grew up in patriarchal families without showing these characteristics.

It is, however, quite possible that our material is not especially suited to checking assumptions about the "authoritarian personality," since the position of the father in the Slavic South is not typically autocratic. The patriarchal family here is at the same time the zadruga family, with considerable rights for all members (especially the married men). The father or grandfather is not the individual owner of the peasant-holding, nor is he the only responsible person in the extended family. The paternal power in the zadruga is by no means absolute. This fact might modify the authority of the father, and therefore does not lead to the unfavorable results which—according to some students of this problem—rigid authority has in an urbanized environment.

To the question whether there are settled and quiet family relations only where strict authority is maintained, the answer is that this is also true in other systems in the Slavic South. The family in some "modern" parts offers almost as peaceful a picture as in the patriarchal regions. The Littoral and Slavonia seem to stand in the lee, protected from the storm. Every single report from those parts stands out in distinction from districts racked by ferment, and presents a picture of life in a more peaceful zone. Here no one fiercely advocates the institution of head-ship, nor particularly attacks it. On the basis of extended rights for the younger people, the two generations live in an atmosphere which is quite bearable. Their desires do not clash, and their rights are largely equal. From the conditions in these regions we can conclude that an anarchic, uncouth situation in any family is to some extent a consequence of "war and revolution," and that more peaceful times may bring to the fore an "inborn" love between father and son, between older and younger generations. We see that, in the Balkans too, outside the sphere of the zadruga and of the patriarchal hierarchy, there are family relations which are good and friendly.

# CHAPTER IV

# Mother and Mother-in-Law[1]

IN ALL the regions investigated, we observed particular love and tenderness toward the mother. Here we are not thinking of the mother's attitude toward children—tenderness in this relationship is universal—but a special tenderness of the children toward the mother. The mother occupied a central position in all her children's most deeply felt emotions as a sort of protectress. In love songs about the yearning of a young man for a girl, or the longing of a girl for a boy of her choice, behind the loved person, we find the mother. We constantly hear the words "ask mother," "tell mother," "mother will not let me," "mother likes you."

It would seem that this markedly affectionate attitude has some connection with the position of women in all the regions, that is, with the subjection of women. Because in the patriarchal setting, seniority by sex is more important than that by age, the mother stood rather low in the hierarchy of this system. Even in later stages of social development she did not achieve equality with men. Her authority was nowhere very high. As it happens, however, this circumstance clearly had a favorable effect on her relationship with her children. She was in a position to give unhindered expression to her affection, for she was not obliged to be aloof, to maintain authority or discipline. At the same time, the children did not build up ambivalent feelings regarding her, as they did regarding the father. In not a single Yugoslav area was there anything like the American situation, where the woman has frequently the primary authority in the family and the obligation of disciplining the children and accepting responsibility for decisions, nor was any antagonism toward the mother found in the Slavic South.

At the same time, however, this relationship between mother and children in the Yugoslav regions, good though it may be, was not always free from problems. In every mother-child tie, there is the seed of tragedy. The mother is always bound to her children by a love in which there may well be a certain biological factor. A

---

[1] The word *svekrva*, mother-in-law, denotes not simply the concept mother of husband or wife, but precisely mother of a woman's husband. The mother of a husband's wife is denoted by a different word. The position of daughter-in-law, *snaha* (or *snaja*, or *snaša*) is so prevalent that it has acquired the meaning of "young married woman."

mother loves her children without regard to external circumstances or even the attitude of the children themselves. But any relationship founded on love has a menace overhanging it, for the loving person is very vulnerable. The mother is particularly exposed to this tragic danger, and this for the precise reason that she always loves her children more than they love her. She is absolutely without any defense against animosity or alienation on their part. In Yugoslavia this danger appeared in the relationship between the mother and a married son and his wife, for as a rule she shared her home with them.

In the stage of social development in which the young couple strive to break up the joint family life, there developed an alienation of the son from his parents, and in this process the daughter-in-law played a fateful role. To her, the husband's mother was a mother-in-law with a senior position of authority, and from that relationship arose conflicts, difficulties, struggles. There were no fewer problems in the relationship between mother-in-law and daughter-in-law in the South Slav village than in the like relationship in any urbanized, industrialized environment. Indeed, there may well have been more. The position of *svekrva*—mother of the husband of a young woman—being simultaneously that of real mother of this son, was never spared either the changes or the strife which attacked the family as such in certain stages of its historical development. As we shall now see, this relationship went through a rhythm of development similar to the changes in some of the other relationships within the family.

## The Mother's Allies

In any environment in which all relationships were in a state of equilibrium and confirmed by tradition, there were no special groupings or alliances within the family, or such as there were were of no great significance. All relationships were amicable and stable, according to duties and custom. Any resentment was hidden away, never breaking out to the surface.

Only when the patriarchal regime began to break up, when clashes and disputes developed, and individual demands forced their way to the surface, did the members of the family group enter into "alliances," which frequently had a militant complexion. Although the mother was always linked with her children, even when they were sharply antagonistic to her, in certain stages she was drawn into alliances of one sort or another. Did she take her place amid the forces of her own generation, associated with the father in defense of traditional rights? Or did she join the forces of the subordinate members of the family, going into league with the dissatisfied children against the only person with authority, the father who heads the family? Or did she take her place in some sort of league of the womenfolk?

To inquire into these matters, two questions were put. These were: "Is the mother more on the side of her husband or her children?" and "Is the mother more on the side of the sons or the daughters?" The reports on the first question, are represented in Graph 11.

Graph 11. Is the mother on the side of husband or children?

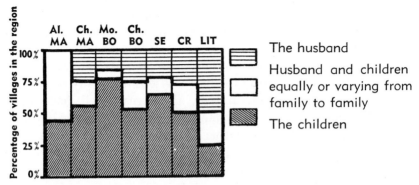

It is very clear from this data that in the South Slav territory studied, there was no predominance of a war between the generations. The following points stand out.

The dignified neutrality of the Albanians. In most Albanian villages the reporters asserted that it was impossible to establish whether the mother leaned more to husband or children. This reveals quite definitely that there were no inner groupings of the family within patriarchal relationships, or that these were of no great importance.

On the other hand, in Moslem Bosnia a particularly close bond existed between mother and children. It would appear that, in the initial phase of the decay of the patriarchal order in this region, there was tremendous pressure on the woman, who sought allies among her children and not her husband, who aimed at maintaining his authority, retaining an Oriental remoteness from her.

Down the Littoral there was a particularly strong bond between husband and wife, one which might be interpreted as a common front of people of like age, were not family life in this region so tranquil and stabilized.

In addition, in all the old-style districts, we found sporadic alliance between husband and wife.

The wife holds more with the husband. The wife holds more with the children in parts where she is more subordinate. But here a wife is valued, for if lost, she cannot be replaced.

*(Skoplje district, Macedonia)*

It varies from one case to another whether the mother is more on the side of the husband or the children, but the saying does run: if you lose a child, God will give you another, but if you lose your husband, it is a branch cut off. *(Mostar district, Herzegovina)*

In the region of great changes, there were many alliances of mother and children against the authority of the father, particularly in Serbia:

Mother and children join in a common front against the father.

*(Kosmaj district, Serbia)*

The mother holds with the children more than the husband. She will hide something from the husband, something of value, food, etc., to sell it without the husband knowing and share the money with the children. *(Posavina district, Serbia)*

Here is an example from the Littoral of the strong bond between husband and wife:

The mother holds more with the husband. This arises from the husband's being absent about the world for long periods. Without exception every woman would rather all her children died than her husband. *(Dalmatian island, Preko district)*

A report from Montenegro indicates the complex of problems of the mother's alliances:

Among us, if one can put it so, we split up two loves. Where sentiment comes in, a mother loves her children more, but if it were a question of the life of husband or a child, she would rather sacrifice the child, for her husband is the provider and protector of the family, including herself, dearer to her as far as life goes. A daughter may also be dearer to a mother than a son, i.e., she gives her more attention, but yet, were life in question, a mother would always decide to save her son.

*(Šavnik district, Montenegro)*

Graph 12 shows the position regarding the second question about the mother's alliances.

Graph 12. Is the mother more on the side of her sons
or her daughters?

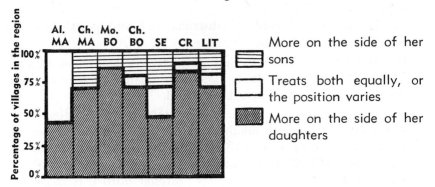

More on the side of her sons

Treats both equally, or the position varies

More on the side of her daughters

The graph demonstrates that in all regions there was a great bond between mother and daughter. Comparison of this graph with the preceding one indicates the parallel course of the curves. Here we find daughters taking the place of children in the first analysis.

The following are some reports from an old-style environment:

While the sons are unmarried, and the daughters too, the mother holds more with her sons, but later, more with her daughters.
(*Nerodimlje district, Macedonia*)

The mother holds more with her children, but as these grow up, the son increasingly separates from the mother, so that she draws closer to her daughters. (*Morihovo district, Macedonia*)

As a rule, if the sons earn and bring money into the home, the mother holds with them. She always protects the girls, her daughters.
(*Tuzla district, Bosnia*)

The mother holds more with her daughters, she prefers a son-in-law to a son. (*Tuzla district*)

The mother holds more with the children, particularly the daughters, if there are any. Often a mother *steals from her husband* and takes things to her married daughters. (*Stolac district, Herzegovina*)

A woman loves her husband, but keeps with the children while she lavishes more care on her daughters than her sons.
(*Bijeljina district, Bosnia*)

Graph 12 shows that in Serbia the mother had closer ties with her son than in other regions. We find the same situation in other districts which had a pastoral economy and tribal culture, e.g., in Montenegro and the Dalmatian highlands. It is hard to say if it was the heroic tradition which in the mother's feelings created greater concern for her sons. For instance, we do not find this complex among the Albanians, or we are unable to observe it for the reason that all feelings among this people were concealed behind a dignified bearing. In Serbia, we can clearly see a struggle of all members of the family against the old authority, represented here by the father. The mother linked herself with the son against the dominance of the father:

> As there is little love between married couples, the mother holds mainly with the children. The mother holds more with the sons, seeing in them future protectors and providers.
>
> *(Posavina district, Serbia)*

In Croatia the strong bond between mother and daughter was often a consequence of the struggle of the young married son and his wife against the parents. Here too we occasionally see a definite struggle between the generations, that is to say, the parents were united in a defensive alliance against the children, particularly the sons, who confronted them with great demands:

> The mother holds more with her children, especially while they are little. When they grow up a bit, she *holds more with her husband.* They form a united front against the children, for the maintenance and defense of their position. *(Varaždin district)*

> The mother holds more with the children while they are small, *more with her husband when the children are grown up.* Later, the mother holds *with her daughters* more than with a son. The son marries and the young daughter-in-law almost always breaks up the peace of the family, but a married daughter always maintains even later a bond with her mother and vice-versa. Out of many reasons, young men are not inclined to marry, whereas it is hard to find husbands for the girls. A young man would gladly marry, but cannot, because there is still an unmarried girl in the house. If a brother marries before his sister, she does not marry, if she is not rich. The older a girl is, the more her parents have to promise to give her if she marries. For these reasons, it usually comes to serious conflicts. Young man and girl alike feel themselves handicapped and maintain that their parents are to blame for it all, for breaking up the land or not promising enough. They are at fault for the young man being a bachelor or the girl unable to find a husband. *(Dugoselo district, Croatia)*

The alliance of mother and daughter is rather in disagreement with the "Oedipus complex" as understood by Freudian psychoanalysis. In not a single region, or at any age, do we find a particularly strong bond between father and daughter. The alliance of mother and daughter is in open contradiction to the patriarchal principle of the preciousness and superior worth of the males. This alliance was indeed an *entente cordiale*, an alliance of hearts. It was not concluded in defense against the demands of son and son's wife—since daughters marry early, this is not of such great importance. And still less was such an alliance concluded for the purpose of acquiring greater rights for women or to get around the male authority. The alliance amounted to a sort of counter-balance to the patriarchal principle of male worthiness, which placed a girl in the lowest rank of the hierarchy. This special love of mother for daughters created a climate which afforded daughters the possibility of favorable development in an environment which consistently undermined a woman's feeling of importance. The loyalty of daughters balanced for a mother that low estimation which is often shown her by the men.

A song from Croatia reveals how, in that "more up-to-date" region, warm feelings of daughters for the mother developed in nearly the same way as in the patriarchal environment:

### A Mother's Tendernesses

A bride sits amid the vines
The bride sings and a bird replies
Among the vines the bride enquires
"O, little birdie, nightingale,
Why dost not sing, winter as summer?"
The little nightingale replies
"Good gracious! bride amid the vines,
Give me now St. Michael's heat
And I will sing, winter as summer,
But why, oh bride amid the vines,
Singest not thou as with your mother?"
Bride among the vines replies:
"O, little birdie, nightingale,
Give me my mother's tender care
And I will sing as with my mother."

Here we should also mention the alliance of grandmother and grandchildren. In all districts, the grandmother spent much time with the children, while the young mothers were busy with arduous labor. Frequently the grandmother had the significant word in the upbringing of the children, who mainly took their wishes to her. This bond with the grandchildren, which was often very strong, played a great part in raising the morale of older women. The case of Aika, described at the end of this chapter, depicts the support which a grandson can offer.

The portrait of Božica, a Bosnian peasant woman, shows moreover how, despite her low standing, a woman could still be the central figure in the family. Despite—or perhaps precisely because of—the lack of attention from her husband, she contrived to enjoy the greatest respect, being the principal influence on the children, and showing particular dignity.

### Božica. Example of a much respected mother

The following is a first-hand account contributed by Zagorka Dragović, a woman teacher in a mountain village of Bosnia.

I know Božica very well indeed, as I have lodged with her for the past three years. She is fifty-four years old. She is not good-looking. but very strong. She wears the peasant costume of her district, is always very clean. Her manner is very civilized and frank. She has five children alive.

She never went to school and is illiterate. Her mother married a second time. She was accounted nubile at an early age by her mother, and very soon began to think she would have to marry. She never really had any girlhood, for she was married when fifteen.

She said: "I had a very nice chance come my way, and knowing I was poor, wasted no time thinking about it, though things weren't at all bad at home, and I might have waited longer." Nobody pressed her, she herself chose her husband, yet before marriage she had only one meeting with him, and prior to this had rarely seen him at all. "I had always held that a good home and good name, and being well known, were more important than all else. Besides, I liked them having a little land, and being a zadruga, so I was not going to stay home thinking it over. Besides, here I had a chance to learn from somebody wiser than myself about things I knew nothing about." Of married life or any sort of love she had no experience, and all that fate brought her, she says, she accepted as being merely as it should be, it was her duty to submit as all her other womenkind had done. That was how she had been brought up. Particular attention was paid to submissiveness and cleanliness in every respect, and moreover she brings up her own family in a like stern ethic; indeed, in some things she goes too far. She herself says that she can quite see that some old fashioned standards should be relaxed, not being any longer suitable for today, yet can never let herself do so, for she believes in her way profoundly and with great conviction.

Thus she married into a zadruga. There were two other brothers in it as well as her husband, these being younger, also the father and mother-in-law. In those days they lived well, as there were no grown-up children, hence fewer needs, so the zadruga could provide in sufficiency for its members. But later, when her brothers-in-law married and they got children, everything began to change, and in the end they split the property up.

She was absolutely submissive to her husband in the first stage of her married life, for he was young, strong, and very cantankerous. Due to his upbringing, he never showed his wife any affection or any attention in front of others, for they would have thought that disgraceful. Her husband was very industrious, "fell on work like a madman," and also never let others go slow. He particularly despised domestic work, cared for neither order nor cleanliness. They were neither clean nor orderly. The mother-in-law paid little attention to that, the principal thing was to carry out the outside work and spin and weave the most necessary things. On that account, she [Božica] was often reproached both by mother-in-law and husband, who would always *take the mother's side*. For this reason she often did housework even by night, which the other zadruga members did not set high.

Her husband was rough even in his most intimate demands, and for those days rather lascivious. She is of rather a cold temperament, so in intimate matters they did not quite fit each other. For this reason this contact, she says, was revolting and afforded her no great enjoyment. Yet she did not dare avoid a single one of her husband's demands, but humbly suffered them all. Often she would remain awake at night, weeping, while her husband, satisfied, long since snored. This was the general attitude of husband to wife—never to reveal himself anywhere as tender or sensitive, for he would be made mock of.

Even after marriage he often went to other villages to marriage parties and other enjoyments, and this used to hurt her, for he never paid any attention to his young wife, left alone beside the cradle with the child "which he had made," thinking it over with aching heart. Later, she grew accustomed to this, for she was "smothered with children," and also saw that he was faithful to her, then at last realized that his place was in company with other men, not drooping about with her at home. What would other men say to him? They would have a down on her, too.

She bore ten children and miscarried once. Of all these, she brought up five surviving children. She gave birth almost always alone, in a damp cellar, two she had in the orchard, some way from the house. The last two births, one being with twin boys, were very difficult, and after them she had difficulty in recovering. She bore children as long as in nature she could. She never tried to do anything against conception. She considers modern women more sensible for avoiding pregnancies, for she thinks excessive bearing is no good to anyone.

Her mother-in-law did not like her much at first because of her cleanliness, all "fiddling with a broom and washing things out," but she did everything to satisfy her and looked after her when she became incapable, particularly when two other, younger, daughters-in-law came into the house. Then the mother-in-law handed over all management of the household to her. Her father-in-law was a terrible drunkard, particularly toward the end of his life. He loved torturing all his daughters-in-law with unnecessary jobs, he would simply invent things, just to wear them out.

Her husband always took his parents' side. Twice he beat her because she took the part of the younger women. She was afraid of his physical force and his spiteful nature, and in such moody fits avoided opposing him. "But for that, when he was in a good mood, I paid him back for everything." Her husband was a miser by nature, so as the children grew up and needs became greater, particularly as to getting things for the girls, he would not willingly understand, and whatever she did get out of him "was all with the greatest pains." For this reason she always had to put up with a lot from him because of his temperament. She realized that he was rather selfish and self-centered and one trait that was particularly hard for her to bear was that he was greedy with food and drink, so would never put up with the least hunger, particularly when food was not yet prepared. Then he would reproach her with being a bad manager and lazy, with all her sweeping and washing out. When he lost his temper he would swear foully and at length, and this she could not bear. Yet she rather praised him than condemned, perhaps because they grew used to one another.

On account of the coarse, uncouth temperament of the father, her children were afraid of him while they were still small, but as they grew up (this concerns only the boys) they would not put up in silence, so the father was more often in a rage, swearing, than previously. The children looked to their mother for protection against him; she defended them and he reproached her with spoiling them. But her children were far from spoiled, as the father, who would spitefully like to hurt her, sometimes said. She brought the girls up very strictly, but did turn a blind eye a little to the boys, although it was never possible to say she had let them go. She had her way in influencing her children, since she knew each of them by nature, by their reactions, and talked to them accordingly. Her children heed her in a way rarely seen. This she says of her grown-up children. Her daughter-in-law is very insensitive and very selfish, and separates her husband from her parents and is jealous of him, particularly with respect to the mother. However, that married son with her still values his mother more highly and is helping her bring up his brothers and sisters. All this is brought about peaceably and without conflict. The father is anyway far from this mental struggle of hers, neither feels it nor understands.

She values her son-in-law highly. He is serious and diligent and quite just in appraisal of his wife. He looks after her and values her and protects her as he does the children, for they live in the largest zadruga in the village. The girls show the parents more attention than does her own son, and this she finds hard, for, as she says, all the same she loves her son and his children more than her son-in-law's as they are somehow nearer to her. In some things she criticizes the grandchildren or rather condemns the parents who "let them go" (spoil them) and provide them with too much of everything and never think that life may demand more sacrifices of them than they will be able later to bear decently.

She does not complain of domestic chores, only when it is shared out and when others perform certain definite periodic tasks. She says there is no work that is hard to her, for "in my own home I am working for myself." She says she would be afraid if she had nothing to work at or for, as those folk, [i.e., Božica and her people] being peasantry, only think of the land and livestock under their noses, and were that to be taken from her—[were she] in some other place—she would be lost. She is still afraid about her children not having anywhere to live, if besides this they do not find some other source of earning. It is her wish while still alive to see at least some hint of an insured future for her children, and she would like not to have a hard old age, thinking here of serious illness.

Božica lives in a family which is one of the poorest, with the least land. She serves as an example in the village. Whenever she visits anybody in the village, all the womenfolk are upset if their house is not in apple-pie order. On one occasion some of a certain household were heard to call out to the mother: "Good Lord! Here's Božica coming, and the house all upside down."

## Mother and Daughter-in-Law
### (Svekrva and Snaha)

The relationship between a mother and her daughter-in-law is never without its difficulties, whatever the environment. Good relations between them are more easily upset and more readily pass into hostility than any other relationship. Clashes between them were frequent in the regions in ferment, which in this regard cover a particularly large area.

In the patriarchal region and that which had achieved a new equilibrium, we did, even in this relationship, find much amiability and agreement. The following report is typical:

> Relations between *svekrva* and *snaha* as a rule are good. The daughter in-law must respect, value, and obey the mother-in-law. The proverb says "There are a thousand women but only one mother."
>
> (*Veles district, Macedonia*)

Though in the patriarchal set-up the positions of mother and mother-in-law were lower than those of the male members of the family, the wife of the head of the house, nevertheless, enjoyed great authority over both her female children and the daughters-in-law. Because the daughters married early and left the home, there tended to be only the "brought in" younger women about the house, among whom there were no great distinctions of rank. As a rule the daughters-in-law were all dependent on the mother-in-law. As the young master of the house, a married son had high rank, belonging to the "ruling caste," and he supported his parents' authority. The bond between a married couple in this environment was not intimate enough to be likely to provoke rivalry between mother and wife. Everything in the household influenced the women in the sense of submission and agreement: The old head of the family prevented any clashes either by tact or severity, and the son acted in the same sense, either by kindness or force.

The demand and expectation of the whole environment that the daughter-in-law should invariably respect her mother-in-law did not result in "forced" pleasantness, but very often in a great affection between the two. A song depicts clearly the attitude of a daughter-in-law toward her mother-in-law in a patriarchal environment:

Our Bogdan has nine vineyards
Sells them all to pay his debts
Yet still cannot get out of debt
So sells his dear old mother too.
Then there speaks Bogdan's own wife:
"Alas, Bogdan, my good lord,
Do not sell our dear old mother,
But sell me your own true wife,
Tomorrow with a troubled head,
You would not cry: "Alas, dear wife!"
Yet would cry: "Alas, dear mother!"

The relationship between mother and daughter-in-law was utterly transformed when the zadrugas began to break up and the young couples engaged in the struggle for independence.

Relations between svekrva and snaha are very poor. Conflicts are very frequent and it is rare for them to get on together. Consequently, bonds between sons and the mother are built up. If a mother-in-law does not agree with her son's wife, the sons then hate the young woman and often ostracize her or knock her about.

*(Andrijevica district, Montenegro)*

The daughter-in-law found it much harder to bear the seniority of the mother-in-law than did a son that of his father, so she urged her husband on in his struggle for independence. The rebellious mood of the daughter-in-law which previously was hidden now came out into the open. She established a sort of fighting front with her husband and often adopted an attitude of open hostility to the mother-in-law. The "young master" then withdrew from his alliance with the "ruling stratum" and linked up with his wife in a struggle for independence.

In districts in which the process of break-up of the zadruga had been completed long since and where the changes proceeded slowly (or where there never had been zadrugas), the relations between mother-in-law and son's wife were more amicable and quarrels were infrequent. Instead of uncouthness toward the parents, one often observed monetary considerations on the part of the younger folk struggling for their own independent livelihood:

Parents are always better; they do not excessively reproach their children for leaving them. The relationship between mother-in-law and daughter-in-law is as a rule good, sometimes, indeed, very good. As a rule, the daughter-in-law will agree with the mother-in-law if she is in good health, but like her less if the mother requires assistance.

*(Novi district, Littoral)*

Graph 13. Good or poor relations between svekrva and snaha

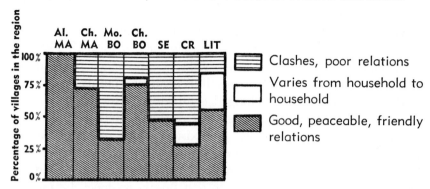

Clashes, poor relations

Varies from household to household

Good, peaceable, friendly relations

Graph 13 reveals a characteristic curve, with great differences between the various regions. The classical patriarchal situation existed only among the Albanians, where there were good, settled relations in all villages. The majority of the reports from this region were like the following:

> The relations of mother-in-law and daughter-in-law are like those of mother and daughter.

In the Orthodox villages of Macedonia, we found frequent good relations. Here are some examples:

> The relationship between mother-in-law and daughter-in-law is good. If there are clashes, they are skillfully hidden. On the whole, sons are on the mother's side. Girls, that is, wives, are indeed brought up so that they do respect the mother-in-law. (*Dojran district*)

> The relationship between svekrva and snaha is very good. Full of love and respect. The snaha is well aware that she should respect her "majka svekrva."[2] The people are on the mother-in-law's side, public opinion supports her. The son is sometimes on his wife's side, if he is too much in love, "under petticoat government," but in the majority of cases he is on the mother's side; there are even cases of him striking his wife for quarreling with her mother-in-law. (*Prespa district*)

> In such clashes, the sons stick to their wives, yet nevertheless do restrain them, to avoid such conflict. (*Djevdjelija district*)

> Mothers-in-law adopt more a dictatorial than a motherly attitude toward their sons' wives. For her a snaha is an incoming woman, whose duty is solely to work. In most cases, public opinion is on the side of the mother-in-law. The mother-in-law more often exploits the daughter-in-law than vice versa. This is the attitude of the mother-in-law toward her son's wife in those homes in which the father-in-law is still alive and master of the house. (*St. Nikola Ovčepolje district*)

[2] I.e., "mother mother-in-law."

The following rather naïve report is characteristic for a patriarchal environment:

> As the mother-in-law and daughter-in-law are regularly together, there is little conflict beause of economic dependence.   (*Žegligovo district*)

Moslem and Christian Bosnian villages approached this question differently from all the other questions regarding family life. Whereas the Christian villages belonged completely to the patriarchal environment, Moslem Bosnia resembled the modern regions. The reason for this may have been the existence here of fewer zadrugas than in the other districts and that in small families conflicts between svekrva and snaha were fiercer than in the large zadruga. We must also suppose that in Moslem Bosnia we have the moment of commencement of the decay of the old-style patriarchal way of life, which was to be seen in a powerful development of the early symptom of the "disease," namely, this clash between mother-in-law and daughter-in-law.

Here is a Bosnian Moslem example in traditional style:

> The sons respect their mother. It is a sin to treat one's mother badly. The daughter-in-law must obey her and never complain. The relationship between mother-in-law and daughter-in-law as a rule is good. Nobody even pays any attention to little clashes. One woman helps the other.   (*Foča district*)

Now two examples from Moslem Bosnia which show the daughter-in-law's resistance to the older woman's seniority and the understanding which public opinion had of that resistance.

> The relationship of daughter-in-law to mother-in-law is slave-like. Young women do not allow themselves to be trodden on without right.
> (*Bugojno district*)

> There is a prickly plant (the cactus) which the people call "mother-in-law's tongue," but the "daughter-in-law's tongue" is narrower and longer. In most cases the people are of the opinion that these two beings never can agree, for they hold that in most cases the mother-in-law is a tyrant to the younger woman.   (*Bijeljina district*)

> Sons respect their mothers. In any case wives have to be obedient. It is rare for a wife to succeed in opposing the mother.
> (*Orthodox village, Derventa district*)

In Serbia, bad relations between mother and daughter-in-law were very frequent, to which the general combative disposition of the Serbian woman undoubtedly contributed. The situation there is characterized by the circumstance that the struggle of the sons for

10. Bosnian market

11. Croatian woman

12. Market at the Montenegrin coast

13. Bosnian village market
14. Serbian woman

independence was directed against the father as family head and not against the mother, who never had much authority within the family. A few instances:

In 80 per cent of cases, the relationship between snaha and svekrva is not good. Before the war, public opinion took the side of the mother-in-law, but now supports her less than previously, though still is on her side. In most cases, a son is good to his mother, but in any clash is on his wife's side. *(Posavina district)*

A widowed mother is respected and helped, and, if she re-marries, there is only tenderness between her son and herself. Everything else is vanishing. Daughter-in-law never agrees with the mother-in-law. Quarrels in this regard are frequent. The mother has to give way.

*(Kosmaj district)*

The son always takes his wife's part. It is very rarely that he proves what people call "a man with a strong hand," who, taking his mother's side, beats his wife. *(Morava district)*

The sons as a rule avoid undesirable scenes between their mothers and their wives, or go to the father, and he, as the elder in the home, then condemns his wife. *(Niš district)*

In Croatia too, relations varied. The first reports show the beginnings of a struggle between the women in the home. Under particularly great pressure, the daughter-in-law rebelled and, moreover, without the support of her husband. This heroic method of woman's emancipation, as we might term it, with resistance in the absence of any ally, was common in the Dinaric districts.

There are frequent clashes between snaha and svekrva. Public opinion approves the action of the daughter-in-law. The mother-in-law exploits her daughter-in-law, and this is revealed by these words, which I have heard spoken: "Why did we introduce you to this home, but to work?" Grown-up sons are obedient toward their mothers, and in particular will obey every suggestion of a widowed mother. There sometimes breaks out a quarrel between mother-in-law and daughter-in-law, but as a rule the sons take the mother's side. *(Dalmatia, Benkovac district)*

The mother-in-law has a fully formed viewpoint and ethic by which the daughter-in-law *must* obey her behests to the full. Clashes are common. Older men and women who have grown accustomed to being slaves and having others serve them slavishly, approve of the mother-in-law's attitude. The younger generation and younger members of the family are on the justified side of the daughter-in-law. In most cases, the daughter-in-law puts up with it and gives way on this or that merely to avoid conflict. *(Gospić district, Lika area)*

109

The relationship between mother-in-law and daughter-in-law is simply barbarous. The mother-in-law is the be-all and end-all of life, and she exploits her position. *(Šibenik district)*

A few examples from central Croatia, where the mother-in-law had lost a lot of ground and the daughter-in-law was on the attack:

If the daughter-in-law is the stronger, she influences her husband, then the son scolds his mother and in such a case it is the daughter-in-law who becomes head of the house on the women's side. Then the mother-in-law is a slave—she labors and attends on the others, while the daughter-in-law sits at spinning or goes visiting her own family, leaving the mother-in-law to look after the children and other things.
*(Zlatar district)*

The sons respect the mother while there is any likelihood of a good inheritance. As soon as the question of inheritance is finally settled, the mother is worth less and, if she needs anything, she is sent to the one who obtained most. Between mother-in-law and daughter-in-law, there are many clashes. Especially if the daughter-in-law has entered the home solely at the son's wish, or has brought only a small dowry. In public opinion the mother-in-law is always the stronger, but when the mother-in-law gets old, the daughter-in-law *has her revenge*. The daughter-in-law is exploited, being the younger. *(Varaždin district)*

This last report shows how property colors relations in connection with the individualism in the economic field long since developed in Croatia.

In the Littoral, there were rare cases of bad relations between mother-in-law and daughter-in-law. The aloofness which existed between parents and the young couple made feasible a relationship of indifference, but there were great individual differences.

Svekrva and snaha are never like mother and daughter, but often put up with one another. Public opinion with fair justice weighs up this relationship and assists the weaker side. *(Kastav district)*

This last report reveals the young couple as learning to fit in with the mother or mother-in-law, who, since she would inherit a great part of the property after her husband's death, had a position of real authority in the Littoral.

Married sons and daughters each look after themselves, and it does not come to disputes later. A widowed mother stays on in the home and enjoys the property, even manages it while able to. At the same time, the son and his wife are more subordinate, they obey her and work.
*(Kastav district)*

As we see, the relationship between svekrva and snaha was rich in problems. The situation was made much more difficult by the fact that the daughters-in-law as a rule live in the home of the husband's parents, and the houses were so cramped that often all members of the family slept in the same room. The men, all born and raised in this house, were accustomed to the close-knit community, but the wives, entering the home as adults, never became completely adapted, at least, not while still young. The patriarchal requisite of absolute submission of the younger person was most completely realized where the older people exercised their influence on the younger from childhood.

As in other relationships in the family, in the relations of mother-in-law and daughter-in-law good, amiable attitudes were more easily maintained when rights are unequal than when they are equal. In this observation one cannot avoid thinking of a set of scales, which rapidly become stable if the amounts in the two pans are of unequal weight, whereas if the balance is perfect, it takes longer for the pans to stabilize their position, and the balanced position is permanently sensitive to the slightest touch or additional weight on either side.

### The Son between Mother and Wife

The mother is pretty well respected, especially when widowed. But in any quarrel between daughter-in-law and the mother, the son is on his wife's side, that is, the daughter-in-law's. "If he would stick up for his mother, there wouldn't be any quarrel at all," say the mothers.

*(Kosmaj district, Serbia)*

The attitude of the son was decisive in the mother-in-law-daughter-in-law relationship. In the patriarchal set-up, the "young master" had his hands tied on the side of those in authority, and, in case of a dispute, supported the mother. In the stage of break-up of patriarchal life, he joined his wife, with whom he was struggling for emancipation. In a region of continued development and new equilibrium, the son was also closely linked with his wife, but, in this sort of environment, that did not exclude his loyalty to his mother.

Graph 14 shows that the authority of the mother-in-law stood or fell with the support of the young master. If, indeed, we compare this graph with the preceding one, showing the attitude of daughter-in-law to mother-in-law, we see that they are largely similar: The space occupied by bad relations between snaha and svekrva coincides with that in which the son takes his wife's side.

111

Graph 14. Whether the son is more on the side
of the mother or his wife

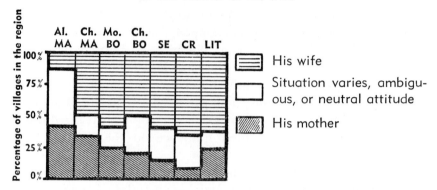

The curve does not definitely bulge at all. This is because young couples were held together by a firm mutual bond in all phases of social development. This points to the conclusion that, except among the Albanians, patriarchal life was nowhere completely intact, and the weakest link in the chain of patriarchal relationships was that between daughter-in-law and mother-in-law. It was the daughter-in-law, who entered the household as an adult, who was the first to rebel against the old order. She drew her husband after her, so that non-submission of son to mother was one of the earliest symptoms of the break-up of the patriarchal way of life.

Solely in the Albanian villages did we find the typical patriarchal situation: Nearly half the villages belong to the group in which the sons were unanimously on the mother's side when the two women did not agree. Typical of this environment is the intermediate area of the graphs, that indicating neutrality or an ambiguous attitude. The young master was compelled to take neither the side of his mother nor that of his wife, for the "parties" were not fighting each other, as there were in any case no decisive conflicts within the family about position.

In all other districts, the son leaned toward his wife and drew away from his mother. A typical report runs:

> Before the war, the son was more on the mother's side, since the war he has been on his wife's side. (*Struga district, Macedonia*)

It would seem, therefore, that support of the mother by the son and agreement between mother-in-law and daughter-in-law were linked phenomena. To ascertain whether these phenomena really were inter-connected, I examined the question statistically, omitting villages with ambiguous attitudes. If we categorize the villages ac-

112

cording to the mutual links possible, i.e., the linkage between support of mother or wife by the son on the one hand, and good or bad relations between mother and daughter-in-law on the other, we get four groups of villages. These groups are typical of stages in the development of family life, and to some extent also of certain regions.

*Group 1.* Among the villages with "settled relationships of patriarchal form" are those villages in which the relations between svekrva and snaha were cordial and the young master also supported his mother's authority. This combination occurred when, by its concentrated pressure, the whole environment tamed the daughter-in-law. Among the Albanians, three-quarters of the villages presented this combination. Examples are:

> Married sons look after and respect their mother, and if there is any clash between mother and wife act pacifyingly, reproaching their wives in the interests of order and peace. The relations between mother-in-law and daughter-in-law are good. The daughter-in-law has to show special attention to her mother-in-law, obeying her and respecting her.
>
> *(Mileševo district, Sanjak)*

> The relationship between mother-in-law and daughter-in-law is good in most cases. Public opinion is on the mother-in-law's side. In the majority of cases, the sons are on the mother's side. On this account they quite often beat their wives.
>
> *(Moslem village, Rogatica district, Bosnia)*

*Group 2.* We can designate the second complex as "the heroic beginning of women's emancipation." Here the relationship between svekrva and snaha was full of struggle and dispute, while the son took the mother's side. We find this situation under exceptional circumstances:

> In many cases the relationship between svekrva and snaha is one of non-sufferance. Public opinion is predisposed according to the nature of the clashes, in the main to be on the svekrva's side. The sons are most often on their mother's side too. In any case where a wife frequently causes quarrels with the mother-in-law, the husband, if there is no great love, has recourse to Sheriat Law (Moslem Law) and seeks divorce. He usually obtains this, as the Sheriat Courts (the *kadis*) most frequently take the husband's point of view.
>
> *(Moslem village, Doboj district, Bosnia)*

As a rule, sons take their mother's side. Divorces that are the wife's fault are frequent because of inattention to the mother-in-law. There are, however, cases of a man's taking his wife's side, and the matter ending in a split. As the daughter-in-law arrives prejudiced in advance against her mother-in-law, relations, though good at first, later become worse and worse, because the daughter-in-law wants to take over leadership and shake off too much bossing.

(*Orthodox village, Tuzla district*)

Rebellion by the younger women was typical of Bosnia, where the break-up of the patriarchal order began only at the close of the First World War, and the pressure of the depression was felt with particular seriousness. The women were far more burdened with work than in former times and constantly complained of excessive work, which they were formerly spared both in the zadruga and the closed Moslem household.

We found the same combination in many Slavonian villages, but here the insubordination of the daughter-in-law derived from the independent mentality of the "girl with a dowry," who brought money and real estate into the family. This mentality of the Slavonian wife, however, also draws strength from the old zadrugas, in which they had relatively great rights, in the special form in which the zadruga had developed here.

*Group 3.* It is the third group, however, which was the most frequent, that of a "united front of the young generation against authority." Here relations between svekrva and snaha were combative, with the son taking the wife's side. In this stage, a merciless struggle against the authority of the older folk came to include the mother, regardless of the fact that she was far from the peak of the hierarchic pyramid.

The mother is looked on as a burden and badly treated. Quarrels between mother-in-law and daughter-in-law are daily occurrences. The mother is always reproached with having given birth to more family than she can maintain. There are many clashes. Public opinion takes the mother-in-law's side. The daughter-in-law is always to blame even though she may not be to blame at all. It is almost invariably the case for the mother-in-law to provoke the younger woman.

(*Ivanec district, Croatia*)

In 95 per cent of the cases sons treat their mother badly, especially if she is a widow, and this they do prompted by their wives. Between mother-in-law and daughter-in-law bad relations are general. The reason is economic. Clashes are frequent although without actual fighting. The daughter-in-law most frequently exploits the mother-in-law.

(*Prelog district, Croatia*)

These struggles took hold of a large part of the villages of Croatia and Serbia, a part of the Moslem villages of Bosnia, and even some Macedonian villages.

*Group 4.* "Harmony without authority" characterizes this group, with relations between the two women good and the son taking the wife's side. Here we are in the more tranquil sphere of stabilized relations of a new sort.

> The position assumed by adult sons between mother and wife is excellent. They, as a rule, tend to take the wife's side. There are no conflicts between mother-in-law and daughter-in-law. The relationship is always good. (*Orthodox village, Jajce district, Bosnia*)

Many villages of the Littoral and of the Christian sector of Bosnia showed this characteristic. This is not solely a modern combination, but, particularly in Bosnia, could amount to a variation on patriarchal relations.

If we count the villages showing these two combinations in which the son's support of his mother is linked with good relations, or the son's support of his wife with bad relations between mother-in-law and daughter-in-law (first and second combinations), we shall see to what extent this link which we have presupposed did indeed exist. It was most clearly shown in Macedonia and central Croatia. Here we have this position:

|  | Macedonia % | Central Croatia % |
|---|---|---|
| Villages in which the son's support of the mother is linked with good relations between the two women or vice versa | 50 | 61 |
| Villages without this link | 25 | 14 |

There were twice as many Macedonian villages with this link than without it, and further, three times as many in central Croatia.

From this we may conclude that amicable and cordial relations between the two women in the family were maintained only when the whole household supported the old authority. The young wife completely adapted herself to the dictation of her mother-in-law, simultaneously developing favorable feelings regarding her, only when all factors in the home supported the mother's authority. If the young wife could count on the support of her husband, it was easy for her to start a struggle for a more favorable position. Then any feeling of loyalty to the mother-in-law was lost and hostility toward her grew. As a rule it was not till she was encouraged by the attitude of her husband, and saw the possibility of success, that the young wife started a struggle for emancipation from the overlordship of the mother-in-law and for a separate economy. Till there was such encouragement, the young wife's discontent was concealed, to become open only if the son—her husband—crossed to her side. Resistance by the young couple destroyed the inner equilibrium of the family, which was re-established only when the principle of the independence and equality of rights of the younger people had won the day.

## *Role of Public Opinion*

Under certain conditions, public opinion had a powerful influence on family life: For instance, in some districts, public opinion exercised pressure on a young man to marry a girl who was expecting a child by him, and it generally was successful in this. Did public opinion have any effective influence in the relations between mother-in-law and daughter-in-law?

The reports from all districts show that there was practically no support for the daughter-in-law from public opinion. In the main, in all regions, public opinion was either divided, that is to say, objective or neutral, or unanimously on the mother-in-law's side. This means that public opinion either exercised a conservative influence, supporting the old authority, or exercised no influence at all.

Many reports state that opinion is divided, neutral or objective. Such answers may mean one of two things. First, they may mean indifference regarding the conditions in this or that household, which, in the region in ferment, was frequently the case.

> Mother-in-law and daughter-in-law rarely agree. All is due to excessive work, which one cannot cope with, so she asks for help. Then there is complaint about the laziness of one or the other. As a rule, the daughter-in-law takes advantage of the mother-in-law. Public opinion is hypocritical, backing both. (*Kosmaj district, Serbia*)

A neutral attitude may have another meaning, namely, it may amount to a dignified reserve. Where standards were unshaken, public opinion did not enter the question, or, since there was harmony in the household, it did not matter which side it took. If a dispute did arise, public opinion supports the side which was in the right according to patriarchal standards. Such divided opinion did not mean indifference but objectivity and responsibility.

> If a mother-in-law has got a name in the village as given to serving out tongue-pie, or being difficult, then public opinion will certainly be on the daughter-in-law's side, but if before the daughter-in-law entered the house she was known to be a quiet, kindly woman, the opposite is the case. (*Cetinje district, Montenegro*)

116

Graph 15 shows three old-style regions where one most clearly sees the significance of public opinion regarding the relationship between the two women.

Graph 15. Whether public opinion supports svekrva or snaha

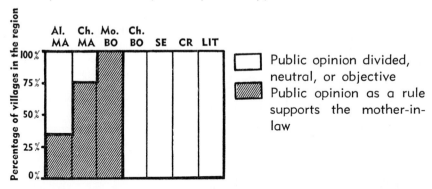

In an environment where patriarchal relations had been preserved, public opinion much more rarely supported the mother-in-law than where patriarchal norms had begun to decay. This means that in an old-style environment public opinion was mobilized only when the old standards are in danger, whereas prior to this it assumes an attitude of restraint. This link can clearly be seen if comparison is made between this graph and the other two graphs regarding the relationship of mother, son, and son's wife.

Further, we can see this link from the following reply:

As a rule public opinion supports the mother-in-law, because it is the daughter-in-law who as a rule infringes the standards of the official ethic and existing customs.        (*Jablanica district, Serbia*)

Graph 16. Relations between svekrva and snaha

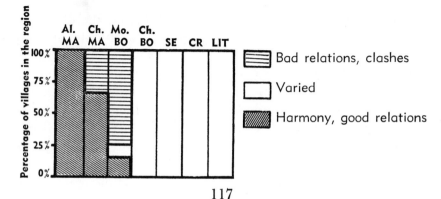

Graph 16 indicates that among the Albanians good relations between the two women were linked with the neutrality of public opinion, while in Bosnia bad relations had become a reason for public opinion to be alarmed. The Christian villages of Macedonia adopted a position in between these two.

Graph 17. Whether the son supports mother or wife the more

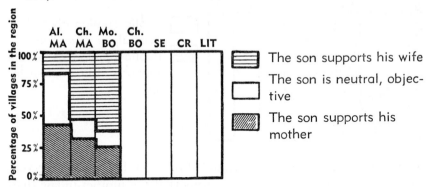

Among the Albanians, the area in Graph 17 which indicates an objective or neutral attitude on the part of the son, and that in Graph 15 which indicates an objective attitude by public opinion, is large. The reserved attitude of the son and of public opinion have the same significance: Where there was harmony between the two women there was no reason for any third party to assume a partisan attitude. In Moslem Bosnia, on the other hand, public opinion is mobilized precisely on account of the bad relations between mother-in-law and daughter-in-law, exacerbated by the son's support of his wife when there was disagreement between the two women. The alliance of the young master and his wife provoked hostile public opinion, which adopted the attitude that the older people should be respected.

When the patriarchal set-up fell apart, however, the disappearance of the authority of the elders proceeded relentlessly, however powerful the pressure of the whole of public opinion. Our graphs reveal that in Moslem Bosnia even those husbands who publicly took the side of the mother or mother-in-law, took the wife's side in her disobedience of the mother-in-law at home. Conservatism in young husbands was no protection for them in their individual struggle against the authority of the elders within the home, for, though the mother was but a third-rate authority, even this now began to seem unbearable. Thus, although in Moslem Bosnia public opinion was

118

unanimous, in the end it had no effect whatsoever. The ethical demand for respect for the elders remained so much hot air. The requirements of submissiveness and humility on the part of the younger folk toward their elders were preserved longer than the zadruga or patriarchal system which once gave them their material basis.

The example of Aika, an elderly Moslem woman, shows that there are the germs of tragedy in the position of mother and mother-in-law even in a patriarchal environment.

### Aika. Example of a neglected mother and mother-in-law

The following account was contributed by Salih Žilić, a male teacher of eastern Bosnia.

Aika is more than sixty years old. She has been a widow for twenty years, and has borne ten children, of whom only three are still alive. This mother has remained in a little cottage which her sons set apart for her. The family is one of the more affluent. The general standing of the family in the village is good, but as individual she stands low, for in the village women have no standing at all. Aika looks older than she really is; she has a masculine appearance, dresses humbly, in much mended but reasonably clean clothes. She is very shy, talks with difficulty, but is said to be as kind as an angel. Her voice is rather deep and harsh, her expression miserable from much grief, which has cut countless furrows in her aged cheeks.

I went to see her at her home. She searched for and at long last found a little roasted coffee which she ground in a handmill, holding it firmly in her old woman's hands.[3] She talked a long time about a window of the old house which looked out on to the street. There, many years back, she had spent sleepless nights, all alone. She was practically a widow, for her husband was then an invalid and her children had gone off to join the army, to war. The first night was the worst to her. She leaned her head on the window-sill, as she relates, and, weeping, stared down the road by which her children had gone. She spent the whole night like that. Afterwards she had a bad chin for some days, where she had leaned it on the edge of the window-frame. She struggled through the arduous years of war in poverty not because of lack of property so much as of sufficient strength to work the land and produce corn. She toiled away, for

[3] Particularly in Bosnia, but also in Serbia and Macedonia, one entertains a visitor with a cup of coffee. It is characteristic that though she goes to her daughters-in-law when she wants coffee herself, she keeps a little coffee at home for ceremonial purposes.

that reason, by herself at the heaviest of field work, for one had to live on, even though every mouthful stuck in one's throat. Everything was hard, she told me, but that war, that was the worst of all. Her children had just grown up and begun to carry on the work, her husband was weak with age, when the war broke out. She suffered and wept much. Witness of that are her tear-dissolved blue eyes and martyred expression.

She comes from a neighboring village. Her father and mother died long ago. Of brothers and sisters she has now only one brother left, but him she loves as she loves her own children. (In these parts there is much love of wives and sisters for husbands and brothers.) She did not go to school and is illiterate. She married her husband of her own free will; that is, account was taken of what she wanted. She had married into a household of intermediate fortune. She and her husband lived alone and worked their farm.

"I knew nothing," she says. "Young folk today know much more than they did then. My man, God be *rahmet*[4] to him, was kind. Upon my word, he never swore at me and practically never laid hands on me. And when I wept because the children were leaving me and going to the war, he reproved me with the words: 'Silly woman, what canst thou do against the Will of God?' I cannot complain that he did not love me."

None of her children were stillborn, but all except three died later. Her husband did not drink alcohol, nor do her children, her sons.

This woman gave birth to her children in the daily round—out in the field, in a room, in a stable, once even out on the road. Working conditions were such that one could not spend time sitting about at home. She cared for her children well, although her husband tended to grumble that she would spoil them. She loved them all equally, male and female. But despite all her care, most of her children died. She had no knowledge of hygiene or proper feeding of children, but did everything according to ancient custom. She believes that it was God's disposal of things for her to have few children left her.

"But now," I said, "things are not hard, your sons all came back from the war?"

"Ah, dear boy, God grant thee long life, to thee and my children, may you all be long-limbed and hale, but my children, of whom I could not have an angry thought, still they are not the same as they

4 "Merciful"—a Moslem-Arabic word.

were when they were younger. They have married, they have got children of their own, and they take account of their own families. And I am but a hewn-off log. They think little about me."

"How do you manage with this house?"

"Well, as you see, I manage to get along. I have a little land, which my sons work, though they charge me for it all. They do not even let my dear little cow have a free feed on their meadows. I find it very hard going, they will not help me as much as they should and, as if I were a bit of rubbish they have cast aside, they squabble among themselves as to which is to bring me a little wood for me to warm my bones and cook my food."

The old woman took her kerchief and wiped her tears away, but when she had done that, she pulled herself together again and wrapped the cloth over her head, for she had a man before her, and, what was more, a man who was not a member of the household, and a woman should never let herself not be properly covered.

That morning she had been to coffee with one daughter-in-law and this daughter-in-law had complained because she had come to her again for coffee, why did she not go to her elder daughter-in-law, for, so she said, there ought to be some sort of order about all this, she could not always make her coffee. With tearful eyes, as if those eyes had never had any other task in life but to weep, she said: "See, I killed myself getting those children of mine on their legs and those women, my daughters-in-law, they do not know that, they rub my nose in the coffee which they did not earn, but my boys did."

"But why ever do you not complain to your sons?"

"Ah, dear boy, as if that would do any good! Besides, I wouldn't think of kindling a fire between them. Let things be! They will come to the same thing some day from their own children, God grant!"

"Are both your sons the same in this?"

"The elder one is more attentive to me, he does warn his wife not to slight me. But he too likes his own family. It is my daughter who looks after me best. But she is married, she is not with me. Now, my eldest grandson, the son of my youngest, he is very attentive to me. He has promised that when he marries, he will take me too into his own home, and will not live with his parents, who hurt me so."

# CHAPTER V

## Brother and Sister

Sister dear, whom have you in the world?
Brother have I and a dear one too.
Sister dear, now tell me the whole truth,
Brother love you or your dear one more?
For my brother I would give my sight
For my dear one triple string of gold
Nor am I sure that I would give so much.
Once through the village, and I found another dear
But through all the world, no brother shall I find
Nor brother is there but of my mother's womb.

*Folk song*

THIS brotherly and sisterly devotion of a special quality is not part of an ancient past, but is still very much alive in many parts of the Slavic South. When I was a social worker with the United Nations Relief and Rehabilitation Organization after the Second World War, this became plain to me. Indeed, every official or welfare worker who has to do with people of many nationalities—emigrants, refugees, prisoners-of-war, survivors of the concentration camps—cannot fail to have been struck by the attitudes of the Yugoslav peasant. So often he will produce somebody whom he introduces as "my brother" (or "my sister"), and even if he does not precisely say so, his whole manner will be eloquent: "I stand surety for this man, I guarantee him." Asked if he really is his brother or his sister, the answer will often be "it's a brother by my uncle," meaning cousin, or "it's a sister from my brotherhood," meaning clan. When he really is able to say *rodjeni brat,*[1] brother by birth, or *rodjena sestra*, sister by birth, his loyalty and readiness to make sacrifices for the protected person exceeds all customary bounds. And where the official concerned knows nothing of the South Slavs, this concept of the brother would surely be sufficient to gain a fair notion of the nature of family life or the tribal system in the man's native land. In fact were the old culture of the Slavic South to die out, leaving only the one song

[1] "Rodjeni brat," meaning "own brother," is emotionally highly charged. *Rodjeni* means "born" or "of kin." The word is connected with the nouns *rod*, "kiths" or "kin," and *narod*, "people" or "nation," and bears a powerful sentiment.

quoted above, it would be possible for a future anthropologist to reconstruct nearly the whole edifice of the patriarchal way of life fairly well.

The brother relationship reflects all the elements of inner-family relationships with particular clarity. We see the high value put upon the blood bond of birth, the distribution of authority, priority by age and by sex, affection and love, rivalry and hatred, harmony and disharmony, indifference and aloofness within the family. The brother relationship is unique within the family. It is a born relationship, between those of similar age group, within the same as well as with the other sex. Here the bond of choice which we find between husband and wife is missing. Here too there is nothing of that factor of chance or of the arbitrary which we find in the attitude of members of the household to the incoming daughter-in-law. There is not the great gulf of years which divides parents from children; nor is there that biological bond which colors the relationship of mother to her children. The relationship between elder and younger brother, or between brother and sister offers us in pure form that very "unknown" which we are endeavoring to calculate or divine. That is to say, it offers us the "family relationship" in both its essential emotional and its hierarchical aspect.

## Sons and Daughters in the Home

The position of sons and daughters in the home, their rank and standing in the family hierarchy, to a great extent determines their mutual relationship.

In the patriarchal family, from birth to death, countless indices point to the higher standing of the male sex. When the patriarchal set-up breaks down, the privileged superiority of brother to sister also breaks down. The rights of males and females are then equal, both in written law and in everyday practice. This tendency toward equalizing the sexes inside the family, however, gets entangled with another tendency, one which means a worsening of the position of the female, namely, that resulting from the girl's loss of value as a marriageable girl. With changed economic conditions, true, the girl acquires greater inner-family rights, but at the same time she loses importance and value as a potential wife. All this is clearly reflected in the brother relationship.

The parents' attitude toward sons and daughters provided the basis for the brother relationship. In regions with a fighting past and heroic tradition, the position of the son was especially privileged.

When a child is born, folk ask "What luck was it?" If the answer is: "A boy," they all pray for him to be fortunate, but if it is a daughter, then, of course joking, but all the same it is characteristic, they say: "God grant it won't live till christening."

*(Šavnik district, Montenegro)*

A son is always looked after more on account of a descendant. Girls are not considered for inheritance. Folk equally pity the man without any children and him who has only daughters.

*(Bar district, Montenegro)*

Sons enjoy greater privileges than daughters. The birth of a girl is looked on as rather a punishment.

*(Korenica district, Lika [former Military March], Croatia)*

The reports from Serbia and from Orthodox Bosnia resemble those from the Dinaric country:

Parents like boys better. Often they feed them better and give them lighter work to do than the girls. *(Sanski Most district, Bosnia)*

When a girl child dies, there is not much mourning, but a boy dying is an irreparable loss. *(Arilje district, Serbia)*

More attention is paid a boy, for "he's my home, my all, a girl is somebody else's home, she leaves, and that's the end of it."

*(Kosmaj district, Serbia)*

In the Dinaric parts of Croatia, we find a complex which was fateful for a woman, due to the pressure of individualistic demands in an area with a heroic tradition.

Sons in the family are welcomed with gladness, a girl is looked on as a sort of ill, a burden. The position of a woman from birth to death is but an uninterrupted string of troubles. *(Gospić district)*

Sons have all the advantages, the parents even sometimes take their advice, whereas the girls are like slaves, made to take a back seat behind their brothers. *(Benkovac district)*

The son is the heir, so has all the rights, even gets better food, which he chooses himself, since he works harder, while the girls have to be content with whatever is given them. *(Metković district)*

The following from Bosnia is typical:

Sons have at least a double advantage.

*(Catholic village, Derventa district)*

Girls were not regarded as real inmates of the home, for they would marry soon and leave it:

Different treatment of sons and daughters is not noticeable at first, but the nearer the girls get to marriage, the less care the parents take

124

of them, they seem unreliable to them, for at any time they may leave them and run off to their young man.     (*Bosanska Krupa district*)

The son as a rule has more rights than the daughter, for he remains at the foundation. He also has an influential word. Whereas a girl is brought up for another and is often badly treated, as she will leave and marry into another home.     (*Županja district* [*Slavonia*], *Croatia*)

In all regions where zadruga life was in decay, the girls had difficulty in marrying, which introduces a new note into the household's attitude toward them. While within the family her standing rose only slightly, the attitude toward the outer world changes, the family spending a disproportionately large amount on her, to make her attractive as a possible bride:

Sons are given greater liberty of movement, much more is spent on the girls' clothing.     (*Koprivnica district, Croatia*)

A report from Serbia reveals both the old and a new tendency toward forcing an inferior position on the woman:

A son may hear everything, see everything, and go about without question. They can count on his good conduct. A girl goes nowhere by herself, nor can she talk to anyone, or leave the house without need.
     (*Kosmaj district, Serbia*)

Another report shows the efforts of the family to marry a girl off:

Parents treat girls more tenderly and better than boys, because they marry very early. Immediately after leaving the elementary school, at most two years later, a girl is considered marriageable. Then everything in her is noted and criticized. For a girl to have as good a reputation as possible, much attention must be paid her. Clothes as fine as possible, but principally, the treatment by parents and brothers must be such as to make it publicly clear that they respect her, as the village will follow suit (and the opposite would be the case). Brothers often go without a suit of clothes in favor of their sister, and a mother treats her grown-up daughter with absolute respect.

     (*Garešnica district, Croatia*)

In the region of continuous development and a new equilibrium, there appeared a tendency to even out the rights of all members of the family. The care of a marriageable girl resembled that in Croatia:

There are no particular differences in treatment, but nevertheless a mother will rather dress her daughter up than her son, but as the son earns for himself by fishing, it will happen that the son is better dressed than the daughter. Here girls require a lot for their wardrobe. Girls have about 20 new blouses and still more kerchiefs. One complete outfit takes from 20 to 24 meters of material. (*Isle of Ugljan, Littoral*)

In some families the daughters are favored, in others the sons. Such is the treatment. Public opinion also means a lot. A son must submit to his father. A daughter may disobey. The parents (the mother) will buy a daughter clothes and shoes rather than a son. Daughters have new clothes, young lads their fathers' cut-down clothes.

*(Biograd-on-Sea district, Littoral)*

In the brother relationship, too, the region with gradual development and new stable relationships resembled the patriarchal environment:

Daughters do less work whereas sons while still quite young, even starting from six years old, are used for heavy work. Girls are better fed and dressed, less beaten and more looked after in their upbringing.

*(Brčko district, Bosnia)*

Both sons and daughters are treated alike and neither has any advantages against the others. *(Vlasotince district, Serbia)*

### Relationship between Brother and Sister

To be able to assess the position of brother and sister in the family hierarchy and differences in their standing, one question asked was whether the brother also had authority over an older sister.

Graph 18. Whether a brother has authority over an older sister

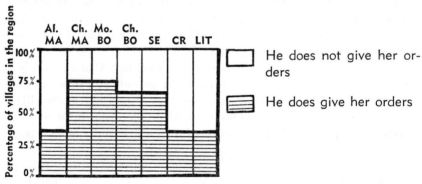

Graph 18 shows a solid block of old-style villages, in which the authoritative position even of a younger brother regarding a sister is to be noted. This block, embracing three-quarters of the villages of the old-style regions, also includes Serbia, which in this regard is considerably distinct from the Croat region. But within Croatia, the Dinaric districts belonged completely to the patriarchal group.

Our second question bearing on this aspect concerned the prevailing "climate" between brother and sister, whether they loved or hated each other or were indifferent, whether there was harmony or disharmony between them. It is not too easy to assess such a climate, for people's ideas of what amounts to "getting on well together" or "not getting on well together" vary in each region, in each separate period. In a patriarchal environment, "good relations" meant that a brother "looks after" and "defends" his sister, covering her and protecting her. This amounts to sanctioned superiority of brother to sister, and in this environment we found that such a protective attitude was highly esteemed. In later stages, the brother's priority begins to be disputed, and his protective attitude provoked resistance on the part of his sisters. Thus the bearing which was "good" in a brother in an old-style environment was "bad" in a modern one. For instance, "good relations" in the Littoral was an expression equivalent to well-intentioned indifference, a lack of rivalry about an inheritance, in other words, a confirmed equality between brother and sister.

The villages split into two groupings, those with good and those with less good relations. Among villages with good, cordial relations are those where we found a friendly relationship, with brother protecting sister and defending her, superintending and counseling her, and such an attitude is represented as favorable.

In the other grouping I have counted "relatively good" relations, "formal" relations, and indifference. The rights of brothers and sisters were equal, or their relations were cordial so long as the sisters obeyed and submitted. Individual differences were great— some agree, others quarrel. There is frequent mention of aloofness between brother and sister, and any great cordiality is lacking.

I have not estimated any grouping with definitely poor relations, for in fact there proved to be few such villages. Those with clearly bad relations were included in the second grouping. Reports from these particular villages speak of domineering, uncouth brothers who order their sisters about, the girls either resisting or being terrorized. Here, although their equality was recognized in principle, there was frequent reference to clashes between brothers and sisters.

Graph 19 makes it clear that the area in which the authoritative position of the younger brother over a sister was established, coincides largely with that in which relations between brothers and sisters were cordial. In the old-style regions, relations are better than in the modern ones, where the rights of brothers and sisters were more equal. It would seem that the established authority of the brother had an inner link with intimate, cordial relations between brother and sister. The brother treats more pleasantly a sister who gives in to

127

Graph 19. Relations between brothers and sisters

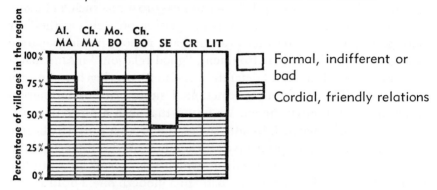

Formal, indifferent or bad

Cordial, friendly relations

him, and the sister has a greater liking for her brother who in the family has a sanctioned position of priority. Rivalry about equality of rights undermines good relationships.

> Sisters are subject to the will of their brothers, particularly if these are younger. Even a younger brother has the right to order an older sister about, for instance, saying the sister is 19 and the brother 15, the brother is still the one to give orders. Thus a sister may only order a brother of under 15 about. Brothers treat their sisters with great tenderness, and sisters love their brothers more than anything else in the world. In everyday life folk say: "Life's hard for a brotherless sister," that is, they consider a sister without a brother rather like an orphan, an unprotected girl.            (*Cetinje district, Montenegro*)

Among the Albanians, we did not find this seniority of the younger brothers over their sisters in so many villages as in the other old-style districts. The following report is typical:

> There are distinctions between the authority of the older and the younger brothers. The older have more authority. The younger are more subordinate. The boys according to age, the girls without regard to age being subordinate to the boys. The boys and girls hold rather aloof from one another. Each [sex] forms its own "class." A brother may beat his sister.            (*Andrijevica district*)

Because of this great aloofness of brother from sister, a brother did not often have the opportunity to give his sister many orders. Apart from this, it appears that with Albanians the authority of the father was so great that no one else in the house had much to say. This can be seen from Graph 18. Whether this situation was characteristic of the patriarchal set-up generally when intact, or whether this was a particular Moslem variant, with the sexes strictly separated, is hard to determine. One thing is certain, among the Moslems of

Bosnia the brothers had greater authority over their sisters than they did among the Albanians. Here are typical reports from Moslem Bosnia:

> Brother and sister are fond of each other. A sister may not court in the presence of her brother any more than that of the father.
>
> *(Travnik district)*

> A sister is always considered to be the junior, even in relation to a brother who is younger. Sisters are subordinate to brothers, but, nevertheless, in the family the brothers protect their sisters. In most cases they get on well together and are fond of each other, particularly while the brother is a bachelor. *(Čajniče district)*

> There are differences in the authority of the older and younger brothers. An older brother is the deputy of his father, hence the lord (except when mentally backward or quite a sop). The brothers are senior to their sisters. A younger brother orders an older sister about, if he has grown up, or rather, when he is physically stronger than she is, or a little before this. The relations between brothers and sisters are good and they respect each other and are affectionate.
>
> *(Brčko district)*

> Unless very young, a brother has priority over a sister, even if younger in years. "There's no brother till your mother bears one," and the attitude of the brother regarding a sister is one of a protector, that of the sister regarding her brother is humble and submissive.
>
> *(Mostar district)*

In the Christian villages of Bosnia, too, the brother was the protector of the sister, and the investigators as a rule emphasize that this is good:

> A boy of three is the elder of a girl of 12-15. This protectorate is imbued with official authority and sincere love. A brother protects his sister. By extant views, subordination and humility is forced on them, but under that is understandable envy and powerful sisterly love.
>
> *(Bijeljina district)*

> The eldest brother orders the younger brothers and the sisters, while a boy who is younger may order an older sister. The male is the elder, but does nothing by force. Sisters do not envy him, for they too hold that as a male he has the right to order them about.
>
> *(Banja Luka district)*

> Brothers are elders to their sisters unless the gap of years is greater than 10. The relationship between brothers and sisters is very fine, they care for each other "like brother and sister." *(Višegrad district)*

> The relationship between the brothers and sisters is one of friendly affection. There are cases of a widowed sister returning to her family

129

and her brothers taking her in and treating her with care, or if a sister is defective, so has no prospect of marrying, here too brothers are exceptionally attentive to her and do all she wants to alleviate her tragic fate. *(Stolac district)*

In the Orthodox villages of Macedonia, the principle of authority by sex was not so clearly marked, but seniority by age was sometimes made much of. Particular respect for the woman as worker and wife in this region also colored the relations between brother and sister:

The relationship between brother and sister is chronological. Younger brothers do not even dare not obey an older sister. Were this to happen, the parents intervene to support the sister.
*(St. Nikola Ovčepolje district)*

If a sister is the elder, all must obey her, both brothers and younger sisters. A younger brother cannot give orders to an older sister. All younger brothers address their oldest sister as *dada*. *(Skoplje district)*

But there were also some villages in this region which spoke of the seniority of the younger brother:

Brothers are always the elders, even if younger. They order their sisters about, the sisters take off their boots, pour water for them when they wash, bring them drinking water, and perform other little services.
*(Sjenica district, Sanjak)*

A younger brother may issue orders to an older sister. The brothers have the seniority, even if younger in years. Brothers and sisters live in great harmony, and help each other in every task.
*(Morihovo district, Macedonia)*

In the order of seniority the brother, even if younger, is above the sister, even though she is older. The relations between brothers and sisters are formal, for the sisters have made their peace with the domination by their brothers. *(Struga district, Macedonia)*

As we see from Graph 18, as far as the question of brother ordering sister goes, Serbia was in the patriarchal grouping. However, this ensured seniority of the younger brother was not linked with a cordial relationship between brothers and sisters, nor with the priority of an older brother over a younger, as in the classical patriarchal regions.

A report from south Serbia clearly shows the patriarchal tone:

A younger brother gives orders to an older sister, the view is that the male is the more capable, even if younger. The relations are typically fraternal. Family love is strong, and this conditions harmony in the relations between brothers and sisters. Here the man who goes away for long periods to earn (*pecalbar*) is prized and all who are not "pecalbars" are of lesser value. *(Vlasotince district)*

130

Another report demonstrates patriarchal relations which have begun to decay:

> By right, brothers are the seniors, and a sister should obey her brother, even if he is a child and she grown up, and to show him honor, take off his shoes, rise when he enters. The relationship between a brother and sister is usually despotic, for the brothers envy them for being fitted out, but before other people a brother protects his sister.
>
> *(Gruža district)*

Seniority still existed but was not so undisputed as in a patriarchal environment.

In the following report, we can see the vestiges of the patriarchal attitude, but at the same time the combative climate typical of an environment in which there are rapid changes.

> Seniority goes by age, though not much heed is paid to that. There are no cases of a sister obeying a younger brother except when she goes to the fair or a festival without her parents, then even a younger brother performs policing functions for his parents and tells them, accuses her. The attitude of the brothers is protective by rule. Although as a rule the brothers are embarrassed on account of their sisters because other lads as a rule tease them about their sisters, so because of that embarrassment the brothers often take it out on their sisters. The sisters have a sisterly regard for their brothers. They hold that brothers as males have more rights, but they do also rebel.
>
> *(Kosmaj district)*

In the Dinaric parts of Croatia, relations were determined by the patriarchal principle, as this example from the former Military March shows:

> Superiority in the family among the brothers is attained by years. Authority belongs to the male children. A younger brother may order his older sister. Here too we see the subordination of the woman—of daughters—first to the father, the mother, then the older, lastly, the younger brothers. At the top of the family pyramid is the "god," the father. Between the brothers and the sisters there is the same relationship as between a man and a woman, with the difference that the sons and daughters are all subordinate to the parents—concretely the sisters are doubly subordinate, to parents and to brother, but the sons only to the parents.                     *(Gospić district)*

With the break-up of the patriarchal family, individualistic trends gained strength, and the seniority of the brother was abandoned. Quarreling and disharmony among the brothers were the same in all parts:

The authority of the older brother is no longer ensured by the mere fact that he is older, hence the superior. Here, too, authority presupposes ability and intelligence, which even the peasant cannot help noticing. Consequently, there are no great differences between the brothers; what is more, there are cases where the eldest brother has no authority at all.        (*Orthodox village, Sarajevo district, Bosnia*)

The attitude of brothers toward sisters in the presence of outside persons is protective; apart from this, 6o per cent of the brothers hate their sisters because of their dressing. "Damn it, always having to spend money on you." Seventy per cent of the sisters adopt an attitude of independence regarding their brothers.        (*Prelog district, Croatia*)

From the following two reports, too, emerges a clear combative spirit, which destroyed all authority within the family and, with this, any patriarchal loyalty between brothers and sisters.

There is little difference between the authority of brothers and sisters. Younger children simply refuse to obey older brothers, if they do not plough and earn. The parents take their part and, to have peace, send them out to pasture.        (*Dugoselo district, Croatia*)

There is no seniority. Among brothers and sisters none can order the others about, they often quarrel.        (*Kutina district, Croatia*)

In regions of gradual development, the brother had no authority over his sister by seniority; neither were there any serious clashes between them. Frequently we find good relations, without regard to whether the brother had a privileged position. Two instances from Slavonia:

Older brothers have the right to reproach, but no right to order. In the main the relation between brothers and sisters is dignified and attentive. Brothers look after their sisters and protect their honor. Generally, sisters have the full protection of their brothers.

(*Nova Gradiška district*)

In the relationship of brothers and sisters, equality of rights rules. Here there is agreement. Those older in years have priority, whether boy or girl. In particular, brothers care for and attend to their sisters, especially if they are younger. Later perhaps it comes to clashes about dividing up the property, if the sister does not get the portion that should be hers. Generally they care very nicely for one another.

(*Slavonska Požega district*)

In the Littoral, a special tone prevailed, one characteristic of a new, well-established pattern: There was no conflict, and at the same time there was less warmth and cordiality between brother and sister:

132

Authority goes by the assistance which the family has from a child, without regard to age. Brothers are subordinate to the parents, but among themselves are equal. Relations between brothers and sisters are good without particular cordiality.                    (*Isle of Krk*)

In the majority of cases there is no love at all between brothers and sisters, but complete indifference. (I think the reason is that they have the same portion.)                    (*Metković district*)

In a patriarchal environment the relationship between brother and sister was stable in a good sense. Relations were exceptionally cordial compared even with other relationships in the same environment. Love and self-sacrifice, as described in the poem quoted at the beginning of this chapter, reached a peak, which can not be exceeded again.

In an environment with rapid change, this relationship was shaken to the roots. Clashes and quarrels undermined brotherly love. In an environment with a new equilibrium, quarrels were certainly rarer and relations more stable, but they had been established with a trend toward greater aloofness and less close affection. Once again a set of scales is suggested, with greater stability when one side is more heavily weighted.

### The Older and the Younger Brother

The priority of the older brother over the younger is not so symptomatic of the patriarchal way of life as was the authority of the younger brother over an older sister. This is to be seen from Graph 20, which shows a curve like that for brother and sister, but with less steep rise and fall, that is to say, with less marked difference between the regions.

Graph 20. Whether there is great difference between the authority of older and younger brothers

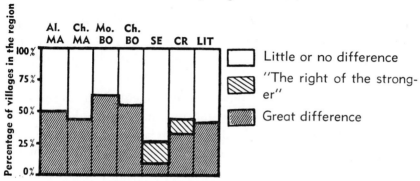

Here the priority of the older brother over the younger in the old-style regions is evident but not occupying as extensive an area as in the seniority of brother over older sister. Nor are the formulations in the reports clear regarding that relationship:

> Older brothers have some authority over the younger. Particularly if the brother is much older, or is head of the house, he is respected just as if he were the father. *(Šavnik district, Montenegro)*

> The older ones have more standing, this shows in better dress; apart from that, the older brothers demand obedience from the younger.
> *(Christian village, Bihać district, Bosnia)*

> There are differences in authority, for the parents keep the younger children at home till the elder marry, do not let them go to jollifications, and dress them more poorly, so for this reason the younger respect the elder. *(Christian village, Sanski Most district, Bosnia)*

The graph reveals a striking detail, that is, kinship of the Croat regions with the old-style areas, with Serbia not in the grouping. In Croatia and the Littoral, it seems that to a certain extent the priority of the older over younger brothers had been retained.

> Younger children respect the older, if there is a big difference in years, and speak to them with the plural of the verb.
> *(Varaždin district, Croatia)*

Another striking feature is the gulf between Bosnia, with its well-preserved hierarchy, and Serbia, with the lowest degree of respect of the younger brother for the elder. A deep chasm divided the rebellious lad in Serbia from the lad full of awesome respect in neighboring patriarchal regions. In Serbia a new factor was outstanding, "the right of the stronger." It was frequently referred to, whereas in other regions, except Croatia, it was rarely or never mentioned. For instance, we have formulations like the following:

> There is no authority of the older brothers. The younger won't give way to it. Unless it is supported with the fist, and then it depends on who is the stronger. *(Kosmaj district, Serbia)*

> There is no authority of the older brothers over the younger. The stronger masters his senior if he happens to be the stronger [sic].
> *(Moravica district, Serbia)*

Whereas in other regions there was agreement about the priority of the younger brother over a sister and that of the older brother over a younger one, in Serbia these two relationships seem to have been in opposition. The reason was, of course, this "right of the stronger." A brother rapidly overtakes a sister in physical strength even though younger, so he assumed his priority and right to order her about, doing so indeed thanks more to his strength than to any patriarchal regulation. Among brothers the situation was different, for when a younger brother equals an older one in strength, he disputed the elder's rights. This right of the stronger can also be seen by the fact that in Serbia there were numerous cases of clashes between brothers and sisters; in other words, they did not adapt themselves without resistance to the patriarchal system. (In this phenomenon, the great militancy of the Serbian woman plays a certain part, as also does the legal position of daughters, who in Serbia are excluded from inheritance.) Characteristic of many family relationships in Serbia was a combination of conservatism and of individualistic destruction of the rules, in short, a tempestuous intrusion of individualism over the borders of the patriarchal set-up.

We see how, under certain conditions, the physically stronger person, but only such, breaks the patriarchal rules. He does so to his own ends, but yet requires respect of those rules by those younger and weaker than himself. In such a case he finds particular support in tradition, which backs the seniority of brother over sister, whether she is younger or older, much more than it does the priority of an older over a younger brother. For in the patriarchal system priority by sex was more important than priority by years.

### Seniority and Brotherly Love

Is brotherly or sisterly love really linked with unequal rights? Do relationships full of cordiality and self-sacrifice really develop better where one party has ensured authority and the other is forced to adapt itself to this? I have endeavored to explore this important question of principle by a statistical examination of the confirmed priority of the brother and of harmony between brother and sister, that is to say, by the degree of correlation between these two attitudes. When one counts all possibilities, the villages may be formed into four groupings, which at the same time reflect four degrees of development.

The first group comprises villages in which the condition of settled patriarchal relationships was predominant. The brother was an authority also for his older sister, yet relations between them were cordial.

The second group is that where the authority of the brother did still exist, yet relations between brother and sister were not so good.

135

The third is that where the authority of the brother no longer existed, but relations between brother and sister were also poor.

The fourth is that of modern, settled relationships, where brother had no authority over sister, yet relations between them were cordial.

Table 1 gives the villages of the various regions arranged according to these categories:

TABLE 1. PRIORITY OF THE BROTHER AND HARMONY
BETWEEN BROTHER AND SISTER

| | Macedonia | Moslem Bosnia | Christian Bosnia | Serbia | Croatia | Littoral |
|---|---|---|---|---|---|---|
| | (figures as percentages of various regions) | | | | | |
| *Group 1* Brotherly authority over sister and good relations (patriarchal stability) | 48 | 52 | 53 | 36 | 9 | 5 |
| *Group 2* Brotherly authority over sister and poor relations | 22 | 26 | 20 | 27 | 24 | 24 |
| *Group 3* No brotherly authority and poorer relations | 19 | 4 | 13 | 32 | 32 | 24 |
| *Group 4* No brotherly authority, but relations very good (stability of new order) | 11 | 18 | 13 | 5 | 35 | 47 |

The first grouping, the patriarchal, prevailed in Macedonia, Bosnia, and part of Serbia. Typical of this is the following report:

Although the older children have more rights and enter all family activities with more rights, and although the younger obey, nevertheless the younger boys give orders to the girls. The saying runs: "even the youngest male is senior to the oldest female." (People think of the future before the boy and his role in the family and in production.) Brothers look on their sisters with slightly more superiority. They get on well together and prepare clothes for festivals. A sister is particularly attentive to her brother. They work as equals at field work, but the brother takes over from his sister at the harder jobs." (*Bosnia*)

The fourth grouping—stability of a new order—was dominant in modern regions. In Serbia, we had the fewest of all villages with this set-up, which signifies stability in relationships. The following is a typical report, this time from Slavonia:

> The older brothers order the younger children without distinction of sex, but the younger never give orders to the older ones. Brothers and sisters agree whenever the parents support equality.

> *(Virovitica district)*

More than half the villages of Slavonia belonged to this grouping, nearly half those of the Littoral, but only one-fifth of those in the Dinaric districts of Croatia.

In an environment with the new equilibrium, we found good relations between brothers and sisters precisely where the brother was not supposed to give his sister orders, that is to say, in those villages in which the principle of equality had received sanction. In such villages, the struggle for the new positions was over. Conflicts ceased precisely because the principle of equality had won. In this environment, "good relations" signifies a sort of good-natured indifference.

The other two groupings, those in which we have quarrels and clashes between brother and sister, mark two stages of development from the old to the new equilibrium. The second grouping, in which the brother still had priority, though under protest from the sister, constituted the first step away from the patriarchal system. This grouping included principally villages of the former Military March and the Dinaric districts of Croatia. These were districts which at the time of this investigation had just entered the stormy phase of break-up of the patriarchal way of life. More than half of the total villages in these districts fell in this second grouping.

Into the third grouping, that in which the priority of the brother no longer held but there was disharmony between brother and sister, come many villages of Serbia and Croatia, where the ethical demand for the authority of the brother over an older sister had already been abandoned.

In the patriarchal environment, good relations rested on a totally different basis from good relations in an environment with the new equilibrium. This we can see if we compare Moslem Bosnia, representing the patriarchal system, and the Littoral, representing the new equilibrium.

In the villages of Moslem Bosnia, in which the brother was an authority for an older sister, in 67 per cent of the villages relations between brother and sister were good and cordial, and in 33 per cent there were poorer relations; in those of the Littoral, however, where the brother was an authority also for an older sister, there were only

17 per cent in which relations between brother and sister were good, and 83 per cent in which they were poorer.

This statistical analysis also demonstrates how, in a patriarchal environment, good relations existed mainly where the authority of the brother was confirmed, but, in a "modern" environment, the opposite was the case precisely where the authority of the brother had been completely lost.

Clearly, relationships between the members of the family had undergone a total transformation in the course of historical developments. In the region with the new equilibrium, equality of the members of the family created the basis for good, amicable relations. At the same time, these never attained the warmth or stability of the brother-sister relationship in the patriarchal environment.

### Relations of Husband toward His Sister and Wife

In the patriarchal environment, we often observed more affectionate feelings and attitudes regarding blood relations, those who are the *rodjeni*, "one's own by birth," than regarding those tied merely by marriage. In an environment in which growth, increase, strength, and well-being were known exclusively on a biological foundation, where indeed there was no other "production" but this, blood relationship was considered of particular importance. In the custom of "keening" for the dead in Montenegro, which consists of the lachrymous chanting of verse, we found mothers bewailing sons, sisters bewailing brothers, but never wives their husbands. Frequently a mother or a sister would cut off her hair and place it on the grave in sign of mourning, but a wife would not do this. In a certain sense, there was a greater distance between husband and wife than between brother and sister. As we shall show below, a whole complex of attitudes and customs prevented intimacy between husband and wife and excluded consultation between them. They were separated from one another both by a barrier of shame and one of patriarchal restraint, whereas in the case of brother and sister, who had grown up together, there was not a single factor to create aloofness. The following examples reveal how great the distance could be between husband and wife:

> There are cases of a wife at first, from shame, not only not going near a husband, but not even addressing him by name, considering this an intimacy. And there is a general avoidance of showing intimacy. This is considered unseemly.　　　　　　　　　　(*Sarajevo district, Bosnia*)

Before the war there were frequent cases of husband and wife together never speaking to each other, or addressing each other by name, but today that is no more. *(Danilovgrad district, Montenegro)*

One thing all have in common, a general characteristic: Husband and wife never show each other any affection, never kiss, or remain alone in a room together; the children taunt the mother when pregnant.

*(Stolac district, Hercegovina)*

I have made a statistical examination of the relationship of brotherly intimacy to conjugal intimacy. In principle, two different linkages were possible between the loyalty of a husband to his own sister and to the wife he had brought into the house: The loyalty to the sister might be in some sort of rivalry with loyalty to the wife, that is, one intimate relationship might exclude the other; or the good relationship to the sister might take the same general form as that to the wife. An indication of intimate relations between husband and wife was that the husband discussed household problems with his wife. Table 2, in which the villages are grouped in four categories, reveals a number of factors typical of the stage which the development of family life has reached, and also typical of the various regions.

The first grouping is characteristic of an intact patriarchal environment. An example from Moslem Bosnia:

The husband does not consult his wife about anything. As a rule he gives orders and she has no right to discuss. Relations between brothers and sisters are good and these respect and love each other.

*(Brčko district)*

In a patriarchal environment the relationship of a husband to his sister and that to his wife rivaled each other. Cordial and stable relations of the patriarchal type succeeded best when the female partner was completely subordinate; the sister, who had been inured to the system from birth, and was adapted to her brother's personality, fit into the system best. For a wife to be submissive to her husband and at the same time have cordial relations with him is a rarer phenomenon. It would seem that cordiality between man and wife was linked at least to some measure of equality of rights, and did not develop particularly well where there was a strict hierarchy.

The first grouping was particularly characteristic of the Moslem form of patriarchal relationships. Included were most Moslem villages of Bosnia. No less than three-quarters of the Albanian villages (not shown in the table) would fit in here.

## TABLE 2. LOYALTY OF HUSBAND TO SISTER AND WIFE

| | Christian | Moslem | | | |
| | Macedonia | Bosnia | Serbia | Croatia | Littoral |
| | (figures as percentages of various regions) | | | | |
|---|---|---|---|---|---|
| *Group 1*<br>Aloofness from wife,<br>cordiality to sister | 37 | 53 | 23 | 8 | 9 |
| *Group 2*<br>Cordiality to wife,<br>aloofness from sister | 19 | 11 | 45 | 37 | 29 |
| *Total*<br>Relationship to wife<br>opposite of that to sister | 56 | 64 | 68 | 45 | 38 |
| *Group 3*<br>Cordiality to wife,<br>cordiality to sister | 22 | 18 | 18 | 36 | 43 |
| *Group 4*<br>Aloofness from wife,<br>aloofness from sister | 22 | 18 | 14 | 19 | 19 |
| *Total*<br>Relationship to wife and<br>sister in agreement | 44 | 36 | 32 | 55 | 62 |

The second grouping is the opposite of the first. Here husband and wife discussed everything, but the relationship with the sister was not so good. We find this complex when a zadruga was in decay, for in a smaller family the conjugal partners were more closely linked, but there was conflict between the brothers and sisters over the share-out of the property. In this category we have Serbia, where at the time of the investigation the struggles connected with the re-shaping of the peasant economy were at a peak, taking the form not merely of the disintegration of the zadruga but consisting also of a change-over from a pastoral economy to an arable one, and further affected by the introduction of dowry property and the granting of a large part of inheritances to the daughter. In Croatia, the culmination of such struggles was a matter of the past.

Taking the first two groups together, we have those villages in which there was opposition between treatment of the wife and treatment of the sister, taken either way. The majority of such villages proved to be in Serbia and Moslem Bosnia. It would appear that

140

Croatian peasants in backyard

16. Croatian women hoeing

17. Open hearth cooking, Lika area, Croatia

here we have a reflection of the Oriental element in the Serbian way of life, such as that found in the strong link between mother and son and the frequent punishment of the wife.

The third grouping shows a uniform picture of good, settled relationships among all members of the family. Here the husband consulted the wife, but the attitude toward the sister was also cordial. In villages with a settled way of life, however, a good relationship toward the sister had a different tone from that of the patriarchal environment. The relationship was devoid of conflict, but it was less cordial. For example:

> Husband and wife consult each other in the main about all matters. Women here are generally an important, not to say a decisive factor in domestic life and on the farm. This makes them very serious and reliable. This is a fairly common phenomenon. Relationships between brothers and sisters are in the main dignified and attentive. Brothers look after sisters and guard their honor. Generally, sisters have their brothers' full support.     (*Nova Gradiška district, Slavonia*)

In these villages it was "civil" or "gentle" bearing that prevailed, and any domination by the menfolk was not particularly emphasized. As we had presumed, this grouping frequently includes villages down the Littoral. Its extension into Croatia may be taken as new proof that here the main attack on the zadruga family was a matter of the past, and serious convulsions of family life were tending to diminish.

The fourth grouping constitutes the opposite of the third. Here the relationships to wife and to sister coincided, but were both poor. The husband did not consult his wife. This grouping is not typical of any single region or any particular stage.

When we add together all villages in which the relationships to both wife and sister coincide, either for good or evil, we find that it is the Littoral which stands out with the most settled relationships, evidencing, moreover, many modern and western elements. Here, too, we also find most Croat villages.

In the patriarchal environment, cordial and warm relations with the sister to some extent excluded cordial relations with the wife, which is what we had theorized. Here the link of the man with "his own" was regularly stronger than that with the "introduced" wife. In the modern environment one standard type of dealing predominated both in blood relationship and that between married couples. The new equilibrium is shown in a strengthening of the link with the wife, without upsetting good relations with the sister. Here, what is more, the circumstance that the wife was not "introduced" into the home as in the zadruga, but the free choice of the husband, played some part. To her belonged loyalty and comradely love by the husband. But relations with the sister were far less cordial and intimate than they were in the patriarchal region.

This problem of brother-sister relations as against those of husband and wife have been studied here from the standpoint of the husband. This is because, in the main, this is how my investigators presented them. However, in folk songs we find abundant material from the woman's angle. The love and loyalty of sister for brother are more striking and impressive than those of brother to sister, for one might have expected that a sister's stern subordination to her brother, even to a younger brother, would be bound to awaken in her certain feelings of resentment. But as the song quoted at the beginning of this chapter shows, in the patriarchal epoch there were no greater loyalty and no greater emotional urge than that of sister for brother. Here is another song which with still greater pathos than the first may serve as second example:

### The Greatest Grief Is That for a Brother

Behind Mt. Neven sank the sun down
The heroes rowed in from the sea,
Young George's wife counted all in,
Counted every man on the ship
But three treasures could not count:
The first treasure George sire
The second treasure her brother-in-law,
The third treasure her own blood brother.
For George sire she cut off her hair,
For brother-in-law she tore her cheeks
But for her brother gouged out her eyes.
Hair when cut will grow again,
Cheeks when torn will heal again
But eyes can never sprout again,
Nor heart be whole for brother dear.[2]

---

[2] Vuk Stefanović Karadžić, *Srpske narodne pjesme (Serbian Folk Songs),* Book I, 1824. The nineteenth-century translation by Sir John Bowring runs:

The sun sank down behind the gold-flowered hill,
The warriors from the fight approach the shore,
There stood young George's wife serene and still:
She counted all the heroes o'er and o'er,
And found not those she loved—though they were three:
Her husband, George, her marriage friend, another,
Who late had led the marriage revelry:

The third, her best beloved, her only brother.
Her husband, he was dead, she rent her hair
For him. Her friend was gone—for him she tore
Her cheeks. Her only brother was not there:
For him she plucked her eye-balls from their bed.
Her hair grew forth as lovely as before,
Upon her cheeks her former beauties spread,
But nothing could her perished sight restore:
Nought heals the heart that mourns a brother dead.

# CHAPTER VI

図図図図図図図図図図図図図図図図図図図図図図図図図図図図図図図図図図図図図図図図図図図図図図図図

# Boy and Girl

図図図図図図図図図図図図図図図図図図図図図図図図図図図図図図図図図図図図図図図図図図図図図図図図

In a strict sense premarital relationships are not family relations, but they are preliminaries for marrying and establishing a family. Although generally they were in accord with the whole style of family life, they seemed to follow to some extent their own laws. In many instances such relations cut straight across venerated rules, shaking to the foundation the entire edifice of patriarchal norms, standards, and authority.

In most South Slav regions, an abundance of folk customs provided opportunities for young people to meet. Among them are church festivals, *kolo* (dancing in the open), spinning bees, gathering for common work for harvest. But as those customs, songs, and dances have been thoroughly studied and described in numerous volumes of Yugoslav ethnographic writings, I considered them outside the scope of my survey. My enquiry was limited to surveying relationships of unmarried people without the ceremonial or institutionalized framework.

The material my interviewers covered included contacts between young men and girls leading toward marriage, as well as sex relations with unmarriageable partners, such as between boys and peasant wives, and between girls and married peasants and gentry. Our material on the relationships between young men and girls was not limited to sex relations, however. Contacts of various grades of intimacy are examined, starting with the chaste life of maidenhood and boyhood. We will see that the strictest seclusion and avoidance did not mean ignoring the opposite sex, but rather a very keen awareness and high appreciation of it, its danger and desirability, hence also a relationship of a special kind.

### Barriers

In love and sexual life, the façade and the reality, the prescribed morals and the facts, are often at variance. Even in an environment in which there was no departure from patriarchal chastity, where the hierarchy was unbroken, where patriarchal regulations were in all respects reflected in actual life, the sphere of sex was an exception. Here more than in any other sphere of life, people found it difficult to conform to the requirements of the collective body. Where the sexes meet, the individual factor in the human make-up refuses to be silenced. Individual preferences are so powerful, so irrational and incomprehensible, that they frequently seem to be determined by fate. The individual preferences of young people often clashed with the desires of their parents and of the zadruga regarding the choice of wife or husband for the young people, this choice being based on standards which were completely alien to the individual desires of the young folk of either sex. The desire of young folk for courtship and for experiments which do not lead immediately to marriage came into conflict with the parents' plans as well as with those moral maxims which demanded modesty, "chastity," and "virtue."

The efforts of parents or of the whole environment to condition young people always have only partial success. All the measures applied to that end have a twofold effect. The erection of powerful barriers—stern prohibitions and incessant supervision—often achieves the opposite result from that desired. Stern prohibitions create great pressures and tension in young people, and this seeks an outlet often in far more serious acts than one finds in a liberal environment. Despite the rigid climate, the borderline is constantly overstepped, as wholesale abductions and elopements demonstrate. The readiness for love is not diminished, but on the contrary is increased.

Folk customs and songs too had a twofold influence. The dancing of the kolo (a chain dance) and, still more, the singing of songs constituted a substitute for intimate contacts and a safety valve for great pressures; but at the same time these activities intensified the inclination for love. The songs themselves make for love contacts, overstepping barriers and circumventing obstructions. They constantly tell of desires which could not possibly be expressed in speech because of the obligatory modesty and reserve which prevailed. But a song can also be sung without its words, it can be hummed or whistled, and the message reach the person intended, once he knows the words which go with the melody. Men could be so moved by songs that in a strict Moslem environment women were not allowed to sing at all if men were in earshot. The children, however, always hear these songs, and themselves begin to sing them long before they have any personal interest in the other sex. With these melodies and the words which go with them, the younger generation absorbs the love yearning which is represented in the songs as the supreme activity of life.

Thus, with the songs, the young folk come to accept the fatalistic view by which any happiness is considered to be liable to bring tragic complications as well as happiness in its train. In this way the younger generation is shaped to that particular preparedness for love which one finds in all regions under Oriental influence.

The tension which exists between the strict surface morality and the hidden desires and passions is steadily maintained and renewed. This tension shows that here the emotions, although hidden—or perhaps just because they are hidden—are much stronger than in a system where sex is emphasized and often exhibited in public.

The following reports show prohibitions and what was considered to be immodest in the conduct of women, unmarried or married. These stern prohibitions reveal a conviction that love is a powerful force, to be kept within bonds only by the strongest counterforce. The first instances are from Moslem villages, where the demands were most strict and were based on the Mohammedan faith. From regulations about dress and bearing:

> All, particularly married women, must keep concealed, so men do not see them. They may not go out much. Not to observe this is disgraceful and mortal sin. *(Bosnia, Brčko district)*

> A woman does not comb her hair in front of men. Or change a garment. She does not appear bareheaded before a man, or adjust her dress or gown, refastening or unfastening or doing up anything.
> *(Bosnia, Cazin district)*

> In the behavior of women or girls, when they move about, it is immodest to have bare feet, uncovered bosom, or to sway or twist the body, or to shake hands or to go with a young man.
> *(Bosnia, Travnik district)*

When this investigation was made, it was still obligatory for the Moslem woman or grown girl to veil her face, though in certain villages this was not so strictly observed as in the towns. This custom walls off women from any contact with men who are not close relations.

Examples of the requirement of quiet bearing and retiring behavior:

> It is immodest to hold converse with men, or for men to hear her singing. *(Macedonia, Galičnik district)*

> Least of all may men hear a married woman's voice. They are not allowed to talk a lot. *(Bosnia, Brčko district)*

It is immodesty if a girl is talkative or loose-tongued, that is, when she uses vulgar words, and this is still greater immodesty for married women, young or old.          (*Bosnia, Travnik district*)

In Orthodox Macedonia we find similar requirements:

A girl may not have conversation with a young man. If they are sweethearts they may allow each other only a few glances, but the girl should look down all the time.          (*Gornji Polog district*)

A girl or a young married woman may not talk to young men, not even when these are married, while in the presence of older men she should be silent. Altogether, silence in young married women is considered a virtue. Such women may not quarrel with neighbors. They must be kind to everybody. Older women enjoy greater freedom in speech and movement.          (*Gornji Polog district*)

Neither a girl nor a married woman may say a word to a man who is not a relation. A girl may not go out alone, but should have somebody of her household with her to look after her. In a kolo she should never join up next to a man, even if he is a relative. There is a special, separate "women's kolo."          (*Struga district*)

Among the moral requirements, the need for modesty, particularly in Moslem villages, was emphasized:

A girl should look nowhere, only at the ground, she should not laugh, stand at the window, or walk in the street if there is a man about. The same goes for young married women, whereas older ones are allowed to do these things.          (*Gostivar district, Albanian village*)

It is immodesty in a girl or married woman to exhibit any lack of restraint, any talk of love or marriage. The greatest disgrace of all is for a girl to laugh when at her wedding; on such a day she should keep her eyes closed and feel shame.          (*Debar district, Macedonia*)

In the patriarchal region with a tribal system, the moral demands ring rather differently. There was less talk of modesty and more of dignity and seriousness as the necessary qualities of a woman. The phrasing reveals that here love was not considered such a danger as in districts under Oriental influence:

The folk do not like extremes in a girl or young married woman, that is, neither for her to be too clever nor too gay, for in such extremes there is a hidden vice. Folk are impressed by serious, reasonable bearing in a girl or woman and for this the expression is "decent." Many describe seriousness in girl or wife in the phrase: "She does not even whiten her teeth," and of a serious girl it is said: 'Blessed the home which gets her.' When a man is offered a girl who is not serious, his

147

reply is: "Get away with you, she's too clever, or she's a gay one." If, however, a man does marry a bad wife who is long-tongued and quarrelsome, cantankerous, the expression is: "Luckless hour when she entered our home." *(Montenegro, Cetinje district)*

Moral requirements were shaped in much the same way even in districts where tolerance regarding premarital and extramarital relations was great, such as in the former Military March. Slight shades of expression, however, do reveal that real life here does not correspond to the strict moral requirements:

When young men are looking for a girl they pay great attention as to whether tongues wag about her or not, so that this greatly influences a young man when he choses a wife. A girl is disgraced by any freedom of movements. It is the general view that a girl should be retiring and subdued, as if she had no life in her. Hence, to find any amusement with young men is greatly frowned upon. They also condemn it if a girl sits near a young man, if she talks excitedly to him and so on. A girl must pay attention to her behavior in the kolo, being circumspect. This means that the girl when dancing should not be too gay, does not let herself go. It is a particular disgrace if a girl goes about with more than one man. Everybody scorns her and says: "She had tried them all" and so forth, and the greatest shame of all is if she has a child.

*(Croatia, Slunj district, Catholic village)*

### Relationships of Girls

Great barriers were erected to maintain a girl's decency or chastity. But although under the pressure of her whole environment a girl from early childhood grows accustomed to renouncing any freedom, nevertheless, concerning contact between the sexes, "conditioning" only reaches certain limits. Graph 21 shows that it was only in the Moslem regions that this absolute demand was really observed, while in all other regions there was a good deal of departure from the rule.

The graph rises and falls, which means that premarital relations in girls were a transitory symptom of the stage of rapid ferment. This result requires supplementary comment, which shall be given below.

Here are reports from Moslem regions:

Morals take first place as concerning honor and the good name of the family. Modesty prevails. *(Struga district, Albanian village)*

Chastity in the girl is here the essential for happiness, as young married women say, and no girls have any sexual relations before marriage. While still unmarried, a girl must be chaste and decent, this is what I

148

Graph 21. Premarital sexual relationships of girls

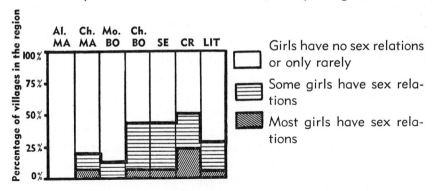

have always heard about the matter, and I have come to the conclusion that it is absolutely true. [The reporter is female.]

(*Bosnia, Sarajevo district*)

The following reports reveal a decay of morals:

Before the war the relations of girls were regarded more sternly. During the war, there were two cases of girls having relations, and those two unhappy girls are to this day taken as the ugliest example quoted by mothers to their daughters, to keep them under control. Here the preservation of maidenly honor is still as firm a notion as ever, both among the women and the men. Virginity is the principal and absolute requirement, and any deception in this respect would be avenged terribly on the girl. However, while maintaining virginity, the young men and girls too know of certain sexual enjoyments which are less dangerous.

(*Bosnia, Sarajevo district*)

It does sometimes happen for a woman or a girl from this village to go to Sarajevo or Mostar, but such a one never returns to the village, for she knows what awaits her. A girl or woman like that, the peasant would without more ado turn out of the place without asking her whether she had lived a decent life or not. (*Bosnia, Foča district*)

The slackening of moral strictness can be seen from the following replies from Christian Bosnia:

Virginity is regarded as important. This is bound to be, without it life would be hard, shameful, for if it is found out, divorce follows. Today, however, when that sort of thing happens, it is let pass, it is concealed and hushed up. (*Brčko district*)

If girls have relations, they marry, but not in the village in which they were born. In such a case they marry anybody, a poor man, a debauchee, a ruffian or suchlike. (*Čajniče district*)

149

In the Orthodox villages of Macedonia, the patriarchal ethic was more often overstepped. Because of the shortage of women in the countryside here, and an old custom that the girls marry late, the girls were in a good position to allow themselves considerable latitude from the requirements of morality:

> Here there is no chance, nor any instance, of a young man and a girl going about together as betrothed, hence the possibility of getting a child from the man and being pregnant before marriage is excluded.
>
> *(Kočane district)*

> The prospect of marriage for a girl who has had sexual relations is in no way diminished, but at the same time they have no opportunity for this temptation to arise, because of the way of living and thinking there.
>
> *(Kočane district)*

> Both girls and women, living as they do, constantly deprived of the possibility, in the most innocent way, of working out their desires, by talking to men, touching, kissing if they find themselves together with a man where they cannot be seen, will not resist his sexual suggestions, for the long stifled passions overflow like a river in spate.
>
> *(Struga district)*

> In sexual regard, both women and men are inclined that way. They conceal their passion. But if they have a chance to meet, there is agreement at once, "and the job's done." Meetings are usually at the well, or in passing, and it only needs a word or two for agreement to be reached, for instance with the poetic sigh "tugo, tugo, lele." They never worry about the consequences. *(Žegligovo district)*

> All the same, sexual relations are developed, though rather concealed. In summer, in the fields, during harvest, then at threshing, at any time, indeed, when folk sleep out in the farmyard or the fields, they have their fling, only it must be well concealed. But in comparison with other parts of Yugoslavia, extramarital sexual relations here are only a very small, insignificant percentage. *(Kočane district)*

The passionate train of thought expressed in these last reports is specifically linked to the old custom of checking whether a girl is virgin at marriage. This custom remained in places in a drastic form, so that we find a special mixture of modesty and frankness about the matter:

> Girls also have relations before marriage, despite the fact that the "commission of women" after the first conjugal night seeks signs of virginity on the bride's chemise. Then the girl has to say with whom she had relations, she is even beaten, and the marriage guests are dispersed; if she was a virgin, the merry-making continues. The husband of an "un-

150

chaste" bride is ashamed of other men, and takes refuge with the cattle.

*(Skoplje district)*

Before the war, if that happened, the bride would immediately be set on an ass as if riding it, but head to tail and in her hands they would put a big bunch of leeks and send her back to her parents. Now this return of a bride no longer happens, as it does not pay. The purchase money to the parents, the wedding gifts, the bride's outfit, and the marriage expenses cannot be wasted. Now when it is found she is not a virgin, she is scolded but not turned out. What is more, a girl who has had sexual relations can find a husband, as there is a great demand.

*(Skoplje district)*

There is a lot of talk whether on the first night the bridegroom will find virginity. While, on the first night, the young couple are locked up in a small room, the wedding guests and the whole village sit about and, in front of women and children, discuss whether he will find it. It does happen that the lad is not able to effect relations the first night. That is surely due to the girl not attracting him, and not knowing her well. In addition, the young fellow has not slept for some nights before; then too, he is not experienced, he is upset, he is afraid. Then young married men teach him what to do and wake up his virility. In the more serious cases, they at once go to the *hodža* [Moslem priest and teacher] or to a witch to free him, for they believe that some enemy woman has "tied him up."

*(Skoplje district)*

The stern demand for virginity, the interest of public opinion in the result, and the general passionate mood created an indivisible whole.

That sexual morals constituted a demand which required particularly powerful support is to be seen from the fact that even in the patriarchal environment we find a relaxation of the obstacles in some places:

Here there is incomprehensible freedom. The older folk take no heed at all of what the younger ones do. There is rarely to be seen such freedom in the relations of young lads and girls. Vulgar expressions, lack in restraint in gesture, winking, teasing, and wrestling of girls and boys together and various other forms of handling of each other for mutual satisfaction astonish one. It is typical of this place that relations even between the young who are blood relations are very frequent and what is more striking still, they are concealed under the excuse of relationships with the phrase "it's all in the family." *(Djevdjelija district)*

Reports from patriarchal districts which never stood under Oriental influence ring much less passionately:

Cases of girls having sexual relations before marriage are very rare, for a girl's maidenhood is valued rather highly.

(*Montenegro, Cetinje district*)

Girls have no relations before marriage. Here it is considered a disgrace for a girl to talk to a young man by herself. The parents (the mother) take strict care of the daughters, as to where they go and when, and where they are. Consequently, the girls have no opportunity for coming into close contact with a man. Virginity is considered important. It is for this reason that sons are married to girls from a decent, moral, home of high standing, and such a family guarantees the virginity of its girls. Generally, girls who have had relations remain unmarried and scorned by everybody. At 35 to 40 they marry widowers and those who are very poor, and who are unable to marry others. (*Serbia, Vlasotince district*)

As Graph 21 shows, the border of patriarchal morals lay between Moslem and Christian Bosnia. In the Christian villages, during the First World War, sexual morals dropped rapidly, and even prostitution spread:

Before the war it was rare for a girl to have relations before marriage. The war and postwar changes in dress, greater poverty, and the need for money for the purchase of textiles, silk, and cloth played havoc in this respect. The poorer girls give themselves to the richer peasants, to gendarmes, excise men, teachers, and other strangers in the village, for a length of silk, for stockings, for creams, and other toilet needs.

(*Herzegovina, Stolac district, Orthodox village*)

Girls in many cases have sexual relations before marriage. Older men have complained to me that in their village there are no virgins older than 16. As reason they give the neighborhood of Hungarian villages, Polish and Czechoslovak. The prospects of marriage are the same as if they had no sexual relations. I know of 13 cases of widows having children. Before the war an unmarried girl never had a child, and would never have been able to marry. (*Derventa district*)

The following report, too, was typical of Bosnia, a real sigh from a conservative-minded investigator:

Only girls who were abducted, but deceived, used to have sexual relations before marriage. The Catholic Church, indeed, brands this and punishes it, but so far unsuccessfully. Before the war and the economic crisis it was the same. They anticipate marriage and feel nothing wrong in it, do not feel it sin. (*Derventa district*)

The largest number of villages with premarital love life were in Croatia. However, the girls did not enjoy this liberty as a sanctioned right. They were frequently involved in conflict between the general circumstances which drove or led them to it and public opinion, which branded them for it. For the girls, who in this phase had difficulty in marrying, there was a great danger in letting a young man have his way, for the lads felt no obligation to marry the girl when they had lowered her value in the marriage market. Examples from the former Military March disclose the hard lot of girls even in this liberal area:

> Earlier, before the war, girls had no relations, but in recent years they do have, the cause, it would appear, not being sexual urge, but the aim of catching the man and persuading him to marry her, for in very many cases the girls have no dowry, so they try this way to force the men to marry them.  *(Gospić district, Lika area)*

> There are very many girls who have sexual relations before marriage. Changes since the war have been great, and since the economic slump greater still. The war taught people many things, among them this. Also the lack of means, prevents marriage, so it is no wonder it comes to relations before marriage. Very great importance is placed on maidenhood before marriage. Particularly, the man, taking a girl, pays attention to it. The prospects of marriage for such a girl are very slight. The more so since the whole village rises up against such a girl as not respectable, particularly the men, who noise abroad what has happened and what has not happened too.  *(Slunj district, Kordun area)*

In the Military March, the erotic climate lacks the tragic note. The Austrian influence weakened the conviction that it was all fate and diminished the melancholic disposition:

> In most cases girls have relations, if they have not married, by about 18. These conditions have remained the same as before, these highlanders were always lively and hot. They have got used to it, and now find it normal. Virginity is not much required, nor in this district is it very greatly respected. If a girl has had relations, it does not matter, provided the man likes her and she has a little dowry.
> 
> *(Dvor district, Kordun area)*

Reports from central Croatia show the importance of property in that part:

> It is rare for girls to have sexual relations before marriage, for they are afraid it will be learned about. Virginity is valued. A case is known of a young husband, the day after the wedding, so beating his wife that she scarcely survived. The village approved of his savagery, saying that she should have married the man she had had dealings with and it was her duty to confess that before she married.
> 
> The prospects of marriage of such a girl are poor. She can marry a widower, or anyone else, only if very rich. In that case the act is per-

mitted because then everybody will pretend not to know about it. Nevertheless, even so, the parents and the rich girl herself are content with a man less well off. (*Dugoselo district*)

The old folk say that since the war every girl has relations before marriage. The older folk, men and women, condemn this. The younger, of both sexes, tolerate it. Such relations do the girls harm, if they are poor. But if they have a good dowry, love relations, no matter with whom, are no hindrance. Virginity is not considered important, it is only a condition if the dowry is small. If a girl has a good dowry, no heed is given to it, and her prospects of marriage are not poor.

(*Varaždin district*)

In a modern environment, thus, the demands men made on girls, in all respects, including that of morals, were greater. The old demands in the new environment, and without the traditional responsibility, have a particular note—a clear hint of male egoism, merciless condemnation of a woman's weakness, and crude material self-interest.

The following report reveals the dark as well as the brighter aspects of the old order, from the recent past in central Croatia:

Before the war there were no such relations. Then, parents looked after a girl and married her to the man indicated by the priest. The priest would not marry a lad if he did not marry the girl whom he had selected. Older girls had to be married first in order not to remain old maids. (*Ivanec district*)

The great responsibility of public opinion regarding the individual girl and the confidence that girl had of her future, used to make up for the lack of individual liberty.

The conservative ideology showed great resistance regarding the morals of girls. Stern demands were maintained even where real life had already undermined the patriarchal ethic. These demands were now principally a burden to girls, who in this phase of family life were much more dependent on the opinion of people than in the patriarchal phase, when the prospects of marriage were much better.

In an environment with steady development, girls were not reproached with premarital relations. Particularly in Slavonia, freedom in love was traditional:

They often have relations. Now, just as formerly. It is not considered important—maidenhood—the principal thing is the dowry. The outlook for marriage is only bad if the girl gets pregnant, if not, much fuss is not made about it. (*Djakovo district*)

154

In most cases, girls have relations, but subsequently marry. Earlier on, girls entered marriage without experience. The parents value virginity, but the young men do not. *(Valpovo district)*

The reports from the Littoral are nearly the same, that is, they show tolerance of the intimate relations of the betrothed couple. The first instance comes from Dalmatia proper, which was a little more conservative than the north Littoral:

Ten years or so ago, there were absolutely no relations before marriage, or very rarely such. In a few cases, girls do have relations, particularly with their betrothed. In the past two years there have been four or five cases of their living together unmarried. Latterly the young men call their girls "wife." *(Isle of Ugljan)*

Girls often have relations, but invariably only with their fiancé or "young man," as they call him here. This is not considered a particular wrong, as it is also not considered a particular wrong when brides go to the altar pregnant. Attention is paid where a girl has relations with any other than her fiancé. A girl's prospects of marriage are slight if she is not married by the man with whom she has had relations. Here one should emphasize that many girls have sexual relations with young men who are their fiancés and get pregnant, but it is rare for the young man not to marry such a betrothed girl. *(Isle of Pag)*

If it is known that a girl has had relations with a man, she will not be able to marry any other man. Girls do have relations before they marry, and in many instances are married in a pregnant state. *(Kastav district)*

In the three years I have spent here, except in the case of sterile women, I have not known a single case of there not having been obvious signs of intimacy before marriage. This is why they marry rather early. The older people condemn such relations until it happens in their own household, then they take it very naturally. One can always find spiteful tongues, but they are unable to hurt the girl. *(Kastav district)*

A girl who has had relations as a rule marries the man in question, but it would rather seem that this is the girls' way of getting married, for when they are pregnant, they are sure of being married. *(Isle of Rab)*

In the patriarchal stage, the liberty of the girls was very limited, but, on the other hand, they enjoyed complete protection. In the stage of stormy ferment, their individual liberty was much greater, but they were exposed to greater dangers. In the stage of a new equilibrium, the girls also enjoyed greater freedoms and more protection, too, than in the stage of transformation. This development through a complete circle is to be seen in Graph 21.

Nevertheless, this graph corresponds only to a certain extent to the true state of affairs, for all the villages in which girls have relations only with their fiancé have here been classified in the group in which girls have no relations at all, or only exceptionally. It is because of this that we have the regional rise and fall of our graph. I adopted this grouping for the reason that there is a difference in principle as well as practically between having relations with one's fiancé and having relations with any other men. The betrothed couples' relations in the Littoral region, as also in some villages of Slavonia, as a rule led to marriage and were not mere trials, adventures, let alone a breaking up of morals. But to complete the picture, here is another graph, in which the villages where the girls have any sexual relations whatsoever, whether with fiancé or others, are classified as villages with premarital relations:

Graph 22. Sexual relationships of girls

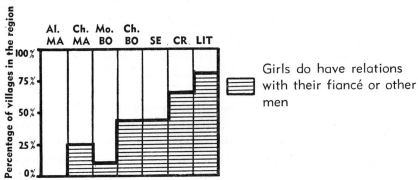

Girls do have relations with their fiancé or other men

Graph 22 reveals a steady growth of individual liberty, as one moves farther from the patriarchal way of life and a subsistence economy. It also shows greater love of liberty of the girl as an achievement of historical development which will last. What, however, is not to be seen in this graph is that freedom in the region with a new equilibrium was limited by a new moral code which in its way was also strict.

### The Protected Status of Girls

Though in the patriarchal environment, views on morals were very severe, we find public opinion on the girl's side if she had broken the moral standards and, still unmarried, was expecting a child. In the environment where the village was a whole and public opinion had some strength, it exerted a powerful and, as a rule, successful pressure on the young man to marry the girl who was expecting his

18. Bosnian youth

19. Bosnian girl with silver ornaments

20.   Croatian girls going to Mass

22.   Bosnian girl

21. Kolo dance in Dalmatia

23. Serbian girl

24. Bosnian girls

25. Sunday gathering, Dalmatia

child. The more modern regions show much greater indifference regarding the fate of such a girl. Graph 23 shows the pressure of public opinion:

Graph 23. Pressure on the man to marry the girl who is expecting his child

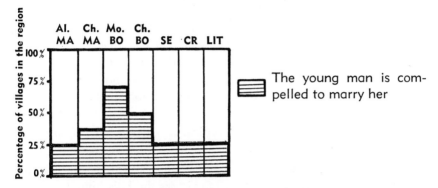

The young man is compelled to marry her

Protection of the girl and pressure on the man was principally to be found in Bosnia and Macedonia. The only reason why no pressure of public opinion was evident among the Albanians was probably the total absence of premarital relations there. In the Christian villages of Macedonia, the pressure of public opinion was most advantageous to the girl:

> In such cases public opinion is aroused. The following typical case happened in this village: a few years ago there was a teacher in the school who satisfied his sexual demands with a young peasant girl, without much concern about the consequences. When the girl became pregnant, the village to a man insisted on his marrying her and he was obliged to do so. *(Žegligovo district)*

> Public opinion compels the man to take the girl in marriage if she is expecting a child. Proofs are sought and, if they are obtained, he is obliged to marry her. *(Žegligovo district)*

Pressure on the man was most frequently mentioned in Moslem Bosnia. This is connected with the circumstance that Moslem Bosnia was in the first stage of abandonment of the patriarchal ethic, but also with the fact that, even if it does not admit women to have the same rights as men, Islam exercises its authority to protect women.

> If the girl is pregnant and she says who it was, a village committee compels the lad to marry her. If he will not, he is boycotted and beaten up. *(Tuzla district)*

157

Public opinion compels a young man in every way possible, by threats—
that they will bring him to court, even beat him, or kill him, which,
if the girl has brothers or near relations, they would indeed do.

(*Brčko district*)

In the Christian part of Bosnia, there were fewer villages where
pressure was brought to bear on the man to do his duty. These reports
come from a conservative area:

Public opinion compels a man, particularly the women do. They boycott him and as a rule he cannot stay long in the village.

(*Stolac district, Hercegovina*)

Public opinion compels the man, and if he does not marry the girl,
boycotts him and makes it impossible for him to marry at all.

(*Višegrad district*)

Reports from Montenegro are typical of patriarchal responsibility
for the girl in the heroic style:

Public opinion compels the man and he loses standing with everyone.
If he does not marry the girl, in some cases she kills him.

(*Danilovgrad district*)

As a rule the man does not admit it, he is ashamed, but he would be
bound to marry the girl concerned, or would incur a blood debt to her
tribe. Such a man is not readily accepted in the community and is
regarded as a bad example.          (*Andrijevica district*)

Two more instances from a region where the patriarchal laws no
longer held, but where, nevertheless, a certain moral pressure on
the man was to be observed. The formulation of the report indicates
that this pressure was neither as energetic nor as effective as in the
patriarchal environment:

Pressure is brought to bear on the man by the girl's parents and older
people in the village. Some girls, in the kolo, drop out when the man
joins in, and others refuse to speak to him. Other men of his age rarely
show any open disapproval.          (*Serbia, Azbukovac district*)

Public opinion compels the man to marry her. Three years ago there
was a case in which the man did not. She married another and the
first one is now scorned by everyone.     (*Croatia, Kutina district*)

Pressure on the man to marry the girl expecting a child by him
was not necessarily revealed in threats or ultimatums. On the contrary, public opinion acted much more reliably when it prevented
such things from arising at all, when it was so strong that it shaped
people's feelings early. Just as the authority of the father was stronger
when he was not obliged to attain a given aim by force, public
opinion was stronger when it did not have to take action. In an intact

patriarchal region, one never had pressure brought to bear on a young man, because there was never any need for it. Nor have we pressure in areas such as Christian Macedonia, because there the girls were in such demand that any young man was glad to obtain one for wife:

> There are no cases of public opinion compelling a man to marry a particular girl. If it does happen that a girl gets pregnant, the man in question marries her at once. He is very glad to take the chance, because it is more frequent for a girl to let a man down than vice versa.
>
> *(Macedonia, Skoplje district)*

This report shows how difficult the question of motivation is. One cannot tell whether the environment acts on the individual by suggesting an attitude of responsibility or by shaping his character and aims in childhood. In the Littoral region, we cannot be sure what it is that compels a young man to marry the girl who expects a child by him, while in other regions the men act in very different ways. Throughout the whole Littoral and particularly on the islands, a girl could count with certainty on the man in question marrying her.

> It never happened here for a young man to refuse to marry a girl who expects a child by him. *(Isle of Ugljan)*

> As a rule public opinion condemns a young man if he will not marry the girl, while his friends and relations try to persuade him to do so, and his parents, even if earlier against it, now give way. Sometimes the young people make use of this method as a weapon to break the parents' opposition. *(Isle of Pag)*

The pressure of public opinion on the man was only necessary and possible in certain situations, namely in the first stage of break-up of the patriarchal system. Earlier, pressure was not needed, later it was ineffective, and later still, when a new equilibrium had been established, once again it was not needed.

## Childbearing out of Wedlock

The question of the protection of unmarried girls who are pregnant has been studied from the negative aspect. Indifference or hostility to such girls often has fateful consequences for them.

Graph 24 gives typical results: Inaction and lack of responsibility for the weaker reached a great height in the region in a state of ferment, while the Littoral had the same attitude as the patriarchal region. Reports varied from unconcern to cynicism and malicious pleasure. Instances from Christian villages of Bosnia:

159

## Graph 24. Lack of concern for the pregnant girl

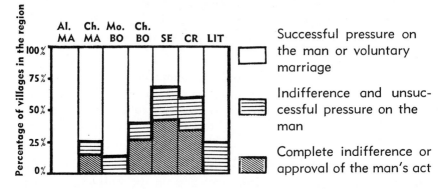

Successful pressure on the man or voluntary marriage

Indifference and unsuccessful pressure on the man

Complete indifference or approval of the man's act

The man is compelled to marry by court and public opinion. Boycotting, if applied, is ineffective, for the girl has nothing in her hands, only in womb or lap. True, the youth's standing is lowered a little, but he soon gets over it. 　　*(Bijeljina district, Orthodox village)*

If it is learned of, pressure is brought to bear. Boycotting is impossible, there are so many girls. 　　*(Derventa district, Catholic village)*

The men say *Bravo*, the chap is proud, the girls try to get him for husband. 　　*(Bosanski Petrovac district, Orthodox village)*

The investigators in Serbia were eloquent about the malicious attitude to the girl:

The man can do everything, he is a male, the girl is always to blame. No talk of a boycott, on the contrary, he is envied, he is "a lad." 　　*(Kosmaj district)*

Public opinion neither brings pressure to bear, nor boycotts, merely values him more, for it is the girl who is to blame. 　　*(Gruža district)*

From Croatia came similar reports, though here more emphasis was laid on the economic standing of the girl, which was decisive regarding her position:

Public opinion does not compel the man to take the girl; what is more, if she is poor, it is on the man's side. 　　*(Velika Gorica district)*

There is pressure on the man, and he too makes a point of marrying her, only now it is he who makes great demands on the girls' parents, knowing that it will not be easy to marry her to another.

　　*(Novi Marof district)*

Two more instances of an almost hostile attitude to the girl:

Public opinion does not force the man to marry. "Why did she let him?" The man is not boycotted, but often looked on as a hero, especially if it is a girl from another village. 　　*(Varaždin district)*

Although public opinion does greatly condemn the girl, it also to some extent tries to persuade the lad to marry her. In this the greatest obstacle is his parents. But if the man refuses to marry her, public opinion exercises no boycott of him, but condemns the girl more.

*(Slunj district, Kordun area)*

The consequences of the irresponsible attitude to the girl on the man's part, and the indifference of public opinion, were abortions and illegitimate children. Graph 25, which shows the proportion of illegitimate children has been drawn from official data. (In the case of Bosnia, I was unable to make any distinction between Christian and Moslem villages, as they were not separated in the official statistics.) This graph shows the same "line of development" as some others made on the basis of data supplied by my investigators.

### Graph 25. Illegitimate births

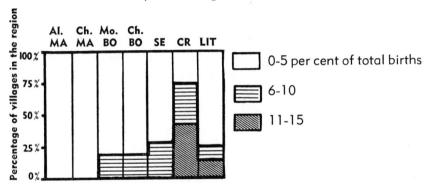

This graph, we see, rises steeply, which shows that illegitimate births were connected with the rapid break-up of the old family system. In the region with a new equilibrium, the number fell sharply, though it was higher than in the patriarchal regions where, in the villages my team examined, there were none at all. In Croatia the peak of the graph is reached, well above the Serbian level. According to the data shown in the chapter "Childbearing," this fact is to be ascribed—at least partly—to the very large number of abortions practiced in Serbian villages.

Illegitimate births are not as reliable a symptom of the rapid break-up of patriarchal life as are many other signs which come and go with this stage. Many circumstances in various spheres of social life effected a rise and fall in the number of illegitimate births, for instance, the religious adherence (in Catholic districts there were in the main many illegitimate births). Comparisons of our regions

161

with European countries suggest certain parallels. Here are the 1931 figures of certain European countries:

### NUMBER OF ILLEGITIMATE CHILDREN
### OUT OF 1,000 LIVE-BORN[1]

| Greece | 11 | Switzerland | 42 | Czechoslovakia | 109 |
| Holland | 17 | England | 44 | Germany | 118 |
| Bulgaria | 19 | Yugoslavia | 49 | Austria | 269 |

(For comparison, United States 104)

It is striking that the countries which first developed world commerce, or first industrialized, such as Holland, Switzerland, and England, had very few illegitimate births, unlike the agrarian countries. On the other hand, where industrialization came late and developed rapidly, such as Czechoslovakia, Germany, and Austria, the figures were higher. One cannot avoid comparison with the Yugoslav regions with steady development, which were also brought into the sphere of world economy at an early date, and where economic changes were gradual, for in these areas there were also few illegitimate births. On the contrary, in regions with rapid ferment, where economic changes began late and were abrupt, we find more illegitimacy, similar to the Central European countries with late industrialization.

However, the only safe conclusion is that in the patriarchal region there were no illegitimate births or very few. In that regime, girls were protected by the single all-embracing social-economic complex of life which guaranteed them marriage, and also by the generally responsible attitude of public opinion regarding the individual. With the destruction of the subsistence economy, the village set-up in the patriarchal world also changed, and the situation worsened for girls. Solely in the Moslem districts did Islam act as a brake and succeed in maintaining protection of unmarried girls; while in the region where a new equilibrium had been established, girls were again protected, although their prospects of marriage were slight.

### Relationships of Young Men

In a patriarchal regime, roles were so distributed that males were allowed to overstep the moral law, or their overstepping was forgiven them. They did not bear full responsibility for seduction, betrayal, or illegitimate children. In this environment, the male and the male

---

[1] *Aperçu de la Démographie de divers Pays*, Institut International de Statistique, L'Office permanent, La Haye, 1936. The figures are for 1931.

162

only was expected to exhibit initiative in everything and to show great aggressiveness as a fighter. Aggressiveness toward women was forgiven him. It was the duty of the girl and woman to look after themselves and also to preserve the ethic. We frequently hear the comparison with the bird of prey and its victims made. It is emphasized that, by its nature, the bird of prey must catch others, and the partridge should look after its own safety.

But male activity, satisfaction of one's passions, were, however, the prerogatives only of the adult males, not of young, unmarried men. In this environment, the young men were retiring in the presence of elder males, and also of the women who lived under their protection. It was the "masters of household," the married men, who had the principal say. The period of activity and full validity of the man only began when he married. This is why it was rare in this set-up for the young men to have relations with girls. Here, to their submissiveness arising from the ancient subordination to the elder men, one must add the tender years of all unmarried men. Apart from this, in the intact patriarchal environment, the young men had no opportunity for much contact with the women, for the girls were most strictly looked after, and married women were absolutely faithful to their husbands. There were no unattached women, except for a few Gypsies. The young man's yearnings found satisfaction in day-dreaming and *ašik*, courtship at some distance.

The sexual abstinence of the young men was one of the most reliable indices of the intactness of patriarchal life in a village, and this was true with Moslems, Catholics, and Orthodox. It was only when the edifice of patriarchal life was destroyed that the sexual morals of young men collapsed, first abstinence itself disappearing, then even the demand for it. Graph 26 offers a simple picture of the changes which took place.

The graph rises steadily with almost incredible regularity from the patriarchal to the modern regions. In this, more clearly than in any other graph, we see the uninterrupted infiltration of new factors into family life. (It also points to the validity of sexual abstinence as a sympton of patriarchal conditions.)

A report typical for the patriarchal world comes from the Sanjak:

Before the war it was the regular custom for the bride not to see the bridegroom at all, not merely before marriage, but even on the wedding day. To do so was "disgrace." When she came before the priest, it was her duty to look straight ahead, not once at the bridegroom, and to speak only through tightly closed teeth. It would happen for a

**163**

Graph 26. Sexual relationships of unmarried men

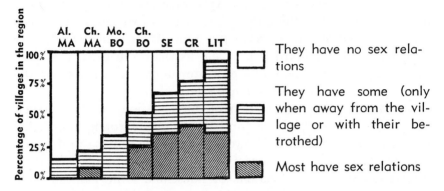

They have no sex relations

They have some (only when away from the village or with their betrothed)

Most have sex relations

couple not to sleep together for two or three months after marriage. The bridegroom would go straight from the church up into the mountain to the cattle, while other people took the bride home. Or one would have a case of a lad being brought to the altar by force, overcome with shame. Even after the war, at first, one could have a case of a bridegroom taking a staff to fight off the company come to put him to bed with his bride. Such ludicrous scenes, with their very ancient notions, were frequent, but they are now only stories of what once used to be. In this respect, people have made quite a step forward, even though this is not a great advance, for more civilized and freer ways of life and thought make slow progress in these parts.

(*Sjenica district, Sanjak*)

From the Albanian villages, the reports are all the same:

The young men have no relations, they always enter marriage without experience.

From the Orthodox villages of Macedonia, the reports are also identical:

In the vast majority of the cases, the young men live in abstinence, probably as many as 95 per cent, for they would be reproached as much as a girl. (*Sjenica district, Sanjak*)

The young men live in abstinence when at home, and even when they go away to work, for they send home all the money they earn.

(*Galičnik district*)

The men enter marriage with no experience whatsoever of sex. At a wedding as a rule a young married man is selected to be the so-called "bridegroom's man" and he instructs him in the secrets of marriage. Similarly the girl is instructed by a married woman."

(*Žegligovo district*)

164

In Christian Macedonia, there were places where the young men lived a more secluded life than the girls. This was no doubt a result of the custom of marrying mere boys to older girls.

In Bosnia, there was more prostitution than in the typically patriarchal region of Macedonia. Nor was it certain that all this prostitution in Bosnia was of recent date. It is possible that a certain amount existed in previous times, this being part of the feudal system and traditions. Nevertheless, in most villages the young men live a modest, retiring life. Examples from Moslem Bosnia:

> The young men live in abstinence, for they have practically no opportunity. They often enter marriage with no experience. Where they do have sexual relations, this is with Gypsies and traveling prostitutes. Public opinion reproaches them, particularly the older folk, but they boast about it to those of their own age. (*Tuzla district*)

> Young men as a rule live in abstinence, since they have no possibility of finding the necessary sexual partner. There are rare cases of resorting to village widows. (*Stolac district, Herzegovina*)

In the Christian villages of Bosnia, too, abstinence was the rule in half of the villages:

> Mixed parties, the kolo, courting with kissing, embracing, feeling each other, yearning for women, in some places the outlet of alcohol—this is, if it can be so called, the sexual life of village lads. Ninety-five per cent abstain. It is therefore obvious that they enter marriage ignoramuses. (*Bijeljina district*)

> Earlier the young men led a life of absolute abstinence. Now there are two cases of having had sexual relations before marriage.
> (*Jajce district*)

> If they have any sexual relations, it is with village or town prostitutes. No more than 1-2 per cent with village girls. This is definitely frowned on. "They hide it like a snake its legs" the saying is.
> (*Bijeljina district*)

Serbia had gone a step further than Bosnia away from patriarchal relationships. Here, however, we do not find things the same throughout the region. In the south there was strict abstinence, as in Macedonia, while in other parts severity had largely broken down, particularly where the men did not marry so early as is the general custom in Serbia.

> Many young men have had no sexual relations with a woman before they marry and so enter marriage quite inexperienced. Discussion of sexual needs is considered immoral. (*Vlasotince district*)

The young men live in abstinence. Hence they enter marriage early, often before they are fully developed. The first marriage [sic] is something quite unfamiliar to them and they enter the state with no preparation whatsoever. (*Vlasotince district*)

Peasant sons up to twenty years of age have absolutely no knowledge of sexual life. In the army they learn a bit, or by chance from a stranger. (The artisan families are rarely so given to abstinence.) They do, however, have their "adventures"—meetings and various bodily contacts. In short, there is abstinence in most cases, for the reason that every girl takes care of herself, as her virginity is her all.

(*Kosmaj district*)

Croatia was a step further still from the patriarchal set-up. In the Dinaric districts, there still existed a patriarchal abstinence, but in central Croatia the conditions resembled those in towns and cities. Here is an example from the former Military March:

In most cases the young men live in abstinence, as the true *momak* [young unmarried man] who enters marriage is as inexperienced as the girl. (*Vrginmost district, Orthodox village*)

This report typifies the exceptional cases, whereas in the rest of Croatia the freer tendency predominated:

All young men have sexual relations before marriage. One or two make the exception. These live in abstinence because they are ugly, or shy, or poor, or for some such reason. The majority are experienced, and very experienced too, when they marry. They mostly have relations with married women, widows, often with their own girl. In the main they take what comes first. Many of them are proud of it and boast to others and count the women they have had. Public opinion takes it all without getting upset, only the older folk grumble a little.

(*Slunj district, Kordun area*)

A report from a district to which holiday-makers come:

The young men do not abstain before marriage. From 15 upward they have frequent sexual relations, and the older they get, the worse they are. The cause is the dancing in the inns, while many lay the blame on outside folk who come to this part for the air.

(*Delnice district, Gorski kotar area*)

In central Croatia, we find the peak of libertinism, with a crude individualistic tone about it all. The premarital sex life of the young men by no means amounted to debauched family life. It was merely a persistent feature of the new age, and the irresponsible forms of these relationships were ephemeral. In regions with gradual development, such as the Littoral, there was far more responsibility in the

166

relations between the young people, with absence of that anarchic quality. Examples from Croatia:

> The young men wander around in gay parties in the evenings, and if they find an opportunity for sexual satisfaction they seize it; only it rarely happens. They live in abstinence because they have no opportunities for satisfaction. This is why they marry early. The girls enter marriage with no experience at all, for it is considered too shameful for anybody to instruct them. This is the influence of the church.
>
> *(Varaždin district)*

> Public opinion condemns young men if they do not live in abstinence and accounts them as foolish, believing moreover that the particular widow has cast a spell over them. The young men are indifferent as to what the public thinks. The principal thing is to have a good time, as the widows feed them well and buy them clothes. Ninety-nine per cent do not abstain; perhaps one per cent enter marriage inexperienced. After consulting twenty-five women, I find that every single one has declared that her husband admitted to her that as a lad he had sexual relations, and they do not know of a single young man in the village who has not.
>
> *(Varaždin district)*

Here is a picture of rampageous life in a Croatian village:

> From an early age, the parents allow their children, in particular the boys, to go about at night, and they have a special word for it, *mračnjariti* [literally, "to go darking"]. There was "darking" before the war too, though not so much as now, when it has gone very far. Before the war the "darkers" would gather from one part of the village at a crossroads and stand about singing. The "darkers"—lads from 14 to 24— gather after nightfall and sing and discuss where each one is going to spend the night. They break up into smaller groups and go to the house of a girl, or more often still, a woman whose husband is in the army or away working, or a widow or divorced woman, if they know of one. While one taps on the window, the others hide. The one at the window calls her softly by her name, tells her he has brought her sweets, or has something important to tell her, or uses some such maneuver. If the girl or woman opens the window, the lad tries his hardest to get inside. If he succeeds, that means he is welcome, and they are soon intimate, but by now another "darker" will be trying to get in too. There have been cases of the "darkers" taking windows off their hinges or breaking the panes, terrorizing the whole house if the woman or girl whom they knew to be alone and without protection did not let them in. Thus it was before the war. Now, since the war, this "darking" is not so dangerous. By politics or other public matters, the village is broken up into sections, and a number of gangs have formed, which arm themselves and

167

often fight, one set of "darkers" hindering the others, trailing them, giving them away, threatening them, stoning them.

In domestic parties too, with a band playing, first in one house, then another, there is wildness, the house full of unrestrained young men. People who have a daughter to marry or perhaps wine to sell will throw a party, and there are many cases of intimacy at carnival time. Particularly if there is a wedding in the village. Many mask themselves concealing who they are and thus approach the womenfolk, some of whom will be half-intoxicated. It is not at all rare for a woman and unmarried girls too to take masks, to the great delight of the "darkers." This is a very old village custom. The masked ones, particularly the men, crawl on all fours, dressed up like bears and commit all sort of excesses. There is much shrieking, confusion, and laughter and many a bruin scarcely escapes whole, as the married women attack him, beating him up and would strip him naked if the other "darkers" did not help him. Many heads of household who like to preserve their standing and authority, when they see the carousal overstepping the bounds, put guards at the doors and in the corridors and insist that the masked ones either leave the house or take off their masks. This is usually after midnight, and the "darkers" disperse.

*(Dugoselo district)*

In Slavonia, love life before marriage was traditional, this being to some extent connected with feudal traditions in this district:

Young men do not live in abstinence, it is their pride to have as much experience and as many love adventures as they can, and they boast to their friends about their successes. They enter marriage very experienced, and it is a rare bridegroom who does not know about the sexual act. The lads have relations with "light women" in the village, at the inns, where there are women who allow them to for money or some small service, and with Gypsy women, merely for "sweets," and often, too, with their own girls, whom later they marry.

*(Županja district, Slavonia)*

In the Littoral, in most villages the young men had pre-marital relations, as Graph 26 reveals. However, this fails to indicate that the premarital relations in this region were in the main with their own fiancées, whom the men would eventually marry. Such relations had the stamp of legitimacy, and were not symptoms of break-up of the patriarchal way of life but indications of a new stabilization. Here are typical reports:

Young men live in abstinence till they are engaged. After this they usually live just as if they were married.       *(Isle of Mljet)*

168

Young men are abstinent till they have chosen the girl whom they intend to marry.                                    (*Isle of Korčula*)

As may be seen, in the patriarchal environment, abstinence was the rule for the unmarried male. With the break-up of the patriarchal regime, freedom in sex entered, no matter whether the changes were steady or fevered. The individualistic trend that developed in economic life entered the love life too, and with it freer choice of a wife, as also of women for brief relations. This greater freedom of the young man in sexual relations, once acquired, was never abandoned. When a new equilibrium ensued, this liberty acquired a new sense, and a closer bond with the wife was formed and also with the betrothed girl. The quality of "adventure" and the cynical aspect disappeared, characteristics which accompanied the period of stormy transformation.

## Trial Marriage

In certain districts there was a custom which might be called "trial marriage." The young couple lived together for a time unmarried, in the lad's home, and married only if they got on well together. If they were not compatible, they parted. This did not spoil their future chances. This practice was very different from the premarital relations which we found between the betrothed in the Littoral, for there they did not live together and as a rule they did marry. A detailed study of trial marriage has not been made, for the reports in response to my questionnaire provided too little material for this, nor is there much about such cases in previous literature on these matters. Here, however, are instances from Slavonia, Bosnia, and the Dalmatian Highlands.

Here *otmica* (abduction) in the literal sense is unknown, but in the figurative sense it is customary. Here there is really no betrothal and marriage, but when a young couple had been courting for some time, one evening he will lay in wait for her with a few of his friends, and if she agrees, she joins him in his hut, if she objects, they stifle her cries and carry her off to his house. The friends then disperse, and the next morning he enters the family circle with her. He goes in first, she follows. Sometimes the family is not surprised, as in conversation the son has been hinting at this for some time; but it can happen that everybody is very astonished, and father and son have it out in the stable afterward. In some places, though very rarely, this unwished-for daughter-in-law is at once driven out of the house, with much disgrace and shame, but as a rule they put up with it, though they do all they can to make it hard for her; then, if she is so foolish as not to go of her own accord, they turn her out. This marriage form has its proper expression, *"prijeći,"* or "to cross over," and it is regarded as legal marriage. Only after the first or second child do they actually have a wedding. If they do not agree, they separate and she is then a "widow," he is a "widower," known as such. Later each, in most cases will marry some other similar "widower" or "widow." It is rare for a real maiden to marry such a "widower," or a lad to marry such a "widow."

(*Podravska Slatina district, Slavonia, Orthodox village*)

Another example from Slavonia shows this custom to be common in a village with three groups of peoples and three faiths in it:

It is interesting that among the Orthodox (Serbs) about 30 per cent take wives without any ceremony. Among the Croats, it is rare (2-5 per cent) ; and it is unknown among the Germans. It is interesting to note that all these marriages are bearable and the parties faithful to each other. It is done to avoid the cost of a proper wedding, for without all the outlay it would be shameful to have this."

(*Našice district, Slavonia*)

Here is an example from a Bosnian village near the former Austro-Turkish frontier:

The so-called *samodošle* ["self-come"] girls frequently live for a month or two in the bridegroom's house before they marry. The rule is that before marriage the couple should live strictly apart, but through lack of rooms they as a rule sleep together in the hay loft over the stables. If the girl does not get pregnant, or the family does not like her, they return her. Such a girl is married again in the same way. There are cases of a girl trying two or three houses, that is two or three "fiancés," till she finds one which fits.

(*Dervanta district, Bosnia, Mixed Catholic-Orthodox village*)

We hear the same from western Bosnia:

There are no unmarried girls, for as a rule they join the man and stay 20 to 30 days, unmarried, of course, then leave him and marry another, while he finds another girl the very same day. One man may try three and more, and the woman the same. This natural marriage is frequent.     (*Bosnia, Bosanski Petrovac district, Orthodox village*)

Here is an example of abduction of the girl and a sort of trial marriage from the Dinaric part of Dalmatia:

Abduction exists, which is to be condemned. It happens when a lad and a girl like each other, but the parents are opposed. Then the lad and his friends, in agreement with the girl, abduct her from her parents' house and take her to the lad's home. Here they live together for some months, only then going to the altar. There are cases of living like that for years, two or three, and having a family, only then marrying. It may happen that during this time the young man goes into the world to earn, and does not return, then the unmarried wife, through ill-treatment, returns with her parents. But then everybody despises her terribly, so even the smallest child addresses the ugliest epithets to her. There are cases of her remaining in the home with the parents-in-law, to wait her husband's return. This form of marriage is called *na ružne*—literally, in ugly ways—and that when the girl goes straight to the altar *na lipe*—in nice ways.

(*Dalmatia, Benkovac district, Mixed Catholic-Orthodox village*)

Here is further instance from the same district:

There are two kinds of marriage. First: a young man sets his eye on a girl in his village or round about. Through a woman he informs her that he likes her. The woman goes to her and brings her some presents and, if she agrees, arranges with her when she is to come to the groom, or rather, where she will meet him and how she will get to him. As a rule, they meet out in the country, or up the mountainside. As agreed with the woman, the girl goes out to work for a few days, either gathering fire wood or as herd-girl. There she meets the young man, and they spend the afternoon together, and in the evening he takes her home. The question now arises, how long she will stay with him? If she finds him what she wants of a man, she stays; in the other case, after a day or two or a month, she runs away from him. This is a disgrace for the man, while the girl has very good prospects and will now easily marry. The opposite can occur: The man finds she is not what he wants (she is disobedient, she does not get on with his parents, and so on), and then he turns her out. This can occur after a day or two, or after a month or two. However, if they suit each other as much as they had thought while they were negotiating, they remain together, and after five to six months or a year they marry, and there are cases of marrying only after three to five years.

Here I should add that as a rule the girl will run away if the man cannot satisfy her sexually. There are women who have thus married two or three times and still run away, and there are also men who have turned out two or three girls.

The other sort of marriage is a ceremonial, festive one. The young man casts eyes on a girl at a fair (if she is a girl of the district), or, if in his village, has had his eye on her for some time) . . . There are several customs at the hearth, followed by a supper. About ten, the young people go to bed while the guests remain for a time. The festivities last two or three days. Now the bride stays in the house. Whether she stays or runs away or her husband turns her out, and what sort of wedding they will have, is now their intimate matter. The ceremonies have been observed, and, if it comes to a wedding, this is only a formal matter without any festivities. I would remark that in cases of this sort there is less likelihood of the girl running away or of the young man turning her out.     (*Dalmatia, Benkovac district, Orthodox village*)

Uncle Milovan, whose tales about love in the Military March are told in the chapter "Extramarital Relationships," related to me a story about an unmarried *snaha*. This story demonstrates that in the Kordun area, too, there were such unmarried daughters-in-law, whose position resembled that of a wife in trial marriage:

An old frontier man of 73 was a friend of mine for hunting, we used to call him *babo* [Dad]. He buried three wives and had many children. Tall, he was, strongly built, young-looking. As we were walking we came upon a young married woman washing linen in the stream. She pleased him and he opened conversation with her. She had been living for three years as daughter-in-law in a household, they had brought her there to marry the son. They needed hands at the farm, but the lad was her junior, and the Orthodox priest would not marry them . . . he would only be eighteen shortly, and then the priest would at last perform the ceremony. After a few days I heard that the old boy had taken over that young woman from the lad. He had talked her into it, ridden up on horseback for her, and taken her off to his *kula*, an old frontier-guard's house like a fort. Then they had a wedding. She bore him a son at once. This was his ninth. Later, this woman told me: "I had lived three years with this lad without knowing what a man was. With the 'old one'[2] I knew I was in the family way the first night. I would rather have his heel than the whole of that young lad."

(*Kordun area, Croatia*)

Such liberty, which in some cases may be designated as trial marriage, existed only where one had a particular combination of Turkish and Austrian influences. There were also some pastoral features and traces of a migratory past. To a certain extent, this climate is the opposite of the classical patriarchal situation, where life was stagnant and conservative, as we know it in the so-called "old-time villages" without any migrations in the last centuries.

## Conclusion

In the patriarchal region, it was the collective demands which dominated, and young people adapted themselves to the maxims of that ethic and the wishes of the older folk. It was, however, only under special conditions that they adapted themselves completely, as among the Albanians, where all circumstances—the continuance of sub-

[2] "Old one" is used as an expression of admiration and esteem.

sistence economy, a majority of males, Islam, and a certain tribal tradition—acted in the same direction. In all patriarchal regions, however, the girls were protected, and so consistently that over-stepping the demands of the ethic did not involve serious consequences for them.

In the phase of abrupt transformation, with unbridled individualism dominant, sexual freedom increased greatly, but so, at the same time, did dangers for the girls, who were now obliged to bear the whole burden of independence and responsibility on their own shoulders. The sexual tension of the males decreased in proportion to the degree to which the girls were sought after, that is their value in the marriage market. In the environment with a new equilibrium, new laws established themselves, which allowed greater individual liberty without serious consequences for the girls.

These clearly apparent tendencies were, however, only one side of the story, one aspect of intimate relationships. The other aspect was the emotional qualities of the contacts, the intensities with which they were laden. For in one area a glance under the veil of a woman might prove so fateful that the second step would be her abduction or perhaps a blood feud between tribes, while in another region even the birth of an illegitimate child would be followed only by cynical remarks of the young father and a chorus of malicious village voices.

The role emotions play in the life of adolescent and mature people, and the specific coloring of these emotions, are not primarily dependent on the stage of development of the various regions, but more on the whole cultural atmosphere. This atmosphere in regions which had culture contact with the West was very different from those under Oriental cultural influence, and also from those which for long periods were engaged in resistance fighting. Since, in our material, such climate reveals itself more clearly in marriage, married life, and extramarital relations than in the boy-girl relations, these aspects will be discussed in the next chapters.

🔲🔲🔲🔲🔲🔲🔲🔲🔲🔲🔲🔲🔲🔲🔲🔲🔲🔲🔲🔲🔲🔲🔲🔲🔲🔲🔲🔲🔲🔲🔲🔲🔲🔲🔲🔲🔲🔲🔲🔲🔲🔲🔲🔲

# CHAPTER VII

# Marriage

🔲🔲🔲🔲🔲🔲🔲🔲🔲🔲🔲🔲🔲🔲🔲🔲🔲🔲🔲🔲🔲🔲🔲🔲🔲🔲🔲🔲🔲🔲🔲🔲🔲🔲🔲🔲🔲🔲🔲🔲🔲🔲🔲🔲

THE universal human tendency to start a family was unbroken in the South Slav villages, the wish for marriage was general. No customs or institutions such as hereditary rules encouraged bachelors. Only in exceptional cases there were lone wolves. Agricultural laborers did not exist to any large extent, and hardly any servants. Individual peasants who became proletarized through debt, moved to the city and disappeared from the village. Lone men and women lacked an economic basis, a status established by custom; their fate was regarded lamentable.

This chapter investigates the circumstances under which it was possible for the people in South Slav villages to marry, and whether there existed insurmountable obstacles in an unfavorable sex ratio. It examines the areas in which the men were in a more favorable position to select a spouse and those areas in which the women were allowed to choose more freely.

## Chances of Marriage

Whether all men and women were able to get married has been dealt with, in this investigation, from the female point of view. The following replies to the question as to whether there were many single women in their village throw some light on the chances of marriage:

> There are no old maids and divorced women in this place. A girl remains single only if she has some physical defect of a grave nature.
>
> *(Bosnia, Sarajevo district, Orthodox village)*

> Marriage chances for women are very slight. Every tenth girl remains single. If a girl is well off she may find a widower or a "similar" suitor.
>
> *(Croatia, Slunj district, Catholic village)*

The first reply comes from a patriarchal district, the second from a region with modern economic conditions. Graph 27 provides a general survey of the marriage chances of women throughout the whole country.

174

## Graph 27. Are there many unmarried women?

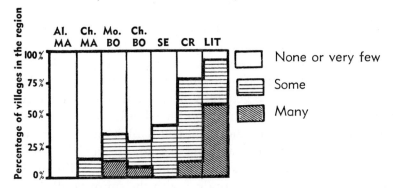

The graph shows an unbroken progression from traditional regions to "modern" ones. It reveals that the chances for girls became increasingly difficult as the region moved away from a subsistence economy and patriarchal way of life. The curve, with its ascending trend in the direction of economically more developed countries, corresponds to the general conditions in the rest of Europe during this period. In 1931, out of 100 women between the age of thirty-five and thirty-nine, the following number was still unmarried:[1]

| | | | |
|---|---|---|---|
| Bulgaria | 2.8 | Holland | 17.4 |
| Yugoslavia | 7.6 | Germany | 17.9 |
| Poland | 12.4 | England & Wales | 20.6 |
| Czechoslovakia | 14.9 | Switzerland | 24.1 |

Replies from the various regions reflect the situation exactly:

There are no spinsters in the village, and only two divorced women. Their marriage chances are good, because we have everywhere fewer women, and they are rated at a high price.

(*Macedonia Alb., Andrijevica district*)

There are no older girls. Divorced women are rarely found, and their chances are excellent. (*Macedonia Alb., Vučitrn district*)

There are no unmarried women over twenty-five years in this village. The husband will never leave his wife because she is absolutely essential for him; she was hard to obtain, and he paid a high price for her. He would only leave her in a case of adultery, but this only happens very seldom. (*Christian Macedonia, Žegligovo district*)

Girls rarely remain single. Older girls have a much better marriage chance than older men. (*Christian Macedonia, Kratovo district*)

---

[1] *Aperçu de la Démographie des divers Pays du Monde, 1929-36,* Office Permanent de l'Institut International du Statistique, La Haye, 1939.

In Macedonia—in the Albanian as well as in Orthodox villages—the situation for the girls was distinctly favorable. In Bosnia the situation was not everywhere as favorable, and in some parts had fundamentally changed within the past years. Fifty years earlier girls in Bosnia still had been so eagerly courted and competed for that special measures had to be taken to prevent fights and manslaughter between rivals. There were generally five to ten suitors for a girl. Catholic Bishops had issued a strictly enforced order that only a man who had secured a permit by the priest could ask a girl in marriage. Once the priest had authorized a young man to court a girl, no other man could obtain a "ticket," as the peasants called it. Without this permit the girl's family would not deal with the suitor at all. If the courtship was rejected, the young man returned the "ticket" to the priest, and it was only then that another man could try his luck. As soon as the families came to an agreement, and the girl had consented formally, a shot was fired through the window to let the village know that the girl was spoken for.

The following reply from Bosnia shows that the situation had not changed everywhere:

> In this village and in the whole township no woman remains unmarried, even if she is lame or feeble-minded.
>
> *(Bosnia, Mrkonjićgrad district, Orthodox village)*

In some Bosnian districts, particularly in Moslem villages, the situation at the time of this inquiry was much less favorable. Many of the Moslem villages had become impoverished during the first Yugoslav era but had remained strictly conservative, so that women were not permitted to look for work outside their homes, a situation which aggravated their distress. As shown in Graph 27, there were villages with many unmarried women.

> There are 24 widows and unmarried girls. Nobody wants us, we are poor.　　　*(Bosnia, Bugojno district, village with 290 inhabitants)*

This is an entirely new tune, unheard of some years ago.

As can be seen from the graph, Serbia belongs to the patriarchal districts in this respect, in spite of the lack of men due to war losses. The change of atmosphere, not yet expressed in the graph, is, however, clearly expressed in replies such as the following:

> In our village it is altogether difficult for girls to get married, yet few remain single up to their 25th year. After this age there is very little chance for them to get married. They are then ridiculed and cited as a warning example to any girl who refuses to get married immediately.

Generally they leave the village to find some work. Their number is small, possibly five or six.

Widowers rarely remarry. Only those with children get remarried immediately. For economic reasons young men find it difficult to get married in our village, because marriage should enlarge the property and there are no girls with substantial dowries.

*(Serbia, Kosmaj district, large village)*

A break between Serbia and Croatia is shown in the graph. In Croatia and the Littoral, chances of marriage were much poorer than in other districts. Money economy had penetrated Croatia one generation earlier, and the Littoral districts several generations earlier than in Serbia, causing great changes. Here are two characteristic replies:

We have some older girls. Their chances of marriage are nil. Only a large dowry would give them a chance, but even then the chance remains slight. *(Croatia, Ivanec district)*

There are many older girls. Their chances of marriage are slight or nil, as they have remained single because they are poor.

*(Croatia, Varaždin district)*

In the Littoral, girls and women feel most disheartened, because poor chances of marriage had existed for a long time; to them it seemed an eternal and unchangeable situation. In Moslem Bosnia, however, where chances of marriage deteriorated only a few years before, people were inclined to consider them as a passing state of affairs. Here is a reply from a Littoral village of 3,000 inhabitants, with some 150 women for every 100 men:

In this village there are about 50 who have remained unmarried.

*(Dalmatia, Šibenik district)*

There is a large number of older, unmarried girls. They have hardly any chances of getting married. They lead a miserable life, earning a little by needle-lace work. *(Littoral, Isle of Pag)*

Marriage chances for widows were everywhere similar to those of the girls. The possibility of remarrying after divorce, apart from the general conditions, also depended on legal provisions. On the whole this was no great problem, as the number of divorced people in the villages was extremely small, except in Moslem villages in Bosnia.

In the first Yugoslav era, legal provisions for divorce and remarriage differed for every region and each religious creed. Divorced women could remarry legally only when they were Moslem or Orthodox, as the Catholic Church did not permit divorce. Catholic women in Croatia, in the Littoral, and in Bosnia had no chance of legal remarriage, and, for a number of other reasons, had very little

177

prospect of it anyway. In Orthodox districts, Serbia, Macedonia, Montenegro, and also Bosnia, there were cases of divorce, as religious impediments were not insurmountable. Moslems could obtain divorces easily, especially if demanded by the man. In spite of this, there were very few divorces of Moslem Albanians in contrast to Moslems of Bosnia. Religious and legal provisions had no decisive significance.

The marriage chances of men did not entirely correspond to the situation of women, as the picture was blurred by generally unfavorable chances of marriage in "modern" districts. The situation of widowed men was particularly difficult in patriarchal districts. One interviewer pointed out that the widowers had no better chances than "robbers and vagabonds."

> We have no older girls or divorced women. Because of a surplus of men, all women get married. There are no divorces whatever. The men are attentive to the women, trying to please them in everything. If the wife dies, the widower cannot marry again. In this village there are more than twenty widowers. Some of them are only twenty or twenty-two years old, but do not think of remarrying, as they cannot find a wife.
>
> (*Christian Macedonia, St. Nikola Ovčepolje district*)

One interviewer tried to explain this in the following way:

> As to your question why widowers find it so difficult to get married again and whether there are any prejudices against them—I have discussed this with many peasants and several reasons are stated.
>
> 1. There are fewer women. The district is infested by malaria and shunned. Women from other districts do not wish to settle here.
>
> 2. Women do not want to take over the nursing of the first wife's children.
>
> 3. In their outward appearance widowers cannot compete with unmarried young men.
>
> 4. However, if a widower is rich, but only if he is not old, he can in exceptional cases find a wife, sometimes he can even find a girl.
>
> (*Macedonia*)

In patriarchal regions, both men and women generally wished to get married. If men could not get married because of lack of women or other insurmountable obstacles, they suffered by the situation to which they could never adjust.

But in a later period, when money economy had infiltrated, marriage was frequently postponed or prevented by economic difficulties. In this case men reacted quite differently. They adjusted to the situation and postponed marriage voluntarily—or apparently so—even for a long time. If it was not "expedient" to marry early, and the delusion of voluntariness was kept up, then something like voluntary bachelorhood developed.

Girls who chose to remain single were to be found only in exceptional cases. In some Catholic areas some girls entered a convent, and in the Dinaric areas (chiefly Orthodox) there were occasional cases of girls making a vow to live "like men." They would replace a son to the father and go to the war against the Turks (as it was formerly). However, these were rare exceptions, and any difficulty in getting married for girls was in general followed by much suffering, disappointment, and unsolved problems.

### Sex Ratio

One factor furthered the marriage prospects of women in the South Slav old-style districts; namely, the surplus of men. Everywhere else in Europe, at the time of the survey, there was a surplus of women for a number of reasons including the losses of men during the First World War. Besides Ireland and Bulgaria only South Slav patriarchal regions showed a surplus of men. (In Bosnia, that is, in Vrbas banovina there were 965 women for 1,000 men.) The villages included in this inquiry gave the picture appearing in Graph 28, which agrees with the official figures.

Graph 28. Numerical proportion of men and women

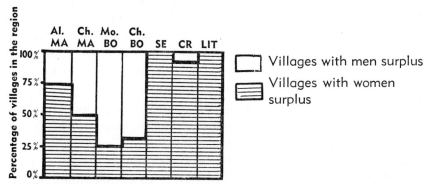

The old-style regions with their large number of villages containing a surplus of men, form a compact block. The clearly defined line of demarcation between the old-style regions of Bosnia and the modern ones of Serbia is remarkable. This line of demarcation corresponds to a new situation, as up to the First World War Serbia, in this respect had belonged to the patriarchal regions. In 1910 there were in Serbia 100 men for 93 women (while at the same time,

179

Bosnia had 100 men for 88 women). The change in the figure of inhabitants in Serbia is due mainly to huge Serbian war losses in the Balkan wars (1912-1913) and in the First World War. In the World War, Serbia suffered the relatively greatest loss of all belligerent countries. The large surplus of men in patriarchal regions before the First World War still affected customs and views even in areas where it had disappeared one generation earlier, particularly in Serbia.

The surplus of women in Serbia, Croatia, and the Littoral was in many villages markedly larger than the surplus of men in patriarchal regions. In Serbia and the Littoral, villages with a large surplus of women were in the majority, including villages having 116 and more women for 100 men. In the Littoral there were villages with 150 women for 100 men.

That women were in a minority was no doubt one of the chief reasons for their good marriage chances in patriarchal regions. The disproportion in the figures of men and women would have a stronger effect in a place where all people wish to get married by any means than in a place where some people prefer to remain single or wish to marry under only favorable circumstances. But the marriage chances of women did not depend on a surplus of men in their own village. Decisive here are the figures for the whole district. In old-style districts, a surplus of men had its effect also on villages with a surplus of women, inasmuch as girls from such villages simply married into other villages. Also, large-scale emigration of men to the cities did not produce a great change if custom required all men and women to marry. This custom is not easily and quickly abandoned. Young men either got married before they left for work in the city (or for overseas) or they returned to their village for a short time to get married. Only if the surplus of women has lasted for a long period, and more especially if it is the result of economic changes, customs with regard to marriage experience a change.

Why the South Slav patriarchal regions showed a surplus of men, and why this surplus had been still greater in former times, despite long wars and guerilla fighting, cannot be easily answered. As this problem had never been investigated, and even official statistics offered few explanations, I had to rely on my interviewers and on some experienced physicians.

The interviewers held two kinds of opinions. One was that the death rate was higher for infant girls because, according to their views, boys were nursed more carefully:

The number of men is larger than that of women. The explanation for this fact is that newly born baby boys receive much greater attention, are better nursed, and their death rate as compared to that of girls is much lower. *(Serbia, Arilje district)*

I have made inquiries with regard to 90 children attending my school as to the death rate in their family, that is among their sisters and brothers, and have obtained the following figures: Of 106 children who have lately died, there were 60 girls and 46 boys.

*(Serbia, Arilje district)*

This argument probably holds good for some areas but not for whole regions. In all regions, relatively more boys than girls died within the first year of their lives.

The other view maintained by many interviewers was that the death rate of women in and after childbirth caused the surplus of men. Several interviewers emphasized that the high death rate of women had its effect on the marriage chances of girls, as women are always in great demand.

An expert of great experience, Dr. Mićo Branisavljević, Jajce, Bosnia, gave me, in the autumn of 1940, the following data: In Bosnia (Vrbas banovina), out of every 1,000 female deaths 230 were due to the consequences of childbirth. In the Jajce district, a typical patriarchal area, of 100 women who died, 56 died in childbirth and confinement. According to his statements, in the Hercegovina (region of Bosnia) and in Macedonia more than half of all women who died, did so in consequence of childbirth. In some places the figure was 70 percent. I had to drop further investigation because of the outbreak of war.

Official Yugoslav figures confirm the assumption of the high death rate of women after childbirth, although these figures do not prove useful in learning the cause of the deaths. In the Yugoslav villages and townships, especially in the old-style areas, obituary notice was given to the roll clerk by a member of the family and almost never by a doctor, as in many of the villages there was no physician. In most cases, death "from unknown causes" was stated; and even when definite diseases were named, such statements remained vague and without proof, a fact which was explicitly mentioned by the Statistical Office.

The figures for death at certain ages confirm, however, the hypothesis of a high maternity death rate. The death rate of women of all ages combined almost equals the death rate of men in all regions. The death rate of women aged twenty to forty, however, is considerably higher than that of men, especially in patriarchal regions.

Among the deceased of all ages, the following belong to the group of twenty to forty years:

|  | *Men* | *Women* |
|---|---|---|
| In Croatia | 11.1% | 13.0% |
| In Bosnia (Vrbas banovina) | 11.3% | 14.2% |
| In Macedonia (Vardar banovina) | 9.1% | 13.7% |

The figures include mortality in towns and villages. The mortality of village women is still higher. The higher rate for women begins for the group of fifteen to twenty year olds.

A whole complex of living conditions seemed to raise the death rate of women in the South Slav patriarchal regions. Working and housing conditions seemed to endanger them more than men. The undeveloped state of medical service because of poverty and economic backwardness also played a part at this period. While there were 7.5 doctors and 55 hospital beds for 10,000 inhabitants in Czechoslovakia, there were 3.1 doctors and 15 hospital beds for the same number in Yugoslavia.[2] Most of the villages had no midwife. Some old customs and superstitions in connection with childbirths had fatal consequences.

One of the most important causes seems to have been the general poverty in patriarchal villages, particularly after the decline of the zadruga and intensified by the economic depression of the thirties. Dr. Branisavljević found that the maternity death rate had further increased since the depression, which indicates that poverty portends a special danger for mothers. (The connection between a patriarchal regime and poverty has been dealt with in the chapter "The Patriarchal Regime.")

Although it may seem absurd, it is a fact that the high death rate of women brings about a more favorable position for women in general. It cannot be denied that marriage chances for girls and women greatly improve when women are scarce. During the patriarchal phase, objective and subjective motivations furthered marriage, and this often caused bitter, even desperate fighting for the woman and led to customs such as bride buying and bride abduction which will be discussed later.

## Selection of Spouse

An old custom still exists in Montenegro that young men woo a girl without knowing the chosen one, frequently also without being

[2] *Economic Development in S. E. Europe,* Introduction by Professor David Mitrany, London, 1945.

acquainted with her relatives. The fact that someone belonging to this family had been a hero in old times suffices to induce the father of the young man to woo for his son. The ancestor through his heroism and renown has secured for the family and the whole tribe, and particularly for the girls, a good reputation all over the country. So when a young man has reached the marriageable age, his father goes about the villages asking: "Tell me my good friend, is there anyone alive of the heroic race of so and so?"—"Certainly, pal, thanks to God there is a full house of them. Their men—honest fellows—have always been heroes, believe me."—"But tell me, are there any girls?"—"Beautiful girls, God knows."

"Thank you my good people, I have had the wish to make friends with them and to become related by marriage. Not without good reason did our elders say that a girl is known by her ancestors. Thank God I have found a good girl for my Mirash."

Nobody asks the youth whether he has seen the girl, whether she will please him, or whether he is fond of another girl in his village. Nobody asks the girl whether there is a young man for whom she feels affection, and whether she would like the young man who has been brought to her.[3]

Who has the decision in selecting marriage partners? What motives are decisive in the selection? In the questionnaire it was asked whether this decision was up to the son or his parents, and which motives were decisive for the selection of the bride. The selection of the spouse was considered from the viewpoint of the male because the choice made by the young man is of much greater importance for his family than for the wife's. As the peasant's son takes his wife to his parents' home, it is essential that he consider their wishes, while the daughter who leaves her parents' house when getting married can more easily afford to disregard their wishes.

In patriarchal regions the bride was chosen almost exclusively and autonomously by the parents of the young man. The procedure as it existed in Montenegro was found also in Macedonia and in the patriarchal areas of Serbia. The young man often took no part in the choice of his bride and hardly any in the wooing.

> The marriage is arranged by the parents jointly with the other members of the zadruga and the closer relatives. The children play no part in this, while almost all relatives and occasionally the tutor are asked for their opinions. *(Macedonia Alb., Struga district)*

The son impatiently waits for a girl to be picked for him, especially if he is over twenty years. Therefore the question of whether he opposes

[3] From "The country where heroism means a dowry for the girl." V. M. in the daily paper *Politika*, Belgrade, 1938.

his parents' is irrelevant. The marriage is arranged by the go-between, a relative of the girl, who is paid for his service.

(*Christian Macedonia, St. Nikola Ovčepolje*)

It would be a mistake, however, to imagine that the choice made by the parents involved compulsion or even brutal force, to which the young man submitted gnashing his teeth. In the intact patriarchal environment, no force was used within the family, a fact stressed again and again by interviewers, as for instance in the following examples from Albanian villages:

Parents do not force their sons. The sons do not interfere, leaving the right of choice to their parents.

(*Macedonia Alb., Garnji Debar district*)

It is not necessary to force the son, as he is used to the custom of accepting the bride chosen by his parents. It does not occur to him that it could be otherwise.     (*Macedonia Alb., Gornji Polog district*)

How is it possible that young men maintained this peculiar attitude, incomprehensible to individualists in the West? Three factors determined this attitude: The part played by young people in the family, their shyness, and their indifference with regard to their objects of love.

In the patriarchal family and in the zadruga, every person had his part, which was his own, in which he felt secure, and which in most cases he would not want to exchange for another. All worries and responsibilities were carried by old people; any initiative was taken by them. The parents and the elder in the house cared for the young people and, as a matter of fact, they did not rest until all their children were provided for, which meant married to the best partner to be found in the whole area.

The young were used to playing the role of minors, being carefree, their initiative confined to dancing, singing, dreaming, and longing. As far as seemed reasonable, childish dreams and preferences were taken into consideration. Young people never had to make decisions and were used to carrying out the decisions of others. (Many people in the zadruga, even middle-aged ones, never handled money because this was not their assigned job.)

In almost all cases parents make arrangement without the participation of their children. An exception to this rule is rare. No force is used but the parents' word is law and the younger ones submit unconditionally.     (*Serbia, Vlasotince district*)

184

In these circles the young were shy, which is the second reason for their unconcern in selecting marriage partners. They were particularly shy vis-à-vis their father and the house elder. The larger the zadruga, the wider was the distance between the young people and the elders. The following scene, which took place in Serbia in the eighteen-sixties, shows this respect:

A young peasant wants to marry a certain girl, and in his despair takes his young sister-in-law in confidence. She wishes to help him and promises: "I will give a hint to your father, and he will no doubt tell grandmother who, in turn, will speak to grandfather, and you will see he will select the girl for you."[4]

The entire institution of the zadruga discouraged the expression of individual wishes without the use of even a trace of force. Perhaps just because no one doubted the wisdom and the benevolence of the elders, no one dared to utter something as ridiculously selfish and private as a personal preference or aversion to a marriage partner.

Young people in "institutionalized" families felt gratitude and obligations toward the responsible elder. Their childish shyness is shown in two passages of short stories by the Serbian author Veselinović. The first is a dialogue between the village schoolmaster and a boy who greatly admires his father. The schoolmaster asks him:

"Will your father get you married in the autumn?"

"I don't know exactly, but I think he may."

"Well, then you will take Marica and be happy."

"Alas, Mitra (the step-mother) says there is a good girl in the Lubanić family in her village."

"You better tell your father that you won't have any other girl but Marica."

"Who—I?"

"Certainly you."

"Not I . . . I could not mention this to him, even if you would give me I don't know what. Not if you would give me the whole village!"

"What if your father takes your stepmother's advice and woos the Lubanić girl for you?"

"I would have to bear it. This would be my fate," he says sighing. "I would not dare to oppose him—no not for anything. It is said: Hard is the life for him who is cursed by his parents!"

"But your father would not go and spoil things for you!"

"Still I dare not mention it to him—no, not even if you'd kill me on the spot!"

[4] Lazar K. Lazarević, *Pripovetke*, Na bunaru (Stories), Beograd, 1898.

"Well, then you better see to it that someone else mentions it to him."[5]

In a second story there is a discussion between a boy and his widowed mother. She proposes that he should get married:

... He hangs his head and blushed.

"I say it is time for you to get married. You are, thank God, grown up and strong. We have a large farm which needs another hand. If the work is well managed the farm will prosper, God willing."

"I don't know, Mother, how to tell you. . . ."

"What don't you know, my child? Can't you tell your mother—so many people say you are sensible. . . ."

"I am sensible but I cannot talk to you about this. . . ."

"Have you got anyone nearer than I am?"

"No, indeed, but somehow I feel ashamed. . . ." While speaking he does not lift his eyes, his face is aglow.

"There is nothing to be ashamed of, dearest. Thank God, you have not committed robbery or a theft. No, we are talking about your comrade for life. God has ordained that men and women should get married."

"Then, mother, I have my girl." He jumps up to run away, but Nera holds him fast.

"Where are you running? Why should you run away like this? Tell mother which girl it is!"

"I can't—if you kill me!"

"Do tell me, my boy!" He hides his head on her shoulder and whispers: "Milica!"

"Ah, Milica! A good girl, and healthy, sensible and a good worker. Oh, that's all right! I myself could not have found you a better one. She comes from such a good family too . . . a good old family!"

The third reason for the attitude of the young people can be found in the nonindividualized, non-differentiated desires and the fatalism that lies behind it. People wish to get married and long for nothing else in their songs and dreams, but the object of their love is rarely fixed, their mood is rather vague. In Slavonia girls say: "Saint Anthony deals out the boys," hoping he will let them have a good and handsome one. But they would seldom undertake to try and find one for themselves.

Numberless magic formulae were used to find out which boy or which girl was entered in the book of Fate. The following saying illuminates this point. The girl hides in the garden at night, listening to the conversation of passers-by. She hopes to hear a name mentioned which would then be her future husband's name. While listening she repeats to herself the verse:

[5] Janko Veselinović, *Slike iz seoskog života* (*Scenes from Village Life*), Beograd, 1896.

Oh Young Moon,
For the sake of your youth!
Gliding over hills and valleys,
You will see my beloved one on your way,
Ordain that he tells his name!

Wishful thinking was often linked to a known person but not firmly, as shown by the childhood reminiscence of a friend of mine, a Bosnian Moslem:

As a little boy I often sat in the home of our neighbor, Hasan. Hasan was always raving about Fata, with whom he had fallen in love. One day, while I was there, he asked his mother to go to the neighboring village to woo Fata. The mother, without losing time, walked to the village, accompanied by her little daughter who later on told me what had happened. The mother found Fata and asked her to marry her Hasan. Fata, for some reason, rejected the offer. The mother could not make up her mind to return home and disappoint Hasan, so she wandered about the village with her daughter. In an orchard she saw a girl whom she liked. She asked her whether she would marry her Hasan. The girl was ready to do so, talked with her parents about it, and agreed.

Hasan had been laying on the wall bench dreaming of Fata. When his mother entered the house, he jumped up, calling excitedly: "Mother, have you brought me Fata?" His mother said: "Not Fata, but another girl." Hasan embraced his mother happily and thanked her. I was very young then, but was much surprised how quickly Hasan was comforted. (*Bosnia*)

Hasan's love has a different significance than love in the era of individualism. His love rather represents a symbol, which, sometimes can be replaced by another symbol. With this mental attitude, Hasan finds no difficulty in being manageable and easily contented. This attitude represents the "ideal picture" of the non-individualistic person who fits into the patriarchal family as a piece into a mosaic. Personal wishes are overshadowed by compliance with the elders.

In reality, however, individualistic tendencies can never be entirely suppressed. No zadruga, at any time, has functioned as smoothly as a bee-hive. Individual inclinations exist in men under any conditions, and therefore cases of heartache, conflict, and restraint can always be found, even though such cases were rare in the patriarchal setting. In the course of radical changes in economic and family life, however, such conflicts accumulate, and force is used more and more openly.

Parents do not use physical force but they influence their sons psychologically, or through the intermediary of another relative in authority.

*(Macedonia, Alb., Struga district)*

The marriage is arranged by the parents through a mediator who often goes from one person to the other in order to transmit messages. The children never discuss the marriage. It often happens that the son is forced, and in the majority of cases he obeys because of his shyness and his customary obedience; another reason is his naïveté.

*(Christian Macedonia, Skoplje district)*

In Bosnia, the independence of the young men is considerable. This situation is brought about by their parents' fatalism. A laisser-faire attitude with the Oriental stamp dominates all Bosnian groups, particularly the Moslems, where the Turkish trend predominates. But also with the Orthodox and the Catholic, tolerance is generally much greater than in other regions, and the high esteem of love, *sevdah*, is traditional. Here love is considered a sanctioned feeling and a legitimate motivation for decisions. The following replies demonstrate this attitude:

Marriage is arranged by the children. However, before taking a wife, the young man requests his father's consent through a mediator, because he is under-age and feels ashamed to ask for this himself. . . . In the case of marriage, the most important point is that the two young people are fond of each other and that they have some means. Everything else is of secondary significance. But even though the son may marry against his father's will, the latter relents later on. "If she is good enough for you, she will do for me."

*(Bosnia, Bijeljina district, Orthodox village)*

At first the children come to an agreement with each other, and then the parents give their consent. To force the boy or the girl is out of the question. The only possibility is that the parents succeed by entreating the children. Within 40 years there has only been a single case of compulsion in this village but later on husband and wife got on well together, I was told. *(Moslem Bosnia, Doboj district)*

At present the children usually talk things over among themselves. Hardly anywhere do the parents object. When marrying off a girl they say: "She could marry into a better family but if she wants it that way we hope she'll be happy—we got rid of a headache."

Neither in Orthodox nor in Moslem families do the parents force their son to marry according to their will, but with all of them one can observe their wish and their attempt by some means or other to get a certain girl as a daughter-in-law. This influences their son to decide in this direction.

In general, one can observe that the parents lose their power over their children, particularly where the sons earn their own money. The father lets them have leadership as a matter of course. Such boys, when getting married, pay the least attention to their parents' opinions, and the parents, therefore, cannot afford to be hostile to their daughter-in-law. Such "snahas" are here no exceptions, and are often the reason for dividing the farm.                    (*Christian Bosnia, Sarajevo district*)

In the modern regions two diverging tendencies were growing: Material interests, and related to this the insistence of parents on their choice of the bride, and from the other side the greater independence of peasant sons and their insistence on their own individual wishes.

Two examples from Serbia:

Mostly the children make the decisions. In some cases the parents still make them. But even if the children do, the parents must be kept informed so that appearances are kept and it looks as though the parents had arranged everything.                    (*Serbia, Kosmet district*)

Parents force the son in most cases, because they try to find a "good" girl with a dowry and also a good worker, while the young man possibly wants a girl whom he likes who does not suit his parents. This is the rule. But after his parents persuade and pressure him into marriage, he settles down to his tribulation. He is well aware that his parents need not be right, but he cannot help himself—the boy is mature, and must get married.                    (*Serbia, Kosmaj district*)

In Serbia the parents lost little of their influence, their former position receiving new support with the opportunity to acquire a daughter-in-law with a dowry. The greatest harshness and inconsideration for the sons' wishes were in regions where zadrugas had disappeared.

Generally speaking, the marriage of today has the character of a purchasing contract . . . even in the villages. The parents rarely ever arrange the marriage with the consent of their children. The children never act on their own initiative.

As a rule, parents force the son to marry the girl of their choice in order to obtain a good worker, thus improving the economic situation of the household. Through the dowry the farm is improved or debts are settled. In both cases a profit is obtained.                    (*Croatia, Gospić district*)

Often the son is forced: "If you don't accept this girl, I won't give you another." The whole neighborhood and all his relatives compel him to obey his parents, as they think this is his duty.

The parents, the relatives, and mediators take care of the marriage arrangements. The children may have discussed them previously, but

the elders settle the amount of the dowry. The elders have the final
word.                                        (*Croatia, Varaždin district*)

The victory of the individualistic principle was secured in the
phase of "new stabilization," where a money economy had gradually
penetrated over a long period of time.

Formerly marriage was arranged by the parents, nowadays the son
chooses for himself with the consent of his parents. The question as to
which girl would be more suitable for the house concerned is discussed.                           (*Croatia [Slavonia], Županja district*)

These individualistic trends in the attitudes of young people contrasted with the indifference encountered in the patriarchal environment. A Montenegrin joke illustrates this attitude:

"What did the people want who came to call yesterday?"
"Why, we have betrothed you to the son of the tribe elder."
"I don't ask to whom, I only ask for when did you settle the wedding."

In general, the parents (and the seniors of the zadruga) have the
decisive word in the patriarchal regions; in the most progressive ones,
the sons decide for themselves. In the regions of abrupt transformation, conflicts over the choice of the bride are very frequent. In
Serbia conflicts occurred in a quarter of the surveyed villages, in
Croatia even in half of them.

### Motives in Selecting Marriage Partners

Although inquiring into the motives of human actions rarely pro-
duces sure results, several questions on motives for choosing a bride
were included in the questionnaire. The results are not without
significance.

The motives for the selection of the bride are displayed in Graph
29 for three regions: One patriarchal, Montenegro; one in abrupt
transition, Croatia; and one with new stability, the Littoral.

In the region of abrupt transition materialistic interest in the
bride was stated most often; love is hardly ever mentioned. Two
examples show extreme cases:

The amount of the dowry has an influence on the selection of the bride.
The girl's father offers a certain sum, but if someone else offers more,
the girl with the larger dowry is chosen.    (*Croatia, Karlovac district*)

The youth usually marries the girl with the larger dowry. There were
cases of the son having "the banns" published in the church but,
having received a message that another girl had a larger dowry, im-

mediately decided for the richer one and had those banns published the same day—the declaration of intention to marry the other.

*(Croatia, Ludbreg district)*

Graph 29. Motives in selecting marriage partners

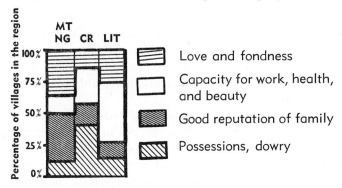

In the graph, the similarity of the patriarchal and the most progressive region is striking; since pecuniary interest as motive of marriage is mentioned seldom, and "love" often. From this fact we may conclude that materialistic interest rises with the beginning penetration of money economy but that it subsides again when conditions are consolidated, to give way to the love motive. However, this assumption is only partly relevant, as regional characteristics are frequently more important than those depending on phases. This is true especially in regard to love.

Montenegro can be considered a typical patriarchal region with a Dinaric pattern. Here materialistic interest in the bride is mentioned only in a few villages. Almost everywhere the "good reputation" of the family and love are decisive factors. The good reputation of the family, rooted in qualities and deeds of relatives or ancestors, is the least individualistic motive imaginable. A reply by a well-informed interviewer demonstrates the conflict for the precedence of the two motives:

Nowadays the boy's love for the girl is the decisive motive. In former times other considerations, namely the good reputation of the family, the respectability and good conduct of the girl.

Eighty years ago, or more, marriages were arranged according to the will of the parents. The young people did not know each other nor were they asked for their opinion. This habit was carried so far that friends who were fond of each other and were on good terms arranged that, if their expectant wives should give birth to a boy and a girl, these two children would eventually be joined in matrimony, so that the friends would become related. In many cases this formal agreement was carried out, and the friends became inseparable. Often parents arranged the marriage with the children taking no part at all as they were convinced that their parents knew better than they themselves what was of value.

Nowadays, however, this custom has been abandoned in many cases; that is to say, people accept each other after having been acquainted personally. But in deference to their parents, they take advice from them, as they wish to obtain their consent and blessing. The parents' authority still has a distinct influence here, although their wish is seldom decisive.

Formerly the main consideration was what kind of girl the man would marry. The girl's reputation was not of as much importance as the reputation of the family, more especially of the father. A man who had failed to distinguish himself in war or who was unreliable or selfish in everyday life found little esteem; he was nicknamed "coward," "good-for-nothing," or "female." From such a father, boys would not accept a daughter, especially sons of heroes and distinguished men. A girl, on the other hand, who was not physically attractive or perhaps even had some bodily defect, was nevertheless desirable, only because her father had distinguished himself in war or civilian life. The girl's mother was likewise subject to inspection as to her descent, that is whether her father was a "proud" man, although the girl's father was of primary importance. Even today people would say: "I would rather marry such and such a girl with only one eye than another girl with two eyes." The qualities of the girl are unimportant; only the father's authority counts. Such views begin to disappear gradually and nowadays the qualities of the girl are more and more considered.

*(Cetinje district)*

In Montenegro, love represented the individualistic motive which permitted the young man's release from all other considerations and limitations. Love became a new motive, gaining in importance.

Chief motives for marriage are the following: Wealth, the good reputation of the family, and, nowadays, in many cases, love.

*(Nikšić district)*

Chief motives for marriage are: The good reputation of the family, the good reputation of the young man, and in recent times also love.

*(Šavnik district)*

In this patriarchal region, the materialistic factor played an even less important part than the graph would indicate. Here, "possession" meant not just money but also a large, influential house. For this reason some replies under the heading "possession" may as well fall in the category of "good reputation." In Montenegro, the phase of individualistic materialistic interests had in a way been passed over. This is characteristic of the region.

In the Littoral, love, in a distinctly individualistic sense, plays a large part.

> In choosing a husband or a bride, fondness and love are, in the majority of cases, decisive. Materialistic motives are of secondary consideration. (*Littoral, Novi district*)

It is difficult to judge whether, in this region, the love motive was so strongly expressed because the economic transformation had already passed and family conditions appear to have become consolidated again, or whether specific regional factors were decisive. The seaside position doubtlessly made it possible for young men to enjoy greater independence, as they could emancipate themselves from the home as sailors and seamen. Likewise the Italian influence, dating from the Venetian republic, strengthened the individualistic factor, securing a more legitimate position for "amore."

In Bosnia love has little individualistic coloring. It has not the stamp of the new but rather of old times. Love is often contrasted with the new, materialistic currents:

> Chief motivation for the selection of the girl is health, beauty, and family, and the fact that she is well versed in household duties. But the prevalent motive is love. Marriage for advantage is still rare.
> (*Mostar district, Moslem village*)

> Love still continues to play an important part, but slowly another motive is creeping in—possessions! (*Brčko district, Catholic village*)

> There are individual differences, but still great value is attached to wealth. Often love is decisive, and the young man kidnaps the girl by force, because he likes her, although he may have never spoken to her.
> (*Sanski Most district, Orthodox village*)

The last reply clearly shows that this is a kind of nonindividualistic love; it is attraction without real personal attachment.

Motives for the choice of the bride, stated as an average of the entire country, are as follows:

| | *Percent of Villages* |
|---|---|
| Property | 75 |
| Capacity for work | 50 |
| Love | 40 |
| Good reputation of family | 35 |
| Health and beauty | 20 |

The concepts "property," "love," and "good reputation of family" change significance in different periods. In old-style settings, "property" also included a family of high standing, while it later meant simply a considerable dowry. "Love" in the patriarchal setting stood for fondness in contrast to materialistic interests, while in the modern circle it had an individualistic tinge, more to distinguish it from "good reputation of the family." "Good reputation of the family," in a patriarchal milieu, meant that one of the ancestors was a hero; in a modern setting it rather implied wealth.

In connection with the development of individualism, material as well as ideal interests might come to the fore. Which motives were decisive in the selection of the wife depended on economic as well as regional-traditional factors, on the date and rhythm of the capitalistic penetration, and of the predisposition of an area for different values. In view of the fact that several motives were competing for prevalence, various results were possible. Thus, for instance, in one area an indication was found of a development which did not correspond with the sequence of values mentioned so far.

> Formerly the chief motive was the good reputation of the family and the capacity for work but nowadays it is the dowry.
>
> Love has not had its turn yet, although occasionally it appears as a rare bird.     (*Croatia, Dvor district, Orthodox village*)

This reply comes from the former Military March, a district with a fighting tradition.

Only one conclusion is certain: Personal attraction by no means became the decisive factor in choosing a wife.

### Bride Price

> It happens at times that a bride can be found for whom no payment is required, but a girl of this kind is avoided by people. The father of a distinguished family told me that he bought one daughter-in-law for 6,000 dinars, and another for 4,000 dinars, while he was not charged anything for the third one. Speaking of the latter he said: "Cursed be the hour she entered my house. She has caused 100,000 dinars worth of damage and she will succeed in splitting the zadruga, the largest and richest in the whole district. If she had been worth any money, they would not have let her go without payment, for something worthwhile is worth paying for."[6]

The remark of this father indicates that the custom of bride buying was very old and widespread. Otherwise he would not have consid-

---

[6] Šaranović in the newspaper *Politika*, Belgrade, 1938.

ered it normal and justified to sacrifice such large sums. He had paid
for two daughters-in-law as much as for about four or five head of
cattle, and this was a large amount for a Balkan peasant in a period
of a serious agricultural crisis. At that time 1,000 dinars was worth
about 18 dollars. Two pounds of bread cost 4 dinars or 8 cents, one
pair of cheap shoes was 150 dinars, slightly less than one dollar. The
dinar had a high value in the village, and there were many peasants
who never had 100 dinars in the house during the depression. In
order to save 3,000 dinars, 45 dollars, a peasant boy had to work hard
in the city for ten years and go hungry most of the time.[7]

Graph 30 shows the distribution of the custom of bride buying.

## Graph 30. Bride price

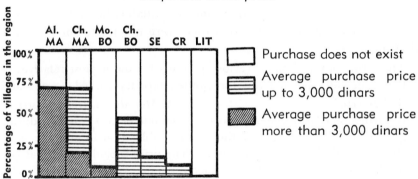

On the above graph, two towers representing Macedonia and the
Christian part of Bosnia stand out as the remnants of a formerly large
block. From the traces of this custom which are found in many districts, it can be concluded that it used to cover a much wider area
than it did at the time of this investigation.

As shown by the graph, in both parts of Macedonia in the majority
of villages a purchase price was paid for the bride. In the Albanian
villages, women were rated at a particularly high price. However, the
Albanians themselves did not consider this sum a purchase price and
protested against its being called that. They always emphasized the
fact that the money paid to the parents of the girl by the young man
was exclusively destined for the couple. With the Albanians, the
purchase money was used only for the bridal outfit and household
goods.

[7] Olive Lodge, *Peasant Life in Jugoslavia*, London, 1941, reporting on this same
period, found that the purchase price for the bride approximately corresponded to the
price for an ox.

Young men as a rule pay 10,000 dinars, which is used for the bride's outfit. In some cases the girl's dowry represents a value higher than the purchase price paid to the family of the girl.

*(Macedonia Alb., Vučitrn district)*

The young man pays the purchase price to the relatives of the girl. The amount depends on the girl's value. At present the price varies between 2,000 and 10,000 dinars. *(Macedonia Alb., Gostivar district)*

In the Christian villages of Macedonia, no strict obligation existed to use the purchase price exclusively to outfit the bride; however, it was customary to return at least part of the purchase price to the groom's family in the form of valuable presents.

The girl brings clothes for herself, her fiancé, and his family.

*(Ch. Macedonia, Djevdjelija district)*

In patriarchal setting "clothes" meant valuable, homemade, richly embroidered costumes, some of which were not worn out during a lifetime.

The term "outfit" implies various presents for the nearest relatives of the man, and also material for clothes, tapestry-worked aprons and similar articles. *(Ch. Macedonia, Debar district)*

In Orthodox circles, the boy gives the girl one or two Austrian ducats (gold coins), and the girl's father has the obligation to give the same amount to his daughter. Here no purchase price is paid to the relatives. Moslems pay between 3,000 to 15,000 dinars.

*(Macedonia, Struga district, Moslem village)*

The boy pays to the girl's relatives 3,000 to 4,000 dinars, he presents his father-in-law with a fur-coat, his mother-in-law with *opanks* (mocassins) and similar articles. He likewise pays for the wedding meal and the other expenses . . . it all depends on previous arrangements. It is, however, essential that some sort of payment is made. The girl receives either a ring or a ducat from her fiancé.

*(Ch. Macedonia, Žegligovo district)*

A purchase price is rarely paid, mostly for the daughter of rather poor people who cannot afford to give her a bridal outfit and also to cover other expenses. Generally 1,000 to 3,000 dinars, seldom larger amounts.

*(Macedonia, Struga district, Moslem village)*

In Macedonia it sometimes happened that the ancient custom of bride buying was criminally misused. From time to time the papers reported frauds; for instance, the parents accepted the purchase price from the man, but induced their daughter to leave him, so that they could sell her a second time. These were, however, exceptional cases that showed the decadence of the old custom.

In the Christian villages of Bosnia, the custom of bride purchase survived surprisingly well, although the influence of the modern state and the penetration of money economy had begun two generations earlier. Prices, however, seemed to be lower than in Macedonia. The following report is typical for the whole region, where the abduction of women occurred frequently and the families became reconciled later on.

> The boy presents money to the girl. The girl's parents receive nowadays up to 1,000 dinars from the richest boys on occasion of the family reconciliation, but often they become reconciled without any payment whatever. (*Ch. Bosnia, Tuzla district, Orthodox village*)

Other examples show some vestiges of this custom:

> The young man in many cases makes a present to the girl as a keepsake or "gift," *belega*. Usually this is a silver or gold coin in a special little box. No purchase money is handed to the relatives of the girl. Only when the girl is fetched from her parents, the father of the boy places some money on the wedding cake and keeps on doing so until the girl's father says: "That will do." Usually 100 to 500 dinars are thus paid. (*Bosnia, Višegrad district, Orthodox village*)

> The boy gives the girl a ring and, if she is poor, some cash, so that she can get her outfit. (*Ch. Bosnia, Stolac district, Catholic village*)

Gifts made by the boy to the girl were in principle distinguished from money and money's worth received by her parents.

> The boy presents the girl with the so-called *Apple*, that is a cash gift according to his financial circumstances—50 to 1,000 dinars. No purchase price is paid for the girl.
> (*Ch. Bosnia, Mrkonjićgrad district, Orthodox village*)

> Before the war the girl received an *Apple* from the boy into which he had stuck a gold ducat. Nowadays this custom has disappeared.
> (*Bosnia, Bihać district, Catholic village*)

The following report shows a gradual conversion of this custom:

> It is the custom for the boy to make presents to the girl, such as an orange, an apple, a cake, a mirror, a kerchief; but in return he receives presents of double the value, for instance a shirt, a ducat (gold coin), woolen socks, and similar articles, all of which are art-needle work.
> (*Ch. Bosnia, Bijeljina district, Orthodox village*)

In Serbia, bride purchase had almost disappeared. The main reason for this does not seem to lie in the surplus of women, for despite this surplus there were very many cases of abduction of girls and elopement. The main reason may be found in the exceedingly great

197

economic changes in Serbia, in the transition from cattle-raising to agriculture, and the rapid penetration of money economy under favorable circumstances. Conservative features of family living had remained here only in customs which did not go against economic trends. The following reply is the only one mentioning bride purchase in Serbia, but it is typical:

> The boy gives the girl some cake and sweets—generally at the fair—worth between three and four dinars. A purchase price for the girl does not exist. This belongs to the past, but nearly all elderly people can remember this custom.        (*Serbia, Kosmaj district*)

All reports from Serbia differ considerably from those from patriarchal regions:

> The girl is looked over by the boy and his parents and, if they like each other, the father of the boy makes the girl a money present according to the means of the bride's father. If the girl is well off, she receives up to 100 dinars, while a poor girl only gets between 10 and 20 dinars. Then the boy presents her with the ring and another gift. The girl makes presents to the boy and his parents, such as a shirt, stockings, a kerchief. The present to the girl generally is of small value. Only a rich boy gives her a necklace or a similar gift. No purchase price is paid for the girl.        (*Serbia, Kosmaj district*)

The following reply is significant of the decadance of old customs:

> The elders of the youth's family call on the girl, giving her a necklace of stringed ducats. Often such ducats are hired for one or two days to be returned to the owner and that is all. After this the girl is, as they express it, engaged by downpayment.        (*Serbia, Kosmaj district*)

Moslem Bosnia was omitted from Graph 30, because Moslem villages, as shown in the graph, failed to conform with the pattern. One of the reasons for this was the poor marriage chances of the girls in this region. The sudden pauperization of the Moslem population in the first Yugoslav era caused many men to leave the villages for the cities, where many of them became still more poverty-stricken, *fukara*, and did not marry at all. The bride buying in Bosnia was, in many cases, merely a supplement to the abduction of women, which will be dealt with later on. In the following reply, the connection of these two customs is shown:

> It happens frequently that girls "steal off" to their suitor against their parents' will. The parents resent it but with certain reservations. Then follow the so-called peace negotiation and they compromise. The boy's parents or friends call on the girl's parents with the peace offer.

Negotiations completed, the boy's parents pay the girl's parents an amount between 100 dinars and 3,000 or 4,000 dinars.

*(Moslem Bosnia, Cazin district)*

The next reply shows a state of transition, and the following one a complete reversion of the situation:

When wooing the girl, the boy always presents the girl with ducats, sometimes with only one. The girl gives the boy some needle work. A purchase price is not paid.     *(Moslem Bosnia, Rogatica district)*

The boy brings some presents, but the girl likewise makes him a present. He hands her gifts worth between 100 and 200 dinars, but accepts from her ducats valued at 4,000 to 5,000 dinars.

*(Bosnia, Sarajevo district, mixed population, majority Moslem)*

In Croatia, bride purchase existed only in one area. General conditions were contrary to those in which bride buying could develop or be maintained. The idea of a purchase price for women was unknown except in the hills of the Dalmatian Highlands, where sporadic vestiges of this custom can be found:

The boy pays a purchase price which varies according to the dowry. This purchase price amounts to about one tenth of the dowry, or sometimes less. Formerly the purchase price was paid in silver coins without any claims on the dowry. There was a saying that silver was given for gold, meaning the girl.

*(Croatia Dalmatia, Knin district, Orthodox village)*

In some Croatian and Serbian villages, the boy handed the girl a certain amount of money. This had not the meaning of bride buying but was a sort of down payment:

The parents and relatives arrange the marriage. The boy calls to give a down payment for the girl; that is to say, he gives her an appointed amount of money. If the marriage does not take place, the party responsible for this has to return double the amount of the down payment.     *(Croatia, Dugoselo district, Catholic village)*

In the Littoral region, where a considerable surplus of women existed, there was no question of purchase price for the bride. The following answer is characteristic for the Littoral and the majority of Croatian villages:

The boy does not pay purchase money; all are satisfied that he had taken her.                              *(Littoral, Isle of Pag)*

### Bride Abduction

A wild fellow on horseback gallops over the mountains holding a girl in front of him. In the background a group of men with smoking guns are in hot pursuit of the kidnapper. Below this picture is the inscription *"Otmica."* This was a painting one could often admire in Yugoslav homes; it represented the popular custom of bride abduction. *Otmica* is the Serbo-Croatian term for capture, kidnapping, abduction of women, and it has a suggestion of war-like violence. However, this term has no criminal connotation. Quite the contrary, Otmica was again and again idealized by artists and praised in folklore.

It was generally known that Otmica was widespread in patriarchal districts, particularly in Bosnia, and that no government in action could stamp it out. The descriptions of older authors are remarkably similar to those brought back by my interviewers. In former periods as during the time of this investigation, the abductors were rarely punished, since the girl herself prevented it by her attitude. Whenever an abductor was brought before a judge, no matter whether he was a Turkish kadi, an Austrian or Yugoslav magistrate, or a member of the armed police, the girl almost always testified that she had followed the fellow of her own free will. During the Turkish era, the Serbian girl confirmed her voluntariness with a special phrase: She had to testify that she had been willing to follow the man "into the mountains and into the water." In the majority of cases she repeated this particular phrase.

Such stereotyped reaction on the part of the girl had several causes: first, an abducted girl found it more difficult to get married to another man. Second, the aggressive man corresponded to the concept of ideal manliness in the region of the Otmica custom, and his action impressed the girl. Third, it often happened that the girl was not altogether innocent in the capture. The transition between brute force used by the young man and semi-initiative on the part of the girl is so gradual that it is almost impossible to establish limits. All expressions in connection with Otmica have a vague significance, because of the ambiguous part often played by the girl.

The activity of the boy can be different. In the case of real abduction, which takes place against the will of the girl, his violence is obvious. Interviewers use such terms as "kidnapping," "waylaying," "carrying off," "capture," and "abduction." Although prosecuted by law, such actions were practiced in many areas. Here is an example from Bosnia:

> Otmica occurs frequently. If, for instance, a girl of means hesitates for a long time, the boy waits for an opportunity and kidnaps her. He

takes her to a hut where they remain by themselves. Later she tells the prosecuting clerk, the police, and her parents that she went with him of her own free will.

*(Christian Bosnia, Bijeljina district, Orthodox village)*

More frequent were cases of Otmica when boy and girl act in agreement. Reports often say: "The boy steals the girl, aided by his comrades." Here is an example from Serbia:

Otmica is rather widespread. Boys and girls come to an understanding between one another. Usually the girl arranges everything with the boy, without everyone else's knowledge. The girl is then, however, received by the boy's family, as if this proceeding was natural and normal. *(Serbia, Kosmaj district)*

Otmica in agreement always indicates an obstinate or rebellious attitude on the part of the girl. Although she did not openly resist her parents, she avoided their authority by allowing herself to be captured. Such an attitude differed widely from her attitude in all other situations of life, and her independence of action was often even greater than that of the young man. While he seldom could choose a girl against the will of his parents, as he had to bring her into their home, the girl could oppose her parents more easily and she did so more frequently. It is true that she exchanged one strict authority for another—her father's for her husband's—but she brought about this transition often in a surprisingly definite form.

A special category is the "fictitious raid," where kidnapping was merely acted out. About this practice there are reports from many districts. It was based on the endeavor by all concerned to avoid the solemn marriage ceremony which, according to custom, required prohibitive expenses. The girl's parents joined the acting or tolerated the elopement—"often their anger is merely simulated."

Besides Otmica there was the custom of the girl's "desertion" to her chosen one, which in various districts had different, traditional names. Interviewers refer to this practice with such phrases as, "the girl steals away from her parents' home," "she deserts to the boy," "she makes her escape," "she runs away," "she breaks away," "she elopes." Although the description resembles an agreed Otmica, interviewers following the interpretation in the various districts strictly differentiate between these two customs. In the case of "desertion" the girl seems to play a more active role than in case of the agreed Otmica.

Graph 31 shows the distribution of Otmica customs in the Yugoslav regions.

## Graph 31. Bride abducting—Otmica

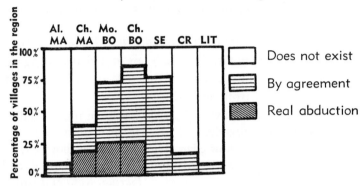

In this graph the curve is semicircular, showing a low at both ends. This is a typical line of development, mostly representing conflicts in the family, where progressive regions show a similarity to the patriarchal ones. The peaceful relations, however, take place on different levels. In this case, Macedonia had not yet practiced bride abduction, because this was a practice that played off the authority of parents, while in Croatia this custom was *no longer* adhered to as here the parents' authority was if necessary openly opposed. In Bosnia and Serbia, however, the revolt against parental authority had only just begun. In addition to this, regional-traditional elements were significant: The Oriental idea of women as a kind of minor and the legal insecurity at the time of the Turkish decay; in Serbia the Balkan tradition of rebels and Hayduks.

Bosnia is the original home of Otmica. Its tradition lives in innumerable folk songs and is suited to the Oriental style of life. At the time of this investigation, real bride abduction occurred frequently. Some interviewers even asserted:

> There are almost more cases of Otmica than marriages on the basis of mutual consent. (*Bosnia, Jajce district*)

Here are some examples of real abduction of girls:

> After declining an offer of marriage the girl is kidnapped. Otmica is carried out by a surprise move. (*Bosnia, Sarajevo district*)

> There are cases of Otmica. Generally a friend of the boy calls on the girl's parents, who do not wish to part with her, and if the girl fails to give her consent at once, she is abducted. This also happens in full daylight. (*Bosnia [Herzegovina] Stolac district*)

> There are cases of Otmica, but they are not frequent. In the majority of cases the boy is assisted by his friends in kidnapping the girl who

202

does not wish to follow him. She is taken to the woods where she is kept as prisoner for some days, ill-treated and deflowered. The girl then submits to her fate and allows to be taken to the boy's home.

*(Bosnia, Sanski Most district)*

Here is an example of an elopement with the girl's consent:

There are cases when a girl marries against her parents' wishes. The girl generally arranges to meet her chosen one at the church fair, and then she elopes with him to his home. The procedure afterwards is similar to the one in Otmica cases. His relatives with some other peasants call on her parents for reconciliation. The girl's mother generally acquiesces, but not the father, so that the daughter is not allowed to face him for years for fear of being beaten-up or even killed.

Otmica is practiced only "pro forma," being an ancient custom. In the majority of cases, parents are aware of it beforehand. After two or three weeks, reconciliation takes place and only then the marriage ceremony is performed. It happens, at times, that the girl leaves the man with whom she has eloped, because she can't get on with him or his parents, or for some other reasons. In this case there are two possibilities: She either marries another man at once, or her parents force her to return to the first man. *(Bosnia, Banjaluka district)*

Other examples reveal the complete change of meaning of the ancient custom under new economic conditions:

The girl steals away from her parents' home in agreement with the boy. This is the most frequent way for girls to get married, because parents thus save the great expense of engagement and wedding. For this reason also, there are no serious clashes. There are no Otmicas; they stopped a long time ago. *(Bosnia, Sarajevo district)*

Otmica has lost its romantic character. It is merely used to conceal material difficulties in connection with the wooing according with ancient custom which is extremely expensive. Strictly speaking, there is no Otmica but only a pretended one. *(Bosnia, Derventa district)*

In Serbia, a strong Otmica tradition existed. At the end of the last century, according to several reports, girls were often kidnapped who had never even seen the boy, for the simple reason that he presumed his wooing would be rejected. At the time of this investigation, only vestiges of this practice could be observed. Although reports from many villages speak of Otmicas, this custom had obtained another, modern veneer, because in Serbia living conditions had adapted themselves to the new economic situation, and this change was brought about quickly and thoroughly. Two examples:

There are plenty of cases of Otmicas, generally because of material conditions, if a rich girl falls in love with a poor boy.

*(Serbia, Kosmaj district)*

Very often girls marry against their parents' will. At first the parents are offended, declining any relation with the eloped girl and her new home. Later on, however, they become reconciled in most cases and become friendly with the other family. *(Serbia, Dobričevo district)*

In Croatia, Otmica existed only in some Dinaric districts with an Orthodox population. There is an important difference between these Croatian districts and Serbia. In Croatian districts, the custom of bride abduction depended on the surplus of men in the village, and had been maintained only in the villages with a female minority. Such villages existed in two areas, in the Dalmatian Highlands and in the rocky "Lika" districts. In these Croatian areas there were Otmicas and desertion in 80 per cent of all villages with a surplus of men and in 24 per cent of all villages with a surplus of women.

In Serbia, the numerical proportion of the sexes played no part. There were as many Otmicas in villages with a great surplus of women as in villages with a small surplus of them. (The number of villages with a surplus of men in Serbia was negligible.) The fact that the custom, which originally had been linked closely with surplus of men, was maintained under entirely changed conditions points to the general conservatism in the relation of sexes, as well as to the guerilla and Hayduk tradition in Serbia.

Let us now turn to the patriarchal regions, which on the graph show a similarity to the modern ones. The following report from Montenegro shows that an unshaken patriarchal set-up offered no suitable base for independent action:

The marriage of a girl against her parents' will is quite rare. In such a case, relations between the young wife and her family remain very loose, even after reconciliation. Even in the man's family she is treated like a stepchild, she is given a derogatory name such as "run-in-girl," and she is respected neither in the house nor by relatives.

*(Montenegro, Andrijevica district)*

In the Albanian villages of Macedonia, bride abduction and elopement occur only in exceptional cases:

Very rarely does a girl marry against her parents' will, but if she does or if she deserts her home for that of her chosen one, then her parents become reconciled soon after her escape, or two, three, or more years afterwards. Or there may arise quarrels, slaughter, and blood feud, especially if the girl had been promised to another man.

*(Al. Macedonia, Struga district)*

Girls usually do not marry against their parents' will. They can only try to obtain their parents' consent through the intervention of relatives. Bashfulness would prevent them from discussing themselves the matter with their parents.

*(Macedonia, Gornji Polog district, village with mixed population)*

In the orthodox part of Macedonia, in accordance with the generally predominant peaceful style of living, abduction of women was less widespread than bride buying. Even in cases of Otmicas, negotiations were entered in order to reach a settlement. A report published in a women's review shows the fusion of the heroic motif and bargaining. It is a story of abduction and counter-abduction:[8]

Cveta is a "deserter" from her home. She left six weeks ago while her father was away from their village on military duty, and she went to Goce's house. Her father was infuriated with his daughter. However, Goce's father for a month prepared the wedding feast for his only son. Goce, accompanied by his uncle, took Cveta to town. Cveta's father, who had been informed of this in time, prepared an Otmica on his part. Thus, returning from town, Cveta was kidnapped by her father. Confusion and consternation reigned in the young man's house—the bride had vanished! The news of the kidnapping came like a flash of lightning from the blue, pervading the whole house with anxiety and grief. Goce's father, irritated like a wounded beast of prey, breathed vengeance. He snatched up his gun and disappeared, firmly resolved to capture the girl or shed blood. Late at night at the house of Cveta's father, through the intervention of an array of Goce's neighbors, a peace treaty and settlement was arrived at. My little pupil who had assisted in the negotiations told us about it at school: "In the name of Goce's father we offered 2,500 dinars for obtaining the girl. Her father only agreed after difficulties. The story goes that this morning other people came offering 3,000 dinars. If we had not received her, they would have taken her." Another schoolboy added: "It was only a matter of money not of the peace treaty."

In Macedonia, cases of desertion from home were frequent, which points to the comparatively great activity of the girls. This was probably due to the fact that, in this region, many girls were marrying younger boys. In the following replies, interviewers strictly distinguished between Otmicas and desertion from home.

There are no cases of Otmicas, only *Begankas*—desertion from home in agreement with the boy's family. Often the entire village is aware of the fact that such and such girl will elope on such a date.

*(Ch. Macedonia, Veles district)*

[8] Minjin, in the review *Žena Danas (The Woman of Today)*, Zagreb, 1939.

Girls sometimes run away from their parents' home. If the parents altogether object to the boy whom the girl desires, then it often happens that she "breaks out." After some time, she and the boy's parents come to an agreement and become reconciled. If a girl makes up her mind to run away, she prepares some clothes in advance, as she would not get them otherwise, and, aided by the boy's friends, she escapes to his home. (*Ch. Macedonia, St. Nikola Ovčepolje district*)

Recently many girls have married against their parents' wishes. They escape to the boys. The parents are angry. The girl does not visit them for years. In the end they are reconciled. Otmicas, real kidnapping of girls against their will, are now very rare, although formerly there were such cases. The boy aided by some friends kidnapped the girl and dragged her into his house. The girl's parents were always the victims of this procedure, because the abductors bribed the Turks—the police force—and the latter threatened the parents if they tried to intervene.
(*Macedonia, St. Nikola Ovčepolje district*)

In all regions, the term "Otmica" had the ring of a stormy, belligerent past and a living tradition, with the exception of Central Croatia and the Littoral. These areas were never or only shortly under the Turkish reign, and here Otmica was not familiar either by name or idea. To be sure, cases of abduction and eloping were practiced, but they were not looked upon as Otmica. The interviewers and their informants decidedly reject the term, and asserted that Otmica is non-existent. In Croatia and the Littoral, women were generally neither courted by many suitors nor least of all kidnapped. As regards the position of marriageable girls, the following reply is characteristic:

Otmicas—kidnapping—do not exist. Girls would rather kidnap a boy if they were able to do so. (*Croatia*)

It is apparent in the case of Otmica that a very old custom, probably of Oriental origin, suddenly expanded. Otmica spread in times of stormy transformation in the villages where there was no lack of a belligerent tradition.

Otmica, typical for regions in transition, and bride purchase, characteristic of intact patriarchal areas are two symptoms of one fact, namely the value of the rarity of women at present or in the near past. In Graph 32, where both customs are presented, the curve shows a plain, descending tendency.

The sudden drop of the curve toward "modern" regions indicates the diminishing value of rarity and the decreased demand for the wife.

Graph 32. Bride abduction and bride purchase

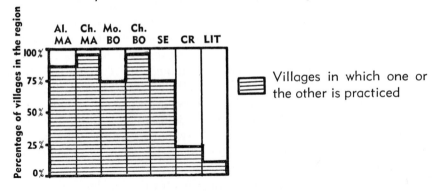

Villages in which one or the other is practiced

## The Dowry

A typical attitude of people toward dowry in a community with subsistence economy, patriarchal regime, and zadruga living can be seen from the following report of a public meeting in southern Dalmatia about eighty years ago.[9] The peasant Andrija had been told that Nikola, the husband of his sister, intended to claim part of Andrija's farm as a dowry. On the occasion of a great church celebration, Andrija, after mass, addressed the assembled people, explaining the matter and asking their advice:

The priest [an Orthodox minister]: "Is it true, Nikola? Has your misfortune confused your senses?"

Nikola: "Well, everyone strives after one's own, and so I want mine."

The priest: "Now then, had not the late Alexa given you his daughter, as is the custom in the whole country and the whole world, or has he sold her to you like a cow? Don't be silly, don't let your mother mourn over you in her grave; don't soil your honor in the face of the whole world so that your name will be disgraced and in everybody's mouth like that of Vuk Branković [the traitor of Kosovo]!"

Nikola: "Steady, priest, in the name of this church let us talk sense. You know that my wife, Marija, is the legitimate daughter of the late Alexa, just as Andrija is his son. Both of them were carried under the same heart and fed by the same breast. Please note that the civil law contains the provision that the paternal or maternal heritage must be equally distributed between the sons and daughters. All are equal before God and the Emperor. If you don't believe me, there are plenty of lawyers in Cattaro: Go and ask whether this is stated in the code of laws."

Now Andrija's other two brothers-in-law jumped up, asking the priest: "Now then priest, by the priests of heaven! Keep quiet and

[9] Vuk Vrčević, *Niz srpskih pripovijedaka (Serbian Stories)*, Pančevo, 1881.

don't forget what you want to say." The older brother-in-law: "Which lawyer, you wretched son! Don't soil the bones of your deceased parents, nor those of our late father-in-law, Alexa. Our blood shall not soil you, may the salt and bread which we have jointly eaten in the house of our parents-in-law turn into leprosy for you! You have got lost, may your senses be blackened! And even though the Cattaro law-courts should adjudicate in your favor, and all the seven kings of the world confirm their verdict, all this will be no use whatever as long as we two sons-in-law are alive and Andrija joins us as a third. We don't send you word through an intermediary, but tell you to your face."

Then follows the speech of the village headman, after which the people talk.

The people: "What you say is gospel truth to us. As long as we keep our old customs, God will help us. If Nikola fails to withdraw his claim but tries to get his way, we shall drive away this black sheep from our pure flock. May he look for a girl with a dowry to feed him."

The priest: "What do you say now, Nikola? Choose as you like, you hawk! But remember the village is always stronger than the bear. You see that some kind of sin has dragged you to an abyss causing you to pick a quarrel with your brothers and the villagers. Pray to God and rid yourself of worldly knavery. Ill-gotten goods seldom prosper! Shake off these silly ideas and these foreign unusual garments. Fly back to your flock and give yourself up to your work! Stick to your handicraft like your father did, and in this way you will be a true brother! Woe to him who has no brother!"

During all these attacks, Nikola was standing there saying nothing, and he did not know what to reply. His wife was standing in a corner among the other peasant women. She had hidden her face in her apron, and was sobbing audibly. As Nikola gave no answer the village elder called out to him: "Speak, Nikola, people have not gathered here to look at you! Speak before something happens to you as, indeed, it should happen. It is all your fault, not ours."

Nikola, after a pause: "Yes . . . what shall I answer you, my brethren? I realize now that I have lost my reason, trespassing against God and you, and that by leading a vagrant life I have harmed myself most of all. My laziness has driven me to extreme distress, and, living abroad, I have become a stranger to myself. Which of you has never erred in this deceptive world, and who will never err? I listened to the priest reading the gospel; he spoke of the prodigal son who squandered all his belongings and then returned to his father naked and barefooted. That's what happened to me. Although you can not all be father to me you may be my brothers in God. My fate now lies in your hands. I ask your forgiveness, and, in the first place, the forgiveness of my brothers-in-law. Accept me as your brother, although I do not deserve it."

So they made their peace. Andrija invited his sister and her husband to his house, entertaining them for ten days and giving them many presents when they left. The other villagers in their turn helped Nikola, so that, in the course of some years, by diligence and work, he gained fresh energy and could settle his debts. He had two sons and a daughter.

As shown by this report, patriarchal peasants considered the dowry the height of injustice and indignity. Nevertheless, within a few decades the dowry was introduced in those South Slav areas where money economy had infiltrated.

As a rule the dowry consisted of an important part of the paternal possessions and, in principle, differed in significance from the "marriage portion" or the bride's outfit. The dowry was closely connected with the heritage due to the daughter. Sometimes the daughter received her entire heritage as dowry in her father's lifetime. Therefore, theoretically the dowry depended on the legal provisions of the right of inheritance. Since laws were not unified, the different civil laws in force before the unification of Yugoslavia—Austrian, Hungarian, Serbian, Croatian, and others—had remained in force in the various historical regions. There were seven different legal areas, plus the Moslem areas, where Mohammedan religious law—Sheriat law—was in force for matrimony and inheritance. The provisions for inheritance differed widely in these eight areas.

In reality, however, these provisions had no decisive effect on actual customs and the practice of dowry and inheritance. The patriarchal regime in particular forcefully resisted modern provisions of the law which conflicted with its maxims and which did not sufficiently consider the zadruga structure of family and economy. The attitude of people in patriarchal regions toward dowry was completely *uniform and uninfluenced* by the eight inheritance laws which were in force: The daughter obtained neither a dowry nor an inheritance. The maxim in these regions was: "It's dowry enough to have found a wife." (*Macedonia, Skoplje district.*)

In Macedonia and neighboring districts, legal provisions in force were in accordance with Serbian or Montenegrin law (the two being similar). According to these provisions, the daughters did not inherit anything after their father's death. They were merely entitled to an outfit when getting married—the so-called "suitable contribution toward the establishment of the household"—a settlement within the scope of the father's means and in accordance with prevailing customs. This "outfit" was, as a rule, a much smaller portion of the inheritance than the portion given to the sons.

For Moslems throughout the country, the Sheriat law was in force, providing more favorable provisions for the daughters than the Serbian law. According to a complicated key that classified the assets included in the estate (house, farm, fields, cattle, cash, and so forth), daughters were entitled to one-quarter, one-half or three-quarters of the inheritance. However, these provisions had likewise no influence on practice where the patriarchal setup remained unimpaired. For the most part, women did not take advantage of their title to inheritance and dowry. Examples from Macedonia show such behavior in its purest form:

> The girl rarely brings a dowry into married life and only if her father dies, and her brothers divide the property. In such cases, she also gets her share but only if she insists on it, which happens very rarely. In the majority of cases the girl brings no dowry. Nor does the husband demand it, because he would be ashamed to accept it from his wife.
>
> *(Ch. Macedonia, Galičnik district)*

> Everything is inherited by the sons. The girl is entitled to a "suitable contribution to the establishment of the household"; according to Sheriat laws, also to a portion of the heritage, but as a rule no demand is made for the latter. The girl brings her outfit, for instance linen, clothes and so forth, in addition to shirts, garments, kerchiefs and similar articles for the other members of the house. She likewise takes along some household articles such as mattresses, chests, blankets, sheets. *(Al. Macedonia, Struga district)*

> No dowry is brought; the girl brings only wedding presents, her own linen, and clothes. Only when there is no heir, she brings a dowry. The outfit is bought from the purchase price paid by the man for the girl.
>
> *(Ch. Macedonia, Nerodimlje district)*

In the Moslem part of Bosnia Sheriat law was in force just as it was in the Moslem part of Macedonia, that is, it was valid for Moslem villages or families. In view of the fact, however, that marriage in Bosnia became so difficult, the dowry customarily was substantial, and it also became the custom that daughters accepted the paternal heritage. The fact that Bosnia had come under the influence of a modern state one generation earlier, breaking off from Turkish traditions, was reflected in this practice. Only now and then the old way of thinking and behavior toward inheritance was maintained. Sometimes marked signs of decadence of the customs were shown as the following example indicates:

> The father-in-law of a friend of mine, Omer, had died. Omer's wife, the daughter of the deceased, had authorized her husband to obtain the

dowry, that is, the inheritance. When everything had been distributed, Omer received from his brother-in-law (his wife's brother) among other things also 15,000 dinars as a return for some portions of the dowry; a very large sum in view of the circumstances of this place. Omer took the money, went to the inn, and said in front of all the people: "I have made up my mind to accept the dowry in defiance of everybody, but I do not wish to derive profit from it and for this reason I will spend the whole of the money on drink." He was as good as his word: He went to Zenica and did not come home before he had spent the whole sum on drinks. His wife does not permit anyone to reproach him, although he drinks to this day in spite of being the father of ten children.

*(Moslem Bosnia, Travnik district)*

However, this romantic attitude of people was disappearing, and the dowry gradually became mandatory. The heritage shared according to Sheriat law was, as a rule, accepted by the wife:

The wife does not immediately bring dowry but only the bridal outfit: blankets, a carpet, jugs, and her needlework as embroidered towels, kerchiefs, trousers, and shirts. Later, after the father's death she accepts the dowry from her brothers. Generally she receives her share of the estate, sometimes she accepts an amount of money for it.

*(Moslem Bosnia, Rogatica district)*

The bridal outfit comprises some beddings and furniture, mostly cushions for the wall benches used in Moslem houses, some copper pots and pans, coffee cups, a glass, and that is all. When her father dies she takes her share in the inheritance.     *(Moslem Bosnia, Brčko district)*

As a dowry she brings goods and landed property, likewise money. Moslems bring ducats and cattle—20 sheep or more.

*(Moslem Bosnia, Mostar district, Herzegovina)*

In the Christian parts of Bosnia, the daughters were in a still better position than Moslem women, because according to Austrian laws sons and daughters enjoyed equal rights. However, if these villages had remained patriarchal, women did not take advantage of the legal provisions but frequently renounced their claims:

After the marriage the wife usually renounces her claim in favor of her brothers. Only a girl who has no brothers usually brings a dowry. The bride brings her "garments," that is to say, her own clothes, and presents for the wedding guests and the husband's relatives.

*(Christian Bosnia, Stolac district, Herzegovina)*

(In the previous Orthodox village a purchase price for the wife is unusual. The groom hands some money to the girl so that she can buy the outfit for her wedding.)

211

Sisters from Orthodox families often do not accept anything. Mostly they bring some clothes and jewelry, rarely property or money.

*(Bosnia, Sarajevo district)*

(In the previous village, with a mixed population of Orthodox and Moslems, the mandatory purchase price for a woman is between 500 and 2,000 dinars.)

The following report shows a device used to nullify the daughter's right of inheritance:

> Often the zadruga is divided, when the father has confidence in his sons, knowing that they are "neither drunkards nor gamblers," and when he is afraid that the daughters might carry the patrimony to their husbands. In such cases the father portions out his estate during his lifetime among his sons, entering this transfer in the register of landed property. *(Christian Bosnia, Bijeljina district)*

In Bosnia, all degrees of transition could be found, from the renunciation of dowry and heritage in the patriarchal style to the insistence on all rights. Here, where ancient customs were partly giving way fast to new ones, there were villages where brides were purchased according to old tradition, while others brought dowries.

In Serbia, the old Serbian laws were in force. In conformity with zadruga rule, the daughters were not entitled to the property of the paternal zadruga, and, consequently, inherited nothing. They had only a claim to a "suitable contribution toward the establishment of a household." This amount was then growing larger:

> The sons inherit everything. Daughters receive nothing whatever, except their bridal outfit. After the father's death, the sons usually share the property. The mother is entitled to usufruct as long as she lives. However, only the sons are legal heirs. As a rule, they separate after marriage and divide the paternal heritage.
>
> The wife, as a rule, brings a dowry in personal chattels or, if she is the only child, landed property. Sometimes also between 800 and 5,000 dinars in cash and her outfit. This money is jointly put by, and, if possible, not spent. Mostly they use it for the purchase of cattle.

*(Serbia, Kosmaj district)*

Although conditions had completely changed in Serbia in the decades prior to this investigation, the law of inheritance had remained unaltered. Yet, influenced by new circumstances, a new practice had asserted itself, which, to a certain extent, was in conflict with the spirit of the inheritance law. Fathers started to furnish their daughters large dowries in order to make it possible for them to get married. A peasant near Belgrade told me, shaking his head:

212

Parents must work hard nowadays, for even the poorest fellow, indeed a cripple, demands a dowry. In the end, however, they all get married. Nobody lives alone.     *(Serbia, surroundings of Belgrade)*

Other reports point out the same tendency:

The girl brings a dowry of money and property; this happened more and more within late years. Young men like to take a girl from a wealthy home, even though she does not get much of a dowry. The sisters obtain much less than the brothers. Here the custom of giving a dowry started only seven or eight years ago. Nowadays the girl obtains landed property or money up to 20,000 dinars.

*(Serbia, Dragačevo district)*

The wife brings property, cattle, sometimes also money, all of which became customary just lately. In any case she must receive a portion of landed property, even though her brothers are alive. The brothers give their sister her share.     *(Serbia, Zvižd district)*

The majority of women bring a dowry. "Some dowry has to be given, then marriage will be possible," goes the saying. Girls from homes with many daughters, especially, obtain dowries. Principally money, but also cattle and an outfit.     *(Serbia, Kosmaj district)*

The girls bring a dowry consisting of either money or landed property. Lately this has been more and more true.     *(Serbia, Dragačevo district)*

In Serbia, it could be observed that economic development anticipated legislation, and that the practices of dowry and inheritance kept pace with this development. Here the situation was contrary to that in Croatia, where progressive laws had been introduced which did not fully take into account the undeveloped economy. Here and there the customs adapted themselves to economic facts rather than to existing laws.

In Croatia and the Littoral, which long had belonged to Austria, legal conditions differed fundamentally from those in the former Turkish provinces. A steadily increasing number of farms became subject to Austrian or Hungarian (respectively, Croatian) law, according sons and daughters equal rights to the paternal inheritance. As long as zadruga estates were undivided, they were subject to a separate zadruga law which conceded to the daughter no claim to paternal property. Within the zadruga, actually nothing was bequeathed because the surviving members of the zadruga remained together. Through their marriages, daughters lost their claim in the paternal zadruga, but, on the other hand, they obtained equal rights in the home of the husband or the father-in-law. In dividing the zadruga, collective property was distributed to single owners, and

213

each of the single owners was from then on subject to the provisions of the civil law, according to which all children had equal inheritance rights.

In Croatia, the legal situation of the woman was therefore more favorable than in Serbia. In most districts, individual peasants including the daughters guarded their legal interests. As a rule the dowry was rather high, often reaching the full extent of the expected inheritance. The law and practice in this region were in accord, probably because the long lasting influence of the Austrian laws of succession and the early penetration of the money-economy. In spite of everything, however, peasants of the few patriarchal districts of Croatia evaded the laws of inheritance regarding female succession. Examples from these areas:

> The sons inherit everything. Daughters are generally "liquidated" by a bridal outfit. As a rule the daughter resigns her portion of the inheritance after her father's death. It is considered a disgrace to take away a part from her brothers.     (*Croatia, Šibenik district, Dalmatia*)

> The father wishes to appoint his sons his sole heirs. He tries to provide for the sons by all means, even though he should have to sell the farm in order to prevent the daughters from participating in the inheritance. Sometimes he is unable to evade the law which makes it mandatory to leave a portion of the heritage to the daughters because the provisions that half of the property must be distributed among the children cannot easily be circumvented.     (*Croatia, Knin district, Dalmatia*)

In most districts of Croatia, however, the practice of dowry and inheritance was in accord with the law. The daughters asserted their claims to the paternal heritage, and the dowry became one of the chief conditions of their marriage:

> Before his death, the father distributes the property in equal portions among his children, that is to say, among the children who have remained at home. Those of his children who have left the house or have married into another house, had been previously endowed with a "dowry"—including sons. The wife brings dowry, richer girls bring some acres of land, a sewing machine, a cow, and their outfit.
>
> (*Croatia, Sv. Ivan Zelina district*)

In the period of the survey, besides landed property, cash payment also was demanded as a dowry, which the peasants found most difficult to provide:

> The wife obtains a field, a pasture, or forest land, likewise money; but in the majority of cases the latter is merely promised. If this remains unpaid within a certain space of time, it often causes quarrels.
>
> (*Croatia, Varaždin district*)

214

In the course of years there was a growing tendency to make cash an essential part of the dowry. However, this process was slowed down and stopped by the depression of the thirties:

As a dowry, the girl obtains money, cattle, and a sewing machine. After the war, during prosperity, the dowry on an average amounted to 40,000 dinars. Nowadays the amount has decreased to 7,000 dinars. As to cattle, a cow is generally handed over.    (*Croatia, Karlovac district*)

In spite of contrary tendencies, the importance of money for the dowry is increasing, even in remote, conservative mountain villages of Dalmatia:

As a rule the wife brings a dowry, cattle, and landed property, but in the majority of cases money. Nowadays this is the main thing. In former times a dowry was likewise desired, but it was not a condition for marriage. Formerly the chief point was a good family, a good reputation, health. Nowadays there is a great demand for the "dowrybearer." The amount of the dowry is fixed by agreement, but more often the following custom is observed:

On the occasion of the groom's formal asking for the bride's hand, the girl or her parents are handed a red bundle in which apples or a hundred-dinar note, or several of them are wrapped up. If this is accepted, it means that the match is acceptable. At the wedding the girl must then bring along as many thousand-dinar notes as hundred-dinar notes had been received by her.    (*Croatia, Knin district, Dalmatia*)

This description combines traditional and commercial elements which were characteristic for Dalmatia.

Quite peculiar were conditions in the former "Military March." Although in these districts economic conditions had abruptly adjusted to a money economy that was furthered by the inflow of dollars sent from America by the numerous emigrants, the traditional fighting mood had not disappeared. The inflow of money to this setup with its backward subsistence economy resulted in peculiar reactions in family life which expressed themselves in the attitudes concerning marriage and dowry:

The dowry is obligatory: If the promised dowry remains unpaid, the daughter-in-law must return to her parents. (*Croatia, Vojnić district*)

The wife brings personal chattels into her husband's home, money, as a rule, and a sewing machine. The husband arranges with the girl's parents that her dowry, for instance 5,000 dinars, will be fully paid to him after the girl is taken from her parents' home. However, to make quite sure that he will obtain the promised dowry, he refrains from having the marriage ceremony performed at once, in spite of having the girl brought to his home and of living with her. It often happens that the dowry remains unpaid for a year or even two years, or that it is not paid at all. All children born to the couple during the interval are illegitimate. Even after the wedding ceremony has taken place, the parents omit to take the necessary steps for legalization, because they don't wish to bother about such "trifles" and to pay stamp duties.

(Croatia, Vrginmost district)

Slavonia, a part of Croatia, rich in corn and wood, had early been included into the sphere of money economy, progressing at the slow pace of the nineteenth century. Hence many zadruga customs had been preserved. In spite of the friendly atmosphere prevailing in Slavonia, however, life was disturbed by inexorable, steadily growing material requirements for marriage:

According to our zadruga law, the wife obtains no landed property; but if a girl does own some landed property, she thereby gains special value. . . . The laws cannot be easily changed but they may be rendered ineffective. New customs are grafted upon old ideas, and this leads to gradual disappearance of the old. Just as our neighbor, each mother wishes to secure happiness for her child. According to law, the girl obtains no landed property; however, the new capitalistic era calls for a dowry. To begin with, ducats are wanted followed by a constantly growing urgent demand for landed property. All girls dream of being an only child, and they sing a song with the verse:

> In father's chest there are one hundred ducats piled
> Alas, I wish I was his only child!

When the first-born is a girl, the mother is tempted to make her "mother's one and only" in order to fulfill the ardent desire of all girls. If the wife fails to give birth to another child, the whole property is left to the girl, and she becomes an "heiress."[10] (*Croatia [Slavonia]*)

In the Littoral, the last traces of zadruga customs were disappearing:

After the parents' death, the whole property of a family goes to the children, sons and daughters obtaining equal portions. If a girl gets married, she receives immediately everything that would come to her by inheritance, for instance, part of the vineyard, of the olive grove, the house, the fishing nets. Consequently the whole country is divided into small plots of land.  (*Littoral, Isle of Mljet*)

From the time that economy with the money nexus penetrated into the village, private property gained paramount significance for each family, as well as for each member within the family. In the

---

[10] Nada Sremec, *Nismo mi krive* (*We Are Not to Blame*), Zagreb, 1938.

patriarchal districts, the village common, which included a large sector of the land consisting of pasture and woods, had played an important part. With the economic changes, the village common was divided up and sold, and each farm could dispose only of its private property. As a result of repeated divisions, the farms became smaller; hence even the smallest lot of ground gained in importance for the single farm. For each person within the family, individual property— what he or she would obtain as inheritance or dowry—became of decisive importance. The material interests of each member competed with the interests of the others, an atmosphere which contrasted with that in the zadruga system. These facts as well as the changes in the numerical proportion of sexes caused a fundamental change in the relationships between the members of the family and between marriageable girls and boys. The sisters claimed the rights against the brothers and the young man made his demands concerning the dowry.

Is it true, as had been said, that the institution of a dowry means that material interests dominate human relations? According to some reports, the introduction of a dowry as requirement for marriage signifies the exchange of selfless bliss for commercialism and selfishness. Things are not so simple. Parents have, at all times, sought security for their children. Even during the zadruga period certain material calculations were not absent when children were given away in marriage; even then the wealthier family offered greater security. The concept that a girl constituted a value "in herself"—a value for which the groom had to pay—did not necessarily constitute a lack of interest in material values, but merely showed that in zadruga times the girl and her family were able to profit from their more favorable position. During that time a marriage meant a heavy burden for the groom, because he had to pay for the bride, while in a later period the roles were reversed and the burden was on the girl's family, which had to furnish a dowry.

Nevertheless, there was a basic difference between the modern and traditional systems. In the patriarchal period, the "buyer" was a collective, the zadruga as such; in the later period, the buyer was a small family. The action taken by an important, well-to-do zadruga in finding a wife for one of its young members had a different significance and provoked different reactions than when a single peasant, the owner of a small farm, gives his daughter in marriage. A wedding could indeed be a heavy burden for a small peasant family, and sometimes it even meant ruin for it to pay out a dowry in cash or to cut up the property. On the basis of our reports it is not possible to give an unequivocal answer to the question whether the dowry was a symptom of the increase of the material element in marriage. There is no doubt, however, that the requirement of a dowry caused many unfortunate phenomena which at zadruga time did not exist.

A little Slavonian song shows the girl's pride in the possession of a dowry:

> From mother the ducats
> From father a grant
> Will allow me to marry
> The fellow I want.

The girl's exuberance is, however, a bubble which is bound to burst when touched by reality. It is a fact that the strict requirements for a dowry and inheritance poisoned family living even in an area with "new stability," as shown by the following report from Slavonia.

### The Portion[11]

I asked the peasant woman of forty-two: Neighbor Oliva, is it really true that a girl who has no heritage has no chance?

Yes, it is true. That is to say, I would not exactly claim that a girl will not marry at all; she must marry—what else should she do? But not the way she would deserve it. Listen how it was with me. You know my Janja. The girl is pretty, virtuous, healthy, good to look at—she was 17. I and my Franjo have saved ducats for her. I brought along to Franjo five big Maria Theresia coins and eight small ones and, as I told you, we got more of them later, and tied 18 big ones and 20 small ones around Janja's neck. The entire village knows how good and hard-working my child is. I expect that she will marry into the most distinguished house of the village, for we, too, are counted among the better ones—as you know our zadruga has 25 acres. Well, you see, the fall came and went, and my Janja remained with us. Never mind, I thought, next year it will happen. Next year Djuka got married and he was the one who would have fitted so well to her—but no one knocked at my Janja's door. Holy Virgin, what will happen to the child?

What was the reason that Janja did not have any suitors?

What indeed! She has no portion, no landed property. There are only a few wealthy boys in the village, and the only sons want to get land. Everyone seeks to enlarge his property. The two or three who would have been suitable for her married—and my child stayed behind. Now I'll tell you everything the way it happened. My first born was a boy and I thought: "I'll get one more, perhaps God will give me a girl."

---

11 Nada Sremec, *Nismo mi krive* (*We Are Not to Blame*), Zagreb, 1938.

You are a mother yourself and you know, how it is that one likes to have a girl better than to have a boy. After all, what's a boy? He is as hard as a stick, and almost becomes a stranger to his own mother once he gets married. And a girl is kind to her mother and is close to her all her life. When I had my second child, it was another boy. Well, we have enough land, enough for two, if they are decent. One of them we can send to the city to school, to become a gentleman, and then it is surely enough land. These are my thoughts night and day while working, and I hope for sure to have a girl when I get my third child—and more I do not want under any circumstances. And indeed, my third child is Janja. We prepared linen and clothes for her, we worked hard, but you know how it is: Ducats for the girl, and acres for the boys. That's all right and the way it should be. She'll get landed property anyway in the zadruga into which she marries. That's why it is the duty of the parents to see that the girl does not marry into a smaller farm than the one she left, and so everything is settled. But you know the song:

What good is a dowry with embroidery and lace—
If she has no land she doesn't get any place.

Everybody is madly longing for a portion. But if a girl has brothers she has no heritage in land. And so my Janja is nineteen, and I can see disaster ahead. I tie two more big ducats around her neck, but it doesn't do any good. Some suitors show up, but what kind! Out of the question for my Janja. Is she supposed to lower herself from 25 acres to 10? I don't even want to hear about it, and neither does my Franjo, and the child just keeps crying. When she reaches her twentieth birthday, I tell her: "Janja, my child, go ahead, wait no longer. Go ahead little lamb, lower your sights as the good God wants it, it probably is His will." So she got married, she is all right but—12 acres are not 25. So you see, if Janja had been my first born, and if I had had no other children, she would have been my only child, our heiress. Then, well, then—God knows whom she would have gotten for a husband, but why talk about it, you know how it is.

## Marriage Age

... Things went also this way with Maxim, the fifteen-year-old shepherd boy from the little Macedonian mountain village.[12] They simply sent word to him from the village that he had to get married and had to come down to the wedding. A peasant who happened to be passing the pasture where Maxim was guarding the sheep brought him the news. He had called out to him from a distant mountain path:

"Your father sends you word to come down to the village. Yesterday they brought you the bride, and tomorrow is the wedding."

[12] From newspaper *Vreme*, Belgrade, 1938.

Maxim accepted this news quietly and without excitement, just as news without special significance is accepted. Holding his stout shepherd's hook in his hand, he leisurely walked down to the village. Before leaving, he had asked a friend to look after his sheep, only until tomorrow, as he would be back by then.

And so it was. While the drunken wedding guests were celebrating his feast in high spirits, he started back to the mountains without greeting his young wife, almost without having spoken to her. He had to go back to his sheep, his young wife he would see some other time.

For Maxim knows very well, just as all the other people knew, that the wedding and everything connected with it had not been arranged for his sake, but that the house, the zadruga, required a fresh, healthy and cheap hand, someone who would help to dig up the ground in the spring.

It often happens that a father keeps begging the village priest for days and weeks to marry his fourteen-year-old boy, who, according to church law and civil law, is not of an age to marry.

If the priest replies that he is not allowed to do so, that he is unable to fulfill the father's wish and, finally, that it would be a sin against the boy, the peasant will not be convinced and will persist in spite of all arguments, with his only counter argument: "There is nobody to do the work, I am in great distress, Sir. . . ."

Marriage ages of boys and girls varied greatly in the South Slav regions. In some parts it was a matter of course that half-grown young people got married, while in other parts it was considered natural that the betrothed couple be mature people. In some districts it was an acknowledged norm that the girl be older than the boy; in others, vice versa. The average marriage age was peculiar in that it changed much more quickly than all other rules and norms, and, after a short time, it hardened into established norms. This means that marriage age was more closely interwoven with economic changes with which it kept pace than were other customs and usages. Graph 33 shows the average differences in age between husband and wife for Orthodox and Catholic regions. It is evident that higher age of the husband was by no means considered normal everywhere.

The situation where the husband is older than his wife was much more frequent in modern areas than in patriarchal ones. In half of the Macedonian villages, the marriage of an older girl with a younger man was considered normal; in many villages the girl was much older than the boy. In Serbia, this situation was found only in a small

Graph 33. Difference in age between man and wife

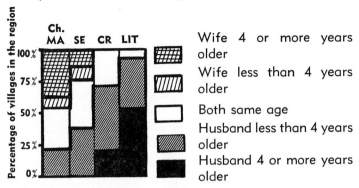

Wife 4 or more years older

Wife less than 4 years older

Both same age

Husband less than 4 years older

Husband 4 or more years older

number of villages. For this custom, which is to be found chiefly in Orthodox areas, the answers include some peculiar explanations:

*Macedonia*:

The girl should always be older than the boy, so as to be *more reasonable*.

Formerly bribes had to be used to get boys of thirteen married. Nowadays rigorous measures are taken; under eighteen years it is impossible by law!

Most men get married at the age of fifteen, sixteen, seventeen, and eighteen years. They rarely get married after completion of military service. After that they cannot find a wife; they are avoided by girls who believe they are old once they had completed their military service. Widowers find it difficult to get married; as a matter of fact it is impossible for them.

In the majority of cases girls are five, six, seven, eight, nine, and ten years older than their future husbands.

Generally speaking, boys get married at the ages of seventeen to twenty. In some cases even fifteen or sixteen years. The boy takes the girl and keeps her in his home until he has the legal right to marry her.

Boys marry very young, from sixteen years upward. Some of them wait a long time because they are unable to find a wife. Some poor men die in old age as bachelors. People of the same age do not marry. Girls are almost thirty when they get married, boys are sixteen and seventeen.

Formerly boys got married very early, say at fourteen and fifteen years. However, as this is not permitted nowadays by ecclesiastical law, they marry as soon as they have reached the legal age of seventeen years. Unless they get married before their military service, marriage is rendered more difficult for them.

Girls get married between twenty and twenty-five years and sometimes later. In the majority of cases girls are older than boys, sometimes by eight to ten years, or more.

*Serbia*:

Men marry before reaching military age, and always girls older than themselves, that is to say girls of twenty-three, twenty-four, or twenty-five. As a rule men are younger. The difference in age differs between one and eight years. The wife is hard working, that is why she must be older.

In most cases people of the same age marry each other, or the man is somewhat older. Formerly it was the other way around, and the girls were older than the boys.

In Moslem and Catholic districts, the situation of older wife-younger husband was the exception. Equal age of husband and wife or the greater age of the husband were considered normal:

*Moslem Bosnia*:

Men marry at the age of eighteen, even earlier when necessary. My pupil of the fourth grade of elementary school married at the age of thirteen. Difference of age between husband and wife is common, and the following rule is observed: If a child of thirteen, fourteen, or fifteen marries (meaning the boy) then the girl is eighteen, nineteen or twenty, and vice versa.

The man usually marries a younger woman, often one who is much younger. The average difference in age is three to five years, but there are also cases where he is ten and twenty years her senior, and that happens frequently.

Men marry not later than at eighteen, girls at fourteen, fifteen, and sixteen. At the age of seventeen they are considered old.

*Christian Bosnia*:

Generally boys marry girls who are one or two years their seniors.

*Croatia*:

Generally married couples are of the same age, or the husband is two or three years older. However, if there is a dowry, then even the greatest difference of age does not matter.          (*Central Croatia*)

They marry between the ages of eighteen and twenty-five, but lately there have been strikingly few weddings. Boys do not like to get married because they are afraid of losing their independence, and their parents dread a young daughter-in-law who might turn their home into hell.

(*Central Croatia*)

Men generally marry after completed military service, that is after twenty-one years. Merely "pet children" that is only children marry between the ages of sixteen and twenty-one. Girls between eighteen and twenty-five. *(Dalmatian Highlands)*

If they marry for love, husband and wife are generally of the same age. If the girl is an only child with a dowry, even if she is older, she will be taken by a much younger, poorer man. If a man returns from America with some money, he often marries a girl much younger than himself, and there are differences in age up to twenty and twenty-five years. *(Dalmatian Highlands)*

Husband and wife generally are of the same age. Often the girl is three or four years older. It is often found that such a girl proves to be more useful in the household. *(Slavonia, Orthodox village)*

Only sons frequently marry before they are seventeen, but in such cases they must obtain the Bishop's permit. In the majority of cases they marry between eighteen and twenty, very rarely after completion of military service. Such men are considered old bachelors. *(Slavonia, Catholic village)*

*Littoral Region:*

Older men mostly marry younger girls, more rarely girls of their own age. Formerly—thirty and more years ago—it used to be the other way around.

Men marry at the age of twenty-five and thirty-five and even at forty. Women between the ages of twenty-five and thirty-five, rarely up to forty.

Usually men are five to ten years older, less frequently fifteen years. Sometimes also the wife is one or two years older, but such cases are rare.

Men marry after completion of their military service at twenty-five to thirty years.

All regions went through great changes as to marriage age. In every single region there were villages where the average marriage age had gone up, as well as villages where it had gone down. Only in a few villages of each region had the average marriage age remained unchanged. What causes brought about such important changes in opposite directions?

The opinion of the interviewers was that there were two causes for the tendency toward earlier marriage. In patriarchal settings it had once been considered important that the men entering marriage were mature for the task of husband, father, and master of the house. The girl likewise was required to have a certain maturity. This situation had now changed however:

Formerly people did not get married so young as they are now, but much later. The husband had to be quite grown up and the wife quite mature, so that the children should be strong. There was a certain chivalry in this conception, because the husband had to command respect, and no one was permitted to hit him once he was married.

*(Macedonia, Albanian district)*

Formerly the view was prevalent that girls were not "mature" for marriage, matrimony, and birth before twenty-five. Nowadays girls are considered mature at fifteen and sixteen. *(Serbia)*

It is noticeable that girls today marry younger than before the war. Peasants tell me that formerly it was considered a disgrace if a girl got married earlier than her twentieth year, and nowadays girls of twenty are said to be old. They also say: "Nowadays she is hardly fifteen and marriageable. The devil is pulling her ears." In this village, boys marry later now than before the war, mostly after completing their military service, at twenty-one or twenty-two years. The result is that today older men marry younger girls. *(Croatia)*

A second reason for earlier marriages was the greater need for working women:

Boys nowadays marry younger, and the reason for this is that there is no zadruga, and the sole owner of a farm needs workers. *(Serbia)*

Today they marry younger than in former years, because the house needs hands. A great many men go as laborers to *pechalba*—and remain out of village as long as they live. Only the women live and work at home. *(Macedonia)*

Since the world war they get married at a younger age. The cause is the need for more workers. *(Sanjak)*

The opposite tendency, to raise the marriage age, also asserted itself in all regions (with the exception of the Albanian areas). The following replies point to this aspect:

The boys and girls nowadays marry later than at the time of the great zadruga families. *(Croatia [Slavonia])*

At present men marry later in life—about five or six years later than formerly. The same things apply to girls. The reason of this is the war or the depression, as boys and girls do not marry because of material difficulties. The depression is stated again and again as the reason, but the real reason lies in the time in which we live, in the desire for an easier life. A dowry is required, but the girls have no dowry. *(Croatia)*

The following reply is rather informative:

Fifty years ago boys married later in life; twenty to twenty-five years ago, however, earlier in life than now. *(Croatia [Lika area])*

This reply points to the fact that in the old, completely intact zadruga economy men married somewhat earlier than at the time of this investigation. Immediately after the break-up of the zadrugas, there was an urgent need for workers on the small farms. Sometimes the sons wanted to marry early just in order to demand the dissolution of the zadruga and to obtain independence. When, after many distributions, a large majority of the farms had been dwarfed, there was no longer such a shortage of workers; on the contrary, every additional mouth to feed meant a burden. The time had come when the farmer's sons could only marry a girl with a dowry. The young peasant could not bring a girl without a dowry into his parents' home, still less could he become independent without the dowry. Inasmuch as girls with a dowry could not easily be found, the time of the marriage was postponed and the average marriage age raised.

In Macedonia and Serbia, marriage age also was frequently lowered, and for the same reason as in Croatia. Here, too, the need for workers increased with the first pressure of the infiltrating money economy. In Serbia, agriculture became more intensive and adjusted to market requirements, and, in Macedonia, many peasants went to the cities to work as laborers. The situation in Serbia and in Macedonia corresponded to the situation in Croatia one or two generations earlier.

Like a delicate measuring instrument, marriage age registers all the subtle economic changes which mold family living in each region. The custom of getting married at a certain age seems to offer less resistance to change than other customs, perhaps for the reason that marriage age attracts little attention.

## The Change of Rôles

Few conclusions in this study are as clear and unambiguous as the worsening of the girl's chances for marriage at the time when villages began to adapt themselves to the invading money economy. And this was so regardless of the date and the rhythm of the adaptation process. The "new time" brought to all South Slav regions a surplus of women as well as a deterioration of the chances for the foundation of a family, and a strict requirement for a dowry.

Although with subsistence economy and zadruga living, the woman was on a lower scale of the patriarchal hierarchy, actually she was indispensable and therefore precious and in urgent demand. Since in this period there were fewer women than men, they were wooed by all possible means including purchase and abduction. But suddenly at a certain historical moment the scene changed and the pretentious and fastidious boy appears on the stage. Now it is he who can choose exactly whom he wishes. He demands a dowry, bargains, sends the wife back if her family does not fulfill its obligations. The boy is now precious, sought after and cajoled, while the girl and her family are in the position of buyers who look for an expensive "ware," difficult to obtain. The girls with dowries are exceptions, and the other girls have poor chances for marrying. They frequently have to resign themselves to taking someone "lesser than they are." The much desired, precious girl has vanished from the stage, the rôles are exchanged.

Yet it is by no means a simple exchange of rôles in which the girl shoulders the burden formerly carried by the boy, and the boy now has the chances formerly offered to the girl. The position of the girl is now far more difficult, for the girl of this period lives on a small and often poor farm, without the backing of the responsible, large zadruga.

The woman is also more dependent on family living than the man in an immutable biological sense. She can cope less than he can with the problem of staying single. She is weaker, more dependent on husband, mother-in-law, children, more exposed to loneliness. The man can work as a laborer in the city to save money in order to purchase a wife, while in most South Slav districts it is impossible for the girl to earn money outside her home. The man can also find satisfactions for his sexual desires which, for the girl are prohibited or dangerous. A girl without chances for marrying cannot do all that. Moreover, the single girl is condemned to living in the atmosphere of harshness and selfishness which now dominates relationships with the village and the family. The bachelor or the widower in the patriarchal era lived in the zadruga, which could support him and grant him much more help and assistance than the impoverished independent family could give to the girl. For these reasons something like voluntary bachelordom is possible for a man, while the girl is condemned to remain single only if need be.

In some places the scene changed almost overnight. It seems as if the boy heaved the sigh: "May my worry pass on to someone else," and the Worry obeyed him. Passing on to the girl, it had, however, become a much heavier burden.

# CHAPTER VIII

## Husband and Wife

WHAT were the positions, the rank and the roles given to husband and wife in the patriarchal regime? Was the wife really so humbled, so much in the background as imagined in countries which lack the patriarchal tradition? Did the break up of the patriarchal order bring the wife alleviation and advantages, or new burdens and difficulties little known in an urbanized, industrialized environment?

I had at my disposal rich material to bring to bear on these problems. My reporters had dealt with all questions relating to the positions of husband and wife with particular thoroughness. Indeed, they accepted this relationship as the central problem of family life, and, in addition to extensive replies to my questionnaire, sent me numerous descriptive pieces to illustrate the position of the woman, including profiles of individual wives who seemed to them typical. Though the majority of my inquirers were young men teachers, they developed their answers to these questions principally from the woman's standpoint.

The reason for this was that the unfavorable factors which weighed down the peasant wife had in some areas accumulated to an intolerable point. Many interviewers were revolted by the position of the wife, while the struggle of peasant sons to acquire greater rights did not seem to them so important, as this question was then already settled in favor of the younger generation. Women, as distinct from the sons, had not even raised their voices to protest against the hard conditions in which, in many districts, they were forced to live. They found in my interviewers devoted and enthusiastic advocates.

We shall see that neither in the "modern" area nor in the patriarchal did the picture quite tally with that which has gained credence in America. Indeed, in parts it is very different, showing most varied features. Not merely life in a completely patriarchal environment, but perhaps still more life in the period of transformation of that setting, offers certain features which surpass the imagination. One needs, if not personal knowledge, at least serious study of the whole dramatic process.

## Subordination of the Young Wife

The position of the wife in the family derived from the position of the snaha (daughter-in-law) in the home of the svekar (father-in-law) and svekrva (mother-in-law). When a girl married, she became not merely a wife. Primarily, she became a snaha, for as a rule marriage meant entering the home not of a husband, but of a husband's parents. The position of the *mlada* (bride or young wife, literally "young female") in the zadruga was the foundation for her later position as wife, even in subsequent periods, when zadrugas no longer existed. But so long as the zadruga was intact, the wife as mlada or *nevjesta*[1] had a special position: Her first year was a sort of examination.

If the girl loved her man, the new situation did not seem too hard to her, nor did she fear her new role much. As we have seen, she accepted all sorts of dangers to flee to the loved one. But marriage for love was not the rule. In all districts, a girl was often "given" to a young man, and the marriage was accepted as duty. True, even in her parents' home the girl was of low rank. But what did matter to her—here "she was mummy's and she was daddy's." She was at least her mother's particular pet, also indeed beloved and protected by her brothers, sought after too at dances and parties. Therefore she sang: "My girlhood was my time of rule, I was an emperor when a maid."

In many old-style districts her main work was the preparation of her own marriage outfit. She was busy ornamenting her clothes with artistic needlework, in which she found great delight and pride. But when she married, she acquired a new status, that of the lowest in rank in a strange home, and many years, even decades, passed before she re-acquired any position of respect comparable with that which she enjoyed as a maid "with mother," and could again do what she liked best to do.

The mood of a girl of the old-style districts before marriage, or, rather, when about to become a snaha, is to be seen from the following passage from a story of Veselinović's describing Serbia of the mid-nineteenth century:

> I was already a grown-up girl and the time had come for me to marry. I quailed before the suitor as a lamb before the knife. I was afraid, yet not afraid. One day the suitors came and asked for my hand.

[1] An alternative word for "affianced," "girl," or "bride," or even "young wife." It is common to all the Slav languages, essentially signifying "she who knows not" or "novice."

I accepted the money payment. Previously there was no choosing at your own will where you would go, but it was where your father and mother gave you to go, like it or not. Oh how heavy my heart was when I took that money in my hand! It was as if somebody had overturned a rock weighing 100 *okes* on me. I went to the loft and hid my face, weeping. It is no joke to renounce everything, your life, your freedom, and go away into a strange home, where you know nobody and nobody knows you, to call a strange mother your own, a strange house your own, make an alien world your own. . . . Their jollification downstairs plucked at my heart, the shots they fired [to celebrate] hit me. . . . I cried and cried and would have cried a long time, had Živana not come.

"Are you crying, Vida dear?" I sobbed away. "Vida!" "Well?" "Why are you crying?" "I must!" "Stop!" "I cannot! Just think what I have now done. An end to happiness. I shall kill myself." "Thou shall not kill thyself. Happiness will come back. This had to be, if not today, then tomorrow. You could never have stayed forever with father and mother—you would have had to seek your own home yourself. Could it be as you want, that would be the best thing. But what's to be done, this is the fate of us all."

"Živana, sister dear! Who can ever grow accustomed to a strange home? Who can fit in with a strange mother?" I cried, through my sobs. "That is not difficult, Vida dear. Do as you are told. Obey both younger and elder. Find fault with nothing that is theirs, always pretend you are content, and you shall become dear to them as if so born." "I know how to work." "I know you do, that is why I say what I do." "I shall do everything, sister darling, to fit in with them, to try to become dear to them." "And so you shall become dear to them!"[2]

I have here examined statistically certain customs regarding the seniors which reflect the humility of the young wife (and to some extent every wife). Changes in such customs are symptomatic of changes in the position of women generally as also in the relationship between wife and husband.

It was a widespread custom for the wife to kiss the hand of the men. The principal person to whom such respect was accorded was the svekar, or father-in-law, as head of the household. Next came the men related to the husband, the *kum*, godfathers, respectively, marriage assistants, "best man," and the visitors. Scarcely anywhere did the wife kiss the hand of her own parents. Graph 34 shows the distribution of this custom.

We see here a sharp line dividing Croatia and the Littoral from

[2] Janko Veselinović, *Slike iz seoskog života* (*Pictures of Village Life*), Srpska književna zadruga, Belgrade, 1896, "Na prelu" ("The Spinning Bee").

229

Graph 34. Whether wives kiss the men's hand

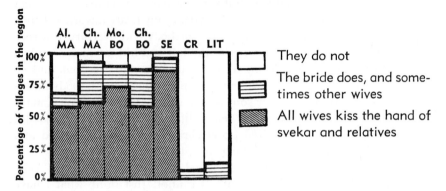

They do not

The bride does, and some-
times other wives

All wives kiss the hand of
svekar and relatives

all other regions. This indicates that the custom must have spread under Oriental influence, for in districts under Western (and at the same time Catholic) influence the custom did not penetrate. Were it a question of an area coincident with the patriarchal way of life, we should not find Serbia in this grouping.

The reports from Macedonia are almost all like the following:

Young brides kiss the hands of all, later only of the elders.

(*Albanian village, Struga district*)

Wives kiss the hand of all elders, visitors, and strangers.

(*Orthodox village, Žegligovo district*)

Only young wives, for the first few months, kiss the hands of all. Later they kiss the hand only of the svekar and other male relatives.

(*Orthodox village, Žegligovo district*)

In Bosnia this custom is most widespread, particularly in the Moslem villages. The first three examples are from Moslem villages:

Wives kiss the hand not only of grown men but even of the children.

(*Čajniče district*)

Wives kiss the hand of the men, and even the smaller boys, if they are marriage witnesses, resp. godfathers (kum), friends, et cetera.

(*Rogatica district*)

Wives kiss the hand of every man, only an elderly wife does not kiss the hands of a younger man.     (*Moslem village, Sarajevo district*)

Examples from the Christian villages of Bosnia:

For half a year after marriage, a young wife kisses the hand of father and brother-in-law, and outside the home also of older men. At meals she kisses the cheek of all members of the household except her husband.     (*Orthodox village, Jajce district*)

230

Wives kiss the hand of all older men. Older women kiss the hand even of lads, if they are relatives, when they come to call.

*(Orthodox village, Sarajevo district)*

Wives kiss the hand only of relatives and kums, but previously of all older men generally. Previously, wives simply had to kiss their husband's hand, also older men without distinction, whether members of the household or other relations. Today that is very rare, perhaps one in a hundred does. *(Orthodox village, Derventa district)*

In Serbia there is much kissing of the hand, particularly in the south.

*Mladas*, brides, kiss the hand even of five-year-old boys. They kiss the hand and rise from their seat to every man. *(Arilje district)*

When it is a festival and there are visitors, the wife also kisses her husband's hands in addition to those of the visitors. And in ordinary, everyday life they kiss the hand of every older stranger who enters the house, or whom they meet on any occasion. *(Dobričevo district)*

It is characteristic of Serbia that the signs of dignity and respect were maintained even when the patriarchal and zadruga way of life were in full decay.

In Croatia, we found very few villages with this custom. In Slavonia, which was under Turkey for 150 years, there were, however, vestiges of it.

Wives kiss the hand of men more in the zadrugas, though not every man, but the husband's father regularly, next his brother, though also other senior men, especially if it is a zadruga household.

*(Županja district)*

If we compare the custom of kissing of hands by the wife with that of kissing by children, we see a strong parallel, except in one region. In Moslem Bosnia there were many villages where the women obligatorily kissed the hand of men, whereas the children kissed only those of their parents. Have we here extreme humility on the part of the women, a humility more emphasized than the submissiveness of the children, or was this because the older children broke free from the old obligations earlier than the women? It is hard to say.

The second custom revealing the humility of a woman before men was the taking off of footwear and washing of the feet. This respect too was mainly shown to the father-in-law, and remained obligatory on a young wife even where the other wives had already given it up. The custom, of course, had some sense as a practical proceeding: There were no baths in the villages, and washing the feet was important to men coming in tired from hard work with mud-soaked footwear. Water had to be brought in and carried out by hand, and this task had been given a ceremonial form. We see the same in the washing of hands, where a younger member of the household was expected to bring water and pour a thin stream of water over the hands of the person washing, though this function had no formal or symbolic significance. In the reports, the removal of footwear was still more frequently mentioned than the washing of feet. In Bosnia, we observed a suppressed but fierce indignation, and in Serbia open resistance to this custom.

Graph 35. Whether the women remove men's footwear

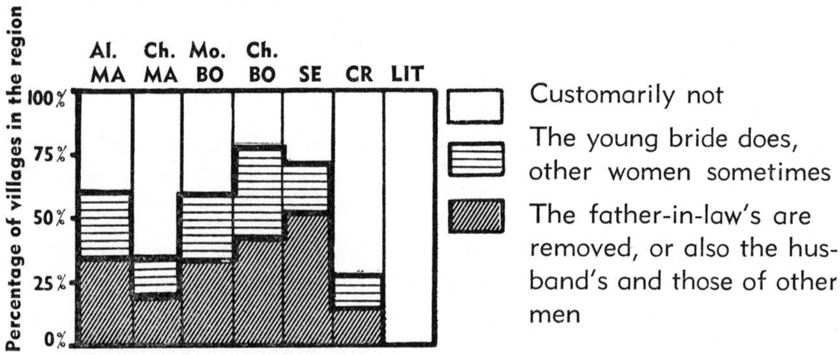

This ancient Oriental custom is, we recall, celebrated in the Catholic Church on Good Friday, yet among the people we found it absolutely nowhere where there had been Western influence. The custom was most extensive in the pastoral areas with tribal culture. In the regions with ancient arable farming—Macedonia, Orthodox Bosnia, and Croatia—it was less widely distributed. Here are examples from Orthodox Macedonia:

> Wives wash men's feet, but only young wives (nevesta). It is proper for male members to wash their feet before going to bed. This is generally done by the nevesta. Or, if there is no young wife in the house, it is done by an older daughter [sister] unless there are younger ones to take her place. But the feet only of the men are washed; women and girls wash their own. (*Albanian village, Struga district*)

> Wives take off the footwear of husband, kum, father-in-law, brothers-in-law, elder men, visitors, gentry. They wash their feet.
> (*Orthodox village, Nerodimlje district*)

> Wives take off men's footwear and wash their feet.
> (*Orthodox village, Prespa district*)

232

Wives as a rule take off men's footwear and lay out these and their socks. *(Sjenica district, Sanjak)*

From Bosnia:

Young wives take off the shoes of the head of the house, and, if there is a snaha, she does it. In the village a snaha is a real slave.
*(Orthodox village, Bijeljina district)*

Before the war it was the custom for a wife the first week after marriage to wash the feet of all the older men in the house, but that custom latterly has worn out. *(Catholic village, Bihać district)*

Wives take off men's footwear, socks, and trousers. A recently married wife will not strip her husband from shame.
*(Orthodox village, Jajce district)*

A reply from a Moslem village of Bosnia shows a rather different custom:

It is the custom for a wife to take off a man's footwear, but if a stranger comes, then the man takes off the guest's footwear.
*(Moslem village, Cazin district)*

Though many of the reporters from Serbia emphasized that this custom was rapidly fading, a count shows that it had all the same been preserved in many villages. In Serbia there was great disagreement between the destroyed zadruga way of life and the formal indication of female humility. With the combative disposition of the Serbian woman, in many villages we can guess the tremendous pressure there must have been to force signs of subordination from the authorities of the family.

The wife takes off the shoes of father-in-law, husband, brother-in-law, washes their feet and cleans their shoes. *(Azbukovac district)*

An elderly woman still takes off an elderly man's footwear and trousers, those homespun, tightly cut trousers which come off with such difficulty. The younger men never do this, each cleans his own footwear. The youngest snaha rubs the mud off everybody's sandals. Now children and the younger lads take their place. *(Kosmaj district)*

In Croatia, we found this custom more frequently than we did kissing of the hand by the wife. Here are two instances from a zadruga environment, from districts which for a time were under Turkish rule:

The snaha takes off the shoes and washes the feet of the father-in-law, of the husband, if he is tired. *(Županja district, Slavonia)*

At the outset the young wife takes off the father-in-law's shoes and washes his feet. This earlier was a customary obligation, but it is now disappearing. *(Petrinja district)*

A report from central Croatia:

Although the wives on the basis of work consider themselves equally industrious, there is still subordination. The wife cleans the shoes, washes the feet, and waits on her husband. This she does because "we're brought to the property" and because it is the custom.

*(Varaždin district)*

In the Littoral this custom does not exist. The following answer is characteristic:

The wife does not as a rule take anybody's shoes off. The wife is not regarded as a servant, but as the housekeeper, the comrade.

*(Isle of Korčula)*

The third sign of women's subordination was the custom of standing at meals, while the men sat and ate. This custom has formal significance only where there is a large number in the home, that is, in a zadruga. While here the standing of women signifies a formal manifestation of honor, coupled with a great aloofness from the men, in a small family it means precisely the opposite, namely, neglect of any formality, as, for instance, when the wife of the head of the house has a bite beside the hearth, leaning against the wall or squatting in a corner. The replies to this question show that we had here only vestiges of a custom once very widespread, but at the time of the survey less extensive than the two above-mentioned customs.

## Graph 36. Whether wives stand at meals

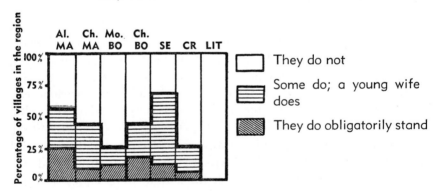

Graph 36 shows that in Moslem Bosnia this custom is not very widespread. This no doubt has a connection with the small number of zadrugas in this region. Examples from various districts:

Before the war, while there were big zadrugas, three tables were laid, one for the men, one for the women, one for the children. After the war, zadrugas are smaller and the wives eat with the men, while the children eat separately. If it is one family, then they all eat together. If there is a visitor, he eats with the head of the house, while wife and children, who eat later, look on. *(Sjenica district, Sanjak)*

The young wife, if her turn, stands. *(Sarajevo district, Bosnia)*

At dinner all girls under fifteen stand. *(Serbia, Vlasotince district)*

In Croat zadrugas, this custom was very widespread (the fact is not evident in the graph because in Croatia there were not many zadrugas left). Nevertheless, from many replies we do see vestiges of the old custom:

All sit down and eat together, but where there is a father-in-law (i.e., if he is well on in years), the women stand, namely, the younger ones (snahas). *(Imotski district, Dalmatia)*

The young wife, or some younger female, holds a candle while the other members of the family dine. In many houses the wives do not eat with the men, they eat after or before, "with the children."
*(Knin district, Dalmatia)*

In the early period the young wife, while she wears a *šamija*, a special kerchief, regularly stands at meals. *(Županja district, Slavonia)*

Replies from central Croatia:

Before the war, but long back, the wives spoke to their husbands in the plural [i.e., formally, politely] and did not sit down to table, but ate standing behind their husbands' backs. *(Koprivnica district)*

Regarding communes [zadrugas] all women used to stand. If one had a babe, all the same she stood and held it in her arm. But today they all sit down. *(St. Ivan Zelina district)*

A wife in a zadruga, even the eldest, may not sit at table with the men, whereas a boy of 15 sits with the men or husbands. If there is meat, the men have the best parts. Today that is vanishing, but it still holds. A wife cleans a husband's high boots, washes his feet, pours for him to wash his face. *(Varaždin district)*

Two reports connected with the subordinate position of the wife, though with no zadruga tradition:

A wife does not stand at meals, except when any male company comes visiting, then she leaves the table. (Only one wife may serve the guest, and then leave at once.) *(Bosnia, Moslem village, Foča district)*

We hear the same from the Dalmatian Highlands:

There are no particular formalities by which a wife shows the man respect. In the household, all sit down to meals together. When any strangers are present, the elder women wait on them, though the men themselves also do this; the younger women, as shy (this is considered highly moral by public opinion), vanish or merely listen from a corner. They wait on the men little.   (*Benkovac district, Dalmat. Highlands*)

In the Littoral, such customs are impossible:

Meals are not begun till all the household are at table.

(*Littoral, Split district*)

Standing at meals is a custom closely tied up with zadruga life; taking off of footwear more with the patriarchal tribal environment; while kissing the hand is linked with an Oriental tradition. All these customs demonstrate the subordinate position of the wife to the male, particularly the head of the household, and they emphasize the position of the mlada as the lowest rank of all in the young wife's new family. Even in the small family, the wife's relationship to her husband is colored by her position as a snaha in the big household. Even today, in many districts, every peasant woman is known as snaha or snaša.

## The Authority of the Husband

Women rise when a man comes up. They are convinced of their inferiority. "A male of five is the senior of a female of fifty."

(*Moslem village, Stolac district, Hercegovina*)

In the patriarchal regime, aloofness between husband and wife was as a rule more emphasized than that between father and son, for the male principle had precedence over the age principle. As a male, the son would some day enjoy high rank, whereas the wife would remain of low rank throughout her whole life. The marks of the wife's subordination were more expressive than those of the respect of son for father. The respect for the husband was particularly great, while the authority of the husband included certain elements of jealous care which were absent in the authority of the father. The freedom and independence of the wife were much more limited than those of sons, and her feeling of importance was undermined more often than that of young lads. In every sense, the authority of husband over wife was higher and broader than the authority of father over sons.

With regard to this matter of the authority of the husband we find a great similarity between all districts which have been under Turkish influence, and this without distinction as to when they were emancipated. Regions formerly Austrian territory differ greatly from regions formerly Turkish, as the reports show.

26.  Croatian mother and children

27.   Croatian women washing linen

28.   Market in Bosnia

Examples from Bosnia:

Formerly the wife received men standing,[3] on the roads she walked behind her husband, nor was she allowed to suckle her child in the presence of husband or of any other man, but always kept her breasts completely covered, and would leave the room while suckling. She dared not comb her hair if there was a man in the room, but had to hide.

*(Sarajevo district)*

There are cases of a wife, at first from shame, not only avoiding being near her husband but even avoiding calling him by name, considering this to be intimacy. Generally a woman avoids showing intimacy. It is considered unseemly to do so.  *(Sarajevo district)*

Women are freer now, and consequently have greater rights. Their position has improved. In the old days, a husband did not even address his wife by name, but only as *you* or even merely calling his attention by crying *hi*! or such words.  *(Mrkonjićgrad district)*

The authority of the husband has certainly diminished somewhat. This is to be seen from the freer movements of a wife. A wife before the war did not go to the market or a shop, did not use the public highways, but looked for concealment and back ways, whereas going out is now frequent.  *(Cazin district)*

The authority of the husband has diminished. This can be seen from the wife's going where she wants, whereas formerly wives did not dare go anywhere till they had asked their husbands.  *(Travnik district)*

Some descriptions of the authority of the husband in Serbia read similarly:

A wife was very shy of her father-in-law and husband, she had to obey them in everything, she had to eat last, a snaja (snaha) even had to kiss a small child's hand, a wife was beaten more. Girls had to marry whom their elders wanted. The authority of the husband has diminished. Previously, a wife did not dare answer her husband back, now she does and is not ashamed.  *(Sokobanja district)*

The changes in Serbia in this regard have been particularly great:

If a boy child has only just begun to walk, he has the right to stand in the presence of mother and grandmother during a prayer, being, as male child, a senior. Piety was greater and respect for the male greater, or rather, fear of God and husband were greater. The authority of the husband has diminished, which can be seen from the fact that the husband seeks agreement with his wife about nearly all domestic matters, even voting.  *(Valjevo district)*

The resistance of the wife to the authority of the husband may be seen from the following reply:

[3] Because of the way the questions were put in the questionnaire, the investigators frequently speak of the authority of the husband in the past.

The authority of the husband has diminished. This is to be seen from the fact that she more often answers back in quarrels, whereas previously she did not even dare say "I can't" or "I've no time."

*(Azbukovac district)*

The authority of the husband has diminished. This is to be seen from his diminished influence in the home. In the most concrete practical way it is shown in his clothing, that is, in his untidiness.

*(Posavina district)*

Examples from Macedonia and the Sanjak:

Authority has not decreased. Here the patriarchal way of life still holds. Even if he does not deserve it, a husband must be highly respected by his wife, for he is her husband, a man. *(Sjenica district)*

The husband used to have greater authority, now he has less. The reason is that now husbands love their wives more and listen to what they have to say, and the wives take advantage of this. There are fewer women, and it is harder to get a wife, and when men do get one, they give way to her. *(Djevdjelija district)*

In Montenegro the height of respect for the husband was to be found in the tribal system, namely, in the past. Here we find a vigorously demonstrative tone, which tends to border on harshness, but here we also find the greatest recent changes:

The wife is subject to the husband in more or less every way. There are popular sayings: "Roof your house, you won't get wet, beat your wife, you won't get tongue-pie." "When my wife asks where I've been, I'll say that I've been sowing salt." There were before the war frequent cases of a husband and wife who never spoke to each other in anybody else's presence, and never called each other by name, but that is no more. The authority of the husband has diminished. This is to be seen from their dealings in company, in a shop, a café or elsewhere, when the husband gives the wife the seat of honour. Beside this there are cases of the wife ignoring the husband's commands, which never happened before the war. *(Danilovgrad district)*

In the old days, sixty or more years ago, the husband was a sort of absolutist, and insisted on subordinating his wife to his authority or will. The mentality of the time was such that the husband, as a man, on all occasions gave expression to his masculinity, so as thereby to demonstrate his lofty standing, particularly military. With such a view of things, he enjoyed complete authority in the family, and this he often applied terroristically, especially toward his wife. It was not that a husband hated or despised his wife, but the age—the collective mentality—made him shape himself according to such a view. It was held that a man was not a real hero or man if he spoiled his wife and treated her nicely. Of such a man it would have been said: "He grovels under his wife's petticoats." There were sly things said if a man called his wife by name (Militza, say) and likewise if a wife addressed her husband (Marko, say). Here they mainly used pronouns, "he" and "she." This again was to hide the intimate relationship, which on the one hand—as they thought—injured the warrior pride of the husband, and on the other the dignity of feminine modesty. It was held to be immodest to praise one's wife, or for a wife to praise her husband. As a real hero and man was considered the man who—in appearance at least—paid not the slightest heed to his wife.

In older times this went so far that it was considered quite a fault in a man if during his lifetime he never struck his wife. Hence husbands in the presence of others were surly toward their wives. I once even heard a tale of husbands making an agreement during the day, when working together, to give their wives a beating the same evening, merely so that their power and authority should be felt. In such instances, a woman would suffer blows or oaths from her husband without protest.

Today, however, people have largely got away from this outlook. On the contrary, if a husband is unable to treat his wife tenderly and humanely, people think him a fool and unworthy of marriage.

*(Montenegro, Cetinje district)*

The investigators, mainly young men, as a rule emphasized the way in which the traditional environment burdened the wife, and how the changes were bringing women alleviation. But from their reports we can see that the break-up of the old family set-up and the anarchic climate often weighed heavily on all members of the family. Here are examples from Christian villages of Bosnia:

It seems that the authority of the husband has diminished. Unfortunately, this is no triumph for the wife, nor emancipation, but it seems the cause is a weakening of morals on both sides. *(Brčko district)*

The wife previously had less influence on the husband, but since the war she has gained all the rights and become quite excessive in her demands. *(Travnik district)*

The authority of the husband has diminished. A wife answers her husband back [criticizes him]. When they quarrel she berates him in public, and sometimes a wife beats her husband. *(Derventa district)*

In Croatia and the Littoral, conditions were very different from those in regions once under Turkish influence. Whether the authority of the husband in Croatia was ever as high as in the districts under Oriental influence, it is difficult to state with certainty. Today in most districts after convulsions lasting for one or two generations, conditions have again stabilized in this regard on a rather altered

basis. It is only in the Dinaric districts that we can see that a patriarchal distance once divided husband and wife.

Before the war a wife could not dream of making any objection to
anything. She had to submit blindly to her husband or the head man
of the zadruga. Today in domestic life the well-intentioned advice or
objection of the wife can have a great effect. Husbands, however, do
not like other people knowing that their wives "boss them." This
change began to show immediately after the war, to become most
marked in the depression.          (*Dalmatian Highlands, Knin district*)

Here is an instance of great changes in the former Military March:

The authority of the husband has weakened, which is to be seen by
the fact that formerly wives did not permit themselves to do before
their husbands what they do today. Thus, for instance, quite a number
swear, use oaths, show themselves when drunk, and so forth, with no
regard to the husband's good name, thereby destroying both his and
their own.                                    (*Petrinja district*)

From some reports we see that there were once hints of feminine
submissiveness also in central Croatia:

The authority of the husband has weakened, for previously a young
wife had to address her husband with the polite formal plural of the
verb, and also had to wash her husband's feet, whereas today all that
has vanished.                          (*St. Ivan Zelina district*)

The reports from central Croatia show a somewhat improved position for women in comparison with the earlier times, while many
indicate that relationships had again become stable, on the basis of
a somewhat curtailed authority of the husband. Expressions used
show that the struggle for position and an influential rôle in the
home was not now acute, but inclined to be past. The following
reply would be unthinkable from a village in which the struggles
about changed positions were at their height:

It was never any different as far as the husband's authority goes, but
formerly the wife herself considered herself inferior. A wife holds that
it would be a most scandalous thing to have a husband for whom she
would have to stand up, thinking she would be a laughing stock to have
a husband whose part she had to take, also acting for the whole family
in case of misfortune, in dealings with the authorities and other people.
The authority of the husband has not weakened. This is clear from the
whole of family life and public life too. A husband who does not know
how to manage his farm and to earn, maintaining his family and having
public dealings with other men, and lets his wife go to meetings, assemblies, the municipal offices, etc., is considered "an old woman" in the

village, or half a man. At meetings, a woman's place is to hold her tongue and she is never asked anything. Her place is in the home, in the bosom of the family, with the children. That is how folk see it, and wives know this and do not stick their noses in where their husbands are discussing some public matter. Were a woman to come to a meeting and join in the discussion, her husband would have to leave from shame and go home. *(Dugoselo district)*

A militant or anarchic note is also lacking in the following report:

The authority of the husband has weakened. This is to be seen in the way women are becoming increasingly equal in making decisions and in conduct of the farm. They were greatly aided in this by the war years, which proved them capable of running the farms on their own and finally by being rather more literate than their husbands, as at school, being mentally more developed, they get more education,[4] and know how to make use of this more practically than the men.

*(Bjelovar district)*

The replies from Slavonia show great changes during the war, though here the position of the wife has always been relatively high:

Once the wife walked behind her husband, for instance, when visiting the family. Now they walk side by side. As a rule the men formerly went about alone, now they go with their wives or the wives go alone. Before the war they rarely sent girls to school. "She's not going to be a parson's wife," was the older folks' excuse. Today they do send them. There was far more suppression of the womenfolk before the war. The authority of the father has decreased. In the absence of their husbands in the world war, the women showed they were the better managers. This has helped a great deal to raise the standing of women in the countryside.

*(Pakrac district)*

The husband's authority in many a family has diminished greatly. The self-confidence of the women was awakened during the war, also the tendency for *priženjavanje*,[5] i.e., for the husband to enter the household of his wife and her relatives. *(Nova Gradiška district)*

Before the war, the woman was much more passive, backward, discouraged. The authority of the husband has decreased. A wife shows her thoughts more freely, and often expresses critical views to her husband.

*(Nova Gradiška district)*

In the Littoral, the expression "authority unchanged" indicated a comparatively high position of the wife acquired at some earlier

---

[4] Children at the time went to school to their tenth or eleventh year, so that in the short school period the girls, being at that age more developed than the boys, sometimes got ahead of them.

[5] The "tone" of this very special verbal noun is rather as if one said that the husband "became a snaha."

period. If at this time any report spoke of there being a change in the authority of the husband in any village of the Littoral, this was rather a matter of the demolition of certain mere vestiges of the man's authority, and on no account indicated the first great attack on the old authority. Down the Littoral, one can observe a strong influence coming in from the cities, also from Italy and from America. The influence of the emigrants was particularly great. These, returning mainly from America or Australia, treated their wives with more consideration and respect. But if relationships between husband and wife have now changed, they are not in violent antagonism to old-world customs of showing respect for the husband:

> I observed that on this island nearly all women married over twenty years address their husbands in the formal plural and always refer to them as "my master." When women go to town with their husband or in the company of more than one man, the men always go ahead in a group while the women follow behind. Of late that has been tending to relax. The younger generations are more educated. They acquire customs from foreigners. (*Isle of Rab*)

> Young wives endeavor to acquire a decisive influence on their husbands, and thereby greater rights in the family. Old women were much subjected, but younger ones are succeeding in getting rights for themselves, for the husbands (the younger ones) traveling about the world acquire other experience, hence respect their wives more.
>
> (*Biograd on Sea district*)

> The wife does all the work, keeps house and looks after the children, and more often than not earns more than the man, taking things to market to sell. In consequence, she is respected as an earner. In addition, former Istria had a large number of schools, and today too there is schooling there which lasts six years (two higher people's classes), and moreover today she is within reach of the town, whence she gets knowledge and indeed also many urban failings. (*Kastav district*)

> There is not a home without one, two, or even more emigrants, hence it remains for the wife to manage the home and do all the work, including jobs which in other districts are exclusively done by men. She is quite equal in rights to her husband. (*Isle of Krk*)

With the break-up of the patriarchal order and of zadruga life, the primacy of the husband vanishes and the status of the wife rises. Apart from its bright aspects, namely, great independence and equality, this change also has a darker aspect, of which I shall speak below.

## Changes in the Authority of the Men

What changes take place in the authority of the men in the home, that is, that of the father and that of the husband? Do sons continue longer to respect their father, or women to respect and obey their husbands? Is it the young men who begin the attack on the authority of the senior, or is it the women who take the first step?

Graph 37, indicating changes in the authority of the husband, is to be compared with Graph 10 on page 89 showing changes in the authority of the father.

Graph 37. Whether the authority of the husband has declined

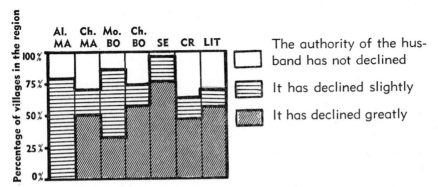

The authority of the husband has not declined

It has declined slightly

It has declined greatly

This graph shows that in most villages in all regions there had been changes in the authority of the husband. Indeed, everywhere except among the Albanians, these were great. If we compare this graph with that showing the authority of the father over his sons, we see a striking difference. Whereas the authority of the father changed most in the old-style regions, that of the husband changed most in the modern regions. This is indicative that the father's authority breaks up earlier than the husband's. At the time of this inquiry, the process of disintegration of the authority of the husband was in full swing in the modern regions, but that of the father's authority had already been completed. On the other hand, in the patriarchal regions it was the father's authority which was in process of breaking down, whereas that of the husband was still intact. For instance, in Moslem Bosnia, there were particularly great changes in the authority of the father, but none at all to be observed in that of the husband. This shows that the primacy of the male sex holds longer than position based on mere age seniority. To bring further

243

light to bear on this problem, I have examined the correlation between the two types of authority in more detail. Here are the
results, set out in tabular form:

### TABLE 1. THE DECAY OF THE AUTHORITY
### OF FATHER AND HUSBAND

| | Macedonia | Moslem Bosnia | Christian Bosnia | Serbia | Central Croatia | Littoral |
|---|---|---|---|---|---|---|
| | | | (The figures represent percentages of the regions.) | | | |
| *First combination* Father's authority unchanged, Husband's authority unchanged | 26 | 35 | 4 | 17 | 16 | 12 |
| *Second combination* Father's authority reduced, Husband's authority unchanged | 39 | 42 | 42 | 18 | 28 | 31 |
| *Third combination* Father's authority reduced, Husband's authority reduced | 31 | 33 | 50 | 59 | 40 | 38 |
| *Fourth combination* Father's authority unchanged, Husband's authority reduced | 4 | — | 4 | 6 | 16 | 19 |

The first combination is the typically patriarchal one—neither
authority has diminished. As we see, the submissiveness of wife to
husband was at its height in Moslem Bosnia.

> Here in the village the authority of the husband has not diminished,
> but the peasants think it has in the towns. There is no difference re-
> garding that of the father compared with pre-war or pre-depression
> days.     (*Albanian village, Vučitrn district*)

The second combination, in which the father's authority has diminished, leaving that of the husband unchanged, we find where the
sons were curtailing their obedience to their father and breaking up
the zadruga in the desire to be independent. This combination is
found in the majority of the villages in the old-style regions. It indicates that in the break-up of the patriarchal order, the first fortress to
fall is that of the father's authority, whereas that of the husband is
only just beginning to be attacked. Here is an instance from Herzegovina, where the sons frequently find hired labor jobs:

The authority of the father has diminished. This is to be seen in the frequent clashes with the children and very frequent arbitrary abandonment of the home, the children going to handicrafts and hired labor. This came about because today many fathers are unable to satisfy their children's material demands. The authority of the husband is not falling off, only that of the father in a minority of cases. The only difference from prewar days is in dress, whereas all the other part of a woman's life in the home and the community has greatly changed. This district is an isolated one, and has not gone through essential changes. Not even the depression period changed the life of the home.

*(Stolac district)*

The third combination embraces villages in which the authority of the father had diminished just as that of the husband had. This combination is typical of regions in a state of stormy ferment, and it means the complete break-up of the patriarchal system of authority. The struggle is either at its height or just coming to its end, and we see the younger people with certain positions won. The sons lead in the struggle, while the wives stand a little to the side. In the end they too get some fruits of the victory over authority. Here is an example from an Orthodox village of Bosnia:

Before the war the authority of the father was greater. Since the war, and at present, it is diminished. This shows in the lack of obedience of the children, in scorn and the outside influence on the child. The authority of the husband has not diminished. The spirit of the age has played its part. The husband is gradually coming to see that his wife is his closest collaborator, and the spiritual horizon of the woman has also broadened.

*(Bosanski Novi district)*

Particularly great changes were taking place in Serbia, whereas in Croatia the storm was already dying out.

The fourth combination embraces those villages in which the father's authority had not diminished, but that of the husband had. This combination takes two forms: In one, in Slavonia, the women's self-confidence developed earlier than that of the sons:

Before the war a woman respected her husband more and was rigorously submissive to him: She had to hold her tongue if her husband swore and scolded her. But since the war all that has changed. Today the women resist and challenge their husbands, even if they do get a beating for it. On the other hand, the authority of the father has not diminished, or only slightly. For instance, a son may not smoke or do anything like that in front of his father, or do anything without asking him. The relationship between parents and children since the war has scarcely changed at all.

*(Pakrac district)*

In Croatia and the Littoral, however, this combination indicated that the sons had gained more favorable positions in earlier stages of development, and for that reason did not seek greater rights. Frequently, they played a conservative role, defending the male privileges. The authority of the father did not diminish, since it had more or less done so earlier, to find stability, so to speak, on a new level. The battle for the economic independence of the sons was already won, and now the husband's authority was being questioned. Only the women now struggled; though the vanguard, being satisfied (sometimes by a merely partial victory), had withdrawn into the background and demobilized their forces.

If we examine each region separately, we see the following: In Macedonia there was a majority of villages with the second combination of relationships, which points to the beginning of a break-up of the family hierarchy. The results in Moslem Bosnia are striking if we add together the villages of the first and second combinations, that is, those in which the authority of the husband was still at its height. We see that in 77 per cent of the villages there had been no change in this respect. The Moslem woman had been unable to shake off the concentrated pressure under which she lived. The economic pressure was tremendous, by reason of the rapid pauperization of these districts, and the women were physically overburdened by their excessive families.

> The position of the woman is determined by the very division of labor. The husband works on the land or at some other work, while the woman looks after the home and everything connected with it. Thus the woman is overburdened with work. In the present-day family the women do not even raise the question of the authority of their husbands, nor make any effort to free themselves from it some day. They are entirely preoccupied with poverty, work, daily cares, and more than anything else by ignorance and lack of enlightenment. Till marriage, in the countryside, life for a woman is more or less bearable. From the day of her marriage to her death, the woman is the slave of everyday cares and sufferings. And while she is the slave of her position, she is also more so that of ignorance and lack of enlightenment.
>
> *(Moslem village, Rogatica district)*

In the Christian villages of Bosnia we find the smallest number of stabilized villages. The patriarchal way of life was breaking down rapidly, and this process embraced almost every village. In Serbia what stands out is the complete destruction of all authority in the home (third combination). Both sons and wives were engaged in a struggle in a more extensive sense than in any other region.

Here the women are even brave—in that they have the sense, at once, to know what to do, and do something which harms the man—they leave the home, or the children. Here there is only a small number of men who also have an eye for other women. The women on the other hand are better at deceiving their husbands and even leave them altogether, then the men beg them to come back. There are women who know how to order men about, women on whose account men go crazy, and of whom people always talk. It is a frequent thing for them to complain to others. The life of women and their neighbors is on rather intimate terms. If a woman is right, she may utter a counter-opinion. But the woman is always half allowed to be right. In the presence of anybody else a woman always bears herself as if she really were humble, yet in every gesture you see a good dose of self-will. (Like a reaction to the existing submissiveness.) That belief in being "worth less" is badly shaken, and though she is poor, she knows how to fight back. There are quite a number of homes in which, in almost all, indeed, it is the wife who has most gumption and manages the home, arranging all its business. Women's work is recognized, but measured with a different yardstick. Those are "women's tasks," which anybody can perform. *(Kosmaj district)*

In Croatia and the Littoral there were relatively large numbers of villages in which the authority of the husband was now being undermined. Here the great drama of the destruction of authority began earlier than elsewhere, so that the fourth act was now playing.

The data reveal the historical process of the break-up of the family hierarchy, with the first act in the Moslem districts, the second in Christian Macedonia and Bosnia, the third in Serbia, and the fourth in the Croat districts.

In this correlation of the authority of the father and that of the husband we observe that we have obtained the same result as when we compared the two pertinent graphs. The authority of the father is the first to be struck at, to be followed later by the authority of the husband. Frequently this latter process begins some decades after the authority of the father has been diminished.

### Rebellion and Resignation to Woman's Lot

Country women and girls take an interest in every movement in the public affairs of the peasantry, but that interest is only of brief duration, for they are prevented from taking an interest in aught but their heavy, coarse domestic chores. Such work, the woman knows, merely makes her stupid and she hates it, but that is how things must be. In most cases the woman is illiterate. Wives who are literate get to know everything and like to read things apart from their husbands, or their children read out to them. When one offers them opportunities, the girls are interested in everything, reading about every question touching their lives and discussing it. There are wonderful examples of intelligent girls. For instance, they read something about women in France, or see pictures in a French magazine, and examine them and listen with great enthusiasm. They approve of equality in the community, and want it. They know about all the modern questions. (Their fathers are politically active and this passes to the daughters, there are more girls than lads in the village.) By reason of their work and their awareness that they can grasp everything just as the men do, they absolutely refuse to believe in their inferiority. They desire equality instinctively and they defend themselves against any attack, though formally they admit that they are accustomed to being inferior since when they were small. . . .

Women rarely allow themselves to be beaten. They defend themselves because, unlike the men, they don't allow anything to happen for which they might be scolded, let alone beaten. They are very careful about this. Only "the worst sort of men" beat. But they do get a box on the ears about twice a year, and this they don't forget. Quarrels take the place of fights. In quarrels the women are stronger than the men. Here the women are uncouth, bold, of masculine appearance and most energetic, assiduous workers and in some cases in every way the better of the men.         *(Serbia, Kosmaj district)*

This is the only report from three hundred villages which describes the women's rebellion against submission in general terms. In the reports from all the other villages, one sees that, though here or there embittered by their arduous position—or by the treatment of father-in-law or husband—the women did not offer much resistance, still less did they put forward any demand for a change in their position. Everywhere, except in Serbia, there is a general feeling of hopelessness and absolute resignation. Graph 38 shows a clear picture.

The line of effort on the part of women to gain a better position shows an exceptionally even curve. The peak in Serbia has both a quantitative and qualitative sense. Here most villages were full of efforts to improve the status of women, and the reasons advanced by the women here had practically reached the level of a set of principles, an ideology.

Graph 38. Do the women try to improve their position?

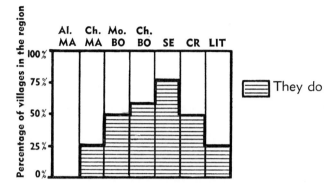

They do

The curve otherwise means that in an old-style region the women do not make any effort to change their position, for stable conditions allow not even the thought of such a change. In the region with a new equilibrium, such efforts are no longer needed, since women have already obtained a more favorable position. The fact that the modern regions of Croatia and the Littoral are on the downward side of the curve means that there is here no such intense effort toward a change of position as there is in Serbia.

The hard role of the women as a rule was expressed in helpless, half-apathetic protests against what pressed hardest on each individually. Such complaints rarely reached the state of any awareness that the life of women generally in the particular district was a hard one. The women supported their individual efforts for greater rights by emphasizing how much they work on the farms, by suggesting their personal abilities or how they economize, or stating that they have added to the property with their dowries. It is almost only this last motivation which stirs the woman's mentality to resistance to complete deprivation of rights.

This revolt of the women based on property was referred to quite often in Christian Bosnia, Serbia, and Croatia. It is significant that, although in Moslem Bosnia and the Littoral women inherit more often than they do in Serbia, in these two regions the investigators much more rarely mention women basing their attitude on their possession of property. It is only in the regions in a state of rapid transformation that this individualistic factor plays a part.

The reports from Macedonia show a state of complete pacification or resignation regarding the position of women:

There is no general movement, solely the desire of each woman individually in that sense. Women do not come to express themselves collectively and under such conditions could not even do so.

(*Albanian village, Struga district*)

Women make no efforts to get greater rights. At least 98 per cent are illiterate. Because of their lack of enlightenment they do not know that there are better ways of living. (*Jablanica district*)

Women are still just like they were before the war. They make no effort to get any rights; by the mere fact of being women, they are considered to be subordinate and created to serve the male. (*Sjenica district*)

In Bosnia, on the contrary, one observes great dissatisfaction among the women. In both the Moslem and Christian villages, they particularly complain of having too much work to do. This is connected with the particularly arduous position of Bosnian peasant women and was a consequence of the great worsening of living conditions after the war in Bosnia and Hercegovina.

To some extent, women demand greater rights on the basis of their labor, which is more intensive than that of the men. A minority of women think that woman by her nature is subordinate to man.

(*Mixed Moslem and Christian village, Stolac district*)

"We work the same as our husbands, still more indeed than they do, and we spend less," ruefully a peasant woman with four children explains to me, while another, in a protesting way, says "*Iksan, iksan,*[6] but the men won't let us have our way."

(*Orthodox village, Bijeljina district*)

Women are held to be inferior, but they feel they are deprived of rights and work far more than the men but through poor enlightenment they do not even think about such matters.

(*Mixed Christian and Moslem village, Sarajevo district*)

The tendency to emphasize individual wishes may be judged from the following:

Women make no effort to get greater rights. It is enough for them to be permitted to go visiting neighbors for a cup of coffee, calling on their friends, and dressing up well when they go out—while they may be dressed any old way at home. (*Moslem village, Brčko district*)

With the end of zadruga life, the patriarchal education with its features of slavish subordination of a woman to her husband ceased. The woman is made equal by reason of her work and her property. There is no ideological "equality movement," but they do demand equality on

6 *Iksan*, "human being," is an Arabic word.

the grounds of their work and property. Today not one will transfer her dowry property to her husband.

*(Orthodox and Catholic village, Derventa district)*

A woman has more rights if her husband, on marriage, becomes an *uljez* (intruder), one who enters the wife's home; then he is "blacker than a raven," otherwise a man must be above a woman in every way.

*(Catholic village, Bihać district)*

It is striking that the reports from Bosnia on this matter are most emotional, in sharp distinction from the Bosnia statements on other matters, which are usually marked by a fatalistic attitude. The burden on the shoulders of a Bosnian peasant woman at this time was almost unbearable. We do not find nearly such sharp protests coming from Macedonia, though there too the women labored very hard, particularly if their husbands were away on long-term labor in far-away places. But in Macedonia the women have some sort of compensation in the high price put on them as workers and housewives.

In Serbia we find a completely different spirit. Though here too there were vestiges of patriarchal views, there was also a definite militancy. In no other region was there such resistance to bad treatment as that exhibited by the Serbian woman. This combativeness arose, no doubt, from a special combination of a generally war-like spirit in Serbia and the traditional scorn for women. The portrait of a Serbian woman Vuka which is given at the close of this chapter describes a type of Serbian peasant woman which is not too rare. The report which commences this section of the present chapter also reveals a woman's demands matured to the point of constituting a general statement.

We find an ambivalent attitude in the following reports:

Young women do try to change their position, but one still feels the older women to be down-trodden; moreover, they condemn such efforts [of the younger women] and assist the men.      *(Arilje district)*

Only affluent women demand equality, for these do not depend on their husbands. All the others admit that they work harder than the men, but "a woman should always submit to a man," for "men and women are different."      *(Gruža district)*

Women seek equality on the basis of their dowry, and this is very often a consequence of the war. There has been such a turmoil that today women's opinions are even listened to, whereas previously they dared not open their mouths.      *(Valjevo district)*

251

This is how it is generally put: "Why dream of such thoughts when they're out of the question?" Solely women of well-to-do houses and those who are progressive in outlook seek equality. Apart from cases where the husbands are advanced, where they have broken with religion, for there too women do want to play a positive part together with the men. Here in this village such women are very rare, but round about there are some. *(Kosmaj district)*

In Croatia the attitude of the women on such matters differs from that of the women of Serbia. The Croat peasant woman invariably rejected any effort contrary to the primacy of the man which is made on general principles. This is the more surprising, since the strong political movement in Croatia known as the "Seljačka Stoga," Peasant Unity, included as an item of its program the raising of the status of the peasant woman. Yet though this party organized social work and promoted peasant women's education, in the main the effort was powerless to change the women's resignation. The difference between the bearing of the Croat and the Serbian peasant woman was partly due to the circumstance that, in an earlier period, women in Croatia were not so oppressed and abased as those in the Turkish and Dinaric districts. The partition of the zadrugas at an earlier date in Croatia afforded women a relatively favorable position, sufficiently so to satisfy them. And as soon as the women had thus to some extent gotten free from the authority of the mother-in-law, a sort of consolidation of inner family relationships took place. The reports reveal the conservative mood of the peasant women here, a mood antagonistic to any feminist move. The first report, in patriarchal style, comes from a Dinaric district:

> However little a woman has, there is no desire and no effort for greater rights. Perhaps some individuals would like to have a try, but these too think it would hurt their husbands' feelings. *(Benkovac district)*

A report from the Kordun, in the former Military March, shows a good measure of awakened, conscious militancy on the part of the women, but at the same time an anti-feminist attitude:

> Talking to girls and married women, I see that there is little desire in their hearts for equality with men. True, the unmarried women hold their own, and won't let the lads best them, and they defend their rights against the men's. But I cannot say that all this could really be described in any sense as a struggle for rights, especially since at the same time we find them taking a decisive stand against even what rights they have got. To the question whether a man has the right to

beat a woman and order her about, the almost unanimous answer will be that he has the right to do what he wants to his wife, since it is he who maintains everything, he earns the money, and he is the man. They are convinced that they can on no account act like men. What makes a woman like this and ties her to her husband is the economic dependence of woman on man. In this village legal customs differ from the written laws by which daughters would be the inheritors of their father's property. Here girls get no land, which is shared among the sons, merely a larger share of the stock, which serves as their dowry.

*(Slunj district)*

Reports from central Croatia:

Women are not subjected, nor do they feel inferior, nor do they want equality, for they already have it. *(Ivanić district)*

Equality of rights is unknown to them, they say: "A husband is the husband and a true woman should obey him. I expect he knows what he is doing." They do not demand equality, and found it funny when I said that was not right for a husband to beat or ill-treat his wife.

*(Varaždin district)*

Twenty-five per cent of the women want to be equal, "we do more work," but 75 per cent are convinced that they are inferior.

*(Prelog district)*

If a rich girl comes into a large zadruga, because of her dowry she demands more respect. *(Pakrac district, Slavonia)*

In the Littoral one observes stability on both modern and old-style foundations:

As a woman is nearly equal to a man, she does not want any more rights than she already has. *(Isle of Krk)*

There are still women who are convinced of their inferiority, but when the talk is of children, the majority of them say: "If you're the father, don't forget I am the mother." *(Šibenik district)*

Young women strive to gain a decisive influence over their husbands, and thereby greater rights within the household. The elder women were very subjected, but the younger ones manage to get rights for themselves, for the husbands (younger ones) travel about the world and gain other experience, so they respect their wives more.

*(Biograd on Sea district)*

Nowhere (except partly in Serbia), did the hidden, but half-conscious, dissatisfaction rise to any higher, ideological level. The struggles went on in the almost hermetically enclosed world of each individual household. True, even the sons, in their struggle for

253

economic independence, did not struggle in any joint, organized way, yet at their disposal they did have certain generally recognized arguments. A young woman, on the other hand, when she rebeled against the tyranny of mother-in-law or husband, had no good justification. The struggle of women for an improved position in the home was gaining strength very slowly indeed, and with much difficulty, out of a realm which was still strictly personal. Indicative of tension and the absence of an open struggle were the nervous symptoms we found in so many peasant women—digestive disorders, hysterical paralysis, and others were common.

Of conditions in the country as a whole, perhaps the following report from a Moslem village may be taken as typical:

> Ideas have no entry in this village. The woman's demand for greater liberty is rather instinctive, and aimed merely at greater freedom of movement about the village. Otherwise, women are not even allowed the right to put forward a demand. They are so beaten down by their upbringing that it is impossible for them even to conceive of being different. (*Tuzla district*)

In such a situation and with such a mood, we are bound to ask how it came about that, nevertheless, the position of women in many districts should have so improved in comparison with earlier epochs. It would seem to be here a case, not rare in history, of a group's acquiring greater rights without ever having fought for them, merely because some other group, fighting for its own aims (and without any intention of satisfying the demands or desires of the first group), by their own victory won rights for this other group too. Though, in the struggle of the married sons for economic independence, the improvement of the position of women was certainly not one of their "war aims," this improvement did in fact result from the destruction of the zadruga. The assault on the fortress of the authority of the father inevitably weakened the defenses of family authority as such. Women acquired a better position in practice before it had ever occurred to them in theory that this might be possible.

In the struggle against the family hierarchy, it was the young males who formed the vanguard. The women came on far behind them. However, after the victory of the men, the women too found themselves rewarded as allies by increased rights and a somewhat more elevated position.

## Vuka:[7] An Example of a Militant Woman

This character sketch was contributed by a woman teacher, Mila Srdanov, from the Shumadia.[8]

We were seated in the kitchen beside a brightly polished wood-burning kitchen range. Vuka was knitting socks and talking:

"You ask me what my life is like? But I have already told you. You know my family, my brother too. In those days ours was the leading house in the village. My father had three children: My elder sister, my brother, who was ailing, younger than me, and myself. My sister married and died. My father too became an invalid, then died. Then my mother and I turned our hands to everything: I began doing all sorts of work at an early age. I used to go ploughing by myself when I was fourteen. I was healthy, strong—and a real little devil. Why, I would pluck up the plough out of the furrow and lump it down again on the ground as if it were a feather. I tell you, I was a real little devil, I was, young.

"You ask about my schooling?"

Here Vuka straightens her back, gives me a sharp look, drops her knitting to her lap, and sighs so profoundly that she quite startles me.

"Ah my dear, why do you ask me that? You know what I'll say: I never saw any school. But I can read and write. My brother taught me. Ah, my dear, what fortune it would have been had I gone to school. . . . If my father had lived, he would have sent me. As it was, I had to be with the livestock, out in the field, or in the house at the chores. Know what I used to do? When my mother left me alone to knit or embroider, I would take a book on my lap and knit blind, not looking at the knitting but reading under it. First I read novels. About love. About girls whom men deceive and abandon. Those I read and often cried, I was sorry for those unfortunate girls. I was sorry for myself, too, because I felt unhappy since I could not do what I wanted, have a school education and learn and know everything. . . . But I also read many other things—newspapers. For these my brother read too. And I was sorry for myself and my ill luck, not being able to live a finer life. . . . I used to go to the town (a little town, the district centre, about half a mile away), but I hated it, and all the townsmen for eyeing every peasant girl.

[7] Vuka or Vukica, a favorite Serbian girl's name, a feminine of "Wolf."

[8] Shumadia was the heart of Serbia around Belgrade, the "home counties" of Serbia—the first part of the Serbian lands to win its freedom.

"Yes, they were strict with me. I was not allowed to go anywhere by myself. Once I was dancing at a fair when darkness fell. All the way home my brother scolded me, and when I got home my mother beat me. 'It's not seemly for a daughter of a proper home to go about loose in the dark' said my mother, warning me.

"There were lads who liked me, but I never gave them a look, for I was sure they were all lying, they would deceive me and leave me. Besides, I could never have a meeting with any of them, they kept me so strictly. For this reason I associated with all the lads equally. For this reason, many were fond of me. There were many fine lads in the village. I did not love any one of them specially. I was somehow always disappointed in them, nor did marriage interest me. I wanted something else, something finer. . . . Do you understand what I'm trying to say?"

She gave me a meaningful look. She was thinking of school.

"Then they married me off. By force. My mother chose a man I did not like at all, whom I don't like even now. Why did they marry me? Because he was alone, because he was rich. Some lads suggested I run away with them. I did not want to. Nor did I dare. My mother threatened to burn my whole marriage outfit. They made a grand wedding of it. I recall it all very well. I was miserable. I felt ill; I had lost weight with fretting. The first days were terrible. Then I began to give way. (Once I thought of leaving him.) I was even affectionate toward him—I thought that would be better. Then I found it very hard."

She sighed.

"It surprises me I did not rot away. Never once a kind word from him."

Her husband was as fitful tempered as an unbroken nag.

"He's the same today. Doesn't care about me. Beats the children, shouts at them. Never like a father, asking them this or that, having a talk with them, making them laugh. He dares not raise his hand at me, though, for he's afraid I would leave him. He's one by himself. Pigheaded. Crazy. Everything is in his hands. Once he tried to start selling the land. Sold quite a bit of it. I set up a wail. He did not say a word, just went his way. I threatened I would leave him. That frightened him, and he gave in. But he drinks like a fish. Then goes crazy from drink. Real crazy. Now he's trying to be decent again. What can I do about it? Where should I take the children, what could I do, without anything to start on? Were everything in my hands, it would all be different. Why, that's the only reason

I put up with it all. Now it is still worse. He is sure I would not leave him, as the children are big and I have nowhere to go. He shouts and swears at the least trifle. He tells me I don't know a thing. . . .

"And what do I do? I am not sincere to him. There is no civilized talk between us. He is not interested in hearing my woes or thoughts, he is not worthy of them. He is not a serious husband or father or even a serious man in village affairs. So how could I tell him my thoughts and cares? I detest him. How could I say anything good of him, the stupid fool."

The whole reason for her hatred of her husband is his inability to live a decent life, worthy of a man, head of a home. She is everything in the home.

"The children take after me. They do not like their father. They have no restraint toward him, they call him odd and laugh at him. And what when we are alone? I detest him even then. Like a stone when he gets on me. I hate him, I can tell you. There was a time when I thought I would leave him and go to another man. When I was younger. But not now. I have had children. One died. A girl. Like me she was. I did love her. I still grieve for her. She died when she was only five days old. That is seven years ago, now I don't have any more. I get rid of them. Twice a year these seven years now. . . .

"How? Oh, by myself. I massage myself. I get it away. I boil herbs and steam myself and it comes away. I don't spend a day in bed. The last time was this summer. It was already getting big. Oh! what bad things I have to do! My womb, you say? I feel it will drop, it will hang loose. What's life to me when I know I cannot bear it.

"Neither he nor I ever had dealings with any others. He doesn't let me go anywhere myself. Why, he doesn't even know about me coming to you. He does not look to me to do anything for him. He often makes mock of me. 'For being so knowing, you're happier so, you've made such a good marriage, you have,' he says."

This is how Vuka tells me her story. I got to know her through her child. She cocks her head a bit on one side and then off she goes, telling me the story, not hurrying. She tells it sensibly and all with point. She would like to learn about everything, simply does not know where to begin. She loves talking about her children. She is very fond indeed of them, very fair to them too, and easy in her handling of them. The children are terribly fond of her. Her first approach to me was:

"I've come to see you, I know you're a girl with schooling. You will give me a hand. . . . And you will teach my child the right things, she being a girl, not to be a martyr as I was. Not to have my rotten life. I see you've quite a lot of books. And the children are all fond of you. You must be kind. Do please teach her the right things. She's a girl, you know yourself the position of women today. Martyrs. I want to make sure she doesn't have that fate."

### Harshness and Beating

There are peoples who live through their whole life without harshness or cruelty to any weaker members of the family. For instance, most Indians in Mexico never strike their wives or their children unless intoxicated. Among the South Slavs, such gentleness is not common. Among them, the lower ranking member of the family is protected against violence and cruelty solely in certain historical stages of development, but in others is exposed to such ill-treatment that it can hardly be believed that we have to do with the same people. Graph 39, showing wife-beating by the husband, makes it clear under what conditions violence shows its face and how it spreads through the whole of an area.

Graph 39. Whether husbands beat their wives

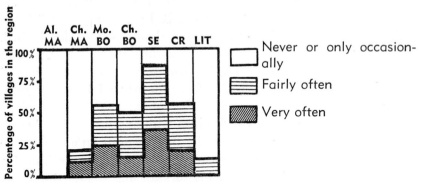

The steeply rising and falling curve, with its low points in the patriarchal region and again in the area of a new stabilization indicates that this phenomenon largely develops during the period of break-up of the patriarchal way of life and the zadruga, and formation of new relationships in the home. Comparison with Graph 38 which indicates whether women try to change their status, reveals a striking similarity of the two curves. There is clearly a link between the harshness of husbands and the resistance of wives: Ill-treatment prompts resistance, while the insubordination of the wives increases the husbands' harshness.

If on the other hand we compare this graph with **Graph 8** on page 77 regarding the punishment of children, we see great differences. With respect to the beating of children, all the regions are much the same, which shows that the application of some measure of force in the upbringing of children is common throughout the South Slav countryside as a whole, and not, like the ill-treatment of wives by husbands, due to disturbed family relationships.

In the patriarchal stage, however, as in the stage of a new equilibrium, the wives were almost entirely protected from beating. Two reports from Albanian villages reveal the men as patriarchally dignified, their authority moreover not open to question:

> It is considered a great crime and a scandalous thing to beat one's wife. Women are not beaten from religious motives, for Islam prohibits it. Islam permits the beating of wives only in three instances: If they go away from the house without asking and obtaining permission from their husbands, if they do not pray to God, and if they do not consent to perform their conjugal duty. *(Prespa district)*

> Husbands beat their wives only rarely and occasionally. They consider this to be right, but if it does happen it is to their shame, not their credit. *(Struga district)*

In Orthodox villages of Macedonia, a similar situation existed. It only came to beating occasionally, out of jealousy, but this was very rare.

> The wife forgives, for if he does strike her, he also caresses.
> *(Sjenica district, Sanjak)*

> In most cases they hold it to be abasing for a sensible husband and that it is wiser to seek a legal remedy, divorce. A husband never beats his wife. On the contrary one sees exceptional leniency in the husbands, unconcern, even indifference regarding the wife's delinquencies.
> *(Djevdjelija district)*

> It would bring shame to a wife to be beaten by her husband, for people would say she had failed to suit her behavior to her husband. Among the Moslems it is the husband's right. *(Debar district)*

In Macedonia, apart from a general patriarchal atmosphere, certain circumstances tended to prevent any cruelty or harshness toward the wife: The wives were often older than the husbands; many husbands went off for long periods of *pečalba* work, and when they returned were happy to have a home again. The shortage of wives and their high price also worked in the same sense.

In Bosnia, the picture changes completely. Calm and patriarchal only a few years previously, Bosnia and Hercegovina at the period of this research were beset by a mood of collapse and chaos. The rapid incursion of money economy, together with unfavorable political factors, resulted in internecine family struggles which were in the main to the disadvantage of the women as the physically weaker, who anyway in these parts by tradition occupied a low status. In Moslem Bosnia one can see two powerful contradictory trends. Of old, there has here been an Oriental fatalism and a sort of indifference which worked against the use of beating; while, in the opposite sense, work a rapid pauperization of this region, which together with this a mood of hopelessness and increased drunkenness, caused attacks of harshness.

Here is a report in patriarchal style:

Men beat their wives, but rarely. Considering the degree of enlightenment here, one could say that the husbands are attentive to their wives. It never comes to real hurt, and there is never beating in the presence of anybody else. *(Brčko district)*

Here is a report which represents beating as a sort of ancient custom, not merely the result of disputes:

The beating of wives is considered the husband's right. In June 1937 there was a case of a woman asking her doctor for advice. She said her husband refused to beat her and she thought there was something wrong with him. "What sort of a man is he when he hasn't once laid hands on me, it's unbearable." *(Jajce district)*

Here are examples of particular subordination of the wife:

The wife is subordinated as much as possible. She may not interfere in any of the husband's doings. People say, "The right hand need not know what the left hand does." "What the husband knows the wife need not." "The man who gives heed to a wife is worse than the wife." The saying is: "If he did so-and-so he was worse than a woman," and "woman is the most backward of creatures." *(Čajniče district)*

Woman is merely a necessary "thing" in the house which one has to keep an eye on. A woman should conceal herself, so the men do not see her at any cost. That is mortal sin. She neither knows nor should know anything. Only obey. She is not to be trusted. "Boast about the quality of the wheat when it's in your barn and your wife when she's in her grave." "Trust neither dog, horse, or woman!" *(Brčko district)*

The complete breakdown of any sort of domestic order, respect, or regard is revealed by the report from a village of mixed Moslem and Orthodox population:

Men beat the women, though it does happen for a wife to be stronger than her husband and beat him, particularly if he is drunk. In quarrels and fighting they don't care who is about, you hear it in the whole quarter. During such scenes one can hear a fine selection of oaths and loathsome expressions. *(Bijeljina district)*

In the Christian villages of Bosnia there was much excessive beating. Statistically, both parts of Bosnia look the same, but detailed examination reveals distinctions. In the Christian villages, the struggle was fiercer, the uncouthness greater, and traditional restraints were more easily lost. Islam was a powerful defense against the complete overthrow of traditional relationships between husband and wife. In the Orthodox villages of Bosnia, a general combativeness, connected with the Dinaric tradition, was often apparent. The vestiges of patriarchal dignity may also be seen in the following report:

Before the war, life had all the marks of the patriarchal upbringing, to be seen in the family and in the community generally. A woman's rights were limited, but she was more honored. The pre-war period had all the marks of patriarchal upbringing, with all the signs of a sound home upbringing, to be observed on many occasions of social and home life. In every more or less important event of home or social life the functions of every member of the family were clearly laid down and carried out with due seriousness. Today there is not a trace of this. *(Orthodox village, Derventa district)*

Yet another report combining severity and fairness:

The husband has the right to beat his wife for three reasons: Unfaithfulness, tongue-pie, and waste in the home. Otherwise it is regarded as shameful and unjust.

*(Catholic village with Orthodox minority, Derventa district)*

The following report shows the combination of patriarchal and modern elements typical of Orthodox Bosnia:

More get beaten than not. Both for jealousy and for bad housekeeping. Or because a wife will not let her parental heritage be spent, while secretly she squanders and distributes the joint property, giving away to her own family. "The first blow is salty," the peasants themselves and their wives too tell me. Resistance or disobedience results in use of mattock or stool. After that of course there are bruises and injuries. They do not so often beat them in front of other people, but quite often in front of the children. With strangers present, however, a husband swallows it and marks it up. "We defend ourselves when it hurts," are the words of an average peasant woman, while she says: "If I am in the wrong, I hold my tongue and bear it." And: "He has the right, for it's his house I am in, his bread I eat, while my work is not admitted," is the complaint of the same wife. The conviction is that it shames the whole house, principally because of the children, who thereby "get a bad name" and find it harder to find wife or husband.

(*Orthodox village, Bijeljina district*)

Fear lest authority be lost is in the following report reminiscent of the punishment of children in Serbia:

In addition to the usual "Long hair, short wit," the peasantry say of women that: "Let a woman have her way, she'll overturn a house on to its chimney," or: "She'd climb up on your head and unload herself down your neck." (*Bijeljina district*)

The following ditty rings cynically enough:

I like an ox which pulls well
And a man who beats his wife,
Lay on a wife, don't spare her body,
Let her innards rot away.[9]

(*Bosanski Petrovac district*)

Old-style and modern considerations are both to be seen in the following report, from the village where Božica lived:

The older men who used to beat their wives considered that the husband's right, but the younger men condemn it. They say they "know other ways and means." I never heard of a single case of beating of the wife even among the Moslems, where the woman is in a worse position than the Orthodox woman, because of the whole complex of their home set-up. But previously, wives were much beaten, the older men themselves say.

(*Orthodox village with Moslem minority, Sarajevo district*)

In Montenegro, the heroic tradition fostered a predisposition toward the use of force. Here patriarchal authority had a specific tone, namely, that there must be some outward marks of authority, and one of these is the beating of wives. But Montenegro was also a region in which much had changed, both in practice and in theory. During the survey, public opinion in the Montenegrin villages had begun to demand considerate treatment of wives. We can see a demonstrative element in the report given before (Cetinje district) and the same appears in the following statement:

As a rule, husbands beat their wives alone (without strangers or neighbors present), but many do not hide it from the children, for the men

---

[9] To cause laughter, this typical little ditty, which is almost untranslatable, is sung suddenly and at the top of the voice during a communal dance. It is here given literally.

want to show that they have the right to do so and to put fear into the children. *(Nikšić district)*

The following report shows certain consideration for the woman, both in a patriarchal and a comradely manner:

Women are not really very often beaten, indeed, more and more rarely. But all the same there is not a woman who has not had at least one beating from her husband in ten years of married life. It rarely comes to injuries (and in such a case divorce follows). In front of strangers and neighbors, they make every effort neither to hear nor to see anything wrong, but it is much more frequent for them to beat their wives in the presence of the children. In certain cases they consider they have a right, for instance, if the wife has committed a crime for which, in the general view, she should be beaten (if she insults her husband's parents, or does anything dishonorable). Beating wives without really important cause is condemned. *(Šavnik district)*

In Montenegro, in all family relationships, there was a direct transition from the patriarchal set-up to certain attempts at progress, in which the phase of much quarreling in the home, which we find in both Croatia and Serbia, was missing.

In Serbia, we find an atmosphere which particularly favored the use of force in the home. Practically all reports emphasize that there was much beating in all families and nearly all peasants definitely approved. The peasants expressed antagonism to beating only in exceptional instances, where there were progressive opinions. In Serbia there were no great differences on this subject between the patriarchal villages and those in a storm of ferment. A variety of factors, new and old, acted unfavorably for women. The fighting Dinaric tradition, the Turkish influence, and the rapid penetration of money economy created a complex of circumstances in which one of the outstanding features was the conviction that there should be severity toward women, with actual use of force. Here are characteristic sayings:

Beat a woman and a horse every three days. *(Niš district)*

If you don't beat a woman she'll go mad in forty days.

*(Morava district)*

He's no man if he has not boxed a woman's ears. *(Dragačevo district)*

A husband should beat his wife so she knows who's the man in the house.

If not beaten, a woman will leap over the house. *(Banja district)*

Bribe your brother and your ox but beat your wife and your horse.

Every woman has an extra rib [thinking here of the one taken from man to make woman] and this needs breaking.

Wave it over the ox, but bring it down on your wife's head.

Wave it over a cur's head, but bring it down on a girl's [i.e., you cannot trust a girl]. *(Kosmaj district)*

The following are reports from a patriarchal environment where beating was used demonstratively:

A husband beats his wife only when the parents complain to the son about insults done them by their snaha. If a husband beats his wife in the presence of neighbors and children, it is considered that he has thereby gained a point to the advantage of his authority. A husband is the master of his wife and it is his right to beat her.

*(Vlasotince district)*

Previously a snaha had to take her father-in-law's footwear off, and serve him in everything, she had to eat last and kiss the hand of a small boy. They beat a wife more, while the neighbors looked on. Girls had to marry whom their elders appointed. *(Sokobanja district)*

And here is a report revealing a decrease in the husband's authority:

The authority of the husband has decreased a little. This is seen by there already being cases of a woman's fighting back when beaten, of deceiving the husband in marital matters, and of not fearing him as she once did, and sometimes of treating casual visitors without his knowledge. *(Jablanica district)*

All these formulations reveal that the militant tradition had a different tone from that of the old-style, stable districts. Serbia was an immigrants' region, settled by incomers from all parts of the Slavic South, people cut off from their old environment, who had developed a powerful tendency to personal initiative and a particular individualism. Legal custom and aversion to the use of brute force in the family were less developed in them than in people in the old-style districts.

In Croatia, other factors operated, and bad treatment had a different quality from that known in Serbia. Any disposition to the use of brute force was unable to gain much headway under Austria. In addition, the Catholic Church influenced people against taking all rights away from women. Nevertheless, the re-shaping of the zadruga here too introduced strife and disunity into the family and prepared the ground for uncouthness and harshness. But it is only in the former Military March and the Dinaric districts (the Lika and Dalmatia) that one observes a combative climate and a tendency to use force comparable with that in Serbia. Here are some reports from those districts:

> Husbands beat their wives, and quite frequently. One can count on the fingers of one's hand the men who have never struck their wives. Woman is simply inured to beatings.     (*Dvor on the Una district*)

> In the main, woman is regarded as a subordinate to her husband, whom she must invariably obey but who may despise and insult her. If any man wants to prove to another that he is not going to allow himself to be humbled or treated anyhow, he will say "I am not your wife."
> (*Orthodox village, Petrinja district*)

> Women are mostly beaten in their young married days, when the husband is easily swayed and obeys whatever mother, brothers, another snaha, etc., or any other may say about his wife. Then, to please them, he beats her. The rest, the minority, beat from jealousy, many others, again, because of a wife's rebeling against her husband's tyranny and arbitrary rule in the home. They beat them mainly with their hands, i.e., boxing their ears or slapping them under the ribs or wherever they can reach. Very often they use hard objects, sticks and such, from which injuries result, and principally to the womb. They also beat their wives in front of strangers. What is more, this is a way of showing off before others. It is a great feather in one's cap to beat one's wife, as this shows that one is the master. Certainly the women defend themselves when beaten, as it is not easy to put up with beating. But when one discusses it with them, they will say: "What else can one do but bear it, as he is the man, so he has the right to do what he wants with his wife." There are few who think differently.
> (*Slunj district, Kordun*)

> Do they beat their wives? I should think they do, and frequently. Mostly when drunk, from jealousy and just to show their superiority to the woman. They beat them with fists, sticks, and belts. This is no shame for a husband. Instead, he is proud. He beats both mother and daughter-in-law. "If she didn't deserve it, she would not get it." One day I heard the following: They had quarreled—husband and wife. She reproached him with spending a lot on tobacco, whereas her skirt was all "windows"—i.e., all in rags. He began to shower the coarsest vulgarities on her, swearing foully by her mother in her grave. And what did she do? She plucked up courage and gave him as good as she got. . . . But then he began to pound her with his fists, till I thought that, slender little thing as she was, she would be broken, crushed. "You dare take my mother's name in vain?" he cried. "You touch her? You?" And he thumps her all over her head and shoulders. "You dare, you misery, don't you know who I am? I am the boss, I have a

265

right to give it to you, but you? Just you get it into your head that I am the boss!" That is her place. Hold her tongue and bear it. She must wait on them.                              (*Orthodox village, Grubišnopolje district*)

The Dinaric parts of Dalmatia had formerly exhibited a typical combative spirit, but at the time of this research had come much nearer to the Littoral villages, which of course are contiguous with them. One can observe these great changes from the following answer:

They only beat their wives by exception, and it does not come to serious injury; that would be shame for both. They never beat in the presence of strangers, rarely that of children, still less that of the neighbors. They fear criticism of public opinion. It is not considered to be the husband's right, the majority consider it shameful. Previously things were different. Let this poem be witness of that:

> Then I took a whippy switch
> And I lashed out twice or thrice,
> Kaia wanted to go to the well,
> Kaia wanted to go sticking,
> Kaia wanted to go everywhere.

There are sayings: "Hit your wife, your potage'll be the sweeter." Or this rhyming jingle:

> Where I glance,
> Off you dance,
> Where my moustache points,
> You stir your joints.

This was the position before the war. Today the position of the women has improved. But even today a woman will get to her feet when an older man comes along the road or bids her good day. They may not cross the road in front of a man, but wait for him to pass. Before the war a woman dared not dream of saying anything against the husband's decisions. She had to submit blindly to the husband or the head of the zadruga. Today the well-intentioned advice or reproach of a sensible woman can do much to decide things in family life. Only the men cannot bear others to know that their wives "dictate to them." This change had begun to show immediately after the war, still more during the depression.                              (*Knin district*)

Though in central Croatia, they also beat women frequently, fierceness and lack of control were slightly less in evidence, except under alcoholic influence.

Women are often beaten, quite guiltless, too, for some consider that a woman should be beaten not to be "spoiled." Otherwise it usually comes to beating through drunkenness, because of spendthrift ways, or when a woman refuses to submit to what the husband has said.

*(Varaždin district)*

Husbands often beat wives, as a rule when drunk. When these reproach them with drinking, wasting money, jealousy, insubordination, "she answers back." They beat them with their bare hands, their feet, a stick or anything else that comes to hand. There are injuries, but the women prefer to hide them. *(Varaždin district)*

This following little scene from the Croatian highlands, related by a man teacher, is typical of uncouthness without great emotion:

There was suddenly a scrap in the inn. A young peasant with great enthusiasm rushed into the fray, when his wife however grabbed his coat, crying, and shrieked: "Don't, you'll be killed!" He turned round on her and hit her so hard that he knocked her down. But, not in the least put out, she just went on shrieking as she lay there: "You keep out of it, you'll be killed!" *(Varaždin district)*

In Croatia, the tradition of zadruga ways with a democratic note and the fact that the split-up of the zadrugas was mainly over, all acted as a sort of brake. The impoverishment which followed on the transference to independent farming made for uncouthness together with drunkenness.

In districts with gradual development and a new equilibrium, we find much similarity to the patriarchal environment. Here was the same settled way of life and similarly the lack of any struggle for dominance inside the home. Down the Littoral the great emigration of the men worked in the same way as the Macedonian labor away from home (*pečalba*) in its influence on the attitude of husband to wife. There were, however, new elements here. Rights between husband and wife were more evened out than in the patriarchal region. This was in the main the result of Western influences coming from former Austria and from Italy, from the Catholic Church, and finally from those returning from emigration, from America or Australia. The first examples are from the northern part of the Littoral:

There are numerous proverbs which come to the same as the well-known: "The wife holds up three corners [of the house], the husband the fourth." There is not a house without one, two, or more emigrants, so it is left to the wife to manage the home and do all the work, even that which in other parts is exclusively the men's task. Hence the rights which the women have. They are quite the equals of their husbands.

*(Isle of Krk)*

The story told in the following report is typical:

Cases of the man beating his wife are very rare. It is generally accepted that men are under the wife's slipper.

Perhaps this story will help you to grasp the relationships of husband and wife. A quarrel had broken out between husband and wife, and the wife was chasing the husband about the house with a broom. To avoid the blows, he got under the bed. She poked at him with her broom, shouting: "Come on out of there, come on out of there!" But he replied: "I'm not coming out, let people see who's the boss in this house!" (*Isle of Krk*)

In Slavonia too there were many villages with the new equilibrium. This area, which with its wheat production and oak forests was the first to find a place in the world market, did not have to adapt itself to the new conditions so rapidly as the other parts of Croatia. The women of Slavonia often based their self-confidence on their dowry and inheritance:

In quite a lot of the Sava Basin villages the wives have an attitude of superiority to their husbands. Particularly in the grape-growing districts. The women are as a rule more sober-headed, so there is quite a lot of mental superiority in them. Hence they rule in home and on the farm; they rule the men. Sometimes that influence is reflected in political and religious matters. Husband and wife consult each other about everything. Altogether, women here are an important, if not the decisive factor in the household and on the farm. For the reason that they are more painstaking and assiduous. (*Nova Gradiška district*)

The combative spirit brought a continuous danger of force and cruelty into family relations. The patriarchal system created a counter-balance. While in the later period advanced ideas about human rights and the equality of all people acted as a brake on violence. In the patriarchal system, the wife was completely protected, but progressive trends at the time of this inquiry had only exceptionally penetrated into the heart of family relationships in the villages.

In this inquiry into beating and ill-treatment within the family, one cannot help wondering whether such violence and harshness had not some basic connection with the brilliant qualities of warlike tribes and peoples. For it is precisely those Yugoslav regions in which we find uncouthness and violence toward women that throughout lengthy periods of history (including the Second World War) consistently resisted any attempt at foreign domination, enemy occupation, and tyranny, and struggled for national liberation with unlimited self-sacrifice. On the other hand, in many Indian tribes

29. Serbian woman

30. Weaver, Croatia

31. Waiting at the mill, Bosnia

32. Making coral necklaces, Dalmatia

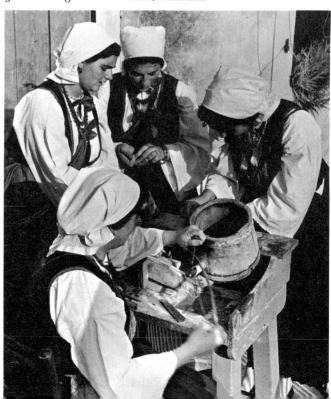

in Mexico, which exhibit particularly noble and humane family relationships, we see that their aversion to force and cruelty, be it solely in self-defense, has a fateful side when it comes to foreign invasion. Their resistance to the Spanish invasion and colonization was insignificant. When they found themselves in the exact situation as the "raya" in the Balkans, they did not "take to the forest"; they did not fight at all against the greatest tyrants. This connection has not yet been proved or even investigated, but nobody who studies conditions in the Balkans and compares them with those in Latin America can help wondering if it is not provable. The comparison reveals the face and obverse of militancy and also of the aversion to the application of any force.

### Disciplinary Right of the Husband

In what environments do people admit that the husband has the right to beat his wife? Where do they question the right? Do they think the husband has the right to discipline the lower ranking members sternly and relentlessly or do they consider it a disgraceful act if the husband beats the wife, an act unworthy of a head of a house, and one degrading for the wife? Do theory and practice in the matter coincide?

Graph 40 gives the answer, both where theory and practice coincide and where they disagree.

Graph 40. The disciplinary right of the husband

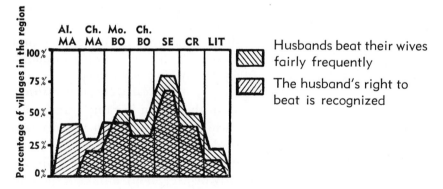

In the first combination, that which we might term a gentle climate (the blank part of the graph), husbands do not beat their wives, or only by exception, nor are they considered to have the right to do so. Examples:

269

Degraded, badly brought-up individuals beat their wives, but this is rather rare. There are cases of injury, this depends on the man's character. If a man does beat his wife, this is usually done in the evening, when they are alone. The peasants consider such acts very low, indecent and signs of a bad character, and they condemn it.

*(Albanian village, Vučitrn district)*

Husbands practically never beat their wives. If this does happen, under the influence of alcohol, as an isolated case, and it does come to boxes of the ears, the whole village publicly condemns such a master of a house. *(Isle of Mljet, Littoral)*

The statistics show (though this is not clear in the graph) that this combination is most frequent in the patriarchal region and that of gradual development. In some parts, the solidarity of the new and the old types is such that one cannot distinguish the exact kind of harmony and stability of life in them. This is, for instance, the case in Dalmatia and Slavonia.

The second combination indicates an uncouth climate (double-crossed in the graph) where women are frequently beaten and the husband has the right to do so:

Women are very often beaten, and it sometimes comes to injuries. The men consider it their right. They are proud of it, boast.

*(Serbia, Jablanica district)*

The peasants consider, and so do their wives, that this is the husband's right as head of the family. If a woman does anything wrong and the husband does not give her a good beating, she begins to despise him, counts him a weakling and strives to assume his place in the home. The village has no respect for such a husband and speaks of the wife as "wearing the trousers." It has been so from olden time. In the opinion of the village, the husband is absolute master in his home, who must see that there is order in the home, and who has the right to punish the members of the family if they do anything very wrong.

*(Croatia, Dugoselo district)*

A large number of the villages in the region in rapid transformation revealed this grouping, in which uncouthness in practice was matched by the theoretical demand for severity.

The third grouping we might describe as a conservative idyll, for the women are not beaten (or only by exception), although the husband has disciplinary rights. Here practice and theory are at variance, and favorably for women. The head of the house acts in the manner of a great-hearted patriarch, who, though he may have the right and the duty of being severe, yet acts by gentle means. Here is an instance from an intact patriarchal village:

**270**

Husbands beat their wives quite rarely. It never comes to serious injuries. They do not beat them in front of others but only when alone, and even then exceptionally. It is the husband's right, but from long disuse has become obsolete, and today the peasants consider it an unworthy means of education, if we may put it so, for the men think they should keep an eye on their wives and continue their education.

(*Struga district, Albanian village*)

The fourth category is what we might call roughness with a bad conscience. Here the wives are often beaten, though this is not considered to be the husband's right, indeed, even often quite shameful. Here practice and theory are at variance, but unfavorably for the wives.

When one talks to the men, the majority today admit that one should not beat one's wife, but yet each of them individually confesses to this sin of beating his wife. (*Serbia, Morava district*)

This group comprises villages which are in process of rapid transformation. Though in some areas there are advanced views, the break-up of the zadrugas and the re-shaping of the family was accompanied by quarrels and cruelty. We find this combination particularly in the pauperized villages of Moslem Bosnia, where the demands of patriarchal dignity conflicted with the harsh life in poverty, and desperation.

To conclude, under certain conditions, there was a contradiction between ideology and actual practice: In the patriarchal area this contradiction was to the advantage of wives, while, in the area in a state of rapid transformation, it often went against them. In the region with a new equilibrium, theory and practice again coincided, and favorably for the woman.

## Roughness and Gentleness in the Family

We may ask if rough behavior in the home prevailed in some districts while more civilized behavior prevailed in other districts. Was there a great deal of cruelty regarding all the weaker members of the family in some regions, while in others the beating of children as well as of wives was out of the question? Was there any connection between the ill-treatment of women and the punishment of children? Statistical examination shows simply that there is everywhere a close correlation between the beating of wives and children. Severity or harshness of the head of the house are, in any environment, the same toward wife and children. Nowhere do we find agreement between husband and wife regarding severity toward the children coupled with a soli-

271

darity between them such as will exclude ill-treatment of the wife. Where we find rough treatment of the children we also find rough treatment of the wife, and where gentle treatment of the children prevails, we find the same regarding the wife.

In our examination of this correlation, the most prevalent treatment was the "gentle" one. The distribution of such villages, in which neither children nor wives were much beaten, round the various regions proves to be strikingly regular. Here we show the combination arranged in a circle which is obviously closed:

Ma. Al.
43%

Lit.                    Mac. Ch.
27%                     27%

Cro.                    Bos. Mo.
21%                     19%

Serb.        Bos. Ch.
5%           14%

At the time of this inquiry, the upper portion of this circle was, so to speak, characterized by a climate of peace. The wheel, however, turns, and it is quite feasible for regions which then had a stormy climate later to be peaceful, while settled regions may enter a phase of change (and this may already have taken place). At the time of the survey, the patriarchal regions were already in great danger of losing their state of peace.

The following description, from a Macedonian village, offers a picture of gentleness and civilized treatment of both wife and children:

The wife is looked upon as the pillar of the household. There is a saying about this: "Let husband use a cart and wife only a needle, she'll empty the house first." In these reports it is striking that the position of a woman in this village is an enviable one, unlikely as this may seem for women in a Macedonian village. However, this village should not be taken as the measure of all Macedonian villages. There are few districts in which the women are in such a position. The reason for its being like this here is in my opinion that here the men engage a lot in *pečalba*. A great number go away a lot for such long-period work. At the moment there are some 72 who are absent, while latterly, before the depression, the number sometimes rose to over 100. When the men are away, it is the women who run the household, while the men, according to their own declaration, observe reasonable abstinence as far as sex goes. When they get back from their period of work, they concentrate all their attention on wife and children. Similarly with the bringing up of children by gentle means: While the husband is away, the wives give all their attention to the children, they are gentle with them; and later, when the husband returns, they cannot alter in this regard. Likewise the fathers. Being away for long periods, five, six, ten, or more years, they do not see the children, and when they do come home pour out all their affection on them and their wives.

(*Village of 812 persons, 427 being men, Prespa district, Macedonia*)

It is a striking coincidence that the two regions here which have a peaceable family life, Macedonia and the Littoral, both had a large emigration of the men. This increased the affection and leniency of the returning men regarding wife and children, features which we find in both these regions of the old-style or new equilibrium anyway.

## Consultation of Wife by Husband

In a patriarchal environment, as a rule, the husband does not consult his wife about anything. There is great aloofness between the two, the wife being considered too immature to examine problems and decide what to do. The husband bears all the responsibility himself, or else shares it with his male relatives. A contributory factor is the circumstance that in an old-style environment all relationships are firmly molded and all situations so stereotyped that it is rare for any very important decisions to be needed. In comparison with the fateful decisions taken by peasants in the stage of break-up of the zadrugas, what decisions there are remain trifling. In the stage of reshaping of the family, the sphere of questions which have to be settled, and in which the wife acquires influence, is rapidly extended. Now zadrugas are splitting up, land is being bought and sold, and here and there children are being sent to school, apprenticed to crafts, or sent to other employment. In an environment with a new equilibrium the matters to be decided on may be still greater, and in almost all of them the wife too takes part.

Whereas harshness and beating constitute a negative aspect, consultation of the wife by the husband reveals a bright aspect of the break-up of the patriarchal order. Consultation of the wife is a sign of yielding of the husband's authority, of abandonment of his autocracy and the raising of the position of the woman.

273

## Graph 41. Does the husband consult his wife?

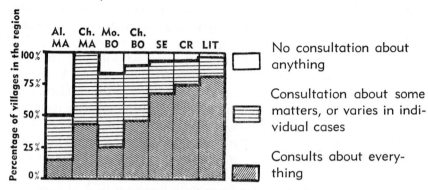

Percentage of villages in the region

Al. Ch. Mo. Ch.
MA MA BO BO SE CR LIT

No consultation about anything

Consultation about some matters, or varies in individual cases

Consults about everything

Graph 41 gives us a simple rising curve with only one break, that of Christian Macedonia. Consulting the wife is an achievement which, once acquired, is never lost again. The bonds between the married couple become increasingly close in direct ratio to the penetration of money economy and the introduction of individual farming, without regard to whether the new factors penetrate and develop in a stormy process or gradually. The first examples are from Albanian villages:

A husband does not consult his wife. Such cases are rare. The wife's place is to obey. The husband thinks of everything. He deals, he sells. There is nothing to discuss in the children's future. That is a subject never spoken of at all. Here fate rules. God has written what the children's future shall be. Nothing can be changed. What is written, is written. And that future written for the children is: pečalba, shepherding, wielding the mattock, marriage. (*Nerodimlje district*)

It is rare that husband and wife discuss anything, if they do, it will only be things connected with her, her tasks or the children.

(*Struga district*)

The husband consults the wife about household and day-to-day needs. He does not consult her concerning honor, an insult, or anything like that. (*Vučitrn district*)

In Montenegro we find a special, heroic, color in the husband's authority.

There is no consultation, for that is considered self-abasement before one's wife. (*Andrijevica district*)

But here too there were great changes. For instance:

A husband does consult his wife about all the more important domestic needs, such as purchase or sale of property, schooling of children, a removal and the betrothal of a daughter or son. (*Cetinje district*)

In the Orthodox villages of Macedonia there was much more consultation than in the remaining patriarchal regions. The reasons were the relatively small number of women and the respect they enjoyed as mistresses of the home, the custom of marrying older girls to young boys, and the pečalba system, through which the wives often had to manage the home themselves.

> Regarding all domestic matters, husband and wife consult each other, but everything is dependent on agreement. And this does exist in these parts. *(Prespa district)*

> The husband does not ask his wife solely about political matters. Regarding all material disbursements he does. *(Skoplje district)*

> A husband never consults his wife. He does everything according to his own whim. *(Prilep district)*

In the Moslem part of Bosnia, women were particularly subjected, and their voice was never heard:

> In most cases a husband does not ask his wife about anything, he does as he finds fit and holds that his wife is not capable of giving an opinion on anything. *(Čajniče district)*

> A husband does not consult his wife about anything. As a rule he issues orders and she has no right to discuss these, or there would be a quarrel at once. *(Brčko district)*

In the Orthodox villages of Bosnia, quite apart from the many disputes, there was rather more consultation between husband and wife:

> In practically all matters, the husband and wife discuss things. Among the Moslems, the husband looks for advice rather aside from his wife, from his relations and neighbors.
> *(Mixed Orthodox and Moslem village, Sarajevo district)*

> In rare instances, husband and wife discuss things. As a rule, the husband has the principal word. A wife may beg her husband as much as she likes not to sell some household good, but it is of no avail if he has once decided on it. *(Orthodox village, Banja Luka district)*

And a report from Serbia:

> Today an increasing number of women participate in agreement with the husband, whereas previously the husband did everything without even informing her. *(Mladenovac district)*

In Croatia, also, despite quarrels, there was much consultation between husband and wife. There was almost as much consultation as down the Littoral, which shows that such consultation was becoming customary while transformation of the family was still in progress.

Probably in Croatia, even in the intact zadrugas, there was more consultation with the wife than in districts with a tribal system.

The following are examples of a sort of preparatory stage of consultation:

> In the main, the husbands determine things, the wives consenting, except in dressing the daughter, where the wife works by herself, secretly. (*Gračac district, Lika area*)

> Wife and husband practically never consult each other; he proposes, she accepts. (*Kutina district*)

The circle narrows, from which the wife is excluded:

> Husband and wife consult each other, but apart, and as a rule keep it secret. Before others they rarely do so. Before others the husband hides any such consultation with the wife, for they would laugh at him. It is rare for the wife to have any decisive word in any consultation. (*Varaždin district*)

> The husband consults his wife about everything which touches house and farm, the upbringing of the children, but not political matters, village affairs, or the community council; here he never does consult her. (*Dugoselo district*)

> Concerning work, a husband consults his wife; but when he spends, he does not ask anybody. (*Zlatar district*)

Reports from economically advanced villages:

> Ninety-five per cent of husbands consult their wives, but hide this from others. (*Prelog district*)

> Husband and wife consult each other about everything; there are even cases where he asks his wife about his craft needs. (*Samobor district*)

> Husband and wife discuss household and family matters. About politics they do not, still less about his purely masculine affairs, about which his wife would tear his hair out. (*Županja district, Slavonia*)

In a region with the new equilibrium, the basis of contact extended still further, particularly in the Littoral. The following description seems to answer the question whether the wife consults the husband, rather than the reverse:

> The husband works a great deal, the wife practically not at all. She takes her own produce to nearby towns, Crikvenica, Novi, and Sušak, selling brandy, figs, oil and wine. She moves about among people more, and in a natural sense is the more intelligent. For this reason, she manages the home and all in it. The husband is there to work, like a servant. This is the consequence of the man's being so worn out by

labor up on the rocky hillside that he does not even desire to worry
his head about other matters when he gets home.

*(Isle of Krk, northern Littoral)*

As we see, the common sector of the life of husband and wife
gradually and continually widened. Despite the frequent quarrels in
certain stages, the conjugal partners gradually grow accustomed to
bearing jointly the new burdens imposed by the individual economy.
Consultation between husband and wife constituted the bright side
of the destruction of the patriarchal system from the woman's standpoint, for now at last she acquired a position more worthy of an
adult.

Is there any link, positive or negative, between uncouthness and
consultation with the wife? Do ill-treatment of the wife and consultation of her exclude one another? The following table sets out the
relationship between these two attitudes.

TABLE 2. THE CONNECTION BETWEEN BEATING
THE WIFE AND CONSULTING HER

|  | | Moslem | Christian | | | |
|  | Macedonia | Bosnia | Bosnia | Serbia | Croatia | Littoral |
|  | (figures are percentages of each region) | | | | | |
| **First combination** "Patriarchal aloofness," Wife not beaten, and no consultation | 36 | 30 | 23 | 5 | 9 | 20 |
| **Second combination** "Aloofness and uncouthness." Wives beaten, and no consultation | 16 | 48 | 35 | 30 | 16 | 10 |
| **Third combination** "Comradely quarrels." Wives beaten, but consultation | 4 | 7 | 13 | 55 | 38 | 10 |
| **Fourth combination** "Comradely harmony." Wives not beaten, and consulted | 44 | 15 | 29 | 10 | 37 | 60 |

This table shows an exceptionally regular distribution of the
various groupings. Patriarchal aloofness prevailed in most Macedonian villages (still more among the Albanians, who are not shown

here). Though women had a relatively good position in Macedonia, dignified aloofness between husband and wife nevertheless remained.

The second combination, aloofness plus uncouthness toward the wife, dominated in Bosnia (and Hercegovina). The stormy transformation of family life in this region resulted in a state of convulsion and uncouthness. Here the traditional scorn of woman played its part. A woman had not much to say, and the husband did not pay attention to her even at this time when the old patriarchal dignity and sense of responsibility of the head of the household have vanished. The Bosnian woman stood under a dual pressure, compounded of the old-style factor of aloofness of the husband and a new element of harshness and lack of concern for her.

The third combination, friendly quarreling, prevailed in Serbia and Croatia. In a period of unrestrained individualism, the old isolation and obscurity of women disappear. Particularly often do we find this combination in Serbia. The traditional combativeness did not prevent the development of a comradely relationship between the conjugal partners. Here the women showed themselves to be particularly self-confident, independent, and militant, so that even though the husband still denied his wife equal rights, he could not disregard her when making decisions.

The fourth combination, friendly harmony between the husband and wife, prevailed down the Littoral, where differences in authority had largely been wiped out. We also come upon this combination in a great number of Croat villages (particularly in the economically advanced part in Slavonia). But this combination was also widely distributed in a patriarchal environment, that of Macedonia. Patriarchal stability and the friendly relations of the new age thus met! This similarity between Macedonia and the Littoral is also to be seen in that in both regions patriarchal gentleness of manners is transformed into stability of a new type, and the stage of fierce strife never fully develops. If we add together the villages with patriarchal aloofness and those with comradely harmony, we find that in the Littoral and Macedonia we have the same proportion—80 per cent. Conditions favorable for women were to be found alike in the most patriarchal environment and in the modern one.

The table thus shows a clear shift of accent from the old-style to the modern. In other words, development was in four stages: From patriarchal aloofness, through aloof uncouthness and general beating, to a new harmony and equilibrium, or from the old hierarchy through a state of chaos to a new order, in which the wife's voice was heard and her counsel valued, and she shared cares, responsibilities, and rights with her husband.

### Lucia: Example of a Comradely Wife

This report was contributed by woman teacher, Darinka Host, from the north Littoral.

Lucia is pretty and very charming. She is thirty-four, but in comparison with her age-group looks much younger. She told me her story with warmth and sincerity while busy at needlework. It is a general characteristic of hers that her hands are never still. She is always at something. She is most painstaking and tidy. She had come to me to be shown some needlework, and it was fortunate for me. We worked together, and I was able at the same time to pursue my inquiry.

Lucia still dresses in peasant costume, though it has lost some characteristics of the past and changed a lot, but the cut is the same, only the material, a print, is bought.

"My dear teacher," she says, "why, I really never was a child. I went to school, but already had to work at home. I was the oldest. I had to look after four younger than myself. I had to do the wash when necessary, cook, and make the bread. Every summer my mother had a child, and after every confinement was bedridden for five months. So it all fell on my shoulders. I shall never forget how when I first made the bread, I was still not strong enough to knead it firm, and my mother would rap me over the knuckles. I did the work for all the younger ones and also got beaten for them all.

"My father had been to the war and immediately after school I had to work at field work and go up the mountain after the sheep. When I grew up I was stronger and had still more to do. Then I also began dancing. A lot of lads ran after me, but I found a fault in each of them and not one suited me. Like that I waited till I was twenty, when my present husband came and we fell in love. We courted three months, then we were married."

She makes much mention of her love for her husband, but always indirectly, for this is regarded as a weakness, even rather disgraceful.

"It was only then that I really began to live. I never had such a bad time since I lived with him. He is kind to me somehow we get over everything else."

She has described to me her first married night, her first pregnancy and her miscarriage after three months, then a second miscarriage and her husband's disappointment that they had no children, for after the second miscarriage she could not at once get pregnant any more. After five more years, however, she had yet another miscarriage, and it was only when she was pregnant the fourth time that she went to a doctor for advice (directed to this by her husband) and at last bore a boy. She describes the pains of birth and says she would rather have never had anything more to do with her husband than have to give birth again, although she is a woman full of temperament. Altogether, she emphasizes that childbirth is horrible, even the first night she told me about was only half as bad. On another occasion she said:

"When I see a woman is near her time I get the shivers and think: Poor dear!"

Despite this, after the first child, eighteen months later she had another. But now she will not hear of it again, and she says she would give a lot to know some way of not getting pregnant any more.

She is very fond of children, and hers are cleverer than those of her friends of the same age. She keeps them very clean. She says to me:

"Let me tell you, love for one's children is very great, neither husband nor anybody do you love like your child."

When she married, she went to live with the parents of her husband, who kept an inn at P. But owing to "lack of care," as she puts it, this began to go downhill, so her husband went to America, where he spent four years. Then there arose quarrels with his parents and she went back to her native village, that is to say, where she is now. When her husband returned from America, he had to go into the army.

"Luckily we had no more children," she says.

Her husband went to look for work, then fell ill and was five months in hospital.

"At the same time I was pregnant and brought to childbed. Not a penny in the house, me in bed with the babe, he in the hospital. Luckily I had my mother, who helped me."

Finally, the husband found a job as chauffeur, where he still works.

"Now, thank heaven, we are all right, except that we are not together (her husband being in the neighboring town of Sušak), "but I am going to take the children and join him when we've saved a bit so we can buy some things for a home."

Our village is connected with Sušak, though it is some hours by steamer or on foot from this town. The peasants sell their grapes, tomatoes, and wild asparagus there. There has been a school here for nearly a hundred years, so there are scarcely any illiterates, except perhaps one or two who have just forgotten their letters. There is little land, so most of the men go away to earn, and the wives stay behind and do all the men's work. But on the other hand, women here are not in a state of subjection.

On the whole there are no rich here, they are all poor and struggle away, working at the rocky soil, to sow a little barley and rye to get some hard black bread. They are very tough and industrious, and inured to misfortune, which, living on this bare rock, is inevitable.

From the number of women with whom I have talked I come to the conclusion that they were more oppressed by their subordinate position before marriage. That is, being subject to their parents. Every girl aims at marriage, even though the majority of them tell of terrible difficulties in married life; for instance, the duties of a mother and the terrors of childbirth, as many of them call it. These arise from the fact that each of them wants to be independent, depending on nobody, the husband later in married life being a comrade with the same rights, except, as many of them insist, that the woman has the greater duties.

## Changes in the Treatment of the Wife

It is not at all easy to obtain a sure answer to the question whether uncouthness toward the wife and ill-treatment of the wife were increasing or decreasing. On the one hand, it is clear that in the old-style regions, which as we have taken it represent the past, there was less beating than in the regions in which the patriarchal system was falling to pieces, but on the other hand one is always coming on data showing that earlier there had been more severity and more beating than during the time of this inquiry. I have endeavored to obtain a solution to this problem in two ways.

First, I have examined the correlation between the zadruga way of life and ill-treatment of the women; that is, whether in villages with zadrugas the women were more or less beaten than where there are no zadrugas.

The table shows a typical shift of emphasis from old-style to modern regions. In the patriarchal region good treatment was linked with the zadruga. The first step away from this way of life was ill-treatment of the women while the zadrugas still existed, then came the break-up of the zadruga and an increase in ill-treatment, and finally a new consolidation of the family without the zadruga and also without ill-treatment. In the patriarchal region, good treatment

## TABLE 3. THE ZADRUGA AND ILL-TREATMENT OF WOMEN

| | Macedonia | Serbia | Croatia | Littoral |
|---|---|---|---|---|
| | (figures are percentages of the regions) | | | |
| *First combination* | | | | |
| Zadrugas and no beating | 64 | 5 | 11 | 26 |
| *Second combination* | | | | |
| Zadrugas and frequent beating | 18 | 30 | 7 | 5 |
| *Third combination* | | | | |
| No zadrugas and frequent beating | 9 | 55 | 47 | 13 |
| *Fourth combination* | | | | |
| No zadrugas and no beating | 9 | 10 | 35 | 56 |

of the women was based on the patriarchal order, while in the modern region it was based rather on equality of the members of the family. This is shown more clearly in the following figures:

| | Macedonia | Littoral |
|---|---|---|
| Total no. of villages in which zadruga and beating are mutually exclusive (combinations 1 and 3) | 73% | 40% |
| Total no. of villages in which zadruga and beating coincide (combinations 2 and 4) | 27% | 60% |

In an old-style region where there were zadrugas, women were not beaten. Down the Littoral the exact opposite was the case. Here we find uncouth treatment of women only in the backward villages of Dalmatia, where zadrugas have been preserved, while in the advanced villages, long since adapted to money economy, there was good treatment of the women. In the region in a state of stormy ferment there is no counter-balance to ill-treatment of the women.

Nor was a simple answer to the question about changes in the treatment of women obtained from the reports of my investigators in answer to the question whether before the war (or before the economic depression) the husbands beat their wives more than today. Shown graphically, the replies present a very complex picture.

Graph 42 clearly indicates two opposing trends, which in every region had different force, according to the predisposition of the region. In many regions the trend which decreased beating seemed to be more powerful than that which brought out uncouthness and ill-treatment.

Graph 42. Changes in the ill-treatment of women

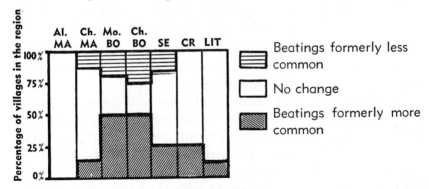

Beatings formerly less common

No change

Beatings formerly more common

This result, however, does not mean that earlier, in the patriarchal environment, men were tougher with their wives than at the time of this inquiry, except in certain districts with a particularly combative tradition. Though even this we cannot assert for certain, for the data of my investigators relate to a recent past, that is to say, precisely to the beginning of the great changes, which tended to bring with them this wave of cruelty and ill-treatment. We find an intact patriarchal system solely among the Albanians, though here we find no signs that previously treatment was any rougher.

It is in Bosnia that we see most clearly all the interweaving trends. The swift changes in this region favored the creation of a fateful complex of the old dependence of the woman and a new inconsiderateness toward her. The first report shows a trend in favor of the woman:

Husbands rarely beat their wives. They consider this a husband's right, but now even that is criticized. Before the war, the position of a woman was worse. Now they are treated more humanly out of purely "natural" reasons.     (*Bosnia, Moslem and Catholic village, Bugojno district*)

Another report, however, shows a trend against women:

The husbands very frequently beat their wives. It comes to minor injuries, but they never go to court about it. Very often the reason is the woman's immorality. Before the war, there was certainly less. Then it was shameful to beat a wife and this rarely happened, and, when it did, every effort was made to keep it quiet. Today the principal reason is the immoral conduct of married women, and there is a great deal of that. (*Bosnia, Orthodox and Catholic village, Derventa district*)

Among the patriarchal regions, the ill-treatment of wives decreased mainly in the Dinaric districts, where previously there had been beating to emphasize the authority of the man.

Before the war, a man had much more right to beat his wife, even without any very serious reason. Since before the crisis this matter has steadily changed in favor of the woman. (*Montenegro, Šavnik district*)

In Croatia, on the other hand, where the family had somewhat settled down after the split-up of the zadrugas, we find that ill-treatment of the wives had also diminished.

The trend toward the raising of the status of the wife (and the reduction of beating) is part of a powerful current, which seized hold of Europe as early as the days of the French Revolution. It undermines the hierarchy of society and of the family, and it does away with degrading treatment of dependent persons.

The opposite trend is connected with the penetration of money economy, particularly with its more recent inroads. This development, which brought the Yugoslav village a high degree of impoverishment, coupled with a growth of alcoholism, a mood of hopelessness, and an indifference for all order, also increased violence and harshness. Therefore, though in this period the position of women rose in one aspect, ill-treatment nevertheless also increased. This was frequently the result of the opposition or clashing of the two trends, the husband not so much beating his wife as having fights with her, which, since she is physically the weaker, culminate once again in her ill-treatment. It was only in a region with the new equilibrium that we find the woman protected against brutality just as she was in the patriarchal environment. Whether the remaining regions will follow the same course as the Littoral in the treatment of the wife one cannot know.

### Conclusion

What was the position of husband and wife in the various stages of family life? To what extent did the reality correspond to the supposition that women had low status in the patriarchal world and a favorable status in a modern environment—a supposition which is generally held in industrialized and urbanized countries?

We can represent our principal results in simplified form by a graph with two lines of development. In Graph 43, I have shown two trends characterizing the position of women: A line indicating protection (or the converse, exposure to ill-treatment), estimated by the beatings received, and a line indicating independence and the part the woman plays in family life (shown by the extent of consultation of the wife by the husband).

## Graph 43. Position of women

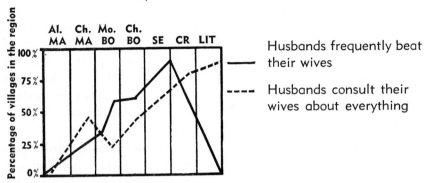

Husbands frequently beat
their wives

Husbands consult their
wives about everything

The lines, which lead from the patriarchal environment to the modern, at first run parallel, then diverge. While the line of uncouthness, with ill-treatment of the wife, starts low and rises steeply in the regions where there were rapid social-economic changes, at a certain point it changes its direction and again falls to a low level. The line of independence, on the other hand, rises almost evenly toward the modern regions, never to drop again. Thus, in the area of a new equilibrium the curves separate.

This graph and the totality of our material together show that the domination of the husband and the low status of the woman in the patriarchal system were a reality which in its extremeness exceeded even anything one may have suspected about those relationships. Nevertheless, the other feature of the woman's position in this same environment is quite different from what was presupposed, for in the patriarchal environment the woman proved to enjoy greater protection and care than in any of the other stages of development of family life, and this to a great extent in practice equalizes out her position, however low this may be in principle.

Further, the presupposition about the trend away from the patriarchal way of life only partly corresponds to reality. The breakup of the patriarchal system—to be sure—brought women greater independence and equality with their husbands and without regard to whether the development was rapid or slow. But together with these alleviations of the woman's lot, there was an increase in unfavorable features in her life, for unchecked individualism exposed her to cruelty and ill-treatment. This was in places so great that these disadvantages make the advantages gained by greater liberty and independence seem inconsiderable.

285

In an environment with a new equilibrium, the unfavorable feature of ill-treatment of women vanished from the scene. Here ill-treatment fell to the low level of the patriarchal environment, while greater independence and participation in decisions continued to increase. Woman here enjoyed liberty and equality with her husband without having to bear the brutalities of a revolutionary period. From this one might draw the conclusion that in the modern region, where the life of women was favorable from both aspects, we had the ideal environment for the woman.

This conclusion would be correct, were there not a third aspect of a woman's life, one which has not been touched upon in this chapter. In the Littoral, the value of a woman as possible bride has been greatly reduced. True, the position of the married woman is favorable, but a great number of women in fact here never reach marriage. In a patriarchal environment, on the other hand, there is a scarcity of women and a great demand for them, due to the absolute desire and need of every man to have a wife, and this is a factor which forms a great counter-balance to any formal subjection or possible low standing of women. True, a woman's status or rank is low in this traditional environment, and in theory she is not important. Yet in actual life we find her highly valued both as wife and as daughter-in-law. On the other hand, in a modern region, though the woman does indeed enjoy equality with the man and is not ill-treated, she is very often completely ignored. Many a woman thus remains alone throughout her whole life and so is lost from any inquiry of this sort and any tabular representation of the position of husband and wife. A whole complex of circumstances combine to make a woman here less important and less irreplaceable than she is in the patriarchal environment.

For these reasons we are unable to find a simple answer to the question whether life in the modern environment is more favorable to a woman than life in the patriarchal environment.

# CHAPTER IX

## Childbearing

FEW human phenomena in the patriarchal environment were so uniform as the wish for children. In the old regions the people knew only a single source of riches—that of biological growth. There was only one means to make life easier and to reduce the heavy physical exertions of the primitive economy—to have "young folks" in the household, children, daughters-in-law, and grandchildren, who were the "right hands," the "substitutes," and the "wings" of their elders. Blood relationship was the strongest bond among the people. All close and beloved people and worldly goods were referred to as "mine by birth." Respect and importance flowed mainly from one source—to be the "elder" and to accept the care and responsibility for younger persons.

All endeavors fused together into a single overwhelming passion— to give birth most willingly and to rear heirs in a blood relationship. This desire for children was not checked by the physical exertion of childbearing and rearing children. In an environment where physical strain was the usual lot and where only strong persons survived the first years of life, physical hardship was of little importance. Material maintenance was no problem because everything was produced at home and the children helped out from an early age. Besides, needs were small. Factors which at times beclouded the marriage relationship did not disturb the relationship between parents and children, which was regarded as the most important and most honorable one.

The desire for children was not qualified: They were wanted not under certain conditions, but at any price and at all times. This striving had something absolute, an almost religious element.

This force, strong as it was, was broken in a particular historical period. The introduction of a money economy brought with it a rationalistic attitude toward life and favored limitation of births. From then on the desire for children no longer had the force and imperativeness that it formerly had. It now attained a relativistic quality—children were desired now only if the farm was large enough to employ and feed them and to provide a dowry for the girls.

It is scarcely possible to discuss this process without touching on the question of human values. Did the patriarchal period, with its desire for numerous progeny, or the rationalistic pecuniary period provide more dignified living conditions in Yugoslavia?

The survey offers ample material for discussion of these questions.

## Birth Rate and Number of Children

Between the two world wars Yugoslavia led the European countries in the number of births.[1] In 1931 there occurred the following number of births per 1,000 inhabitants:

| | | | |
|---|---|---|---|
| Yugoslavia | 34.6 | France | 17.8 |
| Bulgaria | 34 | Switzerland | 17 |
| Poland | 31.6 | Germany | 16.8 |
| Italy | 25.8 | England and Wales | 16.1 |
| Czechoslovakia | 22.1 | | |

Several Yugoslav regions far exceeded the Yugoslav average:

| | |
|---|---|
| Bosnia (Vrbas banovina) | 42 |
| Macedonia (Vardar banovina) | 42.27 |

Some Bosnian districts had birth rates which were even higher[2]

| | |
|---|---|
| Cazin district | 56 |
| Travnik district | 59 |
| Jajce district | 60 |

Official statistics[3] classify the villages or rural districts investigated in my study as shown in Graph 44.

According to the number of births, the entire country was divided into halves. Almost all villages of the patriarchal regions belonged to the categories with the two highest birth rates, while most of the villages from the modern regions were in the two lowest categories. A sharp line separates the two regions.

Bosnia heads the list with about fifty births in half the villages. The birth rate for Macedonia was somewhat lower, perhaps because girls married later there, and many husbands lived for years as laborers away from their villages.

In the modern regions—In Serbia, Croatia, and the Littoral—the birth-rate figures are significantly lower. Serbian family life adapted itself quickly and fundamentally to the great economic changes of

[1] Dudley Kirk, *Europe's Population in the Interwar Years*, League of Nations, Princeton University, Office of Population, 1946.

[2] The figures for districts refer exclusively to villages, as urban communities in Yugoslavia are counted separately. The figures for banovinas, however, include both villages and cities.

[3] *Direkcija državne statistike*, Statistički Godišnjak, 1931.

## Graph 44. Birth rates[4]

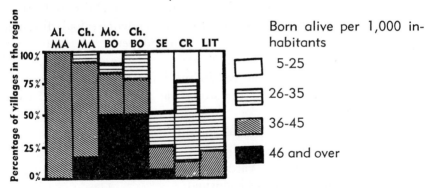

Percentage of villages in the region

Al. Ch. Mo. Ch.
MA MA BO BO SE CR LIT

100%
75%
50%
25%
0%

Born alive per 1,000 inhabitants

5-25

26-35

36-45

46 and over

the last decades. Its drop in the number of births far exceeded the development in Croatia and approached the most modern region, the Littoral.

In spite of the high infant mortality in Yugoslavia—the highest in Europe—there were many children in the families, and the natural population increase was enormous. The following table shows infant mortality and population increase in several European countries, including those with the highest and lowest figures:

### TABLE 1

| | Infant Mortality[5] (Deaths per 1000 births) in the first year | Natural Increase (Difference between births and deaths) |
|---|---|---|
| Yugoslavia | 159 | 15.2 |
| Bulgaria | 147 | 13.9 |
| Poland | 142 | 16.0 |
| Czechoslovakia | 136 | 7.8 |
| Italy | 110 | 11.3 |
| Germany | 84 | 5.7 |
| France | 77 | 1.8 |
| England and Wales | 63 | 4.2 |
| Switzerland | 50 | 5.1 |

What was the result of the two contradictory tendencies which developed simultaneously with the introduction of money economy

4 Of our Macedonian villages, 68 per cent fall in our third category of natality: 35-45 births per 1,000 inhabitants. However, nearly all the remaining 32 per cent belong to the fourth category. In the official statistics the average birth rate for Macedonia (Vardar banovina) is given as 42.27.

5 Dudley Kirk, *op.cit.*

into Yugoslavia, namely the reduction in the number of children by birth control and the increase in the number of children because of the declining mortality rate? The two tendencies had different rates in different regions and developed independently of one another. Thus, for example, in the modern province of Croatia, birth control spread rapidly, whereas infant mortality was not greatly reduced and at the time of the study was higher than that in the patriarchal regions.

Infant mortality:[6]

| | |
|---|---:|
| Croatia (Sava banovina) | 206 |
| Macedonia (Vardar banovina) | 161 |
| Bosnia (Vrbas banovina) | 142 |
| Serbia (Morava banovina) | 113 |

As a consequence of this contradictory development of birth and death figures in Yugoslavia between the two world wars, the ratios in the historical provinces did not approximate one another, but in many respects the differences between them became still greater. The patriarchal regions remained quite undisturbed in their abundance of children, while in the modern regions the number of children dropped rapidly.

Graph 45. Number of children per 100 women[7]

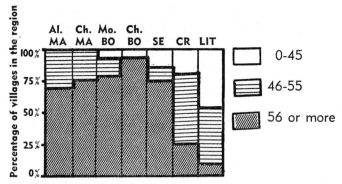

Graph 45 shows a massive block of prolific villages in the patriarchal regions, with a sharp drop in Croatia and the Littoral. With its abundance of children, Serbia still resembled the patriarchal regions. The reason for this is less the high birth rate than the low infant mortality rate—significantly lower than in Croatia and the coast. (Infant mortality in Morava Banat was 113 in 1,000 births; in

[6] *Direkcija Državne Statistike*, Godišnjak, 1931, Definitive Results 1938.
[7] *Ibid.*

Save Banat 206.) As in most questions of family life, in the question of births and child-bearing, the Serbian villages ranged from patriarchal to modern.

## Dangers of Maternity

In old-style areas the death rate of mothers during or after childbirth was so high that it was probably the main reason that women were a minority in these parts of the country. The problem of high mortality among women was discussed in the chapter "Marriage." Here are two descriptions by interviewers from Macedonia of the serious perils of childbirth in a patriarchal environment:

As shown by the figures, which I have compared for men and women in our village, the relative number of women begins to decline from the 15th year of their lives. Most of them by far die because their circumstances do not allow them to observe a minimum of hygienic precepts during and after childbirth. I will just refer to one of two or three examples which I have observed during the six years I have been a teacher in this village. In 1935 a woman, whose husband was in prison for manslaughter of his father, gave birth to a child. She had remained by herself to take care of the agricultural work which requires enormous exertions and strength. Birth took place at the moment when she was threshing grain, a job which requires the highest degree of strength and dexterity. The child was born during night and in the early morning she had to pile up the sheaves in layers, working all day long in the straw under the horses' hoofs. Fortunately, she was strong enough to survive.

Another case which is known to me took place in a field during harvest work. The mother had been cutting wheat the whole morning under a scorching sun. In the evening she withdrew from the others and, hidden behind a block of rock, she gave birth to a child without any help whatever. She did not utter a single cry because of the other people who were not far away from her. Immediately after the birth, she took the child in her arms and walked home.

Only in rare cases birth takes place in the house. Mostly the woman hides in the stable where she remains by herself, because it is considered a disgrace to be delivered in front of men.

*(Macedonia, St. Nikola Ovčepolje district)*

Before the war, a woman had never given birth in the house; always outside in the fields, as she felt ashamed. Then she came back into the house with her baby wrapped in napkins. She had never confided the day and hour of birth to anyone. Often birth took place while she was in the midst of her work. A woman, who now is old, told me how she dropped her newly born baby into the snow but that, thank God, it remained healthy. Last year a young woman died shortly after birth which took place in the field because she felt ashamed to come back to the house. On account of the cold weather she had a hemorrhage, and, after some old women had interfered, it proved to be too late for a doctor's intervention. In this respect circumstances have now improved but not to a great extent. *(Sanjak, Sjenica district)*

## Birth Control

In the Balkans, during the phase of subsistence economy, additions to the family meant helpers in house and field, and were desired. There was more land than could be cultivated by available workers, because there were no paid laborers. Techniques were primitive and time-consuming. There were no markets. Everything was produced in the zadruga. Only large families could survive the struggle for existence or make life somewhat easier for themselves, and every member of the family was a valuable worker. When, however, the money economy began to spread, usually in connection with modern political measures, mortality dropped and the population increased rapidly. The zadrugas were divided. The small farms could not feed large numbers of children. With ready money and available merchandise, more demands were created, poverty was felt more keenly, and the wish to make possible an easier life for the children strengthened the tendency toward birth control.

In all patriarchal regions, the peasants were extremely opposed to birth control. Children were the wealth of the zadruga. If a widow wished to marry again or to return to her parental home, it was only in rare cases that the zadruga allowed her to take along her children. The children were regarded as "acquired in the Zadruga" and therefore had to remain there. With such a valuation of children, the rejection of birth control is self-evident.

As can be seen from Graph 46, abortions increased in frequency by regions, with the greatest frequency in the "regions of abrupt change," in Serbia and Croatia. The graph shows that abortions are phenomena which set in when conditions change suddenly, and that they drop off at a later stage.

Preventive birth control methods do not usually coincide with abortion. This is illustrated by Graph 47.

When curves were drawn, it became evident that the linear direction of the preventive birth control curve was much more pronounced than that of the abortion curve. The peak of such a curve is in Croatia and in the Littoral. The weak retrograde tendency

## Graph 46. Birth control by abortion

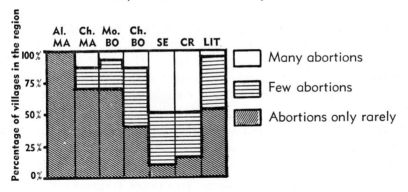

## Graph 47. Preventive birth control methods

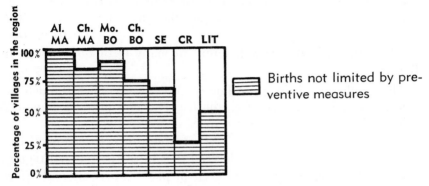

in the Littoral can be explained by the high percentage of husbands living overseas, which makes birth control less necessary.

The number of births is not artificially reduced by the peasants. They desire a larger number of births, as they see in this a source of new workers. *(Macedonia, Djevdjelija district)*

Abortions are not performed. They are considered a *capital sin.* The barrier to preventive birth control probably lies in the husband, who wants to tie his wife to the house and assure himself of her faithfulness. Often ignorance of the means of birth control, and modesty which prevents asking about such means, prevent control. In this village there never were abortions or prosecutions because of abortion. On the contrary, several women have died, because they had opposed a necessary discontinuance of pregnancy.

*(Macedonia [Alb.], Debar district)*

In the Moslem villages in Bosnia the old attitude in favor of many children prevailed at the time of the survey, although the economic

conditions in the first Yugoslav era had changed Bosnia fundamentally:

> Births are not "regulated." . . . "Bread can always be found."

> . . . The women neither carry out abortions themselves, nor is there
> anyone who could perform one for them. The number of births is
> limited only in very rare instances. Barren women attempt everything
> possible to have children, for it is considered a disgrace not to be
> fruitful. (*Moslem Bosnia, Bugojno district*)

In the Orthodox Macedonian villages the influence of religion in
regard to births was not as strong as with the Moslems, but the
fatalistic attitude was the same and intervention was rejected:

> They take precautionary measures. In case of pregnancy they take
> medication—drink something or other. All this developed only after
> the First World War; before the war nothing was "regulated" and
> parents had even fifteen children and thought it was an act of God.
> (*Prespa district*)

The same attitude was still found in many Orthodox villages in
Bosnia:

> The number of births is not limited. Everything, which through the
> will of God is destined to live, will live. The amount of good and evil
> in life is predetermined for everyone.
> (*Derventa district, Orthodox village*)

The interviewers often emphasized that in the patriarchal regions
birth control was not practiced even in places where it would have
been desirable for the peasants to limit the number of children. The
helplessness which these people showed in regard to birth control,
however, was not due to a lack of intelligence but merely illustrated
how new the problem was.

> The number of births is not "regulated." There are cases in which the
> father would like to limit the number of children, but he *does not know
> how*. In the village, an attempt at abortion has never been made. There
> are cases in which the mother has strangled her child after birth. This
> occurs with those women whose husbands are abroad working. This
> is done in secret, but usually the public still learns of it. Up to the
> present, the parents did not wish to limit births at all. Now there are
> some who would wish to do so. The Church has no influence on this
> question. The women do not perform abortions. Apparently they do
> not know how it is done.
> (*Christian Bosnia, Jajce district, Orthodox village*)

The following report came from a village where birth control was
beginning to be used:

With most people there exists a desire for birth control, but due to conventional modesty the women only rarely go to the doctor for advice on prevention of pregnancy. I have heard that at times husbands have visited the doctor. The economic difficulties because of the large number of children are apparent to them sooner. Women themselves perform abortions, drink vinegar, open the womb with the spindle, stretch and strain themselves over a fence. I know of no case where a woman had sought to prevent a pregnancy for egotistical reasons, but rather always only for economic reasons or those of health. Insofar as the men prevent the women from doing this, they act due to fear for the life of their wife or due to ignorance.

(*Christian Bosnia, Sarajevo district, Orthodox and Moslems*)

The following reports from Montenegro are characteristic for that patriarchic area. The influence of the Church is stronger than in other Orthodox regions:

In general, the number of births is not "regulated" in any manner. Abortions scarcely occur and if they do they don't become publicly known. The principal cause for these conditions are the priests who stigmatize abortion as a sin. The second cause is ignorance. But the chief cause is religious influence. Within the last ten years there was one judicial investigation in a case of abortion in the district.

(*Nikšić district*)

The following two answers demonstrate the ascetic undercurrent in this belligerent environment:

Husband and wife attempt to limit the number of children by "shaping their relationship" economically. They suggest restraint to one another by the thought that they cannot support a large number of children. There are cases where the number of births is not limited, especially where only female children are born initially. In the wish for male progeny, the couple continue their activity. Abortion is very rare since it is still regarded as a sin in this village. (*Cetinje district*)

One Croatian region, the Dalmatian highlands, retained many patriarchal features because of the inaccessibility of its barren mountains and because of its close ties with patriarchal Bosnia and Hercegovina:

Births are not regulated by either rich or poor people. Here no attention is paid to the number of births. People are used to saying: "God gave it, so be it." They do not know preventive measures. Abortions are not performed. On the contrary, people desire an ever-increasing number of children. Often one hears mothers say: "The world is wide, may there only be children!" They do not even know that there is such a thing as abortion. If a woman were to perform one, she would be regarded by everyone as a horrible example of vileness.

(*Benkovac district*)

In Serbia and the main part of Croatia, the picture changed. In both regions, more than half the villages belonged to the group of "frequent abortions." The methods of birth control were different in these two regions: In the majority of Croatian villages, preventive birth control was practiced as well as abortion; preventive control was, however, rare in Serbia. Probably the main reason for this difference was that Croatia had more time to adapt itself to the new economic conditions, as the process began earlier here and the changes occurred more slowly than in Serbia.

The following reports show a transitional attitude toward birth limitation. In Croatia the wish for limitation was strong because of economic necessity. Yet moral considerations would not yet allow practice of birth control.

If a woman is barren, the public will always assume that she does not wish to have children and that she knows how to get rid of the child cleverly or that she can perform magic in order not to become pregnant. Abortions are almost unknown. They are performed in strictest secrecy, but at times a whisper still goes around: "So and so did something, otherwise something new would have come." (*Varaždin district*)

In this region the people are very clever in the practice of birth control. Abortions are known but seldom performed. They are kept strictly secret so that usually nothing is known about them. The use of preventive measures is restricted by the resistance of the husband, ignorance, drunkenness, poverty, and modesty.      (*Dugoselo district*)

Abortions are performed frequently and the village knows about it. Peasants often say: "Why have so many poor people in the world?" And the better-off people say: "One is enough and may all be well with this one."      (*Gurbišnopolje district*)

In contrast to the foregoing examples, the following answer is one of the few showing how insistence on marital sexual enjoyment weakens the tendency toward preventive measures. It is from a modern region where family relationships are similar to those in the coastal districts:

Birth control is quite rare although the means are often known. The peasants here are poor and must restrict themselves in everything, but in sexual intercourse they refuse to be limited. The peasants like their wives to be passionate, and they judge the passion of the woman by various distinguishing marks. Thus, for example, they maintain that women with narrow heels are passionate in contrast to women with broad feet. . . . Many pleasures are denied to them, so at least they want to enjoy sexual intercourse fully, naturally, and unalloyed.

*(Croatia [Gorski Kotar], Ogulin district)*

In rich, economically advanced Slavonia there were more abortions than in any other part of Croatia or Yugoslavia as a whole. Three-quarters of all villages in Slavonia fell into the category of numerous abortions. The system of one or two children, which was called the "white pestilence" there, rapidly decreased the population figures. Many Slavonic villages belonged to the type of "new stabilization"— peaceful family relationships as in the patriarchal system but including the practice of birth control.

The women accomplish abortion with the aid of several old women who are skilled in it. There are many abortions, but they are carefully kept secret so that nothing is known. There is, however, resistance to birth control: Reluctance of the husband who usually opposes abortion; ignorance of the methods; and often the influence of the Church [Catholic] which stigmatizes abortions as a sin. The "white pestilence" is fought by the Church, sermons are preached against it. Many are frightened off also by the circumstance that many women have died, since the abortions are performed by inexperienced women and in the most primitive manner. There occur septic infections and serious internal sicknesses and catastrophes.     *(Županja district)*

Many abortions are performed. The public knows of them but does not condemn them very much. Only the old grandmothers are horrified—the younger women not at all; they regard them as a necessity.

*(Valpovo district)*

Prevention is more frequent in Slavonia than abortion:

The married people regulate births by restraint in sexual intercourse. More rarely by abortions. Besides this, a rather large number of newborn children die. The religious influence has been eliminated completely. Both marriage partners are usually in favor of preventive measures. Examples of women who have died are most effective against abortions.     *(Nova Gradiška district)*

The villages in the Littoral had a low number of abortions in common with the patriarchal regions. The lower birth rate in the Littoral was not the result of abortions but of other factors, such as mass emigration of men, higher marriage age, greater number of unmarried women, and preventive measures. Barriers to abortions were the Catholic influence and a general repugnance of the crudeness with which abortions were performed. Technical development and better living conditions favored use of preventive measures.

The following two answers from the Littoral show the aversion to abortions. The second report shows patriarchal and modern elements occurring jointly:

> No case of abortion being performed is known. Births are regulated by the circumstance that the men usually remain abroad for two, three, or five years. *(Biograd district)*

> People here are religious [Catholics] and fear hell more than a family with ten children. Usually the priests at confession forbid any prevention of conception, insisting one must have as many children as God gives. It is the religious influence, pure and simple, which checks birth control, since neither serious consequences to one's health nor legal proceedings because of abortions are known. *(Isle of Krk)*

## Pressure for Birth Control

The following report from Slavonia[8] shows how the pressure for birth control operates and how it affects family relationships:

> "Neighbor, why do you hang your head and act so sad these last few days?"—I asked the peasant's wife in her forties who usually was so happy.

> "Oh, why shouldn't I be sad when everything is going wrong at home? Since my Ivo has been going with Eva, my husband won't speak to me at all, won't even look at me. He says that I'm to blame for everything. I spoil our only child, he says, let him do anything that occurs to him and do not question whether it is good or bad. My boy likes Eva and so I think that if they love one another they ought to be married. And my husband goes around awfully annoyed because his daughter-in-law does not suit him. And with what does he reproach her? She is pretty, she is young, she is decent, she is industrious, she is pleasant, from a decent family—all true, but she does not have any inheritance. That is the terrible thing—she is poor."

> "How large are the possessions of her zadruga?"

> "The zadruga is rich and has fifty acres, but nothing belongs to Eva. Her *mother brought nothing when she was married except 10 large gold ducats* and several smaller coins. And if the mother has nothing, the daughter has nothing either. That's the way things are. And my husband is so mad because I did not forbid Ivo to go with Eva when I knew how matters stood. He says: "You bring disgrace to our house only because you give your only son his own way and don't consider life. The daughter will be the same way the mother was. Where did her mother leave her reason? First she bore a girl. What in the world occurred to her then to have three more, although she herself had brought no inheritance? Has such a thing ever been seen or heard?"

[8] Nada Sremac, *Nismo mi krive* (*We Are Not to Blame*), Zagreb, 1940.

"Well, how should I know what her idea was in having four children? How should I know why she did something that no sensible woman would do? Lord, I wouldn't say anything if she had had one more, but four—that is no way to do things. With two children she still would have been able to get some more ducats for the girl and then one wouldn't care so much that she has no inheritance. And now there is trouble in my house because Eva's mother did not use common sense. Well, how are the children to blame for that? If Eva marries my Ivo, she certainly will not have four children because even if she didn't have a sensible mother, she will have a sensible mother-in-law."

## Effect of Birth Control

What influence did birth control as practiced have on the number of births in the villages of the various regions? There exists a clear correlation between birth limitations by abortions and the birth rate in all areas. If we use Croatia as a typical example, the statistics are as follows:

TABLE 2

| | *Villages with many abortions* | *Villages with few abortions* | *Villages with no abortions* |
|---|---|---|---|
| Villages with low birth rate (0-25 per mille) | 40% | 16% | 0% |
| Villages with medium birth rate (26-35 per mille) | 55% | 64% | 50% |
| Villages with high birth rate (36 and higher per mille) | 5% | 20% | 50% |

The table shows that in the group of Croatian villages with many abortions there are few villages with a high birth rate and many villages with a low birth rate and vice versa. As I have said earlier, many factors can be responsible for low birth rates, but it seems reasonable enough to relate the high abortion figure to the low birth rate in these examples.

Not only abortion but also preventive birth control appears to have a numerically perceptible effect. I found the closest correlation in the Littoral. From this, the conclusion may be drawn that preventive measures were utilized there rather consistently, a result that is not surprising as it corresponds to other observations.

The birth control figures of my interviewers correlate with the official birth figures, which is remarkable because of the difficulties in collecting this material. Abortions are illegal, so every attempt is made to keep them secret. In regions where every type of birth control is condemned on moral grounds, its practice is also concealed. Only the special confidential relationship between my interviewers and the peasants of their villages made it possible to obtain the required information.

## *Attitude toward Childlessness*

The patriarchal man has no illusions that he can master fate. Only fate can endow him with the highest value in life—children. If they are not born or if they die, he stands helpless in the face of his misfortune. Rational—medical—assistance is not available to him.

On the other hand, he lacks the unrest and distress of being personally responsible for every misfortune. Modern man of our technical era is expected to make his own good luck; he blames himself—or others—when things do not turn out well, and he wonders, when death strikes, whether a different doctor or a different method should have been tried. Patriarchal man does not have such self-reproachful feelings. But that is not to say that the values of life mean less to him than to modern man nor that he longs for them less fervently.

The attempts to obtain children by magic show how rarely Yugoslav peasants will resign themselves to childlessness when they really want children. Bitterness toward the barren woman reveals the desperate search for a scapegoat. Agreement with fate is given only by people where the patriarchal way of life is intact, and it imparts to those who adhere to it a near-religious attitude. All groups, however, employ magic formulas varying from religious vows to charms and incantations. Pilgrimages are customary in all religions. The passion for children is also demonstrated by the fact that all obtainable religious aids are tried, regardless of the religious affiliation of the person seeking assistance. Thus Moslem women would light candles to Saint Anthony, and Christian women in Bosnia would obtain from the Moslem priest the Koran talisman with the miraculous "Inscription of Hodja" (*Hodžin zapis*). Only the incantations for love are as widespread and as manifold as the attempts to obtain the blessing of children by magical means. Despite the sometimes obnoxious forms these desperate attempts take to win life's highest values, they are deeply human.

The questionnaire included a question evaluating female barrenness. Answers should reveal not only the intensity of a desire for children but also something about the position of women in the various regions.

Graph 48. Evaluation of barrenness

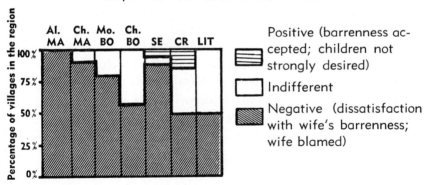

Positive (barrenness accepted; children not strongly desired)

Indifferent

Negative (dissatisfaction with wife's barrenness; wife blamed)

The peak of negative evaluation is in the patriarchal regions, and another high peak in Serbia. The reason for this will be discussed later.

Fatalistic, dignified, resignation was characteristic of the Moslems in the patriarchal environment.

Usually men take a second wife if the first one has no children. They divorce the first wife, or she may remain in the household, according to her own wishes. But no blame whatever attaches to her. Progeny are a gift of God.          (*Montenegro, Andrijevica district*)

They regard sterility of the woman as a punishment of God and accept it.                    (*Macedonia [Alb.], Prespa district*)

The Orthodox part of the patriarchal regions was unfriendly toward the sterile woman.

They do not respect a barren woman, they often make fun of her.
             (*Christian Macedonia, St. Nikola Ovčepolje district*)

The person without children is a woman whom God has punished by leaving her childless.     (*Christian Macedonia, Dojran district*)

They call a sterile woman a "withered stem." All people who have no children take other people's children into their home; they adopt them.
              (*Christian Macedonia, Skoplje district*)

The peasants regard a barren woman as *sinful* and unfortunate. Members of the household and other people reproach her repeatedly.
                    (*Montenegro, Mileševo district*)

The people consider that the childless woman, namely the unfruitful woman, means bad luck and that she has *dragged her husband into misfortune*. They also say: "He has remained a mule."
                    (*Montenegro, Cetinje district*)

In Bosnia, infertility was in some parts accepted fatalistically, in others, bitterly condemned:

301

It is as God wills.                    (*Moslem Bosnia, Foča district*)

An unfruitful wife is regarded as extremely hard luck. It is also believed that barrenness is a punishment from God.

(*Moslem Bosnia, Čajniče district*)

A barren wife is regarded as heartless. She has no child, therefore no heart.                    (*Moslem Bosnia, Travnik district*)

The following answer from Hercegovina criticizes the man:

In most cases the husband is blamed for the barrenness and not the wife. Such males are not regarded or treated as full men. Everything possible is thought up in order to explain their infertility.

(*Stolac district, Catholic village*)

As in Macedonia, Bosnian Moslems could find a way out of their difficulty by marrying a second wife:

The men seek another wife since polygamy is legal.    (*Cazin district*)

Among the Moslems the husband gets a divorce from such a wife. Divorce is very difficult to obtain for the others.    (*Bugojno district*)

The Christian part of Bosnia—for reasons to be explained later— will sometimes express an untraditional viewpoint.

Childless women are well regarded and everyone desires them.

(*Bosanski Petrovac district, Orthodox village*)

In Serbia, the condemnation of female infertility was most severe, although according to birth rate and the frequency of abortions, Serbia was one of the most modern areas. The peculiar thing is that, in Serbia, condemnations of abortion and of infertility did not coincide as in all other regions. Although the condemnation and contempt for the infertile woman was not in direct relation to the desire for a large number of children—indeed, the restriction of the number of children did not at all mean no desire for children—in all areas, severe criticism of infertility ran parallel to the criticism of birth control. Practice of abortion and an indifferent or tolerant attitude toward infertility appear to go together ordinarily, but not in Serbia. A comparison of Table 2, giving the percentage of abortions, with Graph 48, giving the evaluation of infertility, shows that in Serbia alone there was a great distance between the crest of the negative evaluation and the trough of frequent abortion practice. This interval reflects the peculiar combination of conservatism and realism in Serbian family life, which will be discussed later.

Following are some examples illustrating the attitude toward the barren woman in Serbia:

Infertility of the woman is condemned severely and it is a rare case when the woman is not forced into a divorce. *(Morava district)*

The barren woman is despised. Usually the mocking expression is: "He has only wife and mare." One case occurred where a woman who was childless through the fault of the husband, cohabited with another man with the husband's knowledge, until she had a child. Thereafter she was true to her husband as she had been previously.

*(Valjevo district)*

In Croatia, conditions were different. From Graph 48, it is evident that, in half of the Croatian villages, infertility was regarded with indifference or even as desirable. This attitude reflects the new economy, where numerous children are no longer required as farm workers. Even in the villages where infertility was condemned, the reports vary to some extent:

A wife who is not capable of bearing a child is *still* not desired by the peasants. Even though the younger married people do not want to have a lot of children they still do not care for infertility of the woman. They are suspicious of the morals and the health of such a woman.

*(Dalmatia, Knin district)*

Female infertility is condemned by 70 per cent of the peasants, especially by the old ones. The women themselves condemn them, *because they envy them.* *(Prelog district)*

Infertility is considered a virtue for a woman. She does not burden her husband with children. The women envy her. People do not believe that she cannot bear children but maintain that she does not desire to. She has certainly taken or swallowed something!

*(Varaždin district)*

Infertility would be 'convenient' for the peasants. *(Kostajnica district)*

Of the infertile woman, it is said that she is wise and fortunate.

*(Samobor district)*

The answers from Slavonia were even more outspoken:

The women do not seek any remedies whatever for infertility. They would be happy if they were all that way. *(Slatina district)*

The peasants do not condemn barren women. On the contrary, if such women are left widowed, they usually remarry soon, for the peasant needs a wife—and with such a wife he need not be afraid of having children. The farm holdings remain undivided. *(Valpovo district)*

The Littoral showed a similarity with the patriarchal milieu—as it has in other respects. As a new element, a certain feeling of good-fellowship between husband and wife can be read between the lines of the answers:

It is unpleasant for a *married couple* to have no children, and it is a fact that the wife is called some rather derogatory nicknames.

(*Split district*)

The men and the family set great store by children and in the case of infertility they are very sad. (*Biograd district*)

Graph 48 shows the attitude toward childlessness more clearly than the attitude toward infertile women. The factors of accusation or condemnation of the women do not appear clearly. If the answers were arranged according to this point of view, a curve would result which would have a peak in areas of abrupt transformation (in Christian Bosnia and in Serbia). Just as in so many other respects, so also concerning infertility, the woman is worse off in areas of abrupt transformation.

## Conclusions

A distinguished scholar and expert on population problems, Dudley Kirk, remarked in connection with these problems:

. . . Europe entered the modern era with what might be called the primitive phase of population development. . . . Life was as carelessly created as it was destroyed. In normal years it probably showed a considerable surplus of birth over death which, however, was wiped out periodically by disasters of one character or another . . . neither birth nor death control. By modern standards human reproduction, like the production of goods, was inefficient, wasteful and inhuman. . . .[9]

These characteristics are only partially valid in Yugoslavia, however. In view of the high infant mortality human reproduction could indeed be called "wasteful," but in view of the great population increase, not "inefficient."

But the attitude toward childbearing in our regions has no "inhuman" aspect. It results from a need and a desire for a large number of children and not from carelessness. The longing for children, the sacrifices made for the unborn as well as the born ones is in the patriarchal environment much more "human" than the rational attitude in the following period. The attempts of rational planning in an environment without highly developed technology has devastating results. If any attitude toward childbearing might possibly be called inhuman, then it is rather the rational attitude in the phase of abrupt transformation with its mass abortions so dangerous for the mothers' lives, than the irrational attitude in the patriarchal phase.

[9] Dudley Kirk, *op.cit.*, p. 36.

From our material, no conclusion could be drawn to the effect that modern times with the rational approach brought progress to this domain of life to the Yugoslav village. The only conclusion which we could draw from this inquiry is in the negative, namely that the victory of the rational attitude toward childbirth and children does not in every historical constellation have the meaning of progress, whether viewed from the angle of diminishing human sufferings or from the angle of promotion of human values.

# CHAPTER X

# Extramarital Relationships

EXTRAMARITAL and premarital relationships reveal much more about the general character of sex and love relations in our areas than does our material about the relations between husband and wife, since the latter was collected and presented in terms of ranks and roles within the family.

Whereas by reason of the physiological basis of sexual relationships, more or less equality between all persons might be presumed—that is to say, whereas one might expect certain standards to be valid for all people, independently of external circumstances—the data provided by the investigation show precisely the contrary. We know from medical and physiological studies that in reality individual variations, both in needs and capabilities for sexual activity are enormous. Our data, which are not concerned with individual variations at all, further indicate differences in love relationships between various regions and districts. Moreover these differences prove to be greater than those in any sphere of life.

Among our regions were some in which all other aims and strivings appeared to be much more important than a love life. The climate was arid or hostile to all which might be interpreted as sentiment. Here marriages seem to be concluded purely from duty and from conventionality, and other sexual relations were known solely on a monetary basis.

There were, however, other regions in which the language was saturated with expressions and turns of speech from the realm of *sevdah* and *ašik*, both terms derive from Turkish, and mean love in a romantic sense. In these regions abductions and elopements were daily occurrences, and the intense feelings which exist in marriage relationships sometimes flared up in conflagrations of jealousy, or we may find peasant women complaining of their husbands' excessive sexual demands. Love songs of great beauty and a clearly expressed melancholic tone were constantly sung. All that in America is known as *romance* or *romantic love* and looked upon by some sociologists as an artificial creation of Hollywood, grafted on to the community for commercial reasons, here controlled the life of illiterate peasants, the only difference being that it also bore the stamp of fate and a sense of tragedy.

There were also districts in which, though people were as inclined to romanticism as those just mentioned, they maintained a more serene attitude toward it. Fate did not seem to be as ineluctable, and relationships based on the "tender passion" did not necessarily end tragically. A cheerful note even appears in some love songs.

We possess ample material for the study of the love relationships both of the unmarried and married. This, together with that covering the relationships of the married, constitutes a whole. Here reality is stark and unmasked; there many things are concealed. We shall also see by which ethical principles public opinion approved, condemned, or tolerated extramarital sex relationships. We shall try to find reasons for the great differences in this respect between one district and another.

### The Life of "Grass Widows"

Grass widows are in Serbo-Croatian known as "white widows," widows, that is to say, who do not go into mourning.

When a husband goes away on pečalba work, his young wife puts her best outfit away in a chest and takes out her old, threadbare clothes. She dresses very modestly, is "smaller than a tiny fly." The husband sends money and letters from foreign parts, but in the letters makes no reference to his bride; indeed, she does not even get the customary greetings. Years go by, the young wife has borne a child, but the husband is still away earning. The child comes to be three, four, five, or six years old. The father returns home. The first person to see a father coming back after so many years runs to his family for a *muštuluk* or present, and will be given a pair of fine hand-knitted socks. The wife at once withdraws into an inner room and locks the door. Other young wives and girls too come round, and they get into the room through the window, or break open the door. They then remove from the wife the old clothes and kerchief she is dressed in, each tearing off a piece of the kerchief and tucking it into her bosom. No matter, the husband will have brought new ones. They pour water for the wife to wash and take from the chest the outfit she put away there, and dress her. Thus dressed, she must stand in the corner of the room, and kiss the hand of everybody who comes up to her. She does not show herself to her husband at all. She does not go out of the room. Only in the evening he comes to her room. *(Macedonia, Gornji Polog district)*

It is in the marital faithfulness, or unfaithfulness, of the so-called grass widows that we can best study the differences in the sexual life

307

of various environments, for in the main it was women whose husbands were away from the village for long periods who entered such relationships. Marital faithfulness for them could mean sexual abstinence for many years or for life.

In Yugoslavia there are several districts from which it was the custom for large numbers of the men to go to work in distant parts for many years. The principal regions were Macedonia (especially Orthodox Macedonia) and the Littoral. A third area providing emigrants was the former Military March (especially the Lika and Kordun districts). This region is a part of Croatia, and is not treated separately in the present statistics.

It is a strange coincidence that the two regions with stable family living—Macedonia and the Littoral—should be the principal regions from which there was emigration. To some extent this circumstance makes it more difficult to draw conclusions about the link between faithfulness in marriage and the stage of development of family living, for it is not easy to judge to what extent the general stability of life influenced family living and to what extent this was influenced by the women's being accustomed through a number of generations to the emigration of the husbands.

Graphical presentation of the sex relationships of grass widows gives us certain answers to our question about which circumstances influence love life.

Graph 49. Extramarital relationships of "grass widows"

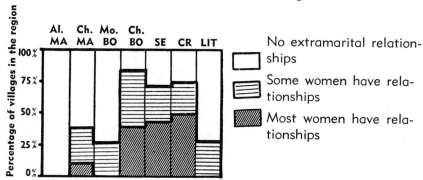

The steep line of Graph 49 gives us a dramatic picture of the tremendous differences between various stages of development. The three regions in a state of ferment are largely identical, while the patriarchal region and the Littoral are again alike, here in the negligible incidence of extramarital liaisons. It would seem that the faithfulness and unfaithfulness of lonely women in the main depends on the more or less rapid penetration of money economy and on the stability of the life of a district as a whole.

The reports from Macedonia present a vivid picture of the life of women whose husbands were away at work. A large part of the menfolk of nearly one-half of the Orthodox villages studied in Macedonia went away to work, in the main to towns in Yugoslavia and other Balkan countries.

> The village is on Mt. Shar. The soil is infertile and the inhabitants are unable to support themselves on it, therefore four-fifths go to work elsewhere in Yugoslavia or abroad, and stay away until they have earned a certain amount in excess of what they send home; then they return and live there till the savings are used up, when they go away to work again.
>
> *(Prizren and Tetovo districts)*

> The wives of men away at work live in complete abstinence in the whole village. Particular attention is paid to their sexual life, lest because of their immoral living a slur were cast on the whole village.
>
> *(Prespa district)*

> As a rule, the women abstain, but there are also cases of entering into extramarital relations with men who are at hand. The peasants as a rule condemn this, but many also approve of it, justifying it by the fact that the husband stays away for years on end, for as long as twenty-five years.
>
> *(Prespa district)*

The following report shows that faithfulness of the women was no result of a negative attitude toward sexual life:

> I will add an interesting joke: If a husband goes away to work, his wife makes notches in the wall every time he owes her something, and when he gets home he has to make good for the shortage, removing the marks one after the other. *(Djevdjelija district)*

The other principal region from which men emigrated is the Littoral. Here, from three-quarters of the villages I investigated, a great part of the menfolk emigrated, in this case overseas. The majority went to America, a smaller number to Australia. There they stayed for many years, in some cases failing ever to return. The sufferings of the lonely wives, their faithfulness to their husbands despite the tolerant views of the public opinion, were strikingly akin to those we see in patriarchal Macedonia:

> Here there is not a household without one, two, or more emigrants, so it is left to the wife to manage the home and do all the work, even that part of it which in other parts is exclusively the care of the man.
>
> *(Biograd-on-Sea district)*

309

The women in this district are real martyrs. There are many cases of young men marrying, then going to sea after a few months, remaining in America up to 16 years. The husband leaves behind a "bride," returns to find an aging wife. Of fifty cases only one had sexual relations. The others were faithful. *(Biograd-on-Sea district)*

The women whose husbands are in America work the property. They are retiring and remain faithful to their husbands, even though they know these are faithless to them. *(Imotski district)*

According to the account of the peasantry, such wives curtail even that little liberty which other women have, for all eyes are on how they behave. The wife who lives in abstinence is highly prized, and those who do not are severely condemned. *(Knin district)*

Such women have dealings with serious men who will not give them away. They rarely go anywhere else. There are cases of women not knowing another man from the age of twenty to death and hoping year in and year out for their husband to return. If the husband helps [sends money to] his wife, she is much reproached; if he has abandoned her, they forgive her, although tongues do wag. *(Šibenik district)*

In most cases, 95 per cent, they abstain and suffer. In rare cases they have dealings with the husbands of local women. *(Krk district)*

The following instance shows that even in Dalmatia it was not any ascetic viewpoint which caused faithfulness to the husbands who were abroad:

Sexual life as such is approved. Sexual life is discussed before even small children, so from infancy up they get to know it, within the family and also with neighbors and in the village generally. Both men and women discuss everything in front of everybody. *(Metković district)*

In Moslem regions, the strictest morals prevailed, especially among the Albanians. However, it is against the precepts of Islam for a man to leave his wife for a number of years. Husbands did not go away for long periods, so the women were less tempted. Particularly in Bosnia, the Sheriat courts enabled women to marry again after the husband's absence of one (or two) years. Divorce is a short procedure, for it is considered that a woman should not remain alone longer. This practice placed the Moslem woman in a much more favorable position than all other women.

The members of the household keep a good eye on the wife. Women abstain from it. If things come to unfaithfulness, the women are not condemned so severely as the husbands are for not having taken their wives with them. *(Macedonia, Albanian village, Struga district)*

310

Women whose husbands are working are much more moderate sexually, for they spend themselves in cares and working for their very existence.
*(Moslem Bosnia, Čajniče district)*

The life of such a woman is hard. She generally marries. The Sheriat court condones absence only up to one year. The peasants do not condemn such a woman. *(Moslem Bosnia, Cazin district)*

Nor was the Christian part of Bosnia a typical emigrational region, even though there were husbands going away to work in one-third of the villages studied. They did not, however, go either for long or far away. But here too the view that a woman should be let alone for tens of years was not held, as the following answer shows:

If a husband does not come home from his work in two or three years, she marries another, even though not divorced from the first. She lives with the new husband for some years without marriage, bearing children to him. After a husband has gone away to work, until she marries another, a woman generally lives in abstinence, but not always.
*(Jajce district, Orthodox village)*

Here, however, are two examples of greater strictness in villages with mixed Catholic and Orthodox population:

Husbands in our village are away only when in the army. Every eye keeps the wives straight, and is on the look-out for consequences. The peasants brand any unfaithfulness. *(Derventa district)*

They abstain. They are afraid of the husband's finding out, for in such case he would cut off their assistance, and on returning he would have his revenge and turn them out, in place of peaceful, contented life. There are not a few such women but I have been unable to hear of a single case of infidelity. *(Herzegovina, Stolac district)*

The following answer shows the combination of old-fashioned romantic-love elements and new elements of libertinism:

On the whole, a woman lives with somebody else, avoiding pregnancy. To this end, they have various methods of protecting themselves against conception. As this is a district which is not self-supporting in its agriculture, the men go off to work when the winter is over. At home remain only boys and old men who are not capable of hard work. The sexual activity of the husband is thus limited. He is only with the wife two or three months, and, because he works hard, even when he is at home he is not active, through fatigue. Women are thus driven to seek satisfaction aside. Generally they find this with good friends who are better off and do not go away to work. Such in this village are "blessed among the women." A woman in this position does not look to exploit

311

a man as is usually the case, but merely to satisfy her natural impulse. The husband knows of this but is not a very stern judge. He turns the blind eye.                        (*Bosnia, Mrkonjić-grad district*)

Serbia, apart from certain districts, did not know the system of working far away from home or emigration. An example of stern condemnation from a district where there were "pečalba" follows:

> In most instances women abstain sexually. A sharper eye is kept on women whose husbands are abroad or working away from home and their most innocent acts are more criticized than the acts of other women.                                            (*Arilje district*)

In Croatia, both theory and practice regarding grass widows differed from those of the coast. The general view in Croatia was that one or two years alone was too hard for a woman. This view is particularly held in Slavonia:

> The life of these women is generally clean, and there is abstinence from sexual intimacy in the first year, but beyond that they find it difficult to resist approaches and [so] submit. The peasants do not reproach them and generally explain things by poverty and hard life.
>                                    (*Slavonia, Virovitica district*)

> If the husband is in America, France, or in the army, she lives with others. It is said that such women have the right to do so. "He's no saint away there either," it is said.          (*Grubišno Polje district*)

> The majority of women whose husbands spend a long time in America have illegitimate children with other young fellows, with widowers, and even with married men. There are cases here of from two to five children got illegitimately and in one case by more than one man. This is not taken to be a great evil. There are moreover cases of the husband's coming back from America and keeping both wife and children.
>                                               (*Ivanić district*)

> The peasants maintain that it is not surprising if, besides other help, a woman wants sexual help when her husband is away and does not concern himself with her at all, and they hold these do so from need, not idleness.                                    (*Dugoselo district*)

The following answer from a Slavonian village is typical of a district with no emigration:

> There are wives who have quite gone to the bad, but their husbands no longer return or send them anything; there are also good women. Generally the peasants say that the former women have sent their husbands away to be able to do what they want.
>                                     (*Slavonia, Vukovar district*)

The former Military March, a part of Croatia, was par excellence a district of emigration, this being partly due to the demilitarization of the March at the end of the nineteenth century and the difficulties in the way of adaptation to independent civilian life. A great part of the men went overseas, mainly to America. However, the reaction of the women was much more decisive than in the coastland or in Macedonia. In this area the importance of love life is held to be self-explanatory. The following replies (as well as Old Milovan stories) reveal the reality and also the attitude of public opinion:

Practically every woman is unfaithful. They say: "Well, and do I know what he does?" And add: "What do you think I got married for?" Customarily here very young men go away, leaving very young wives with at most one child. *(Dvor district)*

Married women have got used to having their desires satisfied, when their husbands leave them . . . difficulties ensue. 70 per cent of such women maintain relations with other men.

*(Lika area, Gospić district)*

If their husbands are in America, France, or elsewhere and do not write to their wives, they find themselves another man and have a sex life, and then live permanently with the man concerned. If their husbands write, they keep a tighter hand on themselves. All the same, it is common knowledge that these women always have relations with other men. Half the peasants approve these relations, particularly for those whose husbands never write, while the other half severely condemns them. *(Slunj district)*

A reply with a cynical note in it:

Every woman becomes the "skirt" of a number of village customers. "Whether she lets them or not, it'll stink." Otherwise they are decent women till it comes to giving their paramours a share of the property.

*(Vrginmost district)*

A woman is faithful if she is in a zadruga. If she is alone, she lives pretty freely. *(Petrinja district)*

Practically all such women have relations with other men. When the men return from work, their wives generally fool them, assuring them that they have been faithful, which the men take at its face value, resuming peaceful life. Nobody reproaches them for that must be done; "God made us like that," say the peasants—"they must do it with somebody," they say. *(Petrinja district)*

Our material indicates that stability of family living and accepted standards, either old or new, resulted in wives' being faithful even under the arduous strain of long separation from the husband. Where conditions were consolidated, marriage was tremendously resistant and abstinence inspired by conjugal loyalty is observed even when the husband is absent many years.

On the other hand, it seems that the phase of economic development was not solely responsible for the great differences between the two strongly ethical regions, Macedonia and the Littoral, and the remaining regions. Regional peculiarities formed by centuries' long developments do seem in this respect to be of greater importance than economic changes which only a few decades before began to differentiate the regions. The conditions in a third emigrational area, the former Military March, were quite distinct from those of Macedonia and the Littoral, and this was the case even when patriarchal life was still very largely preserved. This is to be seen from the stories of Old Milovan about conditions before the First World War, as also from the popular stories and army reports prior to the demilitarization of the March. These show that in some areas there had been of old a more marked tendency toward love life and extramarital relations than elsewhere. I shall have more to say below about the background which favors love relations.

### *Uncle Milovan's Story: Youth in the Former Military March*

"Stana, Mileva, Dara, Milica, all went to school with me. Lovely girls. In peasant dress. I should think so indeed! Married—naturally. But the husband in America, or unable to satisfy the girl. Heavens, some men are hot-tempered, jealous; others human, sensible, when they know they cannot satisfy them.

"Stana was a wild one, hot-blooded. She died young of high blood pressure. Besides, her mother was the same before her. Whenever her mother reproached her, Stana would say: 'My dear mother, don't talk this way. The apple doesn't fall far from the trunk.' She had no children, but a fine farm and garden, a wonderfully run place. But she did like kissing.

"Once I was out hunting with her husband, we two alone. All at once he asked me: 'Have you ever been with my Stana?' I took hold of my gun, how was I to know what he was about, 'Why do you ask?' I said. '. . . nothing special, I'm a bit older, I can't give her all she needs.' 'Are you not ashamed to ask such questions? What would you think, if I were a married man and asked you like that!' He never asked me again nor did I ever go hunting with him again.

"Stana called her husband *Krivonja*, bent thing (not straight, not powerful). 'Whether it is a block of wood or *krivonja* lies down beside me, it's all the same, I just turn over on the other side and go to sleep as quick as I can. I enjoy my heart's play, I do. . . . What do I want with money? I have all I want. I love for love's sake, for the sheer pleasure of it.'

"The principal thing to them is kissing—that's the most important thing—a long time, caressing and kissing. Nothing else matters. Desa was older than me, perhaps thirty when I was a young fellow of twenty. We went to the wood together. When we came out she says to me: 'And what's wrong with me? Am I flesh and bones or a piece of wood? You satisfy yourself in a moment, and what am I? You just behave like my rooster in our chicken coop. Ah, Milovan, my lad, I'd like to meet you when you are 35 or 40.' She never let me touch her again.

"Dara was an attractive wench: Whenever her husband went out, off she went at once into the yard, to look after the poultry, and calls her lover through the orchard, pretending to be scaring hawks. Shouting at the top of her voice 'Sh! Sh! you old hawk! I'm here all by myself!' So loud that her lad up the hill could hear and come down.

"And Mileva. She had two little girls. Her husband was in America. I lived with her two years. She had gone over the border into Bosnia to a Turkish woman who was a fortuneteller to get a charm, so I would love her and nobody else. She caught a bat and got up to other such tricks. 'Do you love me Milovan, my dear?' 'Why so silly, can't you see I love you, my love?' Once when I woke up there she was doing charms and incantations over my head. When she saw I was in love with her—and I put it on a lot, just to please her—she would just cross herself in bliss and cry: 'Thank you, oh Jesus, thank you, Dear Lord!'

"She loved me very much. She got pregnant. She had a son by me, and called him Milutin. A fine lad, black-eyed . . . the very spit of my little grandson today. When they asked her about the child at the parish office, she said it was hers, but she never mentioned me.

"But when the boy asked her, 'Mummy, who's my daddy?' she said, 'Milovan, he is in the town now.' The boy was 12 then, he came straight to me in the town and said, 'Good morning, uncle,[1] I just wanted to have a look at you, I am Milutin.' 'Well, what would you like me to buy you, Milutin?' 'Nothing. I should be ashamed to take it.' But I talked him round, and in the end he accepted a pair of ornamented sandals, *opankas*. And an embroidered waistcoat. And a pair of trousers. And a coat. And a hat. 'Oh, how I would like that

---

[1] "Uncle" was a general, warm term of address to an older man.

one with the feather!' I fitted the boy out from tip to toe. After a fortnight, there he was again, with three pairs of chicken and fifty eggs. 'Mummy sent these—for your love.' Then I sent her back a kerchief and an apron.

"Then her husband came back from America. My old school friend he was. First he came to see me in the town. We were both glad to see each other. He was a sensible sort of man. '. . . I too have been through all sorts of things in America. Nor has she been alone. Thank Heavens it's a boy!" And he brought up Milutin just like all the other children.

"Once I was out hunting with friends, and met Milica, then an old woman, carrying a load of wood from the forest. She was tired—she was nearly seventy. She sat down with her ax to rest. One of the hunters asked her: 'I say, tell us when a woman stops thinking about a man . . . you know what I mean!' 'I don't know,' she said, 'you ask my mother, perhaps she knows.' Her mother was nearly ninety."

### Faithfulness of Married Women

The extramarital liaisons of women whose husbands were at home had a different character from those of the grass widows, and frequently revealed an unrestricted individualism. The reports in answer to the question about the extramarital liaisons of wives in fact present a classical "spiral" development:

Graph 50. Extramarital relationships of wives

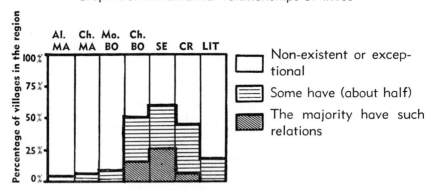

The steep rise and fall in Graph 50 indicates that extramarital relations may be regarded as a symptom accompanying the stormy transformation of family life. We shall see that the incidence of marital faithfulness of wives is, in fact, one of the most reliable signs of intactness of the patriarchal order or, to an equal extent, of stabilization on a new basis.

The following graph complements the preceding one, and indicates the character of extramarital relationships in regard to the gifts or payment accepted by the woman:

Graph 51. Wives' extramarital relationships and rewards

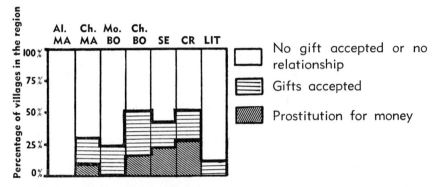

Except that there is no peak in Serbia, Graph 51 shows an outline of steep rise and fall similar to the previous one. Paid relationships became frequent in a period of ferment.

In the patriarchal districts, there were practically no extramarital relationships. These were particularly absent among the Albanians and in Moslem Bosnia. Among the Moslems, public opinion sternly condemned unfaithful wives and considered unfaithfulness a sin. Theory and practice here agree.

In the Orthodox villages of Macedonia there were such relationships, though rarely.

Most women are faithful. They rarely have affairs, and there only wives whose husbands are absent on pečalba work. And merely to satisfy needs.

They accept no gifts whatsoever. They are far from prostitution. It occurs more from love, or they may make each other presents, particularly wives of pečalba workers. (*Prespa district*)

Wives do not accept money, only small presents, sweets, or fruits.

(*Struga district*)

As a rule, wives are faithful, but there are also unfaithful wives, either because their husbands are impotent or very young. They have relations with the man with whom it is most convenient, though also in some cases with whomever it may be. (*St. Nikola Ovčepolje district*)

317

From the villages of the Sanjak and from Kosovo Plain some investigators report customary extramarital relationships:

Wives are faithful just as much as their husbands are to them. They have relationships with gendarmes, traders, teachers, municipal clerks, village youths. Preferably with passing people, excise men, police clerks, tax officials, town youth and men.

Before the war, moreover, the economic conditions in this village were hard. Then too, wives sold themselves for money, but there were also some who had sexual relations without any reward. After the war, every case is rewarded. It is important that the matter should not become known publicly, so that, if the husband does find out, he is a little annoyed at first, then gets used to it.      (*Nerodimlje district*)

When wives quarrel (most frequently because of sexual liaisons) they threaten one another "I'll shave you" (here they have in mind cutting off the hair). I have succeeded best of all and most accurately of all in writing about the evil which marks this village off from others.[2] Here nearly every woman is every man's. I have asked them why such a way of life has spread. They all told me: "Our husbands are to blame. They brought it from America or the army." They talk of diseases: "clap," chancre, syphilis. This last disease is quite common. They call and consider it "the mange." Some treat themselves under doctors' instructions, but the disease is steadily spreading, for sexual relations are frequent. There are numerous cases of the brother-in-law raping the young wife, the father-in-law his daughter-in-law; in short, every man lives with any woman. I do not believe there is a village or town in our country in which there is anything like it. From this are excepted the surrounding villages of the county, that is those villages which adjoin it. This village lives a life which is incredible; nobody would imagine it.      (*Nerodimlje district*)

In Christian Macedonia public opinion did not condemn extramarital relations so sternly as in Moslem districts:

Frequently faithless wives are mocked and are branded in some way, practically the whole village knows they are dishonest.

(*St. Nikola Ovčepolje district*)

Faithless wives are despised. There was a popular song made this very last winter about one, and it is now sung in the whole of this district.

(*Struga district*)

Bosnia fell into two very distinct parts between which there was a deep gulf. Moslem Bosnia in this matter was completely patriarchal. Islam played a great part in the maintenance of a high level of

---

2 The author of this note is a woman.

feminine morals. In the Christian villages of Bosnia, rapid and extensive changes have taken place. In the first instance, the traditional theme of *sevdah*—romance—was striking:

> In most cases the wives are faithful to their husbands. In exceptional cases they have relations with the men whom they loved before they married, but failed to marry.     *(Rogatica district)*

> As a rule wives are faithful, but there are also cases of unfaithfulness. The wives of poor husbands give themselves to richer men for money. The young wives of older men yield to younger men, also for money [sic]; if they are rich they help their lovers.     *(Brčko district)*

Here is a report from a Catholic village:

> It is dangerous in Bosnia to play about with other women. The ax judges. Falseness is remembered two or three generations—girls bear the bad name or good name of their mothers.     *(Derventa district)*

The war particularly shook up Orthodox Bosnia. In places, sexual morals sank catastrophically low, although many other patriarchal customs remained unchanged. Despite the adulterous ways referred to, the first example has a patriarchal quality about it.

> Wives are faithful to their husbands. Cases of women yielding to other men are rare. There are instances of childless women doing so in the hope that some other man may make them pregnant.
>     *(Stolac district, Herzegovina, mixed Catholic and Orthodox village)*

> If they are unfaithful, it is because their husbands do not satisfy them, so they say: "What he cannot do, another can." There were not many unfaithful women. If they were, it was during the war, in the villages, on the insistence of gendarmes or others who forced them to it, also frequently for want of husbands, who were in the army.
>     *(Tuzla district, Orthodox village)*

> Wives are not faithful. They have relations as a rule with the more experienced and older neighbors, who know how to keep the love secret on account of the family, and it is rare for them to have dealings with young, unmarried men. *(Mrkonjić-grad district, Orthodox village)*

> Wives are not faithful to their husbands. They have relations with the man who pays them well.     *(Bosanski Novi district, Orthodox village)*

> Sometimes women have extramarital relations with strangers when they go into the city to sell things. Those are chance liaisons. For them they receive rewards. It is increasingly observed that women sell their bodies for as little as two dinars. If the husband learns, he takes a very sharp line, but his first concern is to insist that the world should not know about it. The only consequence of unfaithfulness is a beating.
>     *(Stolac district, Herzegovina)*

319

It is when they go into the town that most unfaithfulness takes place. In the town for that purpose, there are particular houses which are meeting places, where the peasant women sell themselves. It usually happens on market days. I witnessed a peasant catching his unfaithful wife in the act, and he slashed her badly about her limbs and breast with a knife. She had sold her love to an old man for 10 dinars. So it is with married women, widows, divorced women, as well as unmarried girls, village prostitutes. In nearly every village one can find such a thing as a mother selling herself together with her daughters. There are the village whores. As it is a frequent phenomenon here for young men to marry girls who are their senior, one should make the point that these are quite frequently sexually immature youths, consequently they soon tire of their marital duties. This puts their young wives, full of desire and heat, in a difficult position, and results in real tribulation, nervous troubles, apathy, and so forth. Very soon the wife begins to cast her eyes on other men. The husband becomes jealous. Quarrels, beatings, ill-treatment follow, and their life develops further in this atmosphere. For how long? *(Bijeljina district, Orthodox village)*

From Serbia, even in the patriarchal southern parts, prostitution is reported:

There are cases of unfaithfulness even among the matrons, not only young girls or young women. Sometimes, under pressure, with police officers. These keep a log of the number of women they take, and are not choosy, and have reached the record number of 1,500 a man of thirty-eight or forty being especially eager to collect affairs during his last years of service.

To a peasant an unfaithful wife is a *bitch*. "Kill the wretch if she's no good!" It is a sore point with the peasant. When a man is convinced, a beating follows, sometimes with a weapon, and the knife (Shumadian tradition). A husband does not heed public opinion when he has been disgraced, when his pride has fallen; then his aim is to destroy his wife to the maximum. If any material bond links them, they put up with each other, but there is a gulf between them. In an extreme case, he will turn her out of the house and charge her with adultery. *(Kosmaj district)*

The above report shows the combination of the combative spirit and the modern element of prostitution. The combination of these two elements signalizes the rapid penetration of Serbia by economy with a money nexus.

In one report a teacher maintains that such prostitution had spread in the south of Serbia:

Regarding the disagreement between my data and those of others who have played a part in the inquiry in Serbia, there is an easy explanation. The fact that they were unable to compile the requisite data regarding prostitution does not mean that it does not exist there. It means that they were either not in touch with anybody who could give them the necessary information, or failed to make such contact. Such details are best come by from boastful brandy-loving men, if the investigator can obtain their confidence. In such men, Don-Juanism is as a rule an ideal, and they will very frequently tell all they know down to the least details about such a matter. While on the other hand the women will almost without exception refuse to admit that they have let any man touch them, unless for reasons of love. The reason for this is that this would be counter to the accepted standards of morals in the environment in which they live, and they wish to make out that they are not at variance with these. I know a case of a man, a peasant, losing the list of the women with whom he had relations, and in that list were the names of more than seventy women of the village. The man in question is without any particularly pleasing features, indeed, on the contrary, he is absolutely ordinary. He did not please all those women. Many gave themselves to him for money. There was another case fifteen to twenty days ago. A frontier-guard came to the village on leave. When he wanted to go back to his unit it transpired that he had no money for the ticket. He said that a 'snaša', that is a young married woman, had 'extracted' 700 dinars from him. *(Jablanica district)*

In Croatia, extramarital relations had a different color and were not as a rule considered a catastrophe. Adjustment to a money economy automatically brought with it individual freedom, while the Catholic Church's stand against divorce and new marriage also influenced matters and persuaded people to resign themselves to facts. Nor did the question of prestige become of such great importance as it did in patriarchal regions.

In the Croat regions, where individualism had long since penetrated, public opinion regarding morals was rather indifferent:

Nobody pays any attention to a woman's unfaithfulness. It is ascribed to a restless character. *(Kutina district)*

In the former Military March and in Slavonia, love-making was looked on with favor and adultery tolerated. This attitude did not necessarily mean that the family system was falling to pieces. Here are two reports from the Military March:

Wives are not faithful to their husbands. They have relations with anybody who pleases them more than the husband. They take nothing for this, but even sometimes give the men a present, to keep the liaison going longer and to keep it secret.         *(Petrinja district)*

Perhaps the war has taught them a lot of things, but it was the depression which was largely a determining force. Poverty attacked people all round, and many men returned to their families the easier to be able to bear the yoke of poverty.         *(Slunj district)*

This is one of very few reports which ascribe a regenerative influence on family life to the depression. Here are reports revealing public opinion in Slavonia:

An unfaithful wife is condemned only very slightly. As a rule it is the limp husband who is condemned.         *(Vukovar district)*

It depends on the quality of the husband. If a woman deceives a kind, attentive husband, she is condemned, on the contrary, it is admitted that to some extent she is in the right.         *(Valpovo district)*

Women are as a rule faithful to their husbands. A minority do have dealings, as a rule with a neighbor or a pleasing married man. It would be an insult for her to take money, but she will gladly accept jewelry or clothing as a sign of attention to her. Nor was money ever given before the war and the depression, but help was given to poorer ones in their work and household cares.         *(Virovitica district)*

If a woman has married for love, she is as a rule faithful and never has anything to do with another man. If she has not married for love, she does. She has relations then with men of her village, but more often with various commercial travelers and representatives and with town gentry, as it is more certain that such liaisons will not be known about. For this they take money or various presents for their "toilette," for which they will give anything to be better dressed than others, even at this price. Such women are condemned and the community in which they live looks askance at them. They frequently acquire various nicknames and "tags," such as . . . [three names follow, indicating that a woman is "the gendarmes tart," "the tart of the gentry" or "anybody's"].         *(Županja district)*

Here are reports from central Croatia:

The women of these parts do not go on the market. They enter into sexual liaisons with local men when they go to church festivals, where they stay two or three days, for instance to Mary of Bistrica. For this they accept money and clothing. If a man has no money, he will pal up with the husband and help him in his work.         *(Ivanec district)*

Just as much as the men, indeed, one might say, women are more unfaithful than the men, so their doings exceed 50 per cent. They have relations with married men and young fellows. They do not take money or very rarely, but as a rule have drinks with such men in the inns.

(Varaždin district)

The examples show that here extramarital relations were not something new, unheard-of, or terrible, which in a patriarchal environment would drive the husband to revenge. There are even reports which sound as if they were recording a folk custom.

In regard to extramarital relations, the Littoral was as far from the sternness and dramatic tension of the patriarchal environment as it was from the anarchy and prostitution of regions with rapid changes in progress:

Women generally are faithful to their husbands. There are rare cases of their having relations with one of the husband's friends or friends of the household, but in strict secrecy. Not a single case has been known publicly. (Beograd-on-Sea district)

Women as a rule are faithful so long as their husbands are at home, though while these are away it comes to unfaithfulness with unmarried men and married men. They take no reward for this, indeed, they help the young men. (Isle of Krk)

As we see, the absolute faithfulness of the married woman of the patriarchal environment at a certain stage turns into a sort of anarchy, often for gain, particularly where the money economy has penetrated late and with great rapidity. In districts where money economy entered early and penetrated gradually, we see what might be called the more worthy fruits of individualism. The bond between husband and wife is stronger, as also is the feeling of mutual obligation. Extramarital relations are exceptional cases, and women do not enter into them for material advantage, but usually solely if the husband is absent from home for long years.

## Dangers to Women

Practically everywhere wives' extramarital relations were threatened by sanctions of some sort, hence involved certain dangers. There was particular severity in patriarchal districts with a tribal organization, where adultery amounted to cheating the husband of his authority as head of the family, hence bringing disgrace on the family, the clan, and the tribe:

For unfaithfulness of a woman the sentence is death. As a rule the husband carries it out, to wipe the disgrace from his face and cleanse the sullied honor of himself and his family.

(Vučitrn district, Albanian village)

323

It matters less if others get hold of the fact that a woman has been unfaithful. If the husband knows, or catches her at it, he is ready to kill them both. *(Struga district, Albanian village)*

A husband leaves a faithless wife. During Turkish times, before the war, the husband had the right to cut off her nose, cut out her tongue, or cut off her hair. As a rule everybody gets to know.

*(Montenegro, Andrijevica district, Albanian village)*

The husband beats or abandons the unfaithful wife. Adultery can remain a secret, but rarely. There are cases of the husband's catching the wife in the act and killing them both.

*(Montenegro, Andrijevica district, Albanian village)*

It is important for the unfaithfulness of a wife to remain a secret. If the husband catches the wife in the act, he is considered a coward if he does not kill the adulterer, and will be despised.

*(Montenegro, Bar district)*

The faithfulness of women in marriage remains as before. I think this is because from infancy women are given a stern moral upbringing, and also because the peasants are like the Albanians in matters of morals and formerly used to punish women with death for adultery. Without regard to whether public opinion learned of it, such women were killed, so one cannot recall a case of an unfaithful wife.

*(Macedonia, Galičnik district, Moslem village)*

There were cases in this environment of a man's nobly overlooking a wife's sin and hushing the matter up:

The husband may drive her from the home only if it becomes general knowledge, when even her folk would not take her in. If nobody has known, the matter is quietly smoothed over.

*(Montenegro, Nikšić district)*

In all districts in which the Turkish influence had been strong, sternness was as great as in a region with a tribal system, though with a rather different coloring. It was not the question of prestige that predominated here, but jealousy:

I am aghast at the terrible position and condition of the wife here. I once sent a number of pictures showing women with loads of wood on their backs to the Belgrade paper *Politika*. I had never dreamed that by doing this I should so upset and embitter the larger part of the village. Some even wanted to beat me up, for daring to photograph a wife and, what was worse, publish her picture, this despite the fact that the picture came out so badly reproduced that nobody could have told who is who. However, had it been possible for anybody to recognize one of the women, her fate would have been of the worst. The husband might actually have turned her out of the house and left her. Indeed, such an instance did occur a few years earlier. At the annual feast of a certain monastery, a photographer took a picture of a group of women in folk costume. They did not even know they had been photographed. Those pictures were later on sale in Ochrid with the title: Folk Costume of Ochrid district. One of these pictures was bought by a tourist from Bucharest, and later the husband of one of the women, who had gone to Bucharest, saw this picture. Recognizing his wife in it, he broke off the marriage and left her. The reason given was: "I don't want a wife whose picture anybody can carry in his pocket." *(Macedonia, Struga district)*

It would be a mistake to judge such reactions by assuming that personal liberty and independence were absolute values for wives. One has to perceive what lies behind such jealousy. Though it is concealed from the outer world, there is a very close bond and intense attachment to the wife. As a general rule, the women judged jealousy from this angle and are more easily reconciled to it than to a husband's indifference to sexual life or his wife. This is to be seen clearly in the reactions of a woman from an Oriental environment married to a Western man, especially if they live in countries where independence is looked upon as the greatest value. Such women lack the intense attention (including jealousy) of the husband, all of which are outward manifestations that she is "his." Here is an example of the attachment of a young husband from a district in which the jealousy of the man who goes away to work for long periods is uncompromising:

> In the first years, the man is greatly attached to his wife. He buys her sweets and they pet one another like children. They are shy of each other and of other people who are older than they are. When a girl is married, she becomes the youngest woman in the home and must serve everybody. Then the husband helps her in every way, carries water for her, takes her out to public gatherings.
>
> *(Macedonia, St. Nikola Ovčepolje district)*

Among the Moslems, the marital relationships (and sexual relations generally) were considered so important that there was a short procedure for a wife to obtain a divorce if her husband was away from the home for more than a year. By Sheriat court prescriptions, the marriage was dissolved and the wife may remarry. Endless faithfulness was not expected of her.

Here are some examples of Oriental intolerance:

If a husband were to learn of his wife's unfaithfulness, he would kill her, but there are no such cases because the women are faithful. In the village, there are peasants who are absent from home for a considerable time, as they go to work in the forests as lumberjacks. When such men return home, were any to hear that his wife had uncovered her face to any other man, he would kill her or the man who saw her; this act alone they consider to amount to adultery. For this reason, when alone the women bear themselves very strictly. In 1930, a peasant killed a baker who cracked a joke with the man's wife and wanted to pull her veil aside to see if she was pretty. The husband came on the scene and simply ripped the baker up with a knife. . . . There are cases of a wife going to Sarajevo or Mostar, but such one never returns to the village, for she knows what awaits her. She would simply be driven out by the peasants, without inquiry as to the sort of life she had lived, decent or not.                                           *(Bosnia, srez Foča)*

If a husband learns of his wife's unfaithfulness, he tries to get rid of her, while if he was fond of her he will hate her and beat her. Among the richer peasants he may even kill her. An unfaithful wife is often tortured by her husband, there are cases of his cutting her about madly. In 1925 a peasant was tried for this.    *(Bosnia, Cazin district)*

Wives are faithful. The husband would not even dream of the wife being unfaithful; he would kill her.        *(Herzegovina, Stolac district)*

The consequence of the unfaithfulness of the wife: Expulsion from the home and divorce. It is important whether the village has learned about it.                                     *(Macedonia, Struga district)*

Under Orthodox church law, there was divorce and remarriage, but only under such difficult conditions that peasants rarely made use of the right. Here is an example from Hercegovina, which reveals typical reactions of the husbands in two concrete cases in a Moslem village:

The consequences of unfaithfulness for a wife are fateful. The consequence would be manslaughter or at least abandonment or the departure of the husband to another place. If the matter remains a secret it is settled within the family, sometimes in the form of the husband prohibiting the wife's leaving the house, even to go to church, whereas if it becomes a "public secret," it comes to the consequences I have quoted. In one case the husband drove his wife away from him, and in another he himself left the family and the village never to give a word of himself again.                         *(Herzegovina, Stolac district)*

In Bosnia-Herzegovina, adultery either brought serious tragedy or the matter was hushed up in a style of patriarchal dignity. But there could be hushing up of the adultery of another kind:

326

The unfaithfulness of the wife as a rule leads to divorce. There are cases of the husband's even continuing to put up with it and insisting on keeping it quiet, or pretending not to know; but as a rule, if he does learn of it, a divorce follows. Recently this is no longer put up with, from reasons of material self-interest.          (*Brčko district*)

A report from a village with a majority of men:

The husband forgives his wife's unfaithfulness because it is hard for him to get another wife.          (*Jajce district*)

The following report contains a rather civilized note:

The important thing is for a wife's unfaithfulness to remain a secret. Not to disgrace us publicly.          (*Bugojno district*)

Here and there in Macedonia on account of the scarcity of marriageable girls, one finds a fairly high degree of tolerance.

A husband gives his unfaithful wife a beating, but that is the end of it. He dare not turn her out, because it is hard to marry a second time, so at the same time he consoles himself by the thought that this is her nature, so what can he do about it? He resigns himself to fate, but tries to prevent its happening again, keeps his eye at her more.
          (*Kočane-Skoplje district*)

The unfaithfulness of a wife has hardly any consequences. Husbands make out to their wives that they just don't know about it. But the world at large, the village, gets to know. Nothing can be hidden.
          (*St. Nikola Ovčepolje district*)

In regions with rapid changes—in Christian villages of Bosnia, in Serbia, and in Croatia—the wife's unfaithfulness led to quarrels, tension, and ill-treatment; but fatal results, as in the patriarchal regions, were rare:

A husband will reprove his wife for unfaithfulness, even give her a beating. It is of no importance whether the deed will remain a secret. The man always tells somebody which woman he has had relations with, and sometimes the women themselves talk about it.
          (*Bosnia, Jajce district*)

It is important for a wife's unfaithfulness to remain a secret, otherwise the husband will find every possible way of maltreating and nagging his wife.          (*Bosnia, Bosansko Grahovo district*)

A minority beat an unfaithful wife when they learn about it, and they turn her out, and this without regard to whether the village knows or not. The majority overlook it.          (*Serbia, Kosmaj district*)

The following reports indicate endless conflicts in villages of central Croatia, where there was no possibility of divorce:

Women are faithful, since unfaithfulness is practically impossible for them. Wives are much more closely looked after and more condemned, so they take care. The husband will beat them to unconsciousness with anything he can lay hands on. This is a frightful worsening of her position, which is bad enough anyway. It is very important whether the world at large knows or the matter remains a secret.

*(Varaždin district)*

On account of unfaithfulness, a couple will quarrel their whole life long, even going through it all in front of the children. The important thing is for the world not to know. Husbands say to their wives: "See I don't know about it." Beating and quarrelling to death is a consequence. The husband yields a little if he goes to another woman for intimate relations. The marriage is not broken off.   *(Prelog district)*

Reports from the Military March show much greater tolerance of the extramarital activities of grass widows than of wives whose husbands are at home. In the Dinaric parts of Croatia, a harsh note comes out:

As a rule the wife's unfaithfulness is learned about—then for such a wife begin tortures and reproaches at every whip and turn. . . . If the husband learns and is still away at work, he stops writing to her and never returns.   *(Lika area, Gospić district)*

The husband deals roughly with an unfaithful wife and turns her out. Great fights can occur, and the husband does not conceal the cause from others. If there are not many children, he always turns her out of the home.   *(Dalmatia, Benkovac district)*

The first consequence when a man learns that his wife has been unfaithful is to give her a good beating and threaten more punishment. But if other people have got to know about it, woe to that woman. She is due for beating daily and it may come to her being turned out of the home. This is the final sanction and in their view the worst for the woman.   *(Kordun area, Slunj district)*

But tolerance is reported from the same area in the former Military March:

Most husbands learn of a wife's unfaithfulness, but yet hold their tongues. Definitely most men, a phlegmatic breed, scarcely pay any attention, while the wives here are most often plucky and strong, so men are simply afraid to say anything in reproach, as they may get the worst of it.   *(Kordun area, Dvor district)*

The following comes from a village, the peasants of which go to work in a nearby industrial town.

A wife's unfaithfulness is condemned. Husbands react variously. The majority take it with indifference, having a liaison with some other woman, but the husband who had been faithful beats his unfaithful wife. *(Karlovac district)*

Here is a report from the Dalmatian Highlands which shows a turn of public opinion in favor of the woman:

A husband drives an unfaithful wife from his home, gives her a beating. He will have no more to do with her. Killing is not customary. It is very important that the adultery remain a secret, but that is not easy in a village. . . . The man whose wife is no longer faithful is no longer a man. Such a thing, the peasants say, can happen only to a "silly zany," not to a "real male husband." *(Dalmatia, Knin district)*

In Slavonia adultery need not bring tragedy:

As a rule, the world learns of a wife's unfaithfulness before the husband does, but when he does find out he beats her and turns her out. After a few days he always asks her to come back. *(Vukovar district)*

In the Littoral, there was neither killing nor harsh treatment of the wife for breaking the marriage vow, but there was another form of pressure: The husband who was abroad as emigrant—and only such families had adultery—may leave the wife and never communicate with her again. This possibility was a powerful threat.

When a husband who is in America learns that his wife is unfaithful, he stops writing to her and sending her money. Frequently he does not return at all. *(Isle of Krk)*

Only those wives are unfaithful whose husbands are not at home. When a husband learns that his wife has been unfaithful, he stops communicating with her. In most cases she is abandoned by him.

*(Isle of Korčula)*

Marital faithfulness in the Littoral stood on sound foundations, indeed, foundations apparently firmer than those in the patriarchal regions where there was the threat of death. In an environment with a new family equilibrium, voluntary submission to standards and willing maintenance of obligations gave all relationships a particularly solid basis. Apart from this, however, all villages of the Littoral had an excess female population, so that there was less temptation for women than in the old-world environment.

## Chaste Girls and Faithful Wives

Is there a connection between the premarital love life of girls and the faithfulness of married women? The table below clearly reveals a strong correlation between the two phenomena. But does it reveal anything else?

The first category dominates in all regions, but especially in the

## TABLE 1. PREMARITAL AND EXTRAMARITAL
## RELATIONS OF WOMEN*

| | Alb. % | Ch. Maced. % | Mo. Bos. % | Ch. Bos. % | Serb. % | Cr. % | Lit. % |
|---|---|---|---|---|---|---|---|
| *Group 1* | | | | | | | |
| Girls strictly moral, | | | | | | | |
| Wives strictly moral | 100 | 68 | 88 | 35 | 40 | 33 | 60 |
| *Group 2* | | | | | | | |
| Girls have sex relations, | | | | | | | |
| Wives strictly moral | — | 5 | — | 3 | — | 15 | 5 |
| *Group 3* | | | | | | | |
| Girls strictly moral, | | | | | | | |
| Wives have sex relations | — | — | — | 6 | 10 | 2 | — |
| *Group 4* | | | | | | | |
| Girls have sex relations | | | | | | | |
| Wives have sex relations | — | — | — | 3 | 10 | 2 | — |

\* Only villages reporting frequent liaisons have been included.

patriarchal. In this grouping have also been included relations between betrothed couples known in the Littoral and in certain other villages.

The second category embraces the villages where the girls have relations but married women are faithful. The largest cluster of such villages is in Croatia, where the climate is particularly unfavorable for girls, as the young men strive to seduce them, but will marry only chaste girls.

This category also includes the villages of the pastoral districts, where premarital sexual relations among young people were allowed. Here, when young people do marry, they usually remained faithful. Only in these villages does the situation agree with the theory that, where young people work out their impulses in their youth and satisfy their sexual demands with a wide range of experience, they find it easier than the inexperienced to settle down in marriage. Here are reports from the Dalmatian Highlands:

In most cases, girls have experience before marriage. Perhaps 90 per cent. Joint care of the livestock drives them to it from pure sexual maturity. They place no price on virginity and pretend to have neither heard nor seen anything. What is more, it would seem that the men prefer as wife a girl who has had a number of men. The cases of a girl having a baby before marriage are rare. A girl is always married by somebody who has had relations with her. As a rule married women here are faithful. *(Benkovac district)*

The third category comprises the villages in which the unmarried girls live strictly, while married women do have extramarital affairs. Such villages are rare among those investigated, and only in Serbia were any considerable number found. Here the fact that in Serbia married women were under particularly powerful husband authority probably played a part, so that the wives sometimes engaged in extramarital relations as a sort of rebellion.

Girls have no relations, they are married very young. Great importance is placed on maidenhood. Without this, marriage is as a rule impossible. Very often the wives are not faithful. They generally have relations with neighbors, often the husband's friend or some other acquaintance living farther away, to whom they can go freely. They do not accept presents. *(Moravica district)*

In Orthodox Bosnia, too, we occasionally find this combination, particularly in villages with a male majority:

Unmarried girls have no relations. There was one single case after the war. A married woman is faithful only if ugly, so no man wants her. It is a rare woman who will not have relations with other men. They accept no money, but get fruit and white bread. It seems that it used to be so earlier too. *(Jajce district, Orthodox village)*

In Croatia this category appears under different conditions, that is, in certain economically very advanced villages near the towns:

Girls have to bear themselves modestly and retiringly if they are to marry. The husband is often rough, drinks, and is older than his wife. Wives as a rule have lasting intimate friendships with a young man, often a hired man. The wives are very good housekeepers and particularly tender mothers. *(Dugoselo district)*

The fourth category embraces villages with many premarital and many extramarital relations. We find that this too includes a very small percentage of the villages surveyed.

From these data the only conclusion we can draw is that there is a close correlation between the chastity of girls and the faithfulness of married women. We are, on the contrary, unable to draw any conclusions to support the theory that those women are faithful in marriage who had an opportunity to have free experience before marriage.

## Faithfulness of Husbands

Are extramarital relations of husbands a symptom accompanying the reshaping of the family, as those of wives are? Graph 52 gives a very simple answer:

### Graph 52. Extramarital relations of husbands

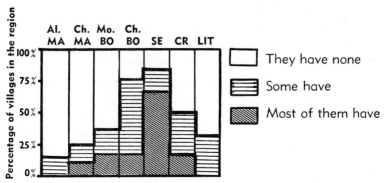

The graph rises and falls steeply, which shows that the unfaithfulness of husbands is indeed a symptom of the rapid break-up of the patriarchal system. The steepness of the graph indicates great changes. When we compare Graph 50, on page 316, showing the extramarital relations of wives, we notice that in the case of the men the rise is particularly steep, and progresses in regular stages, while the gulf between the Moslem and Christian villages of Bosnia, noted on the earlier graph is missing, as is also the similarity between all regions in a stage of transformation.

With regard to rewarded relations and prostitution, there is little distinction between the regions, unless it is that Moslem Bosnia and Serbia stand out a little. In Moslem Bosnia, with its great gulf between the sexes, and the presence of the first stage of break-up of patriarchal life, a married man had practically no other opportunity for extramarital relationships other than with gypsy girls, the singing girls of cafés, or village widows who have become prostitutes.

From Serbia investigators very frequently mention the neglect of family and farm on account of such relations—the sort of situation described by the novelist Borislav Stanković in his novels *Koštana* and *Nečista Krv.*[3] Husbands in Macedonia and down the Littoral also sometimes spent money on liaisons.

[3] The English version is by Alec Brown, entitled *Sophka*, Jonathan Cope, London, 1929.

Judgment of unfaithfulness of the husbands by public opinion was similar to that regarding married women, that is to say, theory and practice agreed. Nevertheless, more villages tolerated the extramarital relations of the men than they did those of married women. In patriarchal districts, unfaithfulness of husbands was sternly condemned and considered a serious crime, even sometimes a sin. The linguistic shade of difference here is of interest: There is frequent mention of men being "condemned," whereas women are "scorned" or "made mock of."

In a region undergoing rapid change, we come, here and there, upon a new element, the view that extramarital relations raise a man's status, do him honor, cause other men to look on him as a hero for this and marvel at his agility. Such approval often had a cynical note. In condemnation of the women's unfaithfulness we found nothing like this anywhere.

The following are examples of condemnation of extramarital relations of husbands from a patriarchal environment:

Husbands are faithful. The saying is: "I won't let mine go, I don't want others." The peasants hold unfaithfulness to the woman to be low, disgraceful, unworthy of a married head of the household. They do not count such to be men. *(Macedonia, Djevdjelija district)*

Husbands are completely faithful. The peasants boycott an unfaithful man and have nothing to do with him. *(Macedonia, Prespa district)*

In most instances, husbands are faithful. The small number who are not are looked upon as bad lots in their villages. Some counsel them to mend their ways. Some enjoy the existence of hatred.
*(Macedonia, Prespa district)*

In the great majority of cases, married men are faithful to their wives. The people here take a very poor view of a married man who has loose dealings with other women, and for this reason the number of such cases is small. *(Montenegro, Cetinje district)*

In Moslem Bosnia, patriarchal dignity favored faithfulness in husbands, but other factors had the opposite effect, particularly the privileged position of the husband, the easy divorce, and the slackening of religious influence. Here are examples of patriarchal morals in Moslem Bosnia and Herzegovina:

Most married men are faithful. About 95 per cent. Unfaithfulness in the husband is condemned. *(Mostar district)*

Husbands are faithful. They are unfaithful only if absent from home, for instance if they have gone to work in Sarajevo or into the army. The

333

peasants hold it against them. Sometimes they even spit on them, merely to disgrace them the more. *(Foča district)*

Two examples of the privileged position of the man and of the great rights allowed him by public opinion follow:

Husbands are not faithful, nor in the view of the local people need they be so. Unfaithfulness is not praised but is not greatly frowned upon.
*(Brčko district)*

The husband very frequently neglects his family and farm when he has such an affair, and it often happens that in the end he turns his wife out. They have relations with prostitutes, gypsy girls, and peasant women of other faiths. *(Cazin district)*

An example of restraint on the man's part due to powerful economic pressure:

Peasants do not spend money on extramarital liaisons. "Food is more important" they say. *(Bugojno district)*

In the Christian villages of Bosnia, there were more cases of husbands' extramarital relations than in the Moslem villages, but less prostitution:

It is done for love, attention, and honor. It honors me that he wants me.
*(Bosnanski Petrovac district)*

It is rarely paid for in money, as a rule in presents, most frequently a two-dinar cake of soap. *(Banjaluka district)*

In Serbia, extramarital relations of husbands were particularly frequent. Many factors contributed to this: The traditional position of authority of the men, inherited from a past under Turkey and in a state of warfare; the arbitrary ways of pastoral folk; the relative lack of wives' rights; and the rapid transformation of the peasant economy and abandonment of the zadrugas. Even in the southern part of Serbia, largely patriarchal, there was much unfaithfulness among the men.

Our first two examples are from the south, where youths married early, taking girls older than themselves:

Husbands are not faithful to their wives. They are not satisfied without a number of women. Men approve such relations. The women suffer in silence. *(Jablanica district)*

The peasants have extramarital relations with other women and in some cases also with girls. Lost youth is made up for after marriage, taking advantage of sexual knowledge acquired with the wife.

*(Vlasontinci district)*

If they are rich again, they are tolerated as decent and worthy of respect. *(Kolubara district)*

The following examples testify to Serbian views of the husbands' extramarital relations:

Extramarital relations of the husband are considered of no acount. On the contrary they are ascribed to his skill and agility.

*(Moravica district)*

Husbands are not faithful. The great majority is not, perhaps 80 percent, though this may be a trifle exaggerated. *(Kosmaj district)*

There can be no guarantee of faithfulness. They find least satisfaction of all in their wives. If in no other way, he will at least get what he wants by the terms of speech he uses. . . . Extramarital relations are in the main between those in marriage, rather than with unmarried persons.

In a joking way a man is reproved, but it is always proof of manhood, strength, and courage. More a virtue than a failing. In such matters, when elder men are concerned, they are very matter-of-fact and objective. *(Kosmaj district)*

In Croatia, there were fewer villages with husbands' having extramarital relations than in Serbia. The circumstance that the breakdown of the patriarchal order was in its concluding phase here played a certain part. Reports from central Croatia reveal the attitude of public opinion:

In most cases, they are unfaithful. Such are mocked yet also looked on rather as fine fellows. *(Varaždin district)*

They have relations with young married women, whose husbands are abroad. They hide this on account of the husbands. It looks as if they themselves feel that they should boast of them. In the village there are two or three women with whom anybody can go. They probably accept money, but not necessarily. Each has three or four illegitimate children. Apart from this, they are peasants belonging by birth to this village, and the children are not subject to any scorn, nor are they themselves except for being poor. *(Garešnica district)*

A report from the Military March:

Married men are not faithful, nor are the wives faithful to the men. The peasants condemn nothing. *(Patrinja district)*

A report from a Dinaric district with a great incidence of emigration which was also true of the Military March:

They have relations with the so-called snašas, who are married women whose husbands have gone to work in America. In the eyes of the peas-

ants the value of such an unfaithful husband is increased. He is a *laf*, a sort of hero. This instance illustrates the hard lot of the peasants' wife.
*(Gospić district)*

An instance of tolerance in Slavonia:

It all depends. It's the opportunity that makes the thief. If a man has a chance he takes another's grapes or his wife. It's all the same to the peasants. They often take no notice, with all their other cares.
*(Županja district)*

Reports from Dalmatia:

Husbands are faithful since they have to be, under the pressure, as they are, of hard economic conditions and public opinion. Otherwise they would soon behave differently. One can observe this underlying attitude of mind.
*(Knin district)*

Are married men faithful? Yes and no, it depends on the man. There is no condemnation of this, indeed, an unfaithful husband is often more respected and sought after.
*(Benkovac district)*

A report from a village from which the men went to town to work or else emigrated overseas:

If men live in their village, they are faithful; if they go away to work, they are not. When they work in a town, they find women enough, and the women seek them out to get their earnings. Some give money for such liaisons and neglect their families, but only a very small number. Most are in South America. The adultery is talked about for a day or two, then forgotten.
*(Imotski district)*

In the Littoral, husbands as a rule had relations only when away from their villages:

Husbands are faithful. They have extramarital relations when they go to Dubrovnik, and, if they know of a woman with whom they can have intimate relations, they gladly visit her. Men do not give any money for such relations. The peasants' view is that men can do whatever they like, and have a sort of right to it.
*(Isle of Mljet)*

Husbands are faithful if they stay at home. Here they have no opportunity to be unfaithful. A small number on rare occasions have relations with prostitutes in the town. These are small outgoings of fourteen to twenty-five dinars. They do not neglect their families. While at home they are always faithful, but when they emigrate they live without abstinence, nor do their wives hold this against them. Such relations can hardly be called unfaithfulness. They are not greatly condemned by the peasants, though a woman will say to herself that he had better have brought those ten dinars home.
*(Isle of Krk)*

In conclusion, we may say that extramarital relations of the men were a symptom of the rapid intrusion of money economy and the rapid break-up of the patriarchal order. Thus they have the same significance as the extramarital liaisons of married women, though they were perhaps less important as symptoms. There is very little adultery by married men wherever one has settled conditions of either old or new style. If the husbands were away from their villages, it is probable that the majority had sexual relations. These, however, were without such far-reaching or serious consequences for family life as those of married women.

### Changes in Marital Faithfulness

To the question whether extramarital relations had become customary in recent times or were of an earlier date, there is no simple answer. In all regions there were many villages in which there had been no change since the war, or before the depression; but in all regions there were also both villages with more and villages with less extramarital relationships than previously. Graph 53 gives us a picture of changes in the faithfulness of married women:

Graph 53. Changes in extramarital relations of wives

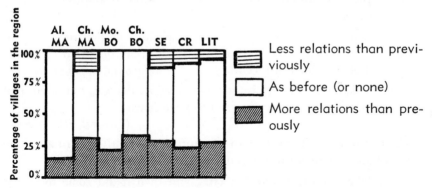

Here we see two opposed tendencies. More villages show an increase than a decrease. The wave of individualism and the spirit of greater personal liberty without exception penetrated all regions, without regard to the previous situation in the region or its phase of development.

A decline in marital faithfulness is to be observed in a minority of villages, and this tendency seems weak. The libertinism which developed during the war and in the postwar ferment yielded a little everywhere, and in every region there were still other particular circumstances which acted against extramarital relations. In Macedonia, there was a gradual decline of the male majority of the population of villages. In Slavonia, through the partition of zadrugas and the diminution of well-being, there was a decay of carefreeness and cheerfulness. Some villages in the neighborhood of the towns abandoned the old customs, for instance, those festive fairdays which were so favorable to love episodes. Down the Littoral, there was an increase of unity in marriage. In every area we see tendencies of greater marital loyalty of the wife, which conflicted with a tendency for more frequent extramarital relations. If we are to understand the complex process of change in the marital faithfulness of wives, a more precise analysis of conditions in each district is necessary.

Our first two examples reveal the increase of extramarital relations during the First World War:

> Before the war there was no adultery of the wives. During the war it began and reached a peak, but since the war it has declined.
>
> *(Bosnia, Bosansko Grahovo district, Orthodox village)*

> Before the war it was less prevalent. During the war there was a lot of it. After the war, things have improved up to the depression.
>
> *(Serbia, Mladenovac district)*

Example from an environment with a gradual reshaping of family relationships:

> Even before the war there were cases of adultery by the wife. This for instance, has been well described by Kozarac [a Slavonian novelist from the end of the nineteenth century].   *(Slavonia, Županja district)*

> The incidence of adultery is the same as before the war, but because of the depression, less money is given to young men.
>
> *(Littoral, Isle of Krk)*

An example of the decline in the number of adulteries in a village which had become an industrial workers' settlement:

> Before the war there were big fairs, and then it did come to sexual episodes. Since the war those fairs have been absorbed in the weekly market, and people go to this for business reasons, hence it no longer has a festive character, and there are no sexual episodes.
>
> *(Croatia, Karlovac district)*

A report from Slavonia shows an increase of marital loyalty in a district where extramarital love was by tradition widespread and permitted:

> A minority are faithful. Most "cast their eyes on others." Among the younger people there is more loyalty. Unfaithfulness in the men is most condemned. Much more than with the older generations.
>
> *(Pakrac district)*

Regarding the marital loyalty of the husbands, we find the same two tendencies as among the women, but the differences between regions are much greater.

Graph 54. Changes in the extramarital relations of husbands

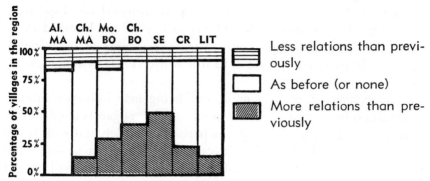

Less relations than previously

As before (or none)

More relations than previously

This curve of Graph 54, with its firm rise and fall, reveals all the drama of the deposition of the head of household. The graph and the reports indicate that the husbands' unfaithfulness was not some symptom of emancipation as it was regarding the women. It was rather a sort of reaction to the head of household's shaken position, the decay of the husband's authority being accompanied by his greater unfaithfulness to the wife. The rising portion of the graph indicates a state of ferment, in which the husband's authority is breaking up, while the descending side represents the process of settling down.

Among the Albanians, this break-up of the husbands' authority had not even begun, and there was likewise no falling off of his position of dignity and personal sense of responsibility. On the other hand, there was an abandonment of a certain element of the arbitrary, an attitude of the master, which proved to be to the advantage of marital faithfulness. In Orthodox Macedonia and the whole of Bosnia, the break-up of the patriarchal family was in its early stage, and connected with this we see an increase in unfaithfulness of the married man. In Serbia, this process had reached a culmination. The striking drop in Croatia and the Littoral indicates that the Croat districts had for some time been in a more or less consolidated stage of development.

Still more clearly than among women, the two tendencies regarding the extramarital relations of husbands cross each other. The penetration of individualistic tendencies into certain districts admittedly

favored extramarital relations, but not unconditionally. It was therefore, not simply a case of the penetration of individualistic and
libertarian tendencies contributing to the parallel entry of a spirit
of leveling out between husband and wife in their duties. The husband certainly abandoned his unlimited arbitrary position as head of
the family, but this on the other hand diminished his disposition
toward marital unfaithfulness. The tendency for the husband to be
more unfaithful developed only when the process of breaking-up
of the zadruga system of life is in full swing. Then extramarital relations become frequent.

The increase of poverty or of well-being may influence marital
faithfulness in various ways. Often we find investigators emphasizing
that increased poverty destroys the patriarchal order, and with it the
monogamistic attitude. Other investigators assert that in one sense
poverty consolidates the family, destroying in the men any will toward
unnecessary effort and any dispersal of energy whatsoever.

We can see most clearly that clash between the tendencies in
Moslem Bosnia, where changes in both senses were great. By Moslem
tradition, the head of the household had a great concern for his
family. He felt responsible for everything and therefore had been
faithful to his wife. However, the traditional sexual liberty of the
head of the household was equally old. New tendencies appeared in
the abolition of the old pleasures of the Moslem gentry and land-
owners—*agas* and *begs*—and the development of new individual
liberties.

It would seem that here we have as many as four interlocking
tendencies. At least this is so if we separate the population into various social strata. Probably earlier it was mainly the agas and begs
who had enjoyed freedom and who also had extramarital relations,
while the peasants were more dutiful and devoted heads of household.
With developments in the first Yugoslav era, and the declassing of the
agas and begs, these now became devoted fathers, burdened by serious
worries, while the peasants, though poorer than before, were inclined
to raise their heads higher, and to free themselves from the restric-
tions of religious ethical laws.

Examples from two villages show the victory of both tendencies.
The first instance shows the former responsibility of the head of
household and the growth of a libertinistic tendency:

> The men as a rule marry at eighteen or nineteen, and enter marriage,
> in the main, quite inexperienced. Before the war they married later
> and gained experience in brothels earlier. Today, married men as a rule

are not faithful to their wives. Extramarital relations are had with various women in inns, and there are cases of relations with married women. They spend quite a lot on this. They neglect their families who go in want of many things. This is not held very much against them, as most men are the same, and look at it as a matter of pride to have as many women as possible. Before the war there was less of this, but before the depression there was more than there is today.

(*Bosnia, Travnik district, Moslem village*)

The other report shows a falling-off of marital faithfulness connected with the growth of poverty during the economic crisis:

Young men live in abstinence unless at work. They say: "It's much harder now for us to get a woman." Married men are faithful "till something comes over us." They have relations "with whoever lets us," mostly with prostitutes. "When there was more money about, there was more running after women." (*Bosnia, Bugojno district, Moslem village*)

### Environments Favorable to Love

A general disposition toward love life exceeding the borders of marriage "by duty" and sexual relations for money is, it would seem, more dependent on regional peculiarities which have developed during the past centuries or thousand years, and through cultural contacts with neighbors and invaders, than on the phase of economic development which is anywhere part of a recent process.

In a patriarchal environment with tribal organization and belligerent tradition, all that is connected with love remained completely subordinate. The aims of national independence and the yearning for respect and glory for the tribe, the family, and the individual as hero, overshadowed all other human aims and completely absorbed men's interest. Only these aims were recognized as legitimate. In such an environment, it was collective aims that dominated, and men remained completely subordinated to the demands of their environment. Independence, initiative, and the possibility of improvisation were lacking in the individual as far as private desires and goals went. Collective tendencies were far too strong for the eminently individual factor of love to be able to develop. Only love between those who are related by blood enjoyed complete moral approval, so that even love between husband and wife remained overshadowed. Loyalty of husband and wife to each other was largely a standardized emotion or attitude, and it also lacked that quality of intensity which characterized any relationship established by a person's own decision. Moreover, the great difference in rank between husband and wife ruled out intimate relationships, for the husband must maintain a gap between him and all the "younger" folk, and the wife must maintain an attitude of awe toward him. The songs sung frequently were the heroic folk songs of epic content, not the lyrical, so-called "female" songs.

In patriarchal regions under Turkish influence, as in Bosnia and Macedonia, the soil for the development of love was much more favorable. Here belligerent goals tended to be in the background, leaving more space for individualistic strivings. The importance of beauty, or *merak*,[4] and enjoyment in the individual sense, taken together with the Oriental tradition were favorable to love. In all districts which had been under Turkish rule, it would seem that the ground was particularly prepared for the sentiments of love. This is not only to be seen in Yugoslav areas but also in many other countries. In the whole of the Balkans (including Hungary), within the former borders of the Ottoman Empire, a predisposition for love emotions in daily life and in songs is clearly to be seen. The same is true in southern Italy with its Saracen past and in Spain with its Moorish past. Even in Latin America, where the Moorish influence worked in watered-down form through Spanish colonizers, we can observe a similar atmosphere. Anyone who has opportunity for comparison will have noted the ineffaceable Near-Eastern element in the countryside near Sarajevo as well as in Sicilian or Mexican towns and villages.

But although in regions which were once under Turkish influence the ground is favorable for love, there was one element which was sometimes so strong that in real life it prevented the development of love relationships. This is the extreme fatalism which no rational factor had weakened.

The fatalistic outlook which up to a certain point favored the development of love sentiments and relationships, if present in extreme form became a hindrance to the realization of such relationships. This was especially to be seen in Bosnia. Complete resignation to fate prevented all activity, prevented too a practical approach to life, prevented compromise in the ordinary affairs of life, and tended to increase hypersensitivity to a diseased degree.

Here love relationships tended to end tragically. It was rare that

4 *Merak* is a Turkish word with a special color, primarily meaning curiosity. In Serbo-Croatian, it has been adopted in the special sense of its secondary meaning of "favorite taste," till it comes to mean "love desire."

people attained their aim in love. Love was to be found principally in songs and expressed yearnings, which became a sort of substitute for real intense experience. The songs which were constantly on people's lips and which incidentally were of superb beauty, all have in them a definitely melancholic note. Love became something idealized but seldom attainable.

In the phase of rapid decay of the old order, however, individualistic and rational factors favored the development of love relationships, but at the same time the crude interests of monetary gain and the extreme rationalistic attitude which in this phase appeared in our regions tended to poison the love relationship. We have seen how, in this stage, love as the motive for marriage is increasingly thrust into the background. But in a region with more gradual development— the Littoral—the soil proved more favorable for love relationships. Collectivistic and individualistic factors had here attained an equilibrium. People clung to general standards, obligations, and considerations, yet at the same time still had the possibility of freedom of choice and independence of action. The danger here is to be found in the over-powerful rational factor, which we see in the shape taken by overseas emigration for decades. Though the betrothal and marital relationships were promising, in reality they were frequently interrupted and whole villages were left without any men in them. In the songs of these parts there was little of that profundity of feeling which we find in regions where the "Turkish hoof" had passed.

The districts in which one can most frequently find love fully realized is Slavonia (including the Syrmia area) and the former Military March. (Voyvodina and Slovenia are left out because they were not covered by the survey.) In Slavonia and the Military March, the Turkish influence played a part over some time, hence impregnating relationships with the individualism of the Orient, and its sense of *merak* and higher enjoyments. Here the Ottomans ruled for 150 years. They only departed in the eighteenth century, which, however, was prior to the complete degeneration of their institutions and culture. Austria, too, subsequently ruling in these parts impressed its own peculiar stamp, influencing people with its tendencies toward a relativistic and a rational outlook. Now military discipline, a more advanced economy, and settled public order removed that sense of being exposed to fate. Extreme fatalism was wiped out. Thereby, so to speak, under Austria, people in the Military March and in Slavonia were equipped to translate their yearnings into actuality. It so happened that also the heroic tradition of the Dinaric people with its specific aggressiveness favored love, once the predominance of political and belligerent aims have been to some extent thrust into the background.

A pastoral economy or past brought in a certain free, almost nomadic element, but only in such measure as to lend the general climate what one might term an artistic quality. Love was further favored by the constitutional factor in the Dinaric people—their health, vigor, and long youth. On the other hand, a factor dangerous to the love relationship was to be found in the combination of the fighting tradition with the rapid influx of money, often from emigrants back from America. This combination often brought about great coarseness toward women. But the general tone is given by the songs sung in this part which reveal both Oriental themes and also a more cheerful tendency in melody and words.

In Slavonia the same factors acted as in the foregoing districts, but here there was also another factor: The gradual economic development and an early attachment to the world economy in this province created a sort of stability and reduced the emotions connected with the transformation of the zadruga. The feudal and Hungarian influences lent gaiety greater legitimacy than anywhere else in the surveyed regions. The relative wealth of this area with its orchards, vineyards, and rich arable land favored the development of a folk culture, of dances full of good cheer and liveliness. Here as a brake on the development of love relationships we find a rational factor which sometimes proved too strong, giving rise to an elaborate system of dowries and inheritances. Slavonian songs clearly reveal all these components to those who know them. The general result is a disposition for love devoid of heavy melancholy.

We can compare the disposition for love with a sensitive plant which, though it will germinate its seed anywhere, after germination requires particular conditions to come to full development. Various factors are required in the soil in the right proportions and the climate, too, must be favorable. The historical development of a region through the centuries can be compared with the soil in which the plant grows, while recent events and the momentary situation constitute the climate. The latter may change in shorter time than the soil.

War, enemy occupation, and political changes, but first and foremost economic developments, may act in such a way as to change the disposition for love relationships at any time. But just as the regional style of the songs sung is slow to change, and the regional character even slower, so even in periods when the climate is unfavorable, such as certain stages of economic reshaping, the soil conducive to love nevertheless remains. These stages of economic transformation are relatively transitory, while the soil changes only slowly and slightly.

図図図図図図図図図図図図図図図図図図図図図図図図図図図図図図図図図図図図図図図図図図図図図図図図

# Illiteracy and Family Relations

図図図図図図図図図図図図図図図図図図図図図図図図図図図図図図図図図図図図図図図図図図図図図図図

As AN indication of the stage of economic development—backwardness or progress—in our regions, illiteracy proved to be very suitable. It can serve as a measuring instrument for the whole civilization and the technical advance streaming from the cities to the countryside, from the centers to the frontier areas. The statistics are both reliable and easily determined, since they were included in the Yugoslav census. They are comparable with figures from other countries where the illiterates were counted. Illiteracy even mirrors faithfully historical influences from East and West, as we will see.

Illiteracy has to be studied without preconceived ideas about "backwardness" in general, particularly in connection with family relations. In a certain sense, the very term "illiteracy" endangers objectivity, as it suggests a disadvantage or even a pitiful state. (The term "analphabetism" used for illiteracy in other languages has the same negative connotation.) If other features of patriarchal life had similar pejorative terms, one would probably look at them also with some prejudice. If the patriarchal regime were called an "undemocratic social structure," subsistence economy "maladjustment to money economy," folk costumes "lack of factory textiles," one would regret or disapprove of this state of affairs too, and, of course, without any justification.

We cannot know in advance if illiteracy has any influence on the family at all, and still less whether there is an unfavorable influence. Finding out whether literacy in any way shaped family relations in rural Yugoslavia will indicate more about the role of the entire complex of technical civilization for the family.

## Number of Illiterates

In the period between the two world wars, Yugoslavia occupied a prominent position among European countries both in the proportion of the agrarian population and the incidence of illiteracy. Table 1 gives the relevant figures on illiteracy for a number of European countries:

First let us examine the illiteracy figures for a number of Yugoslav regions. The figures here relate to the *banovinas*, the administrative

## TABLE 1

|  | Total | Men | Women |
|---|---|---|---|
|  | (figures as percentages of total population)[1] | | |
| Yugoslavia | 45.2 | 32.7 | 57.1 |
| Greece | 40.8 | 23.3 | 57.4 |
| Bulgaria | 31.4 | 19.5 | 43.3 |
| Italy | 21.6 | 17.8 | 25.2 |
| Hungary | 10.0 | 7.9 | 12.0 |
| Czechoslovakia | 4.1 | 3.3 | 4.8 |
| France | 3.8 | 3.4 | 4.2 |
| United States | 4.3 | 4.4 | 4.3 |

areas of this period (for the 1931 Census disregarded historical regions). Nevertheless, some banovinas more or less correspond to historical regions. The figures which follow, however, also include the towns, in which the incidence of illiteracy was less than in the countryside. If the official statistics for the banovinas had not included the towns, the figures would be still closer to my own for the countryside. My figures are based on the number of illiterates supplied me by the State Statistical Bureau for these townships (općine) which are studied in my investigation.

## TABLE 2. PERCENTAGES OF ILLITERATES[2]

|  | Total | Men | Women |
|---|---|---|---|
| Macedonia (Vardar banovina) | 70.9 | 55.7 | 85.5 |
| Bosnia (Vrbas banovina) | 72.6 | 59.9 | 85.8 |
| Serbia (Morava banovina) | 62.0 | 38.8 | 83.7 |
| Croatia (Sava banovina) | 27.7 | 19.6 | 35.1 |

First let us examine graphically the illiteracy of the males, dividing the villages into those in which less than half, and those in which more than half of the males are illiterate.

Graph 55, we see, drops steeply from the patriarchal to the modern regions. The picture falls into two parts: On the one side were the patriarchal regions, in which more than half of the villages had a majority of illiterate males; on the other side were the modern regions, in which less than half of the villages had a majority of illiterate males. Between Bosnia and Serbia exists a great gap.

Graph 56 breaks up the figures into four degrees of illiteracy:

[1] *United Nations Demographic Yearbook, 1948.*
[2] *Final Returns of Census of March 31, 1931*, State Statistical Bureau, Belgrade, 1938.

Graph 55. Illiteracy of the males

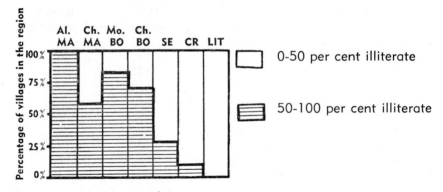

0-50 per cent illiterate

50-100 per cent illiterate

Graph 56. Illiteracy of the males

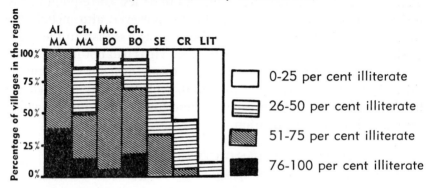

0-25 per cent illiterate

26-50 per cent illiterate

51-75 per cent illiterate

76-100 per cent illiterate

Here we see that we have the highest degree of illiteracy among the Moslems. With the Albanians, it corresponds to a certain stage of economic development. The economy here was mainly pastoral, and there were few schools. In Bosnia and Herzegovina, however, the former Austrian government built many schools. Here the reason for extensive illiteracy among the Moslems is to be explained partly by their hesitation to send their children to schools of "unbelievers," so that in this region there was more illiteracy among the Moslems than among either Orthodox or Catholics. There was resistance to sending girls to school even at the time of this inquiry, in the first Yugoslav era.

On the other hand, the reason that Macedonia was an exception, that is, had a relatively high degree of literacy, is no doubt that Macedonia was a region of an ancient and well-developed agriculture. The pečalba custom also encouraged greater literacy, for lads aiming to go out into the world as laborers made efforts to learn to read and write.

348

In this regard we find Serbia and Croatia among the modern regions, and it was only in the Dinaric districts that the majority of the males was illiterate. The Littoral was also in this respect the most advanced region of all.

Graph 57 examines the illiteracy of the women by a breakdown into two groups.

## Graph 57. Illiteracy of the females

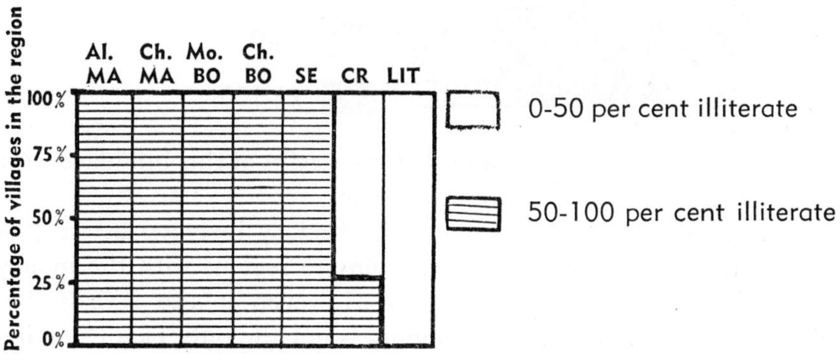

The graph reveals the compact area, covering several regions, in which without exception the villages examined showed a majority of illiterate women. This group even includes Serbia. Five regions with all their villages are included in this group. A profound gulf divides regions formerly under Turkish dominance from those once Austrian.

However to obtain a more detailed picture of female illiteracy, I have divided the degree of illiteracy into five groupings, by splitting up the last quarter into two groups—those villages in which from three-quarters to nine-tenths are illiterate, and the remainder in which over nine-tenths are.

This gives us a new picture. In all the patriarchal regions we now have predominance of the villages in which more than three-quarters of the women are illiterate. On this scale Serbia comes next to the Albanians. On the other hand, although in the Dinaric districts of Croatia there were very many villages with a high incidence of illiteracy, not one belongs to the fifth group. This graph makes clear a distinction between European and Oriental influence on women by pointing up the backward position of women in districts under Turkish domination or those which were preoccupied with the struggle against the Ottoman regime. The graph also shows that the Oriental environment had a much more powerful influence on the

## Graph 58. Illiteracy of the females

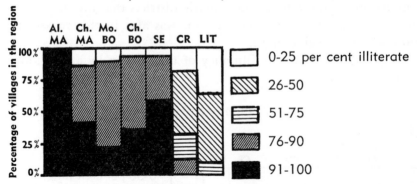

*life of women than of men, and that the results of this influence were far from having vanished from the scene.*

The figures on illiteracy show that literacy increases as we pass from a region with subsistence economy to regions with the money nexus, which is as we presupposed. However, it also reveals that abandonment of subsistence economy is not the only factor making for literacy. Also important is the degree of links with the Western countries, for the Oriental tradition amounts to a brake. This cultural influence is particularly to be seen among women.

We also see a fundamental distinction between the sexes: Literacy spread at a different pace among men than among women. Among the men, illiteracy disappears in step with subsistence economy and the patriarchal set-up, but among the women it disappears only where there has been no previous Turkish domination or struggle against it, another evidence of the strength of the Turkish influence.

To a great extent literacy among women only developed where the Western influence was the decisive one, that is, where there was Austrian rule. Had we included Slovenia in our field of inquiry, this influence would be shown even more clearly, for in Slovenia the illiteracy incidence was only 5.5 per cent, with minimal distinction between the sexes.

### Difference in the Illiteracy of the Sexes

The picture of the spirit or the atmosphere of the family would be still clearer when we look at the education of parents, in the first place at literacy and also at superstitions. The authority of the father and in general of men would become more obvious when we consider the fact that the women are to the greatest part illiterate and actually mentally not so keen and quick-witted as the men. Therefore, the child generally sticks more to the father, finding him more "convenient."

*(Dalmatia, Benkovac district)*

This quotation from the Dalmatian hinterland indicates how differences in illiteracy may influence family relations. What connection did this difference have with the status of the sexes?

The differences are grouped into three categories and are entered in the following table:

1. Small difference in illiteracy between the sexes means that in the village there are 0 to 1.5 times as many illiterate women as men;

2. Medium difference means that in the village there are 1.6 to 2.5 times as many women illiterate as men (about twice as many);

3. Great difference means that in the village there are 2.6 or more times as many women illiterate as men (around three times as many).

### TABLE 3. RELATION OF ILLITERACY OF SEXES
(Ratio)

|  | Alb. Mac. % | Ch. Mac. % | Mo. Bos. % | Ch. Bos. % | Serb. % | Croat. % | Lit. % |
|---|---|---|---|---|---|---|---|
| Small difference | 70 | 28 | 75 | 52 | 4 | 25 | 20 |
| Medium difference | 30 | 62 | 17 | 43 | 38 | 75 | 72 |
| Big difference | 0 | 10 | 8 | 5 | 58 | 0 | 8 |

A small difference in the illiteracy ratio between men and women can have two meanings: Both women *and* men in the village are illiterate or, conversely, both women and men in the village are literate in a great number. Our first group, embracing villages with a small difference in education of the sexes, includes the most backward as well as the particularly progressive villages. In the backward villages of all the patriarchal regions and in Serbia, the men and women were equally illiterate. On the other hand, in Croatian areas and in the Littoral, the villages with a small difference in illiteracy were the especially progressive ones, where literacy of both men and women was high. Villages with an overwhelming illiteracy did not exist in these regions.

Of the Albanian group, most villages belong to the first category, with illiterates of both sexes in the great majority. School education and literacy could not influence family relations under these circumstances.

351

In both parts of Bosnia, conditions were similar to the Albanian settlements, but some villages with a large difference between the sexes did appear. Such newly created distance between the sexes probably had an unfavorable influence on the position of the woman—the domination of the men and the meekness of the women receiving a newly increased emphasis.

In Orthodox Macedonia, there were many villages with twice as high a literacy rate among men—our second category. Literacy entered this region in an Oriental fashion, namely reaching the men well before the women. This fact did not lower the status of women, however; their high price did not seem to be lessened by a difference in the education of the sexes. We shall see later that in Macedonia enlightenment and education had no strong influence on family life (literacy of women does not diminish infant mortality). One of the reasons for this phenomenon was the existence of an old, traditional culture in this region, which at the time of the survey had a greater force than the more recently introduced school education.

In Croatia and the Littoral, a large group of villages proved to be in the intermediate category. Although schools were introduced here relatively early, in many villages there were twice as many literate men as women. Compared to the peasant women of Central and Western Europe, those of Croatia showed a considerable submissiveness which was most probably connected in some way with the difference in education between the sexes. This inequality, like many others in the family in these regions, was largely an accepted state of things, and excited no resistance on the part of the girls or the women. In this region the group of villages with slight differences in literacy between the sexes included villages in which the general literacy was very high.

In Serbia, conditions were unique. More than half of the villages belong to the category where the literacy of men is around three times as high as that of women. Here in places we find that the difference was regarded as one of principle. It was an expression of general hostility to the education of women because it decreases their dependence. We have dealt with the effect of this pressure in the chapter "Husband and Wife," noting that the Serbian woman often reacted vigorously, showed little resignation, and frequently resisted ill-treatment or subordination. Such an attitude, in spite of their lack of education, shows a process of great dynamism. Nothing similar to the power of the concentric pressures on the Serbian woman and the strength of her resistance can be found in the whole of our material on family relations. On the illiteracy of Serbian women, their combativeness, vigor, and resolution can be seen. Their self-confidence, the great influence they exerted on the children despite the pressure brought to bear on them, demonstrates that illiteracy was by no means a decisive factor in their family relations. Here we see that illiteracy had an influence on relations between the sexes only in the sense of being a provocation.

In the other regions the distinction between the illiteracy of the men and the women had various meanings according to other circumstances, but nowhere had it such an eminent importance as in Serbia.

## *Illiteracy and Family Relations*

In order to discover whether illiteracy has an influence on family relations, we shall first look at child mortality in relation to literacy of women in the villages.

There are great differences between various countries and areas in regard to children's mortality: In underdeveloped countries, mortality (especially of infants) is many times greater than in economically progressive ones. The figures on infant and child mortality may change very quickly. In some countries, child mortality dropped by half or one-third in the space of a couple of years. Differences among Yugoslav regions were also great: In Croatia (Sava banovina), mortality of children from 2 to 5 years was below 7 per cent of all deaths; while, in Macedonia (Vardar banovina), it was more than 20 per cent, that is, three times as high. Because of these great differences and also because we know that death rates can drop suddenly, we might assume that literacy would have a clearly visible and favorable effect. However the results are not completely in accord with this assumption.

When inquiring into the correlation between child mortality and female illiteracy the villages were divided, according to the mortality of children of 2 to 5 years, into three groups:

    1. of 1,000 born there were 10-50 children's deaths;
    2. of 1,000 born there were 60-100 children's deaths;
    3. of 1,000 born there were 110-150 children's deaths.

With regard to illiteracy of women, the villages were divided into four groups:

    1. villages with 0- 25% of illiterate women;
    2. villages with 26- 50% of illiterate women;
    3. villages with 51- 75% of illiterate women;
    4. villages with 75-100% of illiterate women.

The results we expected were actually found only in modern regions, the clearest connection being in Croatia. In Table 4 one can see the decline of mortality parallel with the rising of literacy.

TABLE 4. ILLITERACY OF WOMEN AND MORTALITY
OF CHILDREN IN CROATIAN VILLAGES

|  | 1.<br>0 to 25%<br>women<br>illiter. | 2.<br>25-50%<br>women<br>illiter. | 3.<br>50-75%<br>women<br>illiter. | 4.<br>75-100%<br>women<br>illiter. |
|---|---|---|---|---|
| Minimal mortality<br>of children 0-50 (per mille) | 60 | 27 | 0 | 0 |
| Intermediate mortality<br>of children 60-100 (per mille) | 40 | 73 | 88 | 22 |
| Maximum mortality<br>of children 101 (per mille)<br>and more | 0 | 0 | 12 | 78 |

In other regions the mutual link between female illiteracy and child mortality was not so clear as in Croatia. In one region, Macedonia, there was no correlation at all. In this region of ancient culture, villagers with the most school education were not necessarily those with the best sanitary standards. Indeed in this region there were villages far off the beaten track, with a well preserved patriarchal pattern, and also without schools, which in their domestic standards were superior to villages influenced by new civilizing factors.

Enlightenment, school education, and literacy obviously were not the decisive factors for the health of the children in our regions. Which factors were more important, we cannot know without further research, but it is probable that the standard of living played an important role. (Child mortality was highest in the Dalmatian hinterland and in Macedonia.)

To examine further the influence of illiteracy on family relationships, one question from chapter "Husband and Wife" was chosen, namely, the authority of the husband. I inquired where the authority of the husband gave way first, whether in those villages in which the literacy of the sexes was comparatively equal or in those in which there were many more illiterate women. To this end, I sought any correlation between difference in literacy of the sexes and the circumstance that the authority of the husband was relaxing.

The results in no way confirm the supposition that the authority of the husband would disappear sooner in villages with slight differences of literacy than in those with great differences. Either there is no correlation at all between these two phenomena or it is slight. Indeed, in one region, the opposite was the case, for in Croatia the authority of the husband tended to diminish precisely in those villages in which there were very many illiterate women:

1. In villages with slight difference in literacy, the authority of the husband had been maintained in 57 per cent of the villages, and had diminished in 43 per cent of the villages.

2. In villages with a great difference in literacy, the authority of the husband had been maintained in 37 per cent of the villages, and had diminished in 63 per cent of the villages.

Looking for a reason for such a result, which is contrary to our assumptions, we may find it in the fact that every development advances in waves. Where a change is found only in backward villages and is lacking in the progressive ones, one can conjecture that in the latter the wave of development is already spent.

In Croatia, conditions had stabilized during the interwar period, and relationships in the family were no longer changing greatly. In villages with a higher incidence of literacy, the authority of the husband had not diminished. Such villages, often near larger towns, were advanced and had been the first to be caught in the process of economic change. At the time of the inquiry, economic changes were mainly in process in out-of-the-way districts. In these Croatian villages with a high degree of female illiteracy, certain changes were still taking place; whereas in the advanced villages, conditions had settled down again.

In the remaining districts one finds no correlation. This negative result shows that the literacy of women had no decisive effect on the transformation of the family hierarchy in the direction of greater equality.

### Conclusions

The study of illiteracy shows that its influence on the rural family was insignificant. This is in accord with the general impression one receives by direct observation. In Yugoslavia the difference in education between literate and illiterate peasants did not play as big a role as in many other countries. The two groups did not differ in behavior, in speech, or in their outlook on life, nor did they differ in self-confidence, in economic aspirations, or success. In the interwar period, culture and schooling had a weak influence on the peasants in all our regions.

For peasants in most areas, literacy had no special attraction. There was little practical gain or advantage from literacy. Available literature was scarce; aside from popular calendars, newspapers, and in some regions prayer-books, there was little to read. There were very few popular scientific writings, attractive magazines with pictures, or easily understood publications on technical or agricultural matters. Books were too expensive and in the time of the depression completely prohibitive. In some regions there were—it is true—ambitious cultural programs promoted by some of the political parties, but the effect had hardly begun when the war interrupted their efforts.

In certain other countries it was rather different. The efforts of the peasants themselves in overcoming illiteracy were stronger, and the work of organizations in the field did not meet so many impediments. In Mexico, for instance, we can find many similarities to Yugoslav conditions, such as the peasant majority in the population, the economic situation, and the heritage of illiteracy. Yet there the climate for cultural progress was much more favorable. A study from Mexico shows that the percentage of illiterates was similar to that in Yugoslavia but that about half of the literate people had learned to read and write as adults without having gone to school as children. This is in sharp contrast to the Yugoslav situation in the interwar period.

In the first Yugoslav era, there were in general few compensations for the disintegrating traditional culture. Manufactured clothing was far inferior to the traditional peasant costumes in appearance as well as in durability. Shoes were more expensive, less durable—and less comfortable—than the traditional sandals, *opankas*. Modern songs and dances were artistically at a much lower level than the folklore, and the old legal customs had no substitute at all. Even the language was richer in some illiterate districts than in the literate ones. Printed literature has rarely reached the high of the oral poetry of the people. The language of illiterate peasants, Bosnians and Herzegovinians, for instance, is richer and more expressive than that of many educated people, and this not merely in a poetic sense, but even regarding mere accuracy of statement. Hercegovinian peasants, for instance, when ill, were able to describe their sensations so well, and were so precise about the location of pain that—the doctors assert—it was far easier to diagnose their complaints on the basis of their subjective symptoms than those of the average urban patient.

Nor was the climate favorable for schools. Tensions and hostilities within the country were great; a mood of animosity and antagonism was prevalent, as was the fear of approaching war. Teachers were frequently persecuted because of their progressive views. They were transferred to remote places; any activity, even in the cultural field, aroused suspicion. The reasons why the climate for culture and education was so unfavorable, why modern civilization penetrating to the villages showed mainly its darker aspects, were presented in the chapter "Historical Background."

The depression of the thirties, which hit the country only twelve years after the founding of the state, created an additional difficulty for any cultural effort. There was no money for building new schools, or for furnishing them, or even for the employment of more teachers. Many villages were without schools of any kind, and in the others attendance was short. The pupils left school after 3, 4, or 5 years, and often forgot what they had learned. The devotion and sacrifice of the teachers, shown in their untiring collaboration on this survey, could not overcome these difficulties.

The conclusion of this inquiry is that literacy, together with the modern civilization as a whole, was neither a decisive factor nor always even a favorable one in family relationships in our regions. In the period between the two world wars, "progress" in many respects did not mean improvement.

Examining illiteracy did confirm the validity of my method of research. First, we see that our scale of regions reflects reality with regard to the development of civilization. As shown in Graphs fifty-five and fifty-seven the hypothesis that emancipation from Turkish domination was the principal stimulus making for abandonment of subsistence economy and technical backwardness is confirmed. Turkish domination in the past is indeed revealed to be the most important retarding influence, particularly for women. It is notable that this influence had not disappeared even where the liberation from Ottoman rule took place several generations ago.

Comparing the figures for our villages with the average figures for the banovinas, we further find that the villages selected were typical and representative for their regions. Similarity between the curves of illiteracy and the curves based on the data provided by the investigating team show that the data provided by this to be reliable. The complete accord in the percentages of illiterates which we received from the Statistical Bureau and the figures received from my interviewers show that the latter worked conscientiously and were indeed reliable.

# CHAPTER XII

ⅪⅪⅪⅪⅪⅪⅪⅪⅪⅪⅪⅪⅪⅪⅪⅪⅪⅪⅪⅪⅪⅪⅪⅪⅪⅪⅪⅪⅪⅪⅪⅪⅪⅪⅪⅪⅪⅪⅪⅪ

# The Yugoslav Regions

ⅪⅪⅪⅪⅪⅪⅪⅪⅪⅪⅪⅪⅪⅪⅪⅪⅪⅪⅪⅪⅪⅪⅪⅪⅪⅪⅪⅪⅪⅪⅪⅪⅪⅪⅪⅪⅪⅪⅪⅪ

LIKE AN archeologist who is able to determine the place and epoch from which a piece of pottery stems, the student of the Yugoslav family can determine the location of a village—or a questionnaire— from a single clue. The regional life styles are such rounded entities and so distinct that frequently one sentence reveals the whole system. Turns of expression, such as "A soft word opens iron doors," or "The stick comes from Paradise," are often enough to indicate the region of origin.

In all of the reactions and expressions of the South Slavs and in their inter-relationships, one can find signs of the several cultures which marked and shaped them. Roman, Byzantine, Italian, Oriental, and Central-European–Austrian patterns can be distinguished from Illyrian and Slavic backgrounds. With every regional peculiarity the question seems to arise how these various cultures and powers influenced one people, and how the fusion of cultural elements could bring about the regional styles, each of which is a complete entity, and entirely different from the others.

Since the historical outline was given in the beginning of this study, and the differences in family relations have been presented in the previous chapters, we might narrow down the question and ask: Which of the known facts, historical and economic, had an evident and traceable influence on the family in the regions whose characteristics we have learned to know in detail?

## Montenegro

Montenegro lies in the Karst mountains near the Adriatic coast, suited only for sheep raising, but offering excellent opportunities to resist or attack invaders from behind protecting rocks. Biologically, the Montenegrins are well-suited for such a hard life; they are giants in bone structure, health, and strength. The historic roots go back to their Illyric heritage and their contacts with the Turks.

Before the Roman Empire spread across the Adriatic, a powerful state dominated the western part of the Balkans, with its center in the Albanian area. The Romans called it Illyricum, and they needed a century and a half to conquer the Illyrians, who were famous

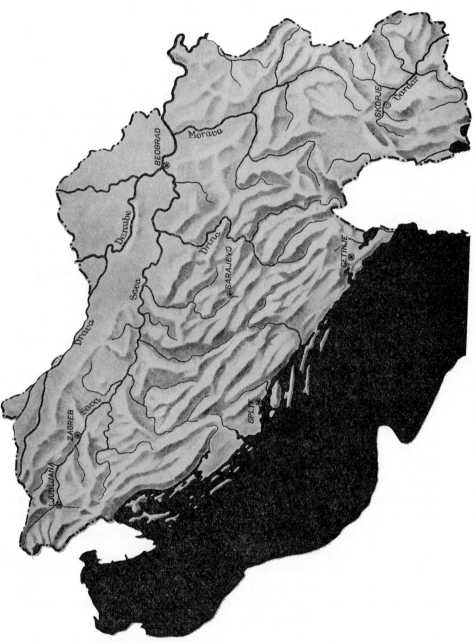

¹ See also map No. 3 "The Historical Regions of Yugoslavia," in Chapter I.

fighters. Especially belligerent were the tribes of the Adriatic coast and the nearby mountains. After they eventually submitted to the imperial power, they numbered among the best Roman soldiers. The battle value of the Roman legions was frequently measured by the percentage of Illyrians they contained. Although the name and the deeds of the Illyrians disappeared from public memory, their fighting spirit remained here a leitmotiv throughout history.

A thousandfold recalled, however, was the historical contact with the Turks. When the Turks invaded the Montenegrin territory, the tribes fought heroically. They were the last of all the Balkan regions to be conquered in 1499, more than 100 years after the Kosovo battle. They were also the first to be liberated, in 1709, having never been really subjugated. Moreover, the memory of the Turkish overlord-ship disappeared completely, and in folk belief and folk epics the Black Mountains had remained always free.

The Montenegrins never adjusted to Ottoman rule or even to their proximity. They became the representatives of resistance fighting for the whole Slav South. For centuries, all their feelings and interest centered on this objective, which dominated their whole life—fighting the Turks. All ambitions and desires for glory of the tribes, clans, and individual men circled around this goal. In these struggles, the tribal system, rooted here from ancient times, received new strength and purpose.

The contact with the West and progressive economy was also overshadowed by warfare, as the European powers supported these militant tribes in their fight against the Turks, furnishing them with modern arms and money. Particularly Russia, the great Ortho-dox power, assisted the Montenegrins generously because Peter the Great, looking for allies, had found in them such enthusiastic fighters. Such assistance for warfare over long periods of time had left dif-ferent marks on the people than money which might have come to them through commercial channels. A higher standard of living or technical progress could never be achieved while their exclusive interest was in fighting.

The Montenegrin reaction to the Yugoslav state was rather strong. Centralism and the failures of the administration caused bitter dis-appointment among this people, who for centuries had dreamed of the "brothers'" liberation. The result of the economic depression in this region of bare rocks was unrelieved starvation. Want and retrogression, poorly organized and apparently incapable adminis-tration, and their helplessness toward these evils caused many of these militant people to become political radicals; and radical changes showed up in their family life.

The patriarchal relationships in the family ceased suddenly, and novel relationships and ways of life emerged instantly. One development, specifically, was striking: The extreme heroic individualism and the tribal collectivism changed, without any interim stage, into an individualism of a new kind and a collectivism of an entirely different sort. Skipped completely was the stage of liberal, rational, or commercial relationships which ordinarily followed the stage of the subsistence economy and the archaic way of life, and which elsewhere in Europe slowly developed for centuries. The family relations here showed a strange break, shifting from patriarchal norms directly to very modern ones.

### Albanian Region

The Albanians and the Montenegrins shared their common Illyrian, Roman, and Byzantine past, but the immigration of the Slavs and the contacts with the Turks set them apart. The Turkish invasion divided the fate and history of the Dinaric tribes. The Albanians, too, fought heavily with the Turks; but, after being conquered, in 468, the majority of them accepted Islam and resisted no further. In the course of time the Albanians became the exponents of the Ottoman power in the Balkans; theirs was the task of holding down the rebellious tribes of the neighboring regions.

In spite of their privileged position in the Ottoman Empire, however, they did not conform to the central power in matters of their own internal organization and autonomy, but lived in the mountains as free tribes. In the period of Young Turks (1908 and 1912), Albania won complete independence.

For long historic epochs, the lives of the Albanians and the Montenegrins centered on fighting. But there was a difference: The first fought as the supporters of Turkish power, the latter as its eternal foes. We do not know why things developed this way. We only know that Islam played an important role in the minds of the Albanians, as in those of their South Slav neighbors. The close ties of the Albanians with Turkey and their attachment to a dying power explains partly their most conservative traits, but not why they conformed with the Ottoman power.

The surveyed villages were in Macedonia (and neighboring areas); the settlers were all Moslems, called *Arnauts* in Yugoslavia. They had immigrated long ago from the Dinaric Alps, many into villages abandoned by the Slav population. Since they had left behind some tribal traditions when leaving the highlands, we did not find with them the purely tribal organization. (Only a few of our villages were from the highlands.) Instead, we found the Oriental strain especially strong.

In Yugoslavia, the Albanians were considered anti-national and an "undesirable element" because of their political role in the past. They suffered much under the policy of state monopolies, the agrarian reform, and bureaucratic hostilities. Yet, although they had dropped from a high position to a rather low one, the effects on family life were hardly noticeable. The subjective reactions to the objective pressures were surprisingly weak. People in these areas did not appear pauperized or declassed; alcoholism and prostitution, squandering of property, and crime did not enter. The patriarchal dignity and responsibility remained; the concentrated pressure could not bend or break them. Many of the poorest boys and men left their native villages in search of labor in distant cities, without straying from the path of patriarchal honor and tradition; and the women who were left behind behaved in like manner.

The standing balance of the stable, patriarchal order, which was still entirely intact when the first blows came, proved its extraordinary staying power. The family relationships remained also completely uninfluenced by the money economy, although many men went away to earn money. In spite of all adversities of this period, family living remained almost completely in its original patriarchal form.

### Macedonia

In the Orthodox villages of Macedonia, we found a patriarchal set-up with Oriental tinge, and without a belligerent note. Macedonia, too, is a highland suitable for sheep raising, but is not as inhospitable and isolated as the Dinaric Alps. The whole region is dominated by the Morava-Vardar Valley cutting through the center of the Balkans, with an old strategical road in a north-southerly direction. Whoever controlled the road was able to control the whole area.

In ancient times, under Philip and Alexander, Macedonia was a major Mediterranean power. During the great migration period, the old population amalgamated with the Slav newcomers but did not completely lose their name and national identity. The Byzantine Empire left many traces of a high civilization; Tsar Dushan's great

Serbian Empire in the fourteenth century had its center in Macedonia, and Macedonia remained the goal of Serbian ambitions ever after. Shortly after Dushan's glorious period, the Turks made their great attacks, and after their victory on the Kosovo Plain, started their domination of the Balkans.

In Macedonia, which was conquered first and liberated last, Ottoman rule lasted for more than five hundred years. The Turks left deep roots; many settled in this region and also promoted the Albanian migration. In 1931, about a third of Macedonia was still Moslem.

Here the Ottoman rule showed its darkest aspect, especially in the period of decline, when the Spahi institution degenerated to a lawless, pseudo-feudal system. The people became in part violently suppressed and exploited raya. An evasive reaction of many Macedonians was the migration to Austria or, later on, to Serbia.

Macedonia was liberated in the Balkan war in 1912, and, in 1913, after the Serbs had defeated their Bulgarian allies, it became "South Serbia." One year later the First World War started, turning Macedonia again into a battle ground. The war wounds never healed completely, as Macedonia had suffered grievously from war damage in destroyed homes, vineyards, mulberry groves, and silk cultures.

The first Yugoslav era brought economic standstill and, during the economic crisis, even regression. Silk culture and other trades never reached the level they had attained before the Balkan wars. The population of most cities decreased, as many Moslems emigrated to Turkey. The state monopolies had a particularly unfortunate effect on the Macedonian peasants who were both consumers and producers of tobacco. European civilization and modern methods which entered Macedonia in this period brought little benefits to the peasantry. The rich, prosperous times were a thing of the past of which gold coins were a memory in every household. Macedonia was the last region to be included in the circuit of modern civilization and money economy—later than the other regions, most of which could not compare with Macedonia's great and prosperous history.

The simultaneous contact with progressive economy, modern state administration, and the West occurred under rather unfavorable conditions after the unification; the standard of living dropped considerably. But although the economic changes were felt as most depressive, the old order was not, or only very little, relaxed. The strict patriarchal rule remained binding for all members of the family, its rigidity being softened by very "human" approaches. The woman kept her unique position which resulted from the combination of the demand of basic submission and humility on the one hand, and the fact that she was needed and desired on the other. Peacefulness and discipline remained characteristic of the Macedonian family. The patriarchal style remained dominant in spite of the influences from the new state and the many difficulties of this period.

## Bosnia and Herzegovina

The geographical setting of these regions is a hill country, somewhat off the major roads, and in the largest part covered by primeval forests (which was still true at the time of this survey). For these reasons Bosnia was less exposed to the storms of history than other Balkan regions.

The most important fact in the history of the Bosnians seemed to be the collaborationist attitude toward the Ottoman invaders. This attitude brought about a chain of consequences. The reasons for such behavior are unknown, but one might have been the religious struggle of the Bosnian state previous to the Ottoman invasion. Bosnia had fought against both the Roman Catholic and the Orthodox churches. The defensive fight against Catholic Hungary was particularly bitter. Bosnia belonged to a Christian sect called *Bogumuls* (or Patarens) which was an additional reason for hostilities of some of her neighbors. The Bosnians favored the Turks, and received the conquerors in 1463 with open arms. As a reward for their acceptance the Bosnian nobility received the right to keep their estates and their feudal order. The Bosnian nobles—the begs—became fervent supporters of the Ottoman Empire. Many of the Bosnians were Islamized. The result of Islamization and migration is reflected in the religious division of the region: In 1931, 44 per cent of the population were Orthodox, 31 per cent Moslem, and 22 per cent Roman Catholic. The Bosnian Moslems were not immigrants, but Islamized natives. The influence of Islam was very strong even among non-Moslem groups, not only in Turkish times but also later.

Bosnian feudalism lasted until the unification, leaving traces of complacency and passivity, but not of fear and resentment as in some other formerly feudal (and pseudo-feudal) areas. The position of the Bosnian peasants had always been more favorable than in the West; personal dependence and services to the beg did not exist, and there was the possibility of buying their own farm. Compared to the European serfs or Macedonian raya, their position was rather advantageous.

There was yet another component in Bosnia—the Dinaric strain and the Kosovo tradition. It was particularly strong in the southern part of the region, in Herzegovina, which was a Karst area with tribal traditions and a militant spirit. Herzegovina rose in revolt against the Ottomans in 1875. The war that followed ended with the Berlin Congress, in which Bosnia and Herzegovina was ceded to the Austro-Hungarian Monarchy. The provinces were occupied by the Austrian army in 1878, and finally annexed in 1908.

A new culture contact took place—with the West, with a modern state and civilization, and with money economy. But strangely enough, there seemed to be a certain continuity in this development, and things changed gradually without a break. The Austrian way of life proved to be somewhat akin to the feudal atmosphere of Bosnia. Austria, the great Western power, with modern military, bureaucratic and civilizing apparatus, sent capable administrators to the new province. Schools and railways were built, medical service organized, and money economy only gradually introduced, planned, and controlled. With the help of exploiting timber, money was brought to the region, and taxes were held low or avoided altogether. Under such a policy the standard of living rose and the old conservatism relaxed. The Bosnians became reconciled to the new power and began to adjust to Western ways. But these trends could not develop very long, as other tendencies prevailed.

About 1910, the resistant component of Bosnia came to the fore in connection with the national movements among other Austrian Slavs. The actions of the nationalistic youth became more and more subversive until the climax was reached with the assassination of Archduke Franz Ferdinand in Sarajevo.

During the First World War that followed, and which was the last war of the Monarchy, nearly the whole progress, achieved in forty years of Austrian rule in Bosnia, was lost. After the assassination of the Archduke, persecution of the population started, especially of the Orthodox, who were considered as subversive. The most inhuman military and police officers were sent by Austria to the provinces, and they used violence and force. The Bosnians were shocked so deeply that this break is reflected in family relationships of every Bosnian population group. It was then that every authority was undermined and the tendency to violence began to rise.

In the first Yugoslav era, the war shock and the war wounds did not heal, and the standard of living sank further, even before the depression. During the depression, people in many districts starved for years. There occurred a reversion to subsistence economy without the old helps and techniques. A mood of dejection was noticeable in all population groups because of the lowered standard of life and administration.

The Christian part of Bosnia and Herzegovina suffered less than the Moslem one. But here, too, the mood was rather pessimistic. This was true even for Orthodox villages, where the belligerent tradition of the Dinaric highlanders dominated over the fatalistic outlook. In these villages, the transformation from patriarchal conditions to a new individualism reached a high point in this era. Formerly personal freedom had been limited by patriarchal rules and relaxed only by the individualistic trends from the tribal sphere; now individualistic features emerged from the sphere of the money economy. The patriarchal discipline slackened considerably.

The Moslems were most pauperized. Here one could see evidence of starvation, alcoholism, prostitution, nervous organic disturbances. Many men went to the cities and there degenerated to the group of *fukara*, which left many girls to remain unmarried. The men allowed themselves greater personal liberty than before, without keeping any of the old patriarchal responsibilities, so that the women found themselves in an extremely difficult position.

The Bosnian Moslems reacted differently from the Albanians, probably because their patriarchal order had already begun to crumble in the previous Austrian era. The decline of the patriarchal relationships gained momentum. The change from the patriarchal order to the individualistic way of life took place under the concentrated pressure of social-economic difficulties and disorganization. Brutalities which occurred in the family, obviously were the consequence of the general situation which drove many to desperation.

## Serbia

In spite of the region's remoteness from the Dinaric highlands, the heroic tradition dominated Serbian life, including family relationships. The geographical setting is a gentle rolling hill country at the crossway of the big Balkan roads (toward Constantinople and Salonika) where two rivers met (Danube and Sava). As a result of this geographical position, Serbia was a battlefield of East and West for centuries. As a result of the hill formation, all immigrants— highlanders as well as lowlanders—felt at home.

Serbia was an area of recent immigration. During the big wars between Austria and Turkey the region was completely evacuated several times, and when relatively peaceful times arrived (from the end of the eighteenth century on) this scarcely populated fertile land attracted many immigrants from various areas, particularly from the Dinaric Karst and from Macedonia. Since guerilla fighters and hayduks still dominated the countryside, most immigrants who settled here also had a militant tradition.

The immigrants came to Serbia not singly but in groups, and as a rule in response to messages received from relatives about good places for settlement. Big zadrugas wandered slowly, the speed set by the grazing cattle, stopping sometimes for months. Because of this kind of migration, the old clan and tribe ties were not loosened and the wanderers did not get lost among strangers; familism remained a distinct trait of Serbian society.

During this migration, the Kosovo memory remained as strong as before. This is shown by the history of their uprisings and early liberation as well as by their attitudes in later periods. T. G. Masaryk,[2] the founder of the Czechoslovak Republic, who was in Serbia during the Balkan war of 1912, describes how the Serbian troops marching into the liberated Kosovo Plain spontaneously removed their caps and stepped silently in their soft *opankas* over the old battlefield in order not to awaken their dead, who had fallen 532 years ago.

Under the Turkish rule, Serbians had a fairly independent internal organization, with open-air assemblies, village elders, and district headmen. These men, called *knez'*, were trustees of the peasants and responsible to them. Turks lived only in garrisons as military and civil servants. There were no *spahis* or feudal lords; the peasants carried arms. The Serbs enjoyed considerably more independence than other peoples in the Ottoman Empire.

They were freer than any settled population could be, and also more than most emigrants to other countries, since there was plenty of fertile land and only a few old settlers, who welcomed the newcomers. The settlers occupied no more land than they could till with their zadruga. Since everyone could have as much land as he needed, there were no hired hands. The largest part of the land was left as common pastures and woods, as cattle breeding was the main branch of husbandry.

2 Dr. T. G. Masaryk, *Die Balkanfrage* (*The Balkan Question*), Veröffentlichungen der Handelshochschule, München, 1914.

The contact with the West developed under very favorable conditions, as did the first contact with trade and money. From their neighbor, the big Austrian Monarchy, Serbians were paid good prices for their products. A current of gold was flowing from Austria to the Serbian peasants. Here prosperity was created, so to say, biologically: In the prolonged period of peace after the upheavals in the beginning of the nineteenth century, the cattle multiplied quicker than the population. Especially the herds of swine were growing, finding excellent pasture in the vast oak forests. As early as the 1830's, hundreds of thousands of pigs were exported to Austria annually. Without investments, without good roads or bridges, capital, credit, or commercial organization, without educated or even literate merchants, commerce grew. Cattle was driven to the border rivers, to the ferries of the Danube and Sava. The influx of money was considerable, and the peasants were the only ones to profit from this trade. As they remained, for a long time, unpretentious in their demands for comfort, wealth accumulated.

After the Berlin Congress of 1878, when Serbia was authorized to build a railway line connecting the Austro-Hungarian network, credit institutions and business enterprises were founded. At the beginning of this century, Serbia emancipated itself from Austria and established commercial connections with other countries. This success gave new support to their feeling of independence.

During the First World War, they sustained heavy sacrifices, suffering the highest percentage of casualties among the warfaring countries. But at the end of the war, in 1918, when Austria collapsed, they were among the victors. At that moment Serbia was the most important component of the Slavic South, having militarily and politically the greatest weight.

In the first Yugoslav era, extensive economic changes took place in rural Serbia. The transition from cattle breeding to intensive agriculture and production for the market brought advance planning, strenuous labor, and high pressure. These shifts were felt as a burden since the peasants compared modern farming to the recent zadruga past, with its rather leisurely rhythm of work. Although in many respects, including family relations, conservatism prevailed, and patriarchal forms were maintained relatively long, they were abandoned wherever they clashed with practical interests. In connection with the economic changes, family life changed considerably also.

In this period, the old-style individualism—a reminder from the guerilla past—fused with a novel type of individualism, stemming from the pecuniary sphere. Patriarchal conditions were eliminated where they were in opposition to economic purposes, such as having many children.

It is possible that the atmosphere in the new state was partly responsible for some of the changes: Personal freedom, for instance, became greater, but mostly for family members high in the "ranks," while remaining limited for the "lower ranks." Patriarchal responsibility was partly replaced by the right of the stronger, and unrestricted passions became even more prevalent than before.

## Croatia

Family relationships in Croatia show a distinct Western coloring. The West influenced the country through Austria, Venetia, and the Catholic Church. Geographical facts are greatly responsible for these influences, as the position of this region in the Pannonian (Hungarian) Plain and at the Adriatic coast exposes it to the north and to the west. As early as the ninth century, the Croats accepted the Roman Catholic Church, while the other Balkan Slavs decided for the East, choosing (in a later period) the Eastern Church. By the eleventh century Croatia had entered a "personal union" with Hungary, under one ruler but keeping her independence. The Littoral areas came under the domination of the Venetian Republic which, like Austria, was also a Western, Catholic power. The influence of the Catholic Church was important also because it strengthened the respective government authority, while the Serbian-Orthodox Church supported national-revolutionary movements (against the Turks, as it were).

Linked with the West, the Croatian peasants were included in the feudal system, which left many traces, one of them being a certain antagonism against *gospoda*, lords or gentlemen. Accordingly, they were suspicious of all "city-like" methods and modern techniques which seemed to be connected with gospoda. This made for a special form of conservatism, distinct from the patriarchal and Serbian one.

The Turkish conquest of southern and central Europe had a twofold consequence for Croatia: some parts became Turkish for one and a half centuries, absorbing many Oriental elements; the rest became Austrian (in 1526), a frontier land toward the Ottoman Empire, the barrier of the West against Eastern aggression. For centuries all Croatian resources were concentrated on defense.

The Military March, under military command, sometimes constituted half of Croatia. It influenced the whole country since it sym-

369

bolized the region's essence—the fighting frontier. In the March, a strict but impartial discipline was introduced, as well as a dictated but well-planned economy. This system had a peculiar effect on the Dinaric people with their rebellious predisposition: While remaining fighters against the Turks they became loyal Imperial subjects. This was in great contrast with the Serbian situation, where fighting against the Turks meant rebellion against the constituted state authority.

Croatia's position within Austria caused a certain political lack of interest on the part of the peasants. The links with Austria and Hungary were voluntary, at least in theory. The constitutional wrangling went on far away in the parliaments of the Monarchy and did not affect the peasants very much. The Monarchy seemed strong and settled, one of the greatest and most stable of the world powers. For the last Austrian generations, the figure of the long-reigning Emperor and King, Franz Joseph I, strengthened the belief in eternal authority. (Revolutionary actions against the Habsburg Monarchy were not carried out by the peasants, and the collapse of the Monarchy left many of them perplexed.)

Modern civilization entered the Croatian village earlier than in most other regions. It was spread by the bureaucracy and the intelligentsia, who were largely educated in Austrian and Italian institutions of higher learning. Western spirit and respect for the capital of the Empire, Vienna, was spread also by the many maid servants who had worked in the cities and the peasant lads who had come home from military service. The level of schools, hygiene, and technique was between that of the Central-European and the Turkish-Balkan civilizations, with their ambition to reach the European level.

The first waves of money economy reached Croatia one generation before Serbia: The first railway was built in Croatia in 1854, and in Serbia in 1884, the first banks founded in 1846 and 1869, respectively. The first and most important merchandise was timber ("Slavonian oak"), which brought but small profits to the peasants. Nor did the building of railways and steamships prove advantageous to them, since the exported wares were not peasants' products, and many villagers dealing with river boats and wagons lost their livelihood. Modern civilization and money entered here, in contrast to Serbia, under rather unfavorable conditions.

The end of the nineteenth century brought many burdens. In the state administration, a modern civil service was built up, which proved costly and required high taxes, to be paid in money. The agrarian world crisis in the seventies and eighties had a catastrophic effect on peasant life and economy. The demilitarization of the Military March in the same period added to the difficulties, as the frontier men had to adjust to changed conditions. As a result of these hardships, a flight from the villages began, both to the cities and overseas. Hundreds of thousands of peasants, particularly from the Karst areas, left home and country, and entire villages were deserted by the men.

The First World War constituted the end of a long historic epoch, making a deep impression on the Croatian peasants. War losses here were much smaller than in Serbia, yet for the Serbs this war meant only one among others, while for the Croats it was the first they could remember, as it broke out after many decades of peace. Moreover, the fact that the seemingly immutable Austrian Monarchy had collapsed profoundly shook the peasants' belief in any authority.

But during the war the peasants selling food came to know the advantages of money. For the first time, they acquired large sums, paid off their debts, bought implements, and began to purchase factory-made textiles and shoes. The money and the feeling of importance as providers of the army and the starving cities greatly blotted out the vestiges of feudal submissiveness.

The peasants' reactions to the new Yugoslav state were rather violent. The deteriorated administration and the lowering of the standard of living caused great bitterness. But in family living no violent changes took place during the first Yugoslav era. The period of my survey was that of a certain stabilization of the family. This era presented an early middle-class period in which individualistic trends, rooted in the economic sphere, were allowed to develop, and the entire family life became deeply influenced by pecuniary motives. But in spite of this individualistic trend, the liberties of the younger family members did not increase very much. The freedom of the young men was severely restricted by their complete dependency upon their parents, the freedom of the girls by their poor marriage chances.

The depression of the thirties did not have as far-reaching consequences as that sixty years before, but was more in the nature of a relapse of a patient who was partly immunized by a previous attack. The Croatian peasants were less affected by the depression of the thirties than the economically more backward regions, which experienced it as a shock, since it was their first of this kind. The former depression had occurred when they were living in pure subsistence economy, and therefore they hardly felt it at all. In contrast to most other regions, Croatian family life changed but little in this period. The crises which the people had lived through previously had made them in a certain way ready for new economic changes, and at the same time immune to their destructive effects.

## The Littoral

In family living of the Littoral, Western ways were clearly traceable. The geographic setting is the coast of the Adriatic, with many islands, excellent for sailing. The Mediterranean, of which the Adriatic is a part, was the center of the ancient and medieval world. Rome early took over these parts of the Illyricum, and Dalmatia became a flourishing Roman province. Later as part of the Byzantine Empire, and still later the Venetian Republic, Dalmatia lay on the main trade and seafaring route between Central Europe and the East, as well as the West. The belligerent elements retreated to the hinterland, the Dinaric mountains, and people in the coast cities and countryside lived a rather peaceful and civilized life.

The "Littoral"—the villages at or near the coast, as defined for this study—belonged in the greatest part to Dalmatia, itself a narrow area on the coast, and to the northern districts, which were under Croatian administration. The position on the Adriatic meant in all periods a strong link with the West. The Dinaric ranges at their back were an inhospitable barrier against the East, and the Dinaric fighters impeded the Turkish invaders from reaching the coast. While these mountains were impassable in winter and times of war, being cut only in few places by cross valleys, the link to the West could never be interrupted, as the gentle Adriatic can be crossed by small boats.

For long periods (and until Napoleon), Dalmatia belonged to the Venetian Republic, the Dalmatians being the republic's best seamen. Through the link with the big sea power, the Littoral was the first South Slav region to establish contact with the world and money economy. One of the results of that old-time progressive economy is the realistic disposition of the peasants toward money and business. Another sign that money economy entered here at an early time was the relatively slow tempo of work which was still observable at the time of this survey, the long siestas of the longshoremen showing the rhythm of an early stage of money economy. The whole life in the Littoral mirrors the orderly administration of Venice and Austria. The autonomous or independent cities (such as Dubrovnik), had a progressive administration, public control of funds, and general compliance with the law. These conditions colored also the life in the villages.

Late waves of money economy had less favorable results in the Littoral. At the end of the nineteenth century, the Littoral's economy suffered a series of heavy blows. The shift from sailboats to steamers meant losses from which this region never recovered, as the sailboats lost their value and the seamen their work. A big part of the valuable Dalmatian vineyards was ruined by a grapevine disease. As wine was the main source of income for the Littoral, the vineyards were planted again, but with a newly introduced grapevine which required more care and yielded less fruit.

The coast dwellers adjusted to the difficulties in a rather rational manner, and by emigrating overseas. The whole way of life acquired a modern, partly commercial tinge.

In the first Yugoslav era, the standard of living dropped here particularly severely, the pressure of the economic crisis was extremely heavy, emigration limitations to the United States had their effect, the Adriatic ports had lost their importance after the collapse of the Austro-Hungarian Monarchy. The sorrows suffered by the Littoral people were succinctly expressed by an old Dalmatian peasant who said to me: "It's a misery since our two kind mothers died—the old grapevine and old Austria."

In spite of all difficulties, this period did not bring about any great changes in the family. Some of the patriarchal forms survived, and the position of women remained untouched by new influences even longer than in regions where the patriarchal regime had been kept intact until recently. As "old newcomers," people were ready for a new adjustment although only to a limited degree. Their family life showed a traditional civilization and peacefulness combined with guarding carefully personal interests. These people were ready for new influences, but remained rather immune to their toxic effects.

Of the surveyed regions, the Littoral was the most Western and adaptable one. This can be demonstrated in an area far removed from our survey material, on the American continent: The flourishing California communities founded by fishermen and fruit cultivators from this region show how early, quickly, and easily the Littoral people adjusted to conditions of a Western industrialized country such as the United States.

As was pointed out in the introductory chapter, historical and political events had such a definite influence on the whole life of the

Slavic South that they cannot be ignored, but must rather be dealt with in detail.

In the chapter "Historical Background," we sought an answer to the question: What historical events and contacts took place in the Yugoslav regions which may have had an influence on intimate human relations and on the family. In this chapter, "The Yugoslav Regions," we asked: Which contacts and events have caused the people of the historical regions to become the individualities we have known them to be by the criterion of family life? In the next chapter, "The Riddle of Culture Contact," a question of more general significance will be explored: Why have certain contacts influenced certain regions with qualities of the infiltrating culture, while the same contacts goaded others to resistance and the emergence of contrary qualities?

# CHAPTER XIII

# The Riddle of Culture Contact

STUDENTS tracing cultural elements in areas where two peoples met frequently found that it is hardly possible to disentangle the web of the newly established culture, as the single elements are greatly changed and have entered into new combinations. Mostly the two cultures form new compounds with entirely new qualities. Yet sometimes the new influences are imprinted on the old base as on a photographic negative, where dark is light and light appears dark. Therefore some elements can be traced, but in their opposites. A rare case of this is to be found in the Slavic South.

In the culture contact in the Balkans there is a good opportunity to inquire into this intriguing problem, as two contrasting styles of life emerged from the contact of the Slavic peoples with the Ottoman Turks. In the Oriental style of countless attitudes and reactions and in every relationship in the family, the Eastern influence mirrors itself in an unchanged picture; while, in the tribal, Dinaric style, everything is mirrored differently, as in a reciprocal picture. The objective facts which hammered or cajoled people into the two patterns have been presented in the chapters "Historical Background" and "Yugoslav Regions." Here I try to define the two styles of life and to examine the twofold result of the single contact.

The Western, Austrian style of life got a little out of focus in this analysis as it is less pertinent to the problem I set myself. But it, too, plays its part in the riddle of culture contact if not pertinent to the answers.

## The Oriental Style of Life

This style of life is a distinct and rounded whole, which displays itself in the entire atmosphere and in countless traits. But it is not confined in the Slavic South: The Oriental style is common to many countries on four continents. In all European regions which have been under Ottoman or Islamic domination, it is to be found, as well as in the Middle East, in Asia, and North Africa, and in Latin America, where the Conquistadors were permeated with Moorish influences. To the observer who is in direct contact with the setting, this style manifests itself immediately, in the shapes and patterns of artifacts, in scents, tastes, and tones. It radiates from the bearing, gestures, and the speech mannerisms of people, and shows up in their philosophy of life.

This style has such a penetrating quality that it can be traced even if Oriental culture had been amalgamated with some other a long time ago or if it crept in completely watered down. In areas such as Slavonia, where the Turkish rule lasted only 150 years and ended in the eighteenth century, it reveals itself in embroidery motifs, and song, in many Turkish works, and in the attitude of people toward love. Hiking through southern Italy, suddenly one has the feeling that the wind carries the well-known fragrance of the Near East. It can be recognized in the shape of a Saracen tower, in an assault of male jealousy, or in a specific kind of feminine modesty. Traveling through Mexico, one finds Islamic motifs not only in architecture but in the style of hoarse sustained singing of the Mexican songs, and in the excitement behind the voice, one recognizes the Oriental tradition. Thrown over the shoulder of an Indian is a native coat woven as a rug and one recognizes the pattern which is known as typical Macedonian. In tracing such motifs, one will learn that they came from the Moors in Spain and were brought by the Conquistadors to the New World. The Oriental style has such an intensity and a piercing force, that it traveled around half the globe and, moreover, in a period when the Moors had already left Spain and the Conquistadors were not in direct contact with them any more.

In certain Yugoslav regions, contacts with the Turks made a deeper impression on family relationships than any other culture contact. This was perhaps caused by the greatness of the Ottoman Empire and its long life, as at one time it embraced three continents with a great many races and nations. Although throughout the whole Slavic South vestiges of it can be found, the style is most outspoken in Bosnia, Macedonia, and the Sanjak. Many consequences of the era of Ottoman greatness as well as of the period of its decline have remained here. Among the latter are the economic backwardness, the low standard of living, and the crude conservatism, which served as a brake to technical progress and was mirrored clearly in the illiteracy of the people.

The traits of the Oriental style are in sharp contrast to the tribal style: Private life is considered more important and the philosophy of life is fatalistic. The differences, of course, are not in the quality but merely in quantity: Man in general is tied to his society in goals, yet he has also individual desires, ambitions, and sensibilities. Every man plans as well as resigns, struggles for his aspirations and renounces to the immutable. But the Oriental plans less, is more easily resigned, and is less dependent on the opinions of others. Universal human tendencies are divided in these two groups according to another key, the accents are distributed differently, the intensity of emotions is centered on other points.

In the Oriental setting, the focus is on personal life. A predominant collective goal, like the struggle for liberation and vengeance for Kosovo, is lacking; the tragic memories of national history are not cultivated, the fighting spirit is not the highest value, asceticism is less emphasized. It is not so important what others think of the individual; the judgment of posterity—"What will the singer say?"—does not enter the mind. The goal is, on the contrary, favorable for feelings from the intimate sphere; personal happiness does not seem a matter for reproach. Enjoyment has a strong artistic tinge: The homes of the Moslems are mostly built on high spots with open views, distant panorama, and vistas which can be enjoyed without strenuous mountain hiking; love songs are sung quietly with no exhibition-istic overtones. The pleasures which are sought cannot be bought for money or have only an insignificant material worth. Besides love and friendship, the beauty of the landscape looms large: The sky at night, a spring, a brook. All of this is enjoyed in quiet contemplation. Song is a part of it and, if possible, the enjoyment of coffee, tobacco, and some plum brandy. Material goods are secondary in the scale of values.

In the calm of the villages, a folk culture of extraordinary beauty grew up. An art of living developed as well as a certain philosophy of life. These achievements with an Oriental tinge can be observed even today in any Bosnian and Macedonian village.

Friendly and extended conversations are part of the art of living and daily enjoyment of the most modest peasants. They are regarded as a general human necessity. Every Bosnian peasant woman visits daily, and usually several times daily, with some neighbor over a "black coffee" in order to talk and laugh for a few moments at least. The conversations of Bosnian peasants and especially of peasant women are frequently works of art, for their speech is full of original and poetic turns of expression.

The fatalistic attitude gives these people repose and a special dignity. People believe that fate should be allowed to take its course, without interference. There is a deep-rooted mistrust of the tireless activity of the people in the West. The people under Oriental influence quietly accept things as they come and endure them with equanimity.

Connected with this is an attitude contrary to every practical or businesslike dealing, which can clearly be seen at the peasant markets or these areas. I wrote in my diary about a market in a town near Sarajevo:

> At the market in Visoko, homemade woolen socks and slippers are sold, with their beautiful traditional patterns. Nearly all women, whether they walk or sit, keep on knitting new merchandise. I ask a woman who is displaying a big bundle of socks and slippers, what the price is. She answers as if frightened out of a deep sleep, "Huh, you're asking me? What, you mean these here? Are they for you?" and similar questions, lost in dreams. No one would think that the woman came here to trade; one would rather suppose that she came only to meet her friends and chat with them. Younger women step up to the older ones, kiss their hands and ask about every member of the family. I cannot help comparing this scene with similar ones from Dalmatia, where I lastly saw women with bundles of woolen socks at the market, but where I marveled at their attentiveness and shrewdness when selling their wares.

Islamic philosophy, with its fatalistic leaning, shaped the Balkan people in a special way, and its influence is lasting. A friend of mine told me once: "If something good comes, I am not especially happy about it . . . perhaps something sad is lurking in the background. If something difficult arises, I am not cast down . . . perhaps a turn for good will come. Nothing is final." This thought gave him a particular dignity and the strength to rise above the most severe crises with grace.

The following presentation[1] of the philosophy of medieval Islam is equally valid as Weltanschauung of the Balkan peasants:

> The strength of Islam is in the roundedness of personality, which at its best it is able to produce. This does not mean universality, nor does it imply that immediacy in relations to the worlds of thought and perception which lends so much quality of repose, of dignity and poise, which could develop only as a result of a static conception of the ideal world and the ideal society. The West is ready to sacrifice the present for the future. We crave not the good life for ourselves but the better life for our posterity. We recognize the supreme value of change, because we are afraid of stagnation and stagnation to us not only signifies death but means betrayal of our one and only task, which is the ad-

[1] Gustav E. von Grunebaum, *Medieval Islam,* Chicago University Press, Chicago, 1946, p. 346.

378

vancement of the race. Such a concept of life requires constant adaptations to new conditions. While the ultimate ideal of perfection remains unaltered, the ideals of the day, that are means rather than ends-in-themselves, compel continuous reorientation. We strive without letup and the effort of our uphill fight which we feel we shall be winning if only we keep at it long enough is the true satisfaction of our lives.

The Muslim's world is at rest, and he is at rest within it. His immediacy to God and his acceptance of the divine order were never, during the Middle Ages, seriously disturbed. Resignation and submission to the inevitable and abdication of searching reason before the inscrutable were rewarded by the consciousness of fitting perfectly and naturally into the great pre-ordained scheme of things that embraces mankind as it embraces the genii, the angels and the stars. The Muslim knows and accepts man's limitations. In fact, he is inclined to underrate man's capabilities. He finds happiness in attuning himself to the will of the Lord as it is revealed in the wondrous world around him. God has vouchsafed him enough of the truth to understand what needs understanding and to trust divine wisdom where understanding ends.

It is remarkable to what an extent the Moslem philosophy of life has spread among the Balkan peasants. It overcame the high barriers of mistrust between raya and Moslems, the hate for the oppressors, and it survived an Austrian period of basic changes and a Yugoslav period of great unrest. The Ottoman state system collapsed, Islam was accepted only in part by the raya, but one of the highest cultural achievements of the Islamic Middle Ages has been grafted on all persons who were under its influence: The great art of enduring life philosophically and of enjoying it. It is an art which has been partially lost in many Moslem lands and one which has been but little developed in the West.

### The Tribal, Dinaric Style of Life

The culture contact between South Slavs and Ottoman Turks did not proceed everywhere as it did in Bosnia, where the sedentary people adjusted to the invading power and absorbed the penetrating culture. With the Dinaric tribes, "acculturation" had the reverse meaning; it meant a most hostile reaction to a provocation. Reciprocal qualities developed here, while in the Oriental style of life Eastern influences manifested themselves unchanged.

The tribal or Dinaric style evolved in opposition to Islam, to Ottoman violence and Oriental culture. Both the tribal social structure and the fighting spirit have their roots in antiquity and are partly heritages from the rebellious Illyrians. As it has already been pointed out, the Illyric tribes living in the rocky Dinaric Alps in proud independence resisted Roman dominance for a long time. Immigrating Slavic tribes interfused with the Illyrians, partly taking over their organization as well as their fighting spirit. Montenegro is organized on tribal principles, and there are traces of this system in Herzegovina and in the Dalmatian hinterland. (In neighboring Albania the same organization of tribes and clans is to be found, with the only difference that in the struggles of the past different goals were pursued.)

However, with the appearance of the Ottoman Turks, the old values were greatly strengthened. The Slavic tribes engaged in a permanent fight against them, and for centuries all strength and resources were concentrated in this fighting. Many characteristics of this style are closely connected with the war contacts with the Turks. Heroic resistance could not have emerged without Turkish power and aggression; and the rounded heroic style as it is known today could not have evolved without the everlasting struggles with the Turks. When the objective of this struggle was reached, the style of life had long been settled and its heroic qualities have remained as dominant values.

The Dinaric style of life has a coloring as intense as the Oriental one, and it manifests itself clearly in Yugoslav areas where immigrants from the Dinaric mountains have settled. This is especially the case in the Austrian Military March and in Serbia.

In this setting, the Kosovo tradition is predominant; the lost battle is incessantly mentioned and hate against the Turks stirred up, although Kosovo was revenged a long time ago. The historical consciousness is so highly developed that many children know the names of their forbearers to the tenth generation.

The principal motif of the Dinaric style of life is the liberation of all Serbs from the Turkish rule. It was not only in the minds of the leaders of the people but it was the leitmotiv with young and old in all strata. A characteristic scene was described by Professor Dvorniković.[2] Once when he was walking in the Dinaric mountains in the Dalmatian hinterland he heard a wailing noise. Coming nearer he found in the Karst rocks two little crying shepherdesses, mourning, as it seemed to him, some death in the family. When he asked them who had died, they answered carelessly: "Nobody—but we are singing and lamenting for Lazar and Milosh, who were killed on the Kosovo

[2] Vladimir Dvorniković, *Karakterologija Jugoslavena* (*Characterology of the Yugoslavs*), Kosmos, Belgrade, 1938.

Plain." These were two of the great heroes of a battle more than half a millennium earlier, and a quarter of a century after the fall of the Ottoman Empire.

As it was pointed out in the chapter "The Patriarchal Regime," tribes and clans are the most important elements of social organization. Collective responsibility is the basis of this system: Every man considers himself responsible for the behavior and the acts of any member of his clan or even of his tribe. If a man is killed, the others "owe blood": They must kill the killer or someone of his clan, and these again must have their revenge. At the time of my survey the spirit of collective responsibility had remained alive, although the vendetta (blood feud) had been abandoned to a great extent.

The whole family and social life was permeated by an aristocratic principle, the belief in the inherited characteristics of the individual, in his *čojstvo i junaštvo* (manliness and heroism), and belief in *soj* (breed) was developed to the extreme. The reputation of family and ancestors was worth more than what a man did himself. Girls, from whom no heroism was expected, acquired their own importance and any opportunity for a future solely by reason of the good name of their family and the heroism of its men. Distinction and eminence were to be acquired by heroism in battle and by some brave deeds of one's ancestors.

The concepts of honor are like those which held among European knights of the Middle Ages. Honor, known as *obraz* (face), is the highest value for which one offers one's life or takes that of another. Nenadović[3] describes the role of *obraz* for the community and the individual:

> Montenegro has no written constitution, but has freedoms and guarantees fitting for heroes. The very formulation of what is allowed and what is not would constitute a limitation. These mountains permit no rules to be imposed upon them. The Montenegrin "face" (*obraz*) is the Montenegrin constitution, and is guarded as a sacred thing. . . . Do we need dead paper with words written on it to make human beings out of people? That's the way they speak and the way they think. In Montenegro public opinion is strong and strict. If you do something, you must consider what the songs will say about it, and the songs have never flattered or lied. We have no ships at sea, no palaces on the coast; we have nothing but our heroism and our "bright face" (honor), and only for these does the world know us and value us. Your face is the face of

---

[3] Ljubomir Nenadović, *O Crnogorcima, Pisma sa Cetinja 1877 godine* (*About Montenegrins. Letters from the Year 1878*), Belgrade, Srpska književna zadruga.

Montenegro; all Montenegro would feel disgraced, is what they often say to one another.

The fact that in this environment the individual is embedded in his community and kin-group does not mean the negation of individual goals and aspirations; they are on the contrary rather more pointed than where the private domain is considered as legitimate. Collective and individualistic tendencies in this setting are of a special type and their connection is of a particular kind. The individual although submerged in his group, is separated from it by his ambition to distinguish himself, to acquire prestige, glory, pre-eminence. His sensitivity with respect to personal success and honor is extreme; he can never ignore public opinion. In connection with the predomination of collective responsibility, every individual keenly feels his obligations to the collective and feels also completely exposed to the judgment of his "brothers." But only here, where everyone knows the deeds of his ancestors, of his father and of himself can he develop his potentialities. This situation is dangerous for his emotional equilibrium, as we will see.

The competition for prestige or fame belongs to the characteristics of this style of life. The individual never loses his personal ambitions and never becomes a cog in a machine. While peasants from other areas (from Croatia, for example) when asked what they are or do, may answer: "Nothing . . . a peasant . . . a laborer . . . nothing," a man from a tribal system would never answer this way, because "nothing" means something terrible.[4] He doesn't want to be a number (except the first). Countless Montenegrin anecdotes show the importance of this heroic-individualistic trait. People shrewdly and with subtle arguments keep proving why someone is a "better" hero than another.

Characteristic of the longing for fame and grandeur is the anecdote which tells how Prince Danilo was discussing with some Montenegrins what each one most ardently wished for. One desired fine weapons, the second splendid clothing, while the third hesitatingly confessed that he wished to be immortalized standing petrified on the highest rock of the Black Mountains, so he would be visible from all directions. The birds in the air, the fish in the sea, the Montenegrins from the mountains, and the travelers on shipboard could admire him standing there.[5]

[4] Professor Rudolf Bićanić, personal comment.
[5] Gerhard Gesemann, *Heroische Lebensform* (*Heroic Style of Life*), Viking Verlag, Berlin, 1943.

The importance of prestige manifests itself in some exhibition of splendor or, under other circumstances, in hiding misery, weaknesses, and failures. There is again an aristocratic element in this wish to keep up appearances, as also in the concealing of poverty, which is characteristic of European nobility. One of my teachers, contrasting the attitude of peasants in Dinaric Herzegovina and in a Croatian area, where Western influence prevails and the style of life is more one of the middle classes, said:

> The peasants of Herzegovina want to show more than they have. A peasant who at home probably hasn't enough to eat will dress up magnificently on Sunday, will mount his horse and ride proudly into the village. The peasants from north Croatia (Drava Valley) often show the opposite tendencies. They have well-equipped farms and houses but complain much more than those from Herzegovina—indeed more than seems justified.

The wish for representation and a sort of conspicuous consumption has probably been one reason that the textile techniques in the Yugoslav countryside are far better developed—indeed to a high art—than all other handicrafts. Several observers have noticed the puzzling contrast between costume and house. A peasant girl, royally groomed with wonderful embroideries and ornaments all over her costume, after dancing the *Kolo*-round, goes home—and her home reveals itself to be a primitive earthen hut without even windows or a chimney. Professor Vukosavljević mentions that in "old settlements" (as distinct from immigration areas such as Serbia) the wish to be well clothed predominates:

> The peasants are fond of dressing well, not only the young ones but also mature men and women. Everywhere clothing is far better than food, better than bedding, better than housing. The poor especially make an effort to dress better. I have often noticed in west Macedonia and in Montenegro that a man would not immediately join a group of his friends whom he saw talking to a stranger. He would first return home and change his clothes.
>
> Men who seem to have scarcely the means of providing food for their families are always well dressed when they appear in public. The village community has its own conventions with respect to clothing. The peasant feels very bad if he cannot dress well. He finds this harder to bear than if he cannot feed himself adequately, "because no one can see what another has in his belly."

"Good clothing" here meant precious homemade garments with artistic embroideries and silver ornaments.

However, personal wishes were modest, except for the desire for prominence in battle and for glory. These attitudes are in sharp contrast with the individualistic trends of a modern, Western environment. I could observe the difference in attitude of two groups during the Second World War in liberated south Italy. In a British Soldier's Club, Allied personnel received tea and refreshments. Twice every day, about five hundred soldiers of various Allied units came there for a snack. Each British soldier studied the bill of fare: "Tea . . . 2 lire; cakes . . . 3 lire; sandwiches . . . 4 lire." With serious concentration, he then made his decision and, when he got to the counter, without hesitation he ordered "two teas, three cakes, one sandwich, please." Their wishes showed great variety, but they were expressed in such a way as to show clearly that it was the result of careful consideration. Yugoslav guerillas also frequented this club. They behaved in an entirely different way from the British but with a striking consistency among themselves. Each tossed a fairly large piece of money onto the counter and merely said: "Give!" When the prices were explained to them, and they were asked what they wanted, each cut the explanation short with a sweeping gesture as if to say: "What nonsense are you talking. Give anything you like!" None of them could or would concentrate on such a trifle as the choice at a snack counter. They did not mind at all what they got or what they paid; to none of them was it worth the slight effort of making a decision. They did not want to be forced to decide in unimportant things, feeling themselves pushed into the conduct of demanding children. Their indifference toward personal preferences was in strong contrast not only to the attitudes of the British but also to their own passionate reactions in politics and battle. Collective goals and only those awakened their interest and emotions.

It is not possible to state for every characteristic of the tribal style whether it developed reciprocally to the Ottoman rule or had existed before. It is known, for instance, that the great value which the Montenegrins attach to the "breed" and hereditary qualities of men is adverse to the Ottoman principle of judging the man exclusively by his individual qualities. It is probable that the Montenegrin aristocratic principle developed parallel with the entire tribal order, but was greatly emphasized in opposition to the Ottoman system. If a feature, however, is common to the whole Slavic South, we can assume it was an older heritage than the culture contact with the Turks. This is the case with certain democratic traits in the entire patriarchal regime, including the tribal setting, which will be discussed later.

## Nervous Disposition

The Dinaric Alps are called by Coon "The Mountain of Giants"[6] because of the peoples' tall frames, deep thorax, and unusual strength (he speaks of the Albanians though). These strong men are, however, robust only in physique, while mentally they are extremely sensitive and susceptible to nervous troubles. An inflexibility of a special kind and an extraordinary sensibility endangers their emotional equilibrium. When people emigrated from the Dinaric Alps, besides their heroic tradition, they also took with them their specific sensitivity and spread it to other Yugoslav regions.

These facts were well known in Old Austria, when, after the occupation of Bosnia and Herzegovina, one regiment from the newly acquired provinces was ordered to the garrison in Vienna. The Viennese were very proud of the big beaming Bosnians who marched through the imperial city like giants in their regimental hats, the exotic red fez. But army doctors soon discovered their weak spot. When in the garrison hospital diagnoses of "nostalgia," "depression," "hysteria" became frequent, their nervous disposition was recognized.

In an article in a Yugoslav Medical Journal, Dr. Dojmi de Lupis quoted some older writings on this subject:

Mattauschek maintains that it is a proven fact that in the case of the Bosnians and Herzegovinians on military duty, and especially among the recruits very frequently temporary or permanent hysteric illnesses are to be found, as well as hysteric complexes and even epidemic hysteric states. He brings proof from the mental clinic of the Vienna Military Hospital for the years 1897-1906. His observations of the childlike gentleness of South Slavs are interesting, as is also the contrast between the magnificent bodies of the Bosnians and Herzegovinians and their poor resistance to illness. He finds astonishing the hysterical reactions of these people when they are injured. According to Dr. Bartel, the same observations can be made with these soldiers in their homeland. Their disturbances are also of a purely psychogenic nature and are probably linked to homesickness.[7]

Similar phenomena were observed by several army doctors in the first Yugoslav period. I remember a characteristic scene in the thirties

[6] Carlton S. Coon, The Mountain of Giants, A Racial and Cultural Study of the North Albanian Mountain Ghegs, Papers of the Peabody Museum.

[7] Dr. Lovro Dojmi, "O veremu" ("On the complex symptoms 'Verem'") Medical News Bulletin, Liječnički Vijesnik, Zagreb, 1940.

when doctors were explaining their experience to a colleague from Vienna. This renowned Viennese specialist for internal disorders, surprised and laughing, asked: "Do you mean to say that in your country diseases, too, have preferences or aversions according to national groups and minorities?" This question was raised because a doctor from the Zagreb garrison hospital had suddenly left the company of his colleagues with the excuse: "I just had a call from the hospital about a new case of pneumonia. The patient is an Albanian. That means it is serious. If he were a soldier from another unit I could remain, but in this case it is too dangerous."

Several doctors explained this puzzling statement to the Viennese doctor. They maintained that the soldiers from strict patriarchal settings had no resistance to illness when separated from "their own," meaning kin, clan brothers, tribe members, or at least men from their community. In greatest danger were soldiers from the Albanian ethnic group who served in cities distant from their villages. When they found themselves in a hospital, suddenly separated from their comrades, they used to give up all hope and lost their desire for life. They demanded nothing, ate almost nothing, and talked to no one. Adding to their difficulties was the fact that they could not speak Serbo-Croatian. Their psychological resistance to illness was nil and the percentage of fatal cases especially of pneumonia were relatively high. Soldiers from other regions also showed characteristic attitudes which affected the course of their illnesses, but those from Dinaric areas and intact patriarchal set-up were the least resistant, particularly when in a "foreign" city.

It is interesting that the soldiers from the Serbian region, although the Dinaric element was strong there, showed completely different attitude in the hospital, and their prognoses were favorable. They easily adjusted to their environment, or else adapted their environments to their needs; the realistic attitude in this situation prevailed with the Serbians over the Dinaric, patriarchal element.

In the Second World War, too, it became manifest that valor and nervous disposition in the Balkans had a certain inner connection. The trends of Dinaric heroism and of nervous reactions continued uninterruptedly and even in an accentuated form. The work of the Swiss psychiatrist, Dr. Paul Parin, offers valuable material.[8] Dr. Parin describes the set of symptoms which in Yugoslavia is called

[8] Dr. Paul Parin, *Die Kriegsneurose der Yugoslawen, Schweizer Archiv fuer Neurologie und Psychiatrie (The War Neurosis of Yugoslavs)*, Vol. LXI. Zurich, 1948, Art. Institut Oroll.

"partisan sickness" or "partisan attacks." These attacks were well known in all regions where partisans fought and after the war in all of Yugoslavia. They were widespread among partisans, auxiliary personnel, and among the populace who came into contact with them. Yugoslav psychiatrists estimated the cases at many thousands. The sickness began as a sort of hysterical attack with headlong falls, unconsciousness, signs of violent distraction, and pretended fighting. Dr. Parin, who worked in partisan hospitals for almost two years, observed hundreds of attacks near and after the end of the war. He gives a detailed description of them and offers an explanation—based on psychoanalysis—for their development and mechanism. Some of his findings are significant for our inquiry.

Only "primitive" yet intelligent people got sick; that is people without formal education. This means that the majority were mainly peasants. Except for Slovenes, South Slavs from all regions, both men and women, took sick. The attacks of sickness never took place at the front, but always behind the lines, only where (according to Parin) aggression could not be directed against the enemy. Parin believes that the strict sexual prohibitions which were enforced in the partisans by the threat of death had much to do with the neurotic situation.

My own observations after the Second World War verified this delicate mental balance of people of the Dinaric areas. As a social worker with UNRRA in Italy, I had to deal with people from many countries and places. Men from Yugoslav Dinaric areas showed a striking instability of mental equilibrium. When they were compelled to be passive, for instance as prisoners of war, they frequently presented a picture of complete helplessness. Previously brave fighters were scared by trifling organic sensations and seemed entirely lost in their organic nervous symptoms.

In the paper in which Dr. Dojmi[9] quotes the Austrian army doctors, he also discusses the nervous disturbances of peasants "at present," that is in the first Yugoslav era, in Bosnia and Herzegovina. This study deals principally with a symptom-complex which the peasants call *verem*. A large part of the patients visiting the rural clinics in Herzegovina had this nervous trouble. The patients complained about various, not very definite, symptoms, especially of palpitations, a feeling of pressure in the stomach, pain all over the body and other vague symptoms. Both men and women are subject

9 Dr. Dojmi di Delupis, *op.cit.*

to "verem," but the women are more often afflicted. The circumstances are described by Dr. Dojmi's patients, as follows:

If you ask them what verem is, most of them answer that it is a sickness caused by grief and suffering, or simply: "It is sadness."

A person gets sick with verem when he weeps for something, when he mourns a loved one, doesn't eat or drink. The pressure gathers in the belly, rises to the pit of the stomach, stops one from eating or drinking, and nothing seems to do any good.

(*Herzegovina, Malo Polje*)

The pit of my stomach hurts and I feel a pressure in my head. I have constant pain. My intestines are like ice and there is a weight in my head. Often I am scared and don't know why; my heart begins to pound and I tremble. Then I get weak and feel exhausted. No work pleases me and I don't care about anything. If I eat, it hurts; if I don't, it hurts too. Something's stuck to the pit of my stomach and hangs on.

(*Herzegovina, Mostar*)

The contrast is striking between the strong and sturdy frames of the peasants in the village clinics in Herzegovina and the emotional and dramatic way in which they describe their troubles in their untranslatable, poetic speech. Dr. Dojmi, with whom I visited these clinics, thought that the intensive self-examination, the observation of the most minute symptoms; in fact, the egocentric mood, is all a part of verem.

People from tribal environments are more susceptible than people from the Oriental sphere, that is people from the Herzegovina area are more so than those from Bosnia. On this point, Dr. Isak Samokovlija (of Sarajevo) made some illuminating observations. Dr. Samokovlija was for a long time district physician in a place in south Bosnia along the Herzegovina border. Although the way of life and the peasant costumes were the same on both sides of this imaginary line, Dr. Samokovlija could often tell simply from their symptoms which patients came from Bosnian and which from Herzegovinian villages. He was particularly able to recognize the women from Herzegovina by their nervous and hysterical symptoms and by their skin. They all had a fine, smooth skin, without scratches or bruises such as are usual with other peasant women. The smooth skin matched their spiritual sensitivity. Dr. Samokovlija's experiences show that the difficult living conditions did not release nervous mass reactions if they were not coupled with certain specific sensitivities linked with the Dinaric tradition.

When we ask how it happens that tough and "hard" people from the tribal areas are so vulnerable and sensitive, the answer is difficult to find. We know that the tribal system had an inflexible structure, the goals were high, and the paths leading to them narrow. Every step from the prescribed course was fateful. Behind the hero lurks fear, fear of not being able to satisfy the high demands, of not being enduring enough, of succumbing in competition or losing face. The rigid tribal organization, with its striving for the absolute, resulted in a special fighting ability and high morals, but often endangered the emotional balance of the men.

It is still a more difficult question why the women of this setting were more exposed to nervous illnesses and disturbances just when the patriarchal regime began to disintegrate than they had been before. One might assume that the women, who carried the heaviest loads in the patriarchal family, would feel the loosening of discipline and of the patriarchal order as the lightening of a burden. For the women in this system had had the very ungrateful role of security valves for the aggression and ambitions of the men. The position of the women made it possible for the men to maintain a mental equilibrium in spite of such extreme competition with each other that it drove them to the edge of madness at times. With women present, there was always someone on hand who was undoubtedly inferior to the man, someone who looked up to him and assured him of his superiority, who under any circumstance acknowledged the higher position of the man and so insured his feeling of domination. (How much the men felt superior to the women is seen from the fact that the term "woman" used to a man was considered the worst possible insult.)

In spite of their low status, patriarchal stability offered some security to the women. While the patriarchal regime remained intact, the women put up with their situation quite well. They shared the reputation of the man or of the family; the sun of glory shone on them, too, at least in a reflected sort of way. Had the women been like slaves, the collapse of the old order would have been a great relief to them. But it is clear from the many cases of nervous disorder during the period of abrupt transformation, that the new conditions meant a heavy burden for them and in many circumstances outweighed the advantages. As long as the patriarchal order was intact, the women resigned themselves to their low status. They were as adjusted to it as they were to the other hard and immutable conditions of life. Their passive resignation to fate enabled them to bear the sufferings of life with philosophical calm. The sudden inrush of the money economy forced them to find individual solutions for problems for which they did not have any guidance in custom and tradition. They found themselves permanently in dilemmas, having to make decisions for instance because of the need to earn money or to regulate births. Under these circumstances, the fatalistic attitude which had helped them to cope with difficult situations was shattered.

The waves of money economy which penetrated into these areas brought very little compensation in the form of technical or hygienic progress as it had to other regions. The standard of living was lowered in this period, child mortality remained on a high level and indeed rose in places. The death of a child is frequently the last drop that makes a glass overflow. The endangered psychosomatic balance of the overburdened woman is upset. This happens most frequently where tribal organization and heroic tradition had prepared the soil for special sensitivity.

But in spite of the fact that in all patriarchal regions the abrupt onset of money economy, connected with modern administration and the economic depression, shattered the patriarchal relationships, nervous disturbances were rather infrequent. The blows were softened by the attitude of *laissez faire*, by indolence or by the fatalistic resignation to fate. In the Dinaric areas such a tolerant, relativistic attitude was lacking, and heavy stress often upset the emotional equilibrium of the people.

### Democratic Elements

Besides the hierarchical and aristocratic components in the tribal organization, strong democratic features were also to be found. The notion that authoritarian and democratic relationships are irreconcilable opposites, as it is presented in many social-psychological writings, has little validity for the Slavic South. While the patriarchal regime was intact, democratic tendencies prevailed; no later stage of family relations has surpassed the democratic trends of the patriarchal era.

For both Montenegrin and Serbian peasants, democratic freedom were by no means empty words; the peasants were dependent on nothing in the world but the decisions of the clan members or villagers. They were dependent on no bureaucracy, no secret diplomacy, no press with which it was difficult to cope, and no remote juridical apparatus. They were not even dependent on economic crises, since they bought almost nothing and had little to sell. They were exposed solely to natural catastrophes such as drought and epidemics, and for these emergencies they had a certain dose of fatalism. But everything dependent on humans was open to their direct influence.

The tribe and village elders were responsible to the villagers and had a high sense of devotion to the people by tradition. The whole administration was not beyond the grasp of the peasants; the open-air gatherings were not larger than could be reached by the human voice. The country seat or the capital were not so distant that one could not walk there or ride on horseback. In 1940 when I spoke to Serbian peasants of the Shumadia district they still had the feeling of self-determination although the German invasion was imminent and threatening. An old fighter against the Turks told me: "It has never happened that there was not freedom in the Shumadia!"

The primitive condition of technology and administration strengthened rather than weakened the democratic element. Since there were neither written laws nor a bureaucratic system, each individual had the possibility of influencing all resolutions in an original, spontaneous and sometimes creative manner, the moral conscience remaining always awake. In some places the resort to written law had been held off a long time in order not to impede the influence of the people. Some sentences show how the people's courts felt responsible for both the injured and guilty parties, and the unusual types of judgment that were passed. The first case was in the 1870's in Montenegro:

A Montenegrin was up for trial. He was found guilty, and the opinion was that he should spend some time in prison. However, the fact that he had parents and little children at home who would perish without him was taken into consideration. Finally they said to him: "Go home! For two years you must not go among people! You must not go two steps from your farm! Twice a year you are all allowed to go to church to communion. Does that suit you, Montenegrins?" "Thus and not otherwise," was the answer of those present in the courtroom.

Another sentence was passed in the 1860's in Herzegovina after the people had discussed the matter for hours in their open meeting, under the leadership of the village priest and village elders. While Stana, a nine-year-old girl, was tending cattle, she was raped by a fifteen-year-old boy. After a long discussion, the meeting arrived at the following conclusion: Little Stana was to remain with her parents. The boy's father was to pay a trustee 184 ducats (gold coins) which were to remain sequestered till Stana was of age. When she was marriageable, she would get the money, with interest, as dowry if the boy's father refused to let his son marry her. If, however, as everyone assumed, the old man would consent to the wedding, he would get his money back. The document was signed: "We have decreed this and have signed it in the spirit of eternal mutual peace. May God rule in a good hour!"[10]

Democratic elements are evident also in the development of landed property. Since there were no written laws, it was always possible to decide independently, and the memory of this was still alive in Serbia at the time of my survey. On one excursion with Professor Vukosavljević and some Belgrade students, the peasants led us up a hill with a good view over the surrounding area and explained to us exactly how private ownership of the land had evolved during the previous 150 years. Their way of speaking was just the same whether they spoke about personal memories or events told them by their elders, for their historical conscience brought past and present almost to a level.

As recently as fifty years ago the region around Belgrade was thinly settled; the peasants in their widely separated farms invited newcomers to become their neighbors. Every zadruga took possession of as much land as it could work, no more nor less. All the rest remained pasture or common woods. As the population increased, the peasants distributed some of these common lots for the sake of more intensive agriculture. The distribution was not definitive, and the peasants paid some token for using the soil. In the last eighty years there were five distributions or redistributions of the lots in this village. Only in 1930, when the registration of landed property was introduced in Serbia and cadastral surveys were completed, did estates really become private property; at the same time the complete freedom of decision and distribution of the peasants of every single village ended.

Democratic procedure, however, was different in the tribal than in the Western sphere. In the former it was assumed that only one course can be the right one; there is no relativity in conceptions, nor unemotional counting of voices to see which proposition has the majority. Although every man had the right to express his opinion, there was always the tendency to reach unanimity. If in a meeting there was one objector to the decision which the majority wished to make, the others urged him to accept their viewpoint. If the

[10] Vuk Vrčević, *Niz Srpskih pripovjedaka (Collection of Serbian Stories)*, Pančevo, 1881.

decision was an important one, the family was asked to work on the man so that he would not endanger an action which all others desired. In whatever way possible, the absolute, the sole truth was aimed at. They aspired to the Eternally Moral, something that must be found even though after endless debates. They seemed to assume that "the sentence was in the air" and all that was necessary was to put it into words. A just sentence was passionately sought.

Even if the head of the tribal organization (and the state) was a strong and willful personality, like the last Montenegrin prince, Nikola, the democratic element was emphasized and the prince was the first to insist on it. A characteristic scene is described by Nenadović:[11]

> Whenever the prince leaves the *Konak* (castle), Montenegrins from all sections swarm about him. Every day countless questions are put to him; legal matters are settled publicly and on the spot. Every few steps someone approaches him, tells him what he wants, questions are asked, objections raised, the necessary explanations given, and the matter is settled. It is not a question of serious criminal cases and complicated lawsuits . . . such are not found in Montenegro. Often a man approaches the prince, who asks, "Have you a request or complaint?" the answer is, "No, sir, I came to see you, for I haven't been in Cetinje for a long time." Once, as Prince Nikola came from the castle, a poor man stepped up to him and said, "Where have you been, sir? I have been here for two full days and have not yet had the opportunity of meeting you!" The prince did not like these words and replied, "Do you see that window at the end of the row? That's where I sleep. If a Montenegrin needs justice at my hands for even a groshen's worth and refuses to come under that window at midnight to call, 'Get up, my lord, I need you,' then that Montenegrin isn't worth that groshen."

Democratic tendencies are obvious in all Yugoslav regions; in the tribal setting they were only accentuated. As was mentioned before, there were strong democratic elements in the zadruga organization of the former Austrian regions (see "The Patriarchal Regime," above), and there are vestiges of the Ottoman heritage of judging a man individually and not by his origin in the Oriental system. The entire patriarchal regime is permeated by the democratic principle, although "democratic" has a somewhat different meaning than in the Western world.

[11] L. Nenadović, *op.cit.*

## The Role of Values

In every historical development there is a mutual influence between objective and subjective factors. Environment and experience shape the people, and the people form their environment and gather their experiences. There are, to be sure, historical events which happen independently of the people concerned, such as invasions, new powers in the neighborhood, new economic systems which penetrate through the frontiers. But people always react in some way: They accept and absorb the influences, or they revise and change them, or else they reject them. At any moment, there are various different courses of action possible, and people make decisions. Which course they will choose is dependent on subjective considerations, that is on inclinations and predispositions which evolved in earlier periods.

The goals of people, their aspirations, purposes, ideals, and values, are the subjective factors. Values can be more easily recognized by looking at the reactions of people than listening to their words and slogans. If some economically backward people or groups complain about the misery of their life, that does not necessarily mean that a higher standard of living is their most cherished value. If they do not care to repair their poor homes, nor to become literate, show indolence toward hygiene and medicine and little enthusiasm to irrigation and tractors, it is evident that a high standard of living is not their most important goal. That does not mean that they do not share the common human values of a better life. They would probably accept with pleasure a car as a present, as well as electric lights and a water supply in their houses. But it shows that they don't want these achievements at any price. They may feel that a poor field is preferable to dependence on an irrigation or implement center, a cabin is better than the need to earn money and pay mortgages or installments, poverty preferable to intensive and hard work. There are many groups and peoples who prefer a moderate working tempo to modern comforts. A stereotyped remark from Dalmatia to anyone who insists on speeding up is: "There is an urgency in dying and not in hoeing."

On the contrary, if people from technically progressive settings speak in a nostalgic way of life without haste and planning, if they almost envy people they see when they travel through southern Italy, Mexico, and Hawaii, that does not mean that their way of life is what they really desire, and that the *joie de vivre* of the people they see is their dominant value. Their attitude shows clearly that there are other things more important to them, such as a nice house with bathrooms and modern kitchen, hygiene, higher education, a car— this is true even if they do not say so, since for them it is self-evident. If they were put in a situation in which they had to make a choice, the things that they would never sacrifice are unmistakable.

People in general experience reality through a subjective lens, according to previously set goals and formerly acquired leanings (Alfred Adler's "tendentious apperception"). Values acquired earlier determine how a group or a people will experience historical events, the way they will interpret them and react to them. Dominant values manifest themselves most obviously in moments of crisis when people make decisions under heavy pressure or when they react without time for second thoughts. When the Germans in the Second World War attacked one European country after another, dominant values of peoples and groups showed up plainly. Some submitted or even collaborated, others waited for a favorable moment to strike, and some attacked the enemy immediately and fought at any price. In Yugoslavia, uncounted people resisted in spite of the greatest dangers from the moment the violence and cruelty of the occupation power became known. The dominant value of the people manifested itself, it could be called national independence or, worded differently, intolerance of foreign domination.

The fate of a culture contact depends on the value orientation of the "receiving" people, especially on their dominant value. For this value other values are sacrificed, and it would not be abandoned under any condition. In spite of the fact the warlike peoples also cherish security, friendly relationships, family, serenity and beauty, and that peaceful groups and peoples abhor brutal oppressors, the former at a certain moment will sacrifice everything for national liberation, while the latter will endure anything in order not to be compelled to sacrifice those things which are the most valued and beloved. Because of their absolute intolerance to an enemy in their country the losses and casualties of the Yugoslavs in the Second World War were very high. (Only the Poles had comparable losses.) Almost 11 per cent of the Yugoslav population perished during the war.[12] This was the price the people paid at that historical moment for their dominant value. This figure suggests that after all during

[12] War deaths among the French were 2 per cent; 2.2 per cent of the population in the Netherlands; 0.5 per cent of the Belgians; 1.25 per cent among the Czechs. Dudley Kirk, *Europe's Population of the Interwar Years*, League of Nations, 1946.

the first Yugoslav era the Dinaric and heroic element had been strengthened in the whole country.

## The Beginning of the Magic Circle

It is quite clear that there is some reciprocity between the historic fate of peoples or groups and their dominant values. Existent values decidedly influence the course of history, historical events strengthen existing values. But if we search for the beginning of the circle we find before us an insolvable riddle. If we ask what the beginning of South Slav history was like, no satisfactory answer can be found. On the one hand we must suppose that all Slav tribes were equal when they moved to the South into their present country. It seems sure that their experience must have become different only after they had settled in the various regions, and this was the reason different value orientations developed. We are compelled to suppose however that the heroic orientation is older than provocation by the invaders, since only people with the ideal of independence and with fighting spirit would have felt the Turkish conquest as a provocation; others accepted the conquerors willingly. It is not possible, I believe, ever to determine which appeared earlier, historical events or dominant values of a people.

Every culture contact generates something new, a whole which is different and more than the sum of its components. This is true even if the components seem to counteract each other, for discord, too, can be a common characteristic. Some results cannot be explained by the qualities of the components. The Dinaric fighting spirit, with its explosive quality, can hardly be found either in the invading Ottomans (the "donating culture," as it may be called) or in the Slavs before the Ottoman invasion (the "receiving culture"). But the new quality, once in existence, decisively influenced further historical development.

The analogy of a chemical compound seems to me more valid for culture contact than the analogy of a mosaic which is so often used. For in creating a mosaic the result can be partly foreseen if the pieces are known, since new qualities will not appear. With chemical compounds, however, new qualities may appear, which cannot be foreseen since they are not inferable from the qualities of the ingredients.

A causal context determining the qualities of the fusion could always be found, but not the reason why certain factors were decisive. Seemingly unimportant peculiarities determine the historical course; unnoticed susceptibilities influence the result; small mistakes of the conquerors bring the powder barrel to explosion. No strategist is able to foresee the bearing of the enemy or the conduct of his own troops with certainty; no inquisitor can be completely sure that the accused will break down. Only in retrospect is it possible to know which factors were decisive in bringing individuals or groups to resistance, resignation, or collaboration.

The reactions of the South Slavs to their conquest could be explained by their Illyrian heritage: Just as the South Slavs were considered dangerous rebels by the Turks and the Nazis, so were the old Illyrians who lived on the Adriatic coast prior to the Slavs, considered nearly incurably rebellious by the Romans. One can adduce the high mobility of the South Slavs through their possession of sheep herds and pack horses, which made it possible to withdraw to the forests much more easily than, for instance, the bulk of the Mexican Indians who were tied to their corn fields for lack of domestic animals, and soon resigned themselves to the Spanish conquerors. Having sufficient food, the South Slavs were able to resist the Turks. But if we accept these statements, we cannot explain why the Albanians, who were also shepherds and heirs to the Illyrians, did not become dedicated foes of the Ottoman Empire but rather Turkish favorites and police troops.

How can it be explained that in the Habsburg Empire the Dinaric fighters became faithful imperial frontier soldiers and the best Austrian officers? How did it happen that they adjusted to the most rigid discipline, never rebelling against Austrian authority, while having a nearly pathological sensitivity to Turkish authority? Why were they as proud of the ancestor who had given reverence to the Empress Maria Theresia of Austria as of the one who had fallen on the Kosovo Plain? Was it some voluntary decision made centuries before that decisively influenced them continually in favor of Austria as a chosen ally and against the Turks as violent invaders?

Why did contact with the Ottoman conquerors make the Bosnians tend toward the Oriental style, while the Montenegrins developed opposite qualities? Why did the Bosnians welcome the Turks with open arms and absorb their influence, while the Montenegrins met them with irreconcilable hate and rejected their influence? How is it that some people succumb to pacification and others do not, that some become active creators of history, others its helpless victims?

The reason why one or another of the innumerable characteristics of two cultures decisively influence the result of culture contact cannot be known. Although the reciprocal relation of dominant values

397

and historical development, of personality structure or national character and historical fate is seemingly easy to discover, the beginning of the circle cannot be stated with certainty.

It may not be chance that the conclusion of this interrogation could be formulated by me only in a negative form. In regard to culture contact, the boundaries of research seem to be rather narrow. If it were possible completely to resolve the riddle of culture contact, we would be able to foresee a great part of the historic developments of the future. Here, however, we come up against the insuperable walls of human knowledge.

# CHAPTER XIV

## Over-all Trends

WHAT tendencies have prevailed in family relations throughout the regions of Yugoslavia as a whole? When we watch the scene from a distance or from some detached point of view, regional differences fade and a vista of the whole area becomes evident.

### Individualistic and Collectivistic Tendencies

In every period at every place, there is one human problem which never fails to appear, since it derives from the twin nature of man as an individual and as a collective being. There are always dramas, conflicts, and dilemmas because of the ambivalence of individual desires and collective obligations. Man as a collective being answers to the demands of his society and shows a tendency to sacrifice himself for the community like the social insects. He is so firmly attached to his fellow-men that the security, esteem, acknowledgment, and glory which the community offers him respond to his inmost desires.

Yet man is an individual who has his own aims and who aspires to personal satisfaction and joy. To reach and defend his personal goals, which may always conflict with those of others, he has developed many aggressive traits. Flowing from individualistic tendencies in human nature is always a certain opposition to collective suggestions and requests. Every child is born with an inclination toward defiance, which cannot as a rule be fought by force. In all children there is a certain resistance to conditioning. Man's capacity for resisting dominating powers, for opposing an established order, for departing from an acknowledged system of values differs fundamentally from conditioned reactions and from inculcated attitudes.

Neither collectivist nor individualistic tendencies can be unlimited within human society. However much collectivist slogans may prevail, individualistic aspirations cannot be subdued, and the more they are subdued the stronger is the counteracting pressure. However early one may begin to "condition" people, however consistently this conditioning may be continued, human beings can never be turned into working bees. But neither can the opposite—the collectivist—tendency be suppressed; this also can achieve its goals against great obstacles. Whenever the pendulum swings in one direction, it is preparing to swing back in the opposite one, though the signs by which this can be recognized are not always obvious.

Man in general can stand only a certain amount of adjustment and subordination to the community. If no outlets remain open for freedom of movement and aggressive impulses, the demands of the community become unbearable pressures. Frequently man transfers his aspirations for freedom (derived from the individual sphere) to the society itself. He desires freedom not only for himself but also, or still more, for his group. He will fight for such freedom with all the passion of one who would liberate himself from iron chains. All the aggression he is capable of is centered in fighting the common suppressor or enemy, and individual goals fade into the background.

The behavior of the individual within the family can be judged correctly only when the broader circles are considered and one has found out how the general human desire for independence manifests itself: Whether in collective resistance against suppression from the outside, or in individual resistance against the demands of one's own community or family.

In the South Slavic patriarchal regions, all desire for independence was expressed in collective resistance to the national enemy. The incessant fight against the Turks, which lasted longer than half a millennium, was not a war in the usual sense, but mainly resistance against the authority of the state, or against an overwhelming neighboring empire to whose existence one never acquiesced. The people were united in pursuing their aims, especially the aim of freedom. Rivalries between men for the sake of prestige and of esteem are part and parcel of this system, and do not contradict the conformism of the "in group."

There was an inner connection between the idea of extreme freedom among the people from the Dinaric areas and conformism within their tribal and zadruga system. When pressure from outside subsided, unity largely disintegrated. The decline of the patriarchal system and of the zadruga seem to be related, to a certain extent, to the fall of the Ottoman Empire. As long as the Turks had to be fought, all aggressiveness was directed against them but, during lulls in the struggle, fighting and vendettas between tribes very often arose. After the foreign enemies and oppressors had disappeared, the zadruga disintegrated as well. There was no power of resistance left.

Fighting against the Turks was, to some degree, an outlet for the inner pressures which resulted from the strict discipline of the zadruga. If this discipline passed the limit a man could bear, he could escape "to the forest," he could become a *hajduk*[1] or a guerilla fighter. After the end of the Turkish wars, when this was no longer possible, it seems to have become much more difficult to put up with collective demands, and the system of the zadruga disintegrated. Though the wars were not directly connected with the zadruga system, they seem to have helped to conserve it. This was the effect of the fight against the Turks both in the regions which belonged to the Ottoman Empire and in the Austrian regions which, as border-provinces, were also permanently involved in fighting, though not in revolt. In the Moslem regions, where there was no fighting against the Turks, the organization of the zadruga was never as rigid as in other regions.

To many generations of South Slavs, from the fourteenth century to the present, it was an unknown experience to conform to the values of a governing power. The character of youth was formed by loyalty to resistance movements. This fight for freedom had another function beyond its consciously pursued aims. This can be seen in the disregard of the immense sacrifices which were made without hesitation in all South Slavic wars of liberation, and from the way the memory of the Serbian defeat at Kosovo was cultivated even after the ultimate victory over the Turks. "The ethics of Veith's Day" (the Day of Kosovo) became a slogan long after the fight was over.

After the fall of the Ottoman Empire, political rivalries among the South Slavic groups were so loaded with passion that they almost destroyed the Yugoslav state. All old standards and values became invalid in the villages, and individual resistance against social rules reached a new high level. But in spite of this, independence and equality among the members within the family were never attained.

In our regions, the collectivistic trend dominated from time immemorial, and it was only a few decades before my inquiry that the individual tendency came to the fore, and then only in certain regions. In the interwar period, the individualistic trend was rising in the whole country. All phenomena connected with the disintegration of the zadruga regime indicate this. However the individualistic period was of short duration and lasted nowhere longer than one or two generations. In this short period the characteristics of the collectivistic period have not been completely lost. They show themselves in a certain generosity, as well as in the lack of interest in

---

[1] A brigand who robbed Turks by preference.

401

minute details of work. Often outspoken indifference is shown for practical viewpoints and technical progress.

It was striking how much better farms were managed by German, Czech, Slovak, and Hungarian colonists, settled in the neighborhood of the old residents of some South Slav regions. These colonists from Central Europe brought with them a certain middle-class tradition which was manifest in their practical minds and in their interest in economic progress, improved skills, and industry. But they were in no way envied or imitated, but rather ridiculed by their South Slav neighbors. The values of the "bourgeois" period—frugality, rational working methods and viewpoints—were never fully accepted by the South Slav peasants.

In the Slavic South, the whole evolution of individualism was cut short. During the brief period that it lasted, all the characteristics of the capitalistic epoch had not developed. All expressions of individualism appeared in a decidedly immature and brusque form, similar to the manners of a teenager who wants to free himself from the family by big words and inconsiderate behavior. In all regions of the country pre-individualistic features prevailed, with the exception of the regions of the "new stabilization," where the marks of a more mature individualism appeared.

The whole individualistic development in its rapid rise and decline could not fully display the typical marks of a capitalistic economy. The peasants were thrown suddenly from fighting with the Turks into the problems of the world depression, from the traditional zadruga economy, with its inherited skills, into a modern economy which would have required businesslike methods. The leap did not quite succeed because in some regions not even a single generation had grown up to enjoy the benefits of the capitalist period before the grave economic depression occurred and the Second World War started, halting this development in Yugoslavia for good. The peasants were in a way cheated out of a whole period of individual freedom and opportunities. They did not enjoy personal independence and higher living standards as did peasants in countries where the development of capitalism was slower.

The contrast to Western urbanized and industrialized countries is obvious, especially to the United States, where the individualistic tendency has had a long tradition and the entire life has been colored by the values of personal independence and happiness for the individual.

## Fate vs. Planning

Another dilemma inevitably appears in the human drama which is never solved completely. An inescapable contradiction arises from the fact that man is forced to plan but is incapable of foreseeing. Man is capable, by thinking logically, of planning in advance and of calculating the consequences of his actions. This capacity involves compulsions: Since man is able to plan, he is compelled to plan, to arrange his present behavior according to the expected future. But though man can and needs to plan, it is rarely within his own power to accomplish his aims. Often in his whole life he does not attain his highest goals, and, if he does attain them, they are frequently taken away from him again. Illness and accidents, rivalries and encroachments by his fellow-men interfere with his projects and desires. At every step he is opposed by powers to which he is not equal and over which he has no influence. And then, being mortal, in the end he is always conquered by death.

Science cannot solve the mystery of personal fate; this ignorance is final. There is no answer as to why a certain man is the only survivor of an annihilated regiment, another the only victim of a traffic accident, why one man is offered so many chances in life while another is haunted by calamities. This riddle of human destiny is probably insolvable, since the struggle of man toward his goals is inescapably tied to his blindness, his ignorance of the future.

If man were to know his future, to foresee with certainty what was to come, his ailments, the hour of his death or of the death of his beloved ones, the obstacles obstructing his way—he would not be able to hope and to strive. His constant pushing forward depends on his blindness to the future: Both form a single, indivisible unity. Yet he must attempt to decipher the future. The future must appear attainable, must be revealed to him in small parts so that he will go on pursuing it. But in its totality it must remain hidden from him. The inner dynamics of the human mind is based on this contradiction.

Men always strive to overcome this contradiction in some way. But although every method ranging from the purely fatalistic to the consistently rationalistic has been tried again and again, the contradiction has never been resolved. The fatalistic attitude results in poverty, helplessness, and dependence on more aggressive groups; the extreme rational attitude results in permanent mental tensions which are felt as a heavy burden. It seems that man is seeking a solution that will enable him to master his problems through active endeavor and at the

403

same time to resign himself to fate, to be prepared for reversals and therefore not be broken by them. But this state of equilibrium has been attained only for short periods.

The rational trend of the nineteenth century which dominated Europe suddenly lost its hold when the First World War broke out unexpectedly after many decades of peace. The belief of the people that man can shape his destiny was then badly shaken as it became evident that their conviction that war belonged to a barbarous past had been a delusion. The vicissitudes of history since 1914 demonstrated to Europeans that planning does not necessarily mean realization.

Illustrative of this is a page of Butterick's Fashion Magazine of 1912, which is full of children's pictures entitled "Future Crowned Heads of Europe." Pictured are the little Russian crown prince and his sisters with wavy hair, the German crown prince with four little boys in sailor suits, Archduke Franz Ferdinand of Austria with his three children, the dark-eyed royal Italian children, the fair-haired Prince Edward of England, and the curly-headed Leopold of Belgium, Bavarian and Saxon princes, and Spanish infantes. Only two or three of these two dozen children have attained what was presupposed and planned, and what had appeared to be certain at the time. All others were caught by a fate which nobody could foresee.

Most Europeans, when their belief in human foresight was shaken, felt a deep shock from which many people of the older generation never recovered. But the Balkan people were not greatly upset by this experience. It only emphasized their fatalistic view of life which had persisted from time immemorial, and which had been firmly based upon the influence of Oriental culture. This view of life was clearly expressed by the words and gestures of Bosnian peasants when they looked at a machine. Shaking their heads, they would say: "What in the world does a German invent!" By "German" they meant a Westerner in general, who believes in mastering destiny by inventions. For these fatalists, all such innovations implied human arrogance and an interference with divine designs.

In the first Yugoslav era, this belief in fate was not greatly shaken. The government was neither able to solve administrative, juridical, and economic problems, nor able to raise the standard of living. This confirmed people's belief that these problems could not be solved by men. At the time of this survey, the doubt about any rational planning was general. The attitude of all Yugoslavs toward fate was completely different from the attitude which seems "natural" to most Americans.

In most South Slavic regions, a way of life prevailed which might be called "speculation on a downward trend." One's attitude toward fate was such that one seemed neither to want luck nor to strive for happiness. On the contrary, one was always prepared for tragic turns or death. Only reluctantly did one resign oneself to being made happy, and one seldom admitted to *being* happy. This would have been considered arrogant.

The proud attitude toward fate does not imply that they did not desire happiness. The fact that there was so much dancing, entertaining, feasting, that so many colorful and precious clothes were made and that so much silver and gold was worn, shows how much gaiety was desired. But a young person who went with a throbbing heart to a Kolo-dance to meet his or her beloved put on an air as if he had to perform a serious social duty.

This is the general attitude; there were, however, several variations in the different Yugoslav regions. The solemn bearing was most accentuated in the Dinaric, tribal setting. There a grave expression was expected of men and women. It meant the highest praise if one said of a girl that "she did not show the white of her teeth." The memory of the Serbian defeat, the incessant singing and talking about the blood bath of Kosovo to whip up feelings of revenge, dominated the Dinaric way of life. For these people not a happy family life, but glorious deeds were the only legitimate objects of happiness. In family life—in the choice of their spouses and the number of their children—they were fatalistic.

But they were fatalists in personal affairs only, not in questions regarding their tribe or the Serbian nation. They in no way felt at the mercy of fate, though they were, by their permanent fighting, exposed to chance more than other men. Since, as guerilla fighters, they held the initiative and wanted to fight, they always thought of themselves as masters of events. They could attain glory by their own efforts—living or dead—and glory in all personal aims was their most important goal.

In the regions that were under Oriental influence, other objectives were prevalent, for example private happiness. Here people strove for joy, longed for love, and did not have the proud defiant attitude toward personal happiness of the Dinaric fighters. Their attitude was rather one of absolute resignation to fate, without any attempt to act against "what is written in the books." There is some connection between a great desire for happiness and consequent fatalism: Since one has conceded, so to speak, that one desires happiness, one cannot despise fate, like a fighter who accepts death willingly. One is humble toward "kismet," and, at the utmost, one tries to influence it by magic spells.

Enjoyment was considered the object of life only in one of the surveyed regions, Slavonia, where love and joy were legitimate and admitted aims. At the time of the zadruga, wish and fulfillment were in full harmony and people danced, sang, ate, drank, wore gold, and loved more than in any other South Slavic region. But when pecuniary influences entered, and the old standard of life could be kept up only by rational methods, this striving for happiness took on a tragic coloring.

Seen from a distance which allows comparisons between different environments, a humble attitude toward fate in expecting happiness was characteristic of the Slavic South. It is rather an Eastern approach. The question "how are you" sounds at time like a well-chosen test for the attitude of people in respect to fatalism and rational planning. When people from the Balkans hear the stereotyped American answers to this question, "just fine," or "wonderful," they think they may well be provoking the envy of men and the revenge of fate, and misjudge their over-confidence. When, on the other hand, Americans hear the complaints and sighs of Europeans (especially from the Slavic South) in answer to "how are you," they seem to them ungrateful and in bad taste, as they seldom see what lies behind the apparent emphasis on the negative aspects of life.

### The Role of the Family

The family, too, is universal, existing in some form in every society. Yet as it plays different roles for the community and for the individual in every environment, we have to ask what role did the family play in the Slavic South. This is not easy to discover, for there is frequently a bigger gulf in this realm of life than elsewhere between what people are and what they appear to be, what they desire and how much is fulfilled. Words which are spoken or printed are often very far from reality.

Among the South Slavs, the family never played a great role officially. The zadruga was prominent, but only as an institution, and as a production cooperative. Family life in a specific sense, particularly marital relations, played a minor role. A wife would never accompany a government functionary at an official ceremony. Pictures of politicians or scientists which were meant for publication would not be taken in his family circle; women and children would seldom be mentioned in biographies. When a peasant spoke of his wife, he would say: "Excuse me . . . my wife. . . ." Of the children was sometimes said, in tribal regions: "according to sin, my son." Something not quite legitimate, which was only tolerated, was attached to all private, intimate, that is to family relations.

In spite of this convention, family relations were emotionally highly charged (see "Brother and Sister," above). In the period of the survey, family relations were so strong that they dwarfed all others. A familial style dominated in all spheres of life. Relations which were impersonal by nature were colored by sentiments of brotherly affection or of brotherly hatred and rivalry. Distant and businesslike relations hardly exist.

At the time of this survey, the attitude of "familism" prevailed in all regions of Yugoslavia. In general, help by relatives was offered readily. In all cities, especially in Belgrade, in cafés and restaurants, you could see officers and clergymen in the company of their peasant relatives. Successful peasants' sons took out their brothers in traditional costumes and paid official visits with their mothers, who could not read or write. By every gesture these peasants' sons showed how important it was for them to support their poorer relatives. The obvious fact that these villagers were badly adjusted to the city was no reason to be ashamed of them. One's greatest pride was to play the protector and the sponsor.

Familism also showed in the assurance with which peasants moved about in the cities. Tens of thousands of peasants in their costumes came daily to the South Slavic cities to visit markets, hospitals, courts, or barracks. None of these visitors would ask for directions or, even less, use maps. Job hunting or migration from village to town or overseas was done with the help of people with whom one had grown up; institutions or impersonal agencies were almost never used. All difficulties were solved by relatives or neighbors who were already acquainted with the city.

This familism also prevailed in "modern" regions. A little scene is characteristic of this attitude; I watched it, not in a patriarchal village, but in a Dalmatian port. In 1942, in the middle of the war, I queued up, with hundreds of people for bread ration cards. Suddenly a girl tried to force her way to the door of the office. The people, who had been standing for hours and were hungry, tired, and irritated, pushed her back indignantly. But she said with self-confidence: "It's a relative of mine in the office, I have to tell him something." After which the people allowed her to pass without any further protest, and were not at all angry when the girl later came out with her ration cards in her hands. Obviously they considered it quite "natural" that she had special privileges with her cousin.

This familism developed into notorious nepotism during the first Yugoslav era. A short recommendation by telephone: "Try to do what you can for him, he's a relative of mine, from my village" sufficed to open all doors. Without such help, however, it was hardly possible to move the doors of the clumsy bureaucratic apparatus on their hinges. Corruption was only partly responsible for this, to a great extent it was "natural" claim of men to be assisted by "their own" people. Since this claim and its acceptance by the officials as well as the public was so general, nepotism could not be fought successfully. Familism takes into account the shortcomings, the unreliability, indolence, and laziness of people. But one relies upon the fact that despite these common weaknesses, men are usually helpful to their "brothers" or clan members.

In America, such nepotism is considered unjust as well as impractical. People are used to institutions which work efficiently, to fair play and objective attitudes toward the public. They are also used to a certain distance among people. One of the preconditions of the good functioning of institutions is an impersonal mood, without high emotions, without expressed sympathy or antipathy to strangers.

These fair but impersonal relations, however, impress people who are used to familism as cold and disquieting. A new South Slav immigrant to the United States—not a peasant at all—said to me, shocked, "It is so strange to find everything done by writing or by telephone. You do not know the person you are talking to, you do not see him, and will never see him. I wanted to go to the shipping agent of a removal company to see the storeroom where my baggage would be left—impossible! I needed a dentist, wanted to go there and ask him when he would have time, and whether he might perhaps treat me at once. Every time my friends shouted at me: 'But why? Who has time for that? That is not done!' A phone call, two short questions, spelling the name, and then I get an appointment in 10 days or they send me some information. Everything I have to decide alone."

It requires a completely changed orientation to skip from a familistic to a rational system of relations. It is not easy to realize that one does not need a brother in order to find work, an aunt to take care of a child, a cousin to get a boat reservation. It needs a great adjustment to gain confidence in institutions and to believe that they really work, that all wheels turn independent of old friendly or familiar ties.

Familism, where it is established, is preserved by mutual effects of subjective and objective motives. The continuous intervention by the family interrupts every orderly administration; on the other hand, the poor performance of impersonal "agencies" increases familism, since one cannot get along without help from relatives.

Again there is a sharp contrast to the United States, where all instances support the "pursuit of happiness." Officials appear at every ceremony with wife and children; politicians, military men, and scholars are photographed in the circle of their family; in the shortest biographical note all members of the family are mentioned. On the covers and pages of magazines, family pictures are shown, husband and wife with tender expressions, and children happily united with their parents. Yet this, too, is partly a conventionalized picture, not completely in accord with reality. As independence within and from the family is one of the highest values, there are many people who remain or become single and "unattached," as the figures for households of one person show. The high quality of American institutions and organizations strengthens the feeling of security and self-sufficiency, making the independence of the individual possible. In spite of this, the longing for intimacy seems to be wide-spread and many people yearn for the intimate family life of three generations which they may have seen in less "developed" countries. They take for granted the perfect and smooth functioning of American institutions, but they do not feel they have resolved the difficult problem of loneliness, which is discussed over and over again.

In the Slavic South, however, close family ties are not noticed or are not appreciated. The positive aspects of familism are overlooked, and aims which contrast to irking reality are longed for and discussed endlessly. To them, personal independence and efficient institutions seem to be the most desirable goals.

### Rhythm of Changes

In the Slavic South, the changes through the centuries remind one of high and low tides. In all recorded history, there have been far-reaching changes which came in waves. In quiet times, all family and community relationships in the village seem to be standardized. The conduct of most people harmonizes with established norms and values. Society is homogeneous; individual differences are negligible. Men resemble one another in the same way as the villages of a region are alike. Children conform to their parents, whose demands and views they accept without resistance. In each new generation, the characteristics of the older generation appear anew, and to these belong, as a rule, an inflexibility toward new influences. For centuries the attitudes of men remain almost the same, forming characteristic regional patterns.

This low tide picture changes abruptly when a new power conquers the country or a new economic system penetrates it. Under the influence of great changes, when men are threatened by new dangers or enticed by new opportunities, that which stood firm for centuries breaks down in a few years. The homogeneity of the community, which, in fact, only appeared to exist now disintegrates completely. Many people react in new ways and adopt new attitudes. The traditional character of the people, considered unchangeable from time immemorial, seems to change with one stroke.

An impression of a great and sudden change is given by the fact that the stream of events lifts to the top men whose characteristic preferences correspond to the new situation. Those who, according to their predisposition, fit into the new system, gain status, influence public opinion, create new standards and new fashions. One by one, others follow; they give up old habits and begin to swim in the new stream. The types who profit by the events—in a good and in a bad sense—have, by suggestion, an effect upon others. According to their example, the habits and the character of youth are formed; a new generation grows up which differs greatly from its parents.

But this impression of great and sudden changes is not borne out by reality. Only a certain number of men have "changed" and, of adults, almost only those who were previously inclined to the new trend. In such moments of strong pressure, minorities which do not actually represent the character and the tendencies of the majority frequently float to the surface, while great groups different from the new types are pushed into the background, lose their status and their influence. They may reappear when the new order has somewhat slackened or when another change sets in. Deep changes in the character of a region develop only when a new generation is raised under the influence of new conditions of life and of the new patterns. Despite appearances, however, even this generation is not quite homogeneous; many individuals deviate openly or secretly from the official pattern; they maintain a continuity with former periods, and in them lie seeds of new changes.

If the South Slav people had really changed, they would not show the same face again and again after generations. Nor would regional characteristics remain so marked that, even overseas, someone who knows the setting can distinguish a Montenegrin from a Dalmatian, a Serb from a Bosnian, and would know where a certain man stems from even before he has spoken.

Stormy historical events have repeated themselves throughout the centuries, and, in a certain sense, the country seems to have altered little. Frequently the observer has the impression that up to now the Balkans have remained the same as they were when the Romans fought the rebellious Illyrians.

Such a rhythm of change is similar to low and high tides: The rocks on the coast are covered by waves during the high tide or a storm, but they reappear in their old shapes when the waters fall. This comparison, however, does not fit completely: The rocks after a storm are unchanged, while people are not. The generations who lived through times of revolutionary changes carry marks which cannot be erased.

In comparison with the Balkan scene, American development seems to have another rhythm altogether. Life in the United States gives the impression of a river flowing in one direction. This continuous streaming does not, however, imply a calm movement. Quite the contrary, everything seems to rush tempestuously; there is forward pressure in every field especially in the technical one. But in spite of the rapid development, it does not seem that fundamental changes occur. The Constitution has remained almost unchanged since it was written, historic figures have not been removed from their monuments, neither the dollar nor street names have been changed. The flag with its stars and stripes is typical of the rhythm of change in America: It has remained the same in color and pattern, but gradually stars have been added. The changes are rather of a technical nature than changes of principle.

However these impressions of low and high tides or of a current streaming in one direction, respectively, are to a certain degree deceptive. Historic development seems to follow a spiral course: To a certain extent it both rises and turns in a circle, rather than following a pure cyclic movement or flowing as a current with no

411

countercurrent. Today young Americans may not be quite as unlike their grandfathers as one may conclude from obvious differences, nor were the guerillas of the Second World War exactly the same as the guerillas of Roman or Turkish times.

# CHAPTER XV

# The Reshaping of the Family

IN THE last chapters, the space dimension of this study was considered, for the regional diversity and the life styles influenced by East and West are in a certain sense space aspects of the whole picture. Now we shall turn to the other aspect of this study, the time dimension, to the stage of development in which each region was caught at the moment of inquiry. A study of the time dimension might make possible some conclusions of more general significance.

In the period of the survey, great changes were taking place in many parts of the country. The transformation of the family became central to our research not only because a large number of the surveyed villages were typical for the great changes in the interwar period but—what is more important—because the study of chaotic and anarchic relationships offers opportunities for more wide-ranging observations. Just as the construction of a building is easier to understand when it is being dismantled than when it is intact, so it is with human relations. Rules and regularities are most easily revealed at the moment they are disintegrating, when the adhesion is loosening, when malfunctions appear.

Family relations in a process of transition, however, posed certain difficulties for investigation. Since the process occurred in different regions at various times, each village was in a different stage in this process. Not only did newly emerging patterns have to be found but also the transformation process itself, different in each region, discovered.

Just as the decay of the folk costumes has its rules, so, too, has the break-up of the traditional familial relationships. In some South Slav regions, the men, and in others, the women first gave up folk costumes; in some areas woolen garments, in others linen clothing was first replaced by factory merchandise; here the pure style of the cut was first abandoned, and there the patterns of embroidery and weaving. So it was with family life. In one region the married sons were the very first to demand economic independence and rebel against family authority; in another, the daughters-in-law undermined the zadruga with their dowries; and, in a third, the young men broke down patriarchal morals by seeking intoxicating individual freedom

413

by erotic means. The sequence of events depended upon the specific circumstances under which new elements invaded the area, and upon the predisposition which had developed in each region in earlier periods.

Studying the process of change, it became clear from the start that one of the most dramatic, conspicuous, and significant phenomena is an upset equilibrium in the family, the suddenly aggravated conflicts. In this connection two questions arise: First, is the discord in the family due more to the process of transformation or to the traditional regional peculiarities, that is, to a certain predisposition for feud and violence? And, second, has the new equilibrium in one region, in the Littoral, some prognostic value, indicating the direction in which the development of the other regions will move?

### Patriarchal Order—the Point of Departure

The differences between life styles as discussed in the last chapter are significant only from a certain point of view. From another, they disappear almost completely. All patriarchal regions had many things in common. Despite tensions or struggles between the tribal groups and the peasants under Oriental influence, all of them were, nevertheless, in some way related to each other. When a Bosnian Moslem or a Montenegrin asked: "What will Europe say to this?" or "How will Europe react to this?" The questions may be motivated by contrary hopes, but the foreignness with respect to "Europe" (meaning the Western powers) was almost the same.

Breathing in the patriarchal atmosphere, one sometimes has the feeling that the two variants—described in the last chapter—have in common a certain nomadic element from far-distant times; an element that links, in spite of many differences, the shepherds from the meadows of the Dinaric Alps with the shepherds of the Arabic desert. These people seemed to lack many features which were considered typical of other European peasants, such as an interest in the details of husbandry, in practical solutions and improvements at the farm, and in untiring work. On the other hand, the artistic interest was incomparably stronger than the technical and so was the poetic expression of these people, their singing habits, their hospitality, their joy in looking over wide spaces, and a general sweeping generosity which is hard to describe.

Yet another factor levels the differences in life styles: In the patriarchal stage there was a free meeting of different cultures; not only

414

Oriental features and those of the tribal regime, but even Austrian and Hungarian elements fit in quite effortlessly. Expressions or pieces of uniforms from the former Austrian Military March seemed by no means out of place. The situation is similar to Latin America, where there is also a blend of Indian and Spanish (and even Moorish) motives, melted into a new entity.

However, traits connected with a money economy appear as a foreign element, contrasting sharply with the patriarchal tradition. Just as in textile patterns in which Slav and Turkish motives blend into one, while a printed cotton blouse made in a factory strikingly differs from the traditional homemade style, so it is also with the newly developing relations among the people of this area. The interest in "production," dowry, inheritance, civil law suits is much more alien to the patriarchal way of life than any cultural element that was introduced during the era of subsistence economy. The patriarchal villages of different variants resemble each other in many respects much more than villages which are in different phases of development. There is a big gap between the patriarchal villages in Herzegovina and the villages on the coast which have adapted themselves to a money economy, even though they are geographically so close that one can walk from the one to the other in a matter of hours.

The following characteristics can be found in all regions in the patriarchal stage of development:

The zadruga is the norm everywhere, except among the Bosnian Moslems. Sons, even when married, do not separate from home during the father's lifetime.

The woman has a scarcity value. In all patriarchal regions the mortality of women is higher than that of men, and so there is an excess of the latter. The head of the house tries to find brides for the younger males as soon as possible because women are absolutely necessary for farm work. The customs of bride purchase and "otmica" have their roots in this. The woman is appreciated as a worker and as a wife. She brings neither dowry nor inheritance to her marriage. All girls get married; even widows usually remarry. On the other hand, men find it difficult to get a wife and in some areas widowers cannot marry at all.

In this phase, there is a need and a longing for large families. The children are not overburdened with work, as in later phases, but they are necessary as herdsmen. Birth control is unknown; barrenness is regarded as a great misfortune or a punishment of God. The number of surviving children is high.

415

The family hierarchy is strictly observed. At the head of the zadruga is the father, who is obeyed and shown honor, often in ceremonial form; the younger people conform to authority which is maintained "naturally" without coercion.

The hierarchy is built up according to age and sex. Authority by sex is more important than that by age, especially in the tribal regime. The elder brother commands the younger ones and especially his sisters, even the older ones. A sister willingly obeys her brother and is deeply devoted to him.

As a wife, the woman has a secondary position, but she dominates as mother-in-law. The married son supports the authority of his mother, and the daughter-in-law usually submits. The mother is frequently closely tied with her daughters in an *entente cordiale*.

Patriarchal sex-morality is rigid and, as a rule, there are no premarital love affairs. The girls are protected and chaste, and, generally, the young men, too, enter marriage without sexual experience. They are often younger than their brides. Public opinion enforces morality and also protects any girl who is in danger of being deserted by a youth by exerting successful pressure upon him.

Male authority is great; the woman shows her husband and, even more so her father-in-law, her deference by various tokens of submissiveness; the husband has the right to punish his wife, but rarely strikes her. His conduct is that of *noblesse oblige*. The husband keeps his distance; he does not consult his wife, but neither does he mistreat her. The brother-sister relationship is often more cordial than that between husband and wife.

Marriages endure, and marital fidelity is the norm; it is seldom broken, especially not by the woman. The stability of all obligations is great, the scope of individual action narrow.

Illiteracy is the norm, especially for the women, but this does not necessarily imply a general backwardness. The patriarchal setting is not a fruitful soil for alcoholism. Excessive drunkenness runs counter to the moral ideals and the dignified bearing of these people.

In the patriarchal milieu, personal freedom is limited by a strict code of rules of conduct; this is especially strict for women and for the younger members of the family. There is little room for individual wishes and actions.

### Burdens of Independence

The peasants who, in spite of impediments and resistance, succeeded in breaking-up their zadrugas had high hopes for the future.

They did not foresee the difficulties which awaited them, the risks of an independent small farm, the dependence on the market. To the observer, however, the consequences of the break-up of the zadruga were obvious. In the field, the phenomena following the collapse of the zadruga economy sometimes presented themselves as dramatically as if a film director had made a sequence of scenes in sharp contrast in order to make visible the consequences of the change.

On one of my excursions to Bosnia in 1940, I went to the Jajce district, where 80 per cent of the men and 90 per cent of the women were illiterate. There I found in the oak woods a large zadruga which seemed an embodiment of the patriarchal idyll.

The young married couple whom I was visiting with friends was quietly squatting, Turkish fashion, in the grass under a tree. They were happy, chatting, and laughing, and seemed in no way harried or over-tired. This was all the more surprising as nine tiny children fluttered around them like chicks. The mother was the second wife of her husband and he was her second husband—both had been widowed for a short time. The children were from two (or three) different marriages, which is why they were all so tiny and near in age. The peasant woman did not seem troubled; she laughed continuously, although she had eight children of her own, had lost four, and was now expecting a new one.

There was one room for each conjugal family. In the little room where a dozen people slept, there was no furniture at all except a loom. The floor was barely six feet below the new ceiling, of which they were all very proud, since until recently there had been no ceiling at all. The clothing of old and young was homemade. Everything they wore was made of material that had been grown there, and spun, woven, dyed, sewn, knitted, and embroidered at home. The heaviest task for the women was the weaving of all the necessary linen and wool, blankets, mats, and bags. No time was wasted on cooking. This was done in a tiny hut where the rocky floor was not even smoothed and which contained no utensils. In a copper kettle the corn mush bubbled on the open hearth, and was stirred by two of the bigger girls. These primitive household conditions were no burden to the housewife; organically and in every way she was completely equal to her task.

A few days later, I went to the Shumadia district in Serbia and visited old Nana's village (see the chapter "Patriarchal Regime" above). It was striking how worn out and exhausted the women there looked. The wives of Nana's grandsons, 17 and 19, were young mothers, but had already lost their fresh looks. When we were sitting at the nicely set table of their respectable home, I was haunted by the picture of the Bosnian cabin in the forest with the laughing people before it. Slowly it became clear to me that the refrain which I heard over and over again from the mouths of young and old women alike—"we have no substitute"—was a sigh for the lost zadruga.

From the vivid descriptions of the Serbian peasants, the difficulties of rational working methods and of the production for the market became obvious. The sturdy figures and proud bearing of the Serbian men in their brown homespun woolen clothes appeared to be a match for every hardship, and one felt that they were fighters or sons and grandsons of fighters. However, when they talked of the altered economy, one sensed a helplessness—things were not developing the way they wanted; somehow they felt deceived and caught unawares. All of them complained that the work was much more strenuous and demanding than it had been before.

A few decades ago, there had been a lot more fallow land and pasturage, and the relatively small amount of tilled land was worked quite primitively. Ploughing and hoeing was done only once a year. The pigs were driven out to forage in the large oak and beech forests, and much less corn was needed than at the time of my interviews, when the pigs were fed in pens. Hence there used to be fewer corn fields and also less hoeing. Men used to work in the fields only after their marriage, when eighteen, nineteen, or twenty years old; now, however, even twelve-year-old boys performed heavy labor in the fields. The development went so quickly that every peasant noticed the changes in himself, and felt the heavy burden of it.

In another village, where they had begun to cultivate vegetables for the city, a few years before they had succeeded in organizing rational production for the market. But the more the agriculture became organized the more worn out the peasants seemed to be, especially the women. Men and women went to bed at 9 o'clock, and the women, who usually took the vegetables to market, often had to get up after two or three hours of sleep in order to be on time in the early morning. After selling their wares they rushed back to the village and worked in the fields till evening. The women complained about the increase in work even more than the men. They also told about the rivalry and competition of the housewives in furnishing their homes, in dressing their children and in providing bridal portions for their daughters.

418

Also, in a third village, where fresh milk for the city was the chief product, they complained about increased demands, especially in regard to the dowry of the girls, which was insisted on to an increasing extent: "for formerly the boy was worth one *dukat* (gold coin) and the girl a hundred, but now the girl is worth only one *dukat* and the boy more than a hundred!"

The peasants were completely unprepared for these difficulties. They had no reserves whatever, so that any new burden could ruin them completely. While peasant farms in Western Europe were much bigger, possessed better buildings, more stock, and, in part, money reserves, and were connected with credit institutions and insurance companies, all this was lacking here. The Yugoslav peasants had a standard of living near to the physiological minimum; starvation in the spring and until the new harvest was a regular occurrence in many areas. The technological backwardness from the time of the Turkish wars had never been overcome; the birth rates had dropped less than mortality rates. The minute plots of land, which resulted from the zadruga division and later divisions of inheritances among the many children, were not sufficient to give security to the peasant families. Any accident destroyed such a farm and family. If a cow died, if the harvest was ruined by drought or hail, if a tax payment fell due, or a fine had to be paid, catastrophe was unavoidable.

The fact that the whole peasant farm was based upon a single married couple was a constant danger. If the husband or wife died, if they were sick or unable to work, if they became drunkards, committed adultery, were imprisoned, even if the husband had to go into the army, then the farm was ruined. The peasants felt these dangers particularly acutely, because they compared them with conditions in the zadruga, which had always provided substitutes, aid, supervision, and support for the individual and also for the conjugal family which was part of it.

The dependence on the market was a factor of particular insecurity. The individual peasant suddenly felt his dependence on supply and demand and on politics, which meant an additional risk. All economic changes, both domestic and foreign, now affected them. All Dalmatia starved when Dalmatian wine could not be sold; entire Croatian districts went into debt if there was a stoppage in the export of eggs and fowl; all Bosnia trembled because of a conflict of exporters, when wagon loads of fresh Bosnian plums were not unloaded at the station in Vienna and began to rot, thus endangering further exports. The economic world depression deeply shook all parts of the country and brought years of famine to many areas which had become partly dependent on selling their products.

The dangers were especially strong because the village community too had broken up at the same time as the zadruga. In all patriarchal regions, the tribe, clan, or community had had its own organization, or at least a moral authority. The coherence was especially strong in the regions of tribal organization, in the Austrian Military March and in Serbia, with their village and district organizations. All this was weakened by the same influences which had destroyed the zadruga. The peasants suddenly found themselves seriously vulnerable on dwarfed peasant farms without any support or assistance.

The family conflicts did not disappear when the zadrugas were broken up. The pronounced pecuniary interests which had shared in the break-up remained to further endanger friendly relations in the family. The relations among brothers and sisters became dependent upon possessions and inheritance, the attitude to a fiancée or a wife took on a tinge of interest in money, and even regard of one's mother was influenced by her gold coins and her dowry. Economic rivalries within the family shattered its peace. Even where there was no conflict within the family, the selfish note became more prominent in the family egotism. Families now lived more separated from one another, and the village community no longer acted as a regulative element. The economically dependent members of the family were exposed much more than formerly to the tyranny of the privileged members.

All these negative phenomena in family life showed a special aggravation in regions where a money economy was introduced suddenly. Ruthlessness became a principle, the battle of everyone against everyone increased, the right of the stronger triumphed, and strife became the norm. In the regions with gradual, continuous development, all these phenomena appeared in a milder form, but they did not fail to appear. Here, too, was the economic regression which caused many men to emigrate overseas and in a way abandon their families, and relationships became influenced by pecuniary interests.

### Benefits

If the hopes in the economic sphere were deceptive, in another sphere they were not. Under the changing conditions, the status of dependent family members rose, the strict discipline was relaxed. But, while the new difficulties were realized immediately, the people

420

did not feel the benefits so soon. When the sudden changes occurred, the women who had been most completely engulfed by the patriarchal family did not know what was happening.

The precious woman, royally groomed, remained only in songs and in ethnographic museums. Now, though, she had been caught up in a whirlwind, the beauty of her clothes spoiled, disunity entered her home. Her husband was becoming rough, frequently drunk; there are quarrels with his parents, the children are obstinate, their debts are growing, everything is in a turmoil. In the earlier period, if there had been worrying and suffering, if the equilibrium was disturbed, everything soon came into balance again. A sign that the rhythm of life was undisturbed was the singing that accompanied the work and rest of women of the patriarchal era. The women then did not feel the unrest which comes with the hope that things could be changed, the efforts of moving the surroundings, the disappointments of failed attempts. Now the storm tosses the woman between dependence and revolt, between the husband's tyranny and his indifference, between heavy economic pressure and the temptation to spend money.

But the woman in this phase is not only confused and harassed, she is also, in a certain sense, more serene. The walls which seemed eternal have crumbled, the net in which she was caught has holes. Slowly she lifts her head. She begins to shape her life more actively, to discard the old customs of female submissiveness. Although a woman seldom lives through these big changes with open eyes, her breathing is nevertheless freer.

With abrupt transformation, the economic development and the status of women diverge. The economic circumstances change with great speed, yet the habits of people and the traditional relationships remain longer conserved. Old habits and customs remain as they would float in the air, and the old female submissiveness has a long life, much longer than the zadruga organization and the protective attitudes of public opinion.

In the period of the major changes, there exists between temptations and dangers of the independent farming a high tension. From one side insecurity threatens, from the other side independence and freedom is pulling. The two centrifugal forces which disturb the equilibrium of people in this period move in different directions. Recorded as graphs, the lines of security and the lines of personal freedom diverge like the blades of a pair of scissors. The next two graphs speak a plain language.

On Graph 59, two curves are entered in the regional tables: The curve of the slavish dependence of the woman and that of feminine insecurity. Feminine subservience is represented by the custom of kissing the men's hands, and insecurity by the fact that many girls remain unmarried.

Graph 59. Feminine subservience and insecurity

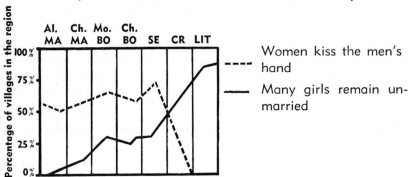

Women kiss the men's hand

Many girls remain unmarried

The graph shows the intersection of the lines. The insecurity of the women increases with the social situation unfavorable for establishing a family in the economically progressive regions, while the symbols of submission are lost along with the collapse of the family hierarchy. There is a lag, however; security vanishes from the life of the whole family, but individual freedom is increased for the dependent family members. In regions where a money economy began with a stormy development, as well as in regions where its penetration was slower, both tendencies reveal themselves and irrevocably change the relationships which prevailed during the time of a subsistence economy.

In Graph 60, this divergence is represented in the development of Croatian villages during the ninety years previous to this study. The factor of feminine submission is shown by the custom of having women stand during meals, and the security factor by the attitude of the public, which forces a man to marry a girl who is expecting a child. In Croatia, the custom of having the zadruga women stand during meals was very widespread. Illegitimate children were rare. At the time of the survey, the zadruga custom had disappeared, but there were a great many illegitimate children. The graph is constructed according to probabilities, except for the right column, where the survey results are entered.

422

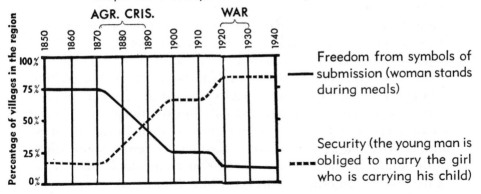

Graph 60. Development in Croatia, 1850-1940

The lines cross; the signs of greater freedom increase, while the line of security diminishes in the economically progressive regions.

The inner connection of positive and negative elements was responsible for the great dynamicism in the period of a penetrating money economy and the adjustment to it.

### Abrupt Transformation

Family life in the Slavic South developed differently than it did in the West. It did not, as in Western Europe, gradually adapt itself to the unfolding money economy or develop along with it. Neither was there anything resembling the evolution that occurred in the United States, where generations of Americans and successive waves of immigrants were carried along by the momentum of the expanding economy and followed new paths with great optimism. Almost everywhere in the South Slav regions, the patriarchal family structure collapsed suddenly, with all the characteristics of catastrophe and revolution. Zadruga and village organization fell apart under the pressure of influences which were felt by the peasants to have come from outside.

True, through the expansion of a money economy, a certain amount of prosperity had come initially to Croatia, Serbia, and Bosnia; the standard of living had risen, mortality and illiteracy were reduced. At the time of the investigation, however, these benefits had faded away, or had even been reversed. Almost everywhere the standard of living had fallen below that of a generation before, and an atmosphere of failure, deceived hopes, and pessimism prevailed.

The phenomenon of collapse and rebellion is the main impression when one studies family relations in the state of quick transformation. The most common and also the most significant characteristic of this phase is the extensive discord or disunion in the family which suddenly appears. In this moment the problematic of human relations becomes evident. When a centuries old, time-honored order is prevalent, when the economy is balanced, and the relationships standardized, the level of the quarrels in the family is low. Within a carefully delimited sector struggles and rivalries occur and are sanctioned by public opinion, and only in exceptional cases do the waves of violence, hate, and resentment rise high. In the restricted area, activity and aggression are worked out in heroic competitions of the youth, in the authority of the senior and the mother-in-law of the zadruga. In other sectors everything is peaceful.

In the phase of abrupt transformation, the phenomena of family strife and disunity appear. The scope of individual action and reaction broadens, and space becomes too narrow for the immensity of human aggression and willfulness. The level of discord in the family rises to great heights. The possibility and the need for individual solutions nullifies all rules and all consideration for the weaker members.

Conflicts and clashes within the family occur under the influence of certain socio-economic conditions with a regularity that seems like a law of nature. Just as pathological conditions have their norms, as bacteria have their laws of spreading, as an epidemic has its prescribed path, so the disturbance of equilibrium in family relationships has its order. Each individual conflict or brawl between a married couple because of a trifle is largely dependent upon the historical phase of the village where it occurs. In the obstinacy of the woman, in the bitterness of the man, in each of their reactions is reflected not only their individual characters and the history of their relationship but also the history of their area and their village.

The simile of an epidemic which breaks out after a disastrous earthquake suggests itself. At a certain moment, conflicts within families increased as if their members had been struck by an infectious disease. The effects of the disease were different for persons in different settings. People in environments which until then had not been touched by the "epidemic" succumbed helplessly, while persons in areas where the "disease" had appeared earlier seemed better able to cope with it and resisted it more effectively. The "virulence" of the bacteria also appeared to vary in intensity at different periods; in the last century the disease was not as contagious as after the First World War, and especially during the

1930's. In those regions where the infection had appeared first, a certain amount of immunity to reinfection had developed, and a slow process of convalescence had taken place. Only one region appeared to have regained an equilibrium.

There were two centers of abrupt changes: Croatia and Serbia. The following examples—quoted from questionnaires—from a Croatian and a Serbian village will show the differences as well as the common traits of two variants of unrestrained individualism.

### A VILLAGE IN CROATIA

The peasant farms are situated partly along the road and partly on the surrounding hills. The peasants supplement what they need for their living as hired labor in the nearby mine and through seasonal work in the fields. The married sons often separate from their father. As a rule, in such separations, litigation results, since the father is willing to give them only the most necessary possessions. There is a rhymed saying: "The son would like to keep the bowl and the winecup and drive his father out to the pig trough." When the parents have transferred their possessions to the children, they run the danger of being "left to the beggar's staff." Another saying goes: "He put down his spoon before he had finished eating."

There are a large number of unmarried old maids. Their chances of marriage are slim or, to be more exact, do not exist at all, since they remained unmarried in the first place because of poverty. There are many widowed but no abandoned (divorced) women. If a widow or a girl has children, she has no chances of marriage. If a rather large dowry is available, neither children nor advanced age, neither physical defects nor scandals matter.

Today the men marry at an earlier age than formerly, for economic reasons. Their possessions are supposed to be augmented by marriage.

The marriage is arranged by parents, relatives, intermediates. The boy and the girl often discuss it, but the parents negotiate concerning the dowry. Parents have the deciding word. They often force the son into marriage: "If you won't take this girl, you won't get another!" All the relatives and neighbors exert pressure on him to obey his parents, in the conviction that it is his duty. As a dowry, the woman brings to the marriage plots of land, money or a house. A dowry is the only prerequisite for contracting a marriage. The amount of the dowry is determined exactly before the marriage.

The wife manages what she gets when selling products in connection with the dowry. But she must give something to her husband "whenever he needs it." This is the reason for a great deal of strife and conflict.

The husband consults his wife concerning all household matters, but only when they are alone, . . . he does not want anyone to know about it. Infertility of the woman is not regarded as a fault but as an advantage.

The women do not demand any equality of rights and considered it amusing when I said that it was not right for a husband to mistreat and beat his wife. "The man is the man and a proper wife must obey him." "He knows what he is doing."

The men often beat their wives—regularly when they are drunk. In reply to my question as to the reasons, I received the answer: "Because of drunkenness, extravagance, jealousy, disobedience." The man not only beats his wife but also the other women in the household. Public opinion does not condemn beating women. Even if the woman is provoked, she must keep quiet. "If she has a long tongue" she is beaten.

Girls have to be bashful. If they openly look a man in the face during a conversation, they are considered wicked.

Many girls have premarital sexual relations. Virginity is valued and is a prerequisite for marriage . . . if the dowry is small. With a large dowry, however, virginity is unimportant.

Village public opinion by no means forces a youth to marry a girl who is carrying his child. He is not boycotted at all, but often is even regarded as a "hero," especially if the girl is from another village.

The young men usually have premarital sexual relations. They do not enter marriage unexperienced, since they have rarely lived abstinently. They have relations with the village maidens, wives, and widows—also with prostitutes during their military service, or if they work in the city. The public does not consider this wrong. They do not keep these relationships at all secret, but rather boast about them and like to relate sexual episodes.

The married men are not faithful to their wives; they have sex relations with other village women, with widows, waitresses, and also prostitutes if they go to the city. After the war there is more infidelity than before, especially on occasional visits to the city.

Married women are faithful; for them it is almost impossible not to be so, since they are watched continually and they would be very severely condemned also. Because of this they are very careful. If the husband learns of his wife being unfaithful, he beats her sometimes until she is unconscious. It means a terrible worsening of her situation, which already is very difficult. It makes a great difference also whether the public learns of this adultery or whether it remains secret.

Abortions are performed rarely. They are kept secret.

Parents beat the boys more than the girls. The children are beaten as long as the parents think themselves stronger. The children resist and also attack the parents, especially if they expect no inheritance.

The mother feels a closer relationship to the children than to the husband. She is especially intimate with her daughters as long as they are small. When the children are grown, then she is closer to her husband. They then form a common front against the children in order to protect and maintain their position. Children often resist the demands of their parents. They complain about being oppressed by their parents—secretly while they are young, then openly as they grow older. As a rule they revenge themselves on their fathers. If he has divided his possessions and they can receive nothing more from him, then they do not restrain themselves at all. In such cases the word of the old man has the least importance, especially if he is unable to work.                    (*Varaždin district*)

### A VILLAGE IN SERBIA

The village is situated on very fertile soil. Before the war (First World War) 80-100 per cent of the peasants lived in zadrugas. In the ten years after the war all the zadrugas were divided. There are about 5 per cent unmarried old maids. It is very difficult for them to get married.

In 60 per cent of the cases, marriage is agreed on by boy and girl, but usually with the knowledge and consent of the parents. Even if they marry against their parents' will, a reconciliation occurs later. It is customary for the boy to give 100 to 500 dinars to the girl's parents, depending upon his means.

Some husbands beat their wives, but in about 50 per cent of the families it never occurs. In 70 per cent of the families the husband consults his wife about his work, and purchases, and sales. Beating one's wife is not regarded as disgraceful, but as a man's right. Often they do it before others in order to demonstrate their manliness. Before the war, the men beat their wives even more. Frequently the peasants do not allow their daughters to attend school. They feel that women shouldn't read books "because they know too much anyway."

Only in the rarest cases do girls have intimate relationships—

perhaps 2 or 3 per cent of them. Virginity has great significance. 80 per cent of the young men live abstinently.

In half of the cases husbands are faithful to their wives. Before the war, there were fewer extramarital affairs.

Women are usually faithful to their husbands, but there are cases of conjugal infidelity. If they have relations, they have them with whomever they like. Usually they do not accept gifts or money except when they have become prostitutes. In 50 per cent of all pregnancies an abortion is performed in one way or another. The public knows about it, but does not condemn it unless the woman dies.

Except for the sexual relationship, husband and wife only very rarely have affection and love for one another. Even if the women have an extramarital affair, the partners usually are united only for sex and not by love and tenderness. The men are coarse. Sexual relationships are discussed in a cynical manner. Curses and insults are full of sexual expressions.

The father's authority has been reduced somewhat. Sons now are freer than formerly in their conversation and in their behavior toward their father. They decide for themselves about many personal matters such as choice of a bride or purchase of clothing.

Mothers are closer to the children than to their husbands, since there is so little love between marriage partners. The mother favors her sons more than her daughters, since she regards her boys as future protectors and bread-winners.

Grown sons show little devotion for their fathers, except where the fathers have money. Seventy per cent of the peasants' sons force their fathers to divide the farm and are successful in doing so. Earlier, before the war, the younger people showed much more respect for their elders, even if it was only empty formality in many cases. Now they show respect only when they are materially dependent on their fathers. (*Shumadia district*)

Although in regions of abrupt transformation, everything was in a state of flux, and although there were considerable differences between the Croatian and Serbian variants, it was easier to find symptoms and characteristics for this phase of family life than might be expected. The characteristics of this phase are the following:

The dissolution of the zadruga is the first sign of the disintegration of patriarchal life. Along with the appearance of money economy, the mass division of the zadruga spreads from district to district, and

428

as a result the entire subsistence economy breaks down, and so do all obligations within the family.

The conditions for entering into marriage become easier for men, more difficult for women. In this phase, the sex ratio usually changes in favor of the women but actually affects them adversely. The girl now has to possess a dowry and heritage in order to be able to marry; on the other hand, the man easily can find a wife.

Abundance of children has become a burden for the family. Birth control spreads irresistibly, chiefly by means of abortions. The birth rate has dropped significantly, as well as the average number of children in families.

In connection with the breaking-up of the zadruga, the family hierarchy also crumbles. The authority of the father is especially reduced. Respect for him disappears, the sons resist his authority. Severe conflicts between father and sons frequently break out about division of the property, even fights with brutal excesses on both sides. The father often attempts to maintain his authority by force. The children resist beatings as soon as they are physically able to do so.

The position of mother and daughters-in-law undergoes a great change. Although in places traditional symbols of the submission of the young woman remain, the docility and obedience of the snaha frequently disappears. As a rule she is the first to break through family discipline and to take her husband along with her. The peasant son, who along with his wife carries on a struggle for economic independence, ceases to support his mother's authority.

The brother-sister relationship changes fundamentally. The sisters no longer obey their brothers. Conflicts occur, frequently because of the sister's dowry. A fight about seniority and the heritage often develops between the older and younger brothers. These fights are decided according to "might makes right."

Relationships between young men and girls become freer. For the girl this freedom often has serious consequences. The young men enter into intimate relationships with them without any obligations, and thus reduce or destroy the girls' marriage chances. Often the girl and her illegitimate child are abandoned by the man. In this phase, public opinion does not support the girl, and does not influence the father of the child in her favor; if it tries to exert influence, it is rarely successful.

The authority of the husband wanes. The wife receives greater rights, although on her part this battle is scarcely ever waged consciously. With the loss of his high position the man also drops his dignified and responsible attitude toward his wife. Brutal beatings occur, especially while drunk, and also abandonment or "driving away" of the women. In spite of all this, the importance of the woman increases, and the husband often asks her for advice. The relationships and conflicts between married couples often take on the character of comradely arguments.

The relationship between man and wife becomes closer as the man's bonds to his relatives weaken. Individualistic tendencies to some extent color the marriage relationship. The individualistic factors in this period, however, usually have the significance of money interests and are not especially favorable to the choice of a spouse according to personal inclinations. Mercenary marriages occur frequently, marriages for love no more frequently than in the patriarchal phase.

Conjugal fidelity becomes shaken. As all binding obligations within the family loosen, monogamous attitudes weaken. In individual cases, circumstances result which almost mean the disintegration of the family, for example, if the husband wastes money because of extramarital affairs, or if the wife becomes a prostitute. However, such cases are exceptions. The weakening of marriage is evident chiefly in the husband's infidelity. Also, in this phase, the women suffer severe punishment for infidelity.

In this economic phase, all civilizing organizations, especially the school system, develop, and illiteracy decreases. On the other hand, alcoholism increases in connection with the disappearance of economic security from the peasant's life.

For this phase, great changes in all relationships are characteristic. Since the old norms are torn down at a rapid pace and the new ones are built up only slowly, a chaotic tone prevails.

As a result of the unrestrained individualism, which is the rule, personal freedom is assured only for those who are strong physically and economically.

## Continuous Development

While patriarchal family life has been known and studied for a long time, and family life in abrupt transformation almost forced itself on the observer, the phase which I called "New Stabilization" was unknown and had to be newly defined. It was surprising to learn that this phase of family life had as uniform and pure a style, and as solid an internal structure as the other two phases, despite its

430

peculiar composition of elements from the patriarchal and transformation phases.

In this phase of family life also, from a single attitude or gesture,
from a single answer, a conclusion can be drawn regarding a whole
series of modes of behavior or a whole complex of stereotyped relationships and automatic reactions.

Characteristic of this phase is the peculiar combination of old-style
and modern elements. Every gesture, every phrase of the people
indicates that the style oscillates from patriarchal to modern. The
peaceful relations within the family, the mutual fidelity and loyalty
of the spouses, the respect of the chidren for their parents are
reminiscent of the patriarchal atmosphere. On the other hand, the
relatively elevated position of the women and the younger people,
the realistic attitude toward money, the greater sexual freedom and
liberty of movement of the young folk resemble elements in the
phase of "abrupt transformation."

The atmosphere of this setting has more Western coloring than
in other regions. As in Western Europe and in America, the economic
factor had a strong influence upon family life, and through long
periods of time this influence brought progress. Then, when economic and political reverses occurred, the reactions of the people
were not stormy or catastrophic; people adapted themselves to the
situation and made the best of it, without hatred, despair, or neuroses.

Two examples—quotations from questionnaires—show typical
attitudes:

### A COASTAL VILLAGE

The village lies on a steep slope of the sea coast on the northern
Adriatic. Many people emigrate to America. Almost 40 per cent of
the population is hungry from Christmas until May. If they have
some *polenta*, corn meal mush, or if the weather is favorable for
fishing, they are lucky.

Wine and brandy are important products. During the week, that
means, at work, wine is regarded as food, on Sunday it brings pleasure and contentment. Circumstances haven't changed on this score;
they also give no indication of changing.

There were zadrugas in this village, but they had already disappeared by the end of the last century.

The men marry between twenty-five and thirty years of age, many
even later. If they had emigrated to America as youths and then
come back after thirty years with dollars, they get married in the

village and return again to America—with or without their wives. In former times they used to marry younger. The many seamen and emigrants marry only after they have saved up something. Formerly most of them stayed in the village and married early.

There are many unmarried maidens. Their marriage prospects are slim.

Young men and girls seldom marry directly against their parents' will, but such cases do occur: The girl's parents often oppose marriage simply so that they won't have to provide a bridal portion if the marriage takes place. At the same time, they quarrel with the young man's parents. Six months after the marriage, everyone is reconciled and they continue to live peaceably. The goal was attained—they didn't have any expenses.

The woman handles the money in most cases. It can be said that the woman handles up to 90 per cent of all the money that enters the house. Here the wife is the boss in the family. She can even contradict her husband in front of children or strangers. The man works much harder than his wife. The woman goes to the nearby town with the products; she sells brandy, oil, figs, wine. She has more contact with people than her husband. She also has greater natural intelligence. The man stays at home and works almost like a servant. This is because the man is so exhausted by working in the stony, rocky soil that he doesn't want to bother about anything when he comes home. Very rarely does it happen that the man beats the woman. Indeed, it has been common knowledge for a long time along the whole coast that the people of this region are lenient to their women and that the women are much more skillful and that they run the house.

Morals are quite strict. Virginity of the maidens is not especially protected, because girls who have had a love affair cannot marry anyone other than the boy with whom they had lived. They know themselves that it is very difficult to get married if they were engaged and then broke off. The boy also has trouble finding another girl.

Married men usually are faithful to their wives—they don't even dare think of another woman. Married women are 100 per cent faithful. Even if the men have emigrated, their wives are faithful in probably 95 per cent of the cases. They are abstinent and endure it.

There is no birth control because it is regarded as a mortal sin and the word of the spiritual leader is regarded as holy. Abortions seldom occur. People are very religious—Catholic—and fear Hell

432

more than a family with ten children. "One must accept as many as God gives."

Children are not brutally beaten, older children especially are not beaten. Parental authority is respected, and serious strife scarcely ever occurs. If the father is unable to work, the property is divided, the father stays in his own house and each child feeds him in turn— each week he eats his meals with a different one.

The mother feels close bonds with her husband. The bonds between mother and daughter also are especially close.

I do not know when this subordinate position of the man had its start. In any case, it existed before the war (First World War). The father's authority in regard to the children has not decreased recently.

### A DALMATIAN ISLAND

The island is stony. The village is located in the rocky Karst. Many peasants are stone masons. A great many emigrate to other countries. There are no zadrugas. Usually only the parents live together with their children.

The men marry late, from twenty-four to thirty years of age; girls marry from eighteen to twenty-four. There is quite a large number of unmarried old maids. The chances of marriage are slight. This is also true of widows.

The woman is not regarded as a servant but as a housewife and comrade. She does not kiss the man's hand, and she sits at the table at the same time as the man.

Girls frequently have relations with their chosen men. Virginity before marriage has great value, but if it is lost with her fiancé, this has no further influence upon a normal marriage.

The young men live abstinently until they have chosen a girl whom they desire to take as a wife.

Husbands usually are faithful to their wives. Women likewise. Only some women, whose husbands are abroad, are unfaithful. However, even most of these women live abstinently.

In most cases the younger people respect their elders. It is a disgrace to raise one's hand against an elderly man or to make fun of him.

Parents affirm their authority mainly by "kindly advice," and they are supported by public opinion.

Features of this phase are not difficult to determine, since all elements are adjusted to set customs and rules even when they are not derived from prehistoric times. The characteristics of the phase of "New Stability" are as follows:

There are no zadrugas. In most villages, they had been divided up several decades previously; in others, there apparently had never been any. There is much less fighting and strife between married sons and parents than in the areas of abrupt transformation. The young married sons no longer struggle for independence and division of the property at any price. Often three generations live together without zadruga rules but also without conflicts.

The marriage prospects of the girls are worse than in the other phases. Dowry and heritage are granted to the daughter to the full legal extent. Although the material interests are perceived clearly, the selfish and brutal note is very rarely pronounced. Material interests by no means form the main motive in the choice of a wife.

An abundance of children means a burden. In this phase there are significantly fewer births and fewer children than in the other phases of development. Limitation of births is not carried out mainly by means of abortions as in the phase of abrupt transformation.

The father's authority is not as great as in the patriarchal phase. The sons also have fewer conflicts with him and no resentments as in the phase of abrupt transformation. The sons, who enjoy great privileges, as a rule show a polite, sometimes even a devoted attitude toward the father. The father is rather lenient toward the children. Brutal beatings scarcely occur.

The mother's position is changed to the extent that she has closer ties to her husband than in earlier phases. The mother-in-law, the svekrva, does not possess unqualified authority. Relations between mother and daughter-in-law, as a rule, are friendly. The married son also is more attached to his mother than in the abrupt transformation phase.

Progressive as well as conservative elements appear in the relations between young men and girls. Freedom in erotic matters has become greater. Premarital sexual relations are frequent but without a libertine or cynical note. Usually boys and girls who have been intimate marry one another. Public opinion does not exert strong pressure to make a young man marry the girl who carries his child. The man does it voluntarily in most cases.

The position of married couples is old-fashioned in the sense of stability and progressive in the sense of greater equality of rights for the women. It is not customary to beat women; if it occurs, it is condemned by public opinion. The woman plays an important role within the family.

In a sense, the ties between married people are more intimate than they had been in earlier periods. In the choice of the marriage partner, besides the possession motive, love and sympathy play a certain role. While the links of a married man with his relatives become looser—usually indifferent with his sister—they become closer with his wife.

Marriage is stable, almost more so than in the patriarchal epoch. Fidelity of married women is the rule, even if the husband is absent for years, although public opinion exerts no pressure in this respect. The men also usually remain faithful to their wives, especially as long as they stay in the village. In its monogamous attitude, this setting agrees perfectly with that of the patriarchal one.

In the reduction of illiteracy, a progressive factor is evident.

The stability of norms in this phase of new equilibrium is similar to that of the patriarchal regime. However, there is more equality of rights between family members than in other periods. The valid norms themselves apply to the enlarged sector of individual freedom. In this phase, all relationship of new origin adopted legitimate forms and ceased to be objects of conflict.

Can family life in the phase of new stabilization be regarded as the future form of the family which is in abrupt transformation? In other words, can we conclude, in analogy with regions which have had a continuous development, that the family will also consolidate again in other regions in accordance to rules similar to those in the villages observed here?

Family life showing "new stabilization" occurred mainly in the Littoral regions: These regions, however, developed under very special circumstances. Thus, all conclusions on a basis of analogies must be drawn with great caution. A development such as that in the Littoral can never be repeated; the penetration of money economy can occur nowhere in such an early period of development and never as by such gradual stages. One can no longer expect anywhere the formation of peculiarities of the Littoral region with the unity of conservative and progressive elements, of friendliness and realism.

In spite of these considerations, however, the evolution of a new stability in the Littoral appears to correspond to a general tendency rather than to any regional peculiarity. The question whether the characteristics of new stability are conditioned mainly by regional tradition or by the phase of development can be decided with certainty only if the method of investigation is developed further. Therefore, in order to come nearer to a conclusion about the character of conflict and violence in the family, I worked out a technique for a "differential diagnosis" of the evolutionary phases.

## Evolutionary Types

From the start of this study, the impression of phases of development was strong, and during the research work these phases became ever more real to me. Yet they were not defined so clearly that I could indicate to which phase any single village should be classified. To make this possible, it was necessary to find those features of each phase that were typical enough to define it exactly and to promote it to an evolutionary type with strictly delimited borders.

Beginning with the patriarchal regime, I looked for the characteristics common to all villages which had given the general impression of a patriarchal style. After experimenting with a large number of questions, five were chosen as the surest indications of a patriarchal regime. They were formulated, in accord with the phrasing of the questionnaire, as follows:

1. All girls marry. There are no old maids or only in exceptional cases.
2. Birth control by abortion does not exist, or only exceptionally.
3. The attitude of the sons toward their father is full of respect or at least polite. Serious conflicts between father and sons do not exist.
4. The brother gives orders, even to his older sister.
5. Young men live abstinently; those with premarital relations are exceptions.

Of these characteristics, the two most consistent and of greatest symptomatic value for the patriarchal regime are the devotion of the sons to their father and the sexual abstinence of the young men. In no patriarchal area were there deviations from these norms.

Each village—that is, every questionnaire—was then examined, and each had to satisfy the stipulated requirements in at least four questions before it was designated to the patriarchal type. The most important questions were examined more thoroughly and judged more strictly. After the selection was finished, the villages of the patriarchal type were entered in the regional table. Graph 61 shows the break-down of the patriarchal villages by region:

436

## Graph 61. The Patriarchal type

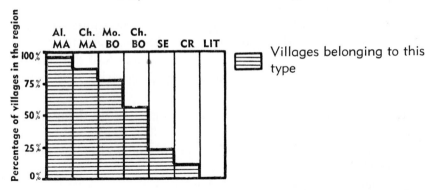

Villages belonging to this type

The graph shows that our supposition was sound; in the old-style regions, patriarchal family life was dominant in the largest number of villages. The relative number of patriarchal villages decreases with striking regularity as the distance from the old-style regions increases; the curve does not stray in a single place from its over-all direction.

This graph also proves that the place given to the various regions on the basis of the principle of seniority was well chosen, and the great difference which shows up in the graph between Serbia and Bosnia proves that it was correct to include Serbia among the "modern" regions.

Next, the trends of the abrupt-transformation phase were examined. Five characteristics were chosen as appearing regularly and as symptomatic. They were formulated as follows:

1. Birth control by abortion is widespread.
2. The attitude of the sons toward their father is without respect; conflicts between them are frequent.
3. In choosing a wife, many conflicts arise between the son and his parents.
4. There is much unfaithfulness among married women.
5. Marital unfaithfulness of men is increasing.

The attitude of sons toward the father, the abortions, and the infidelity of wives were of the greatest symptomatic importance, and these questions were given particularly thorough consideration.

There was no question of determining the boundaries between the abrupt transformation and the patriarchal types of villages since they are so fundamentally different that there are almost no borderline cases. Classifying the questionnaires to this type was no more

437

difficult than with the patriarchal type—a sign that it is really a life style with a definite profile.

For the delimitation of the type of "new stabilization," which developed under conditions of continuous development, it was necessary to find symptomatic traits for both components of this style, the moral-conservative and the economically progressive. I chose the following indices:

1. There is no zadruga. Married children live by themselves or with their parents without zadruga rule.
2. The men marry relatively late, usually only after the military service.
3. There are many unmarried women.
4. Many young men have premarital relations.
5. Married women as a rule are faithful.

Although these indices do not reflect the characteristic tranquility and consolidation of this phase, they are, nevertheless, well suited to delimiting it as a type. The late marriage of men, the absence of zadrugas, and the poor marriage chances for the girls are symptomatic of the adjustment to money economy. The intimate relations of young men are signs of greater individual freedom, while the faithfulness of wives represents the stable, moral element and a connection to the patterns of the patriarchal setting.

In trying to establish the boundaries of the type of new stabilization, two different kinds of dubious cases were found: In Dalmatia a transitional form between the patriarchal type and the type of new stabilization; in Slavonia a transitional form between the type of new stabilization and that of abrupt transformation. All villages of the type of new stabilization were in the western part of the country and were Catholic. None were from the typically Balkan areas.

The villages of new stabilization and those of abrupt transformation were entered in one regional graph; Graph 62 has a surprising regularity.

In this graph, the nearly equal steps suggest the durable and irrevocable drifting away of family relations from the patriarchal norm without regard to the rate at which subsistence economy is disintegrating. Both types of adjustment to the "new economy," although different, are nevertheless related, creating an indivisible entity. The regular growth of the solid areas in these graphs shows that the hypothesis of stages of development was sound and the sequence of the historical regions in the scale was correctly chosen.

Graph 62. Two types of family life

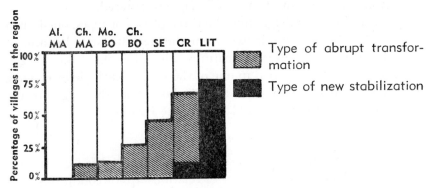

Type of abrupt transformation

Type of new stabilization

When all the villages had been divided into these newly created categories, I realized that the partition of the tables or graphs into three types was not enough for the interpretation of the statistical results. The tables had to be broadened in order to make the tendencies in family life—"the evolutionary lines"—clearly visible.

A principle related to the regional one—national-denominational grouping—offered a possibility. The patriarchal type was divided into the Moslem and the Christian groups, and the type of abrupt transformation into Serbian and Croatian groups of villages. The new table according to types was divided into five parts:

Patriarchal type of family life, Moslem variant (Pat. Mo.)
Patriarchal type of family life, Christian variant (Pat. Ch.)
Type of abrupt transformation, Serbian variant (Tr. Se.)
Type of abrupt transformation, Croatian variant (Tr. Cr.)
Type of new stabilization (N. St.)

In each of these groups, villages from different regions and areas were entered. While the regional principle was abandoned, a national-denominational element was introduced, which was a factor of decisive importance for all relationships and had also an evolutionary note. The order of "seniority" was not difficult to decide, I was in doubt only about the first place in the table, but I soon found that the Moslem variant of the patriarchal type belonged at the head of the scale.

To the Moslem patriarchal group belonged villages from Macedonia, Bosnia, and other areas; to the Christian patriarchal group, villages from all regions except the North and the West of the country. To the two variants of abrupt transformation, villages from all regions except the two extremes—Albanian settlements and the

Littoral—were designated. To the group of new stabilization, villages from the coast and from Slavonia were entered.

In classifying the villages into the three phases or types, one-fourth of the villages were eliminated from the new statistics because of their doubtful and transitional natures. Three-fourths of the villages, however, could be included in one of the three clearly defined types. This was the first success of the new method. The advantages for the solution of the problems raised will be shown soon.

## Lasting Changes

Using the new method, several changes of family life were statistically reexamined. First a number of relationships or conditions were worked out which, when investigated with the regional method, showed results leading farther and farther away from the patriarchal base. The curve on these regional graphs seems to strive toward the infinite as it runs through all regions in an uninterrupted direction. These conditions stray more and more from the patriarchal norm regardless of whether the economic changes occurred gradually or abruptly. The newly established relationships are not symptoms of a temporary crisis but are permanent traits connected with money economy, never returning to previous patterns.

The first example is from the realm of individual freedom and sex morals. Graph 63 shows the premarital intimate relations of young men and can be compared with the Graph 26, page 164 in the chapter "Boy and Girl."

Graph 63. Sex relations of unmarried men

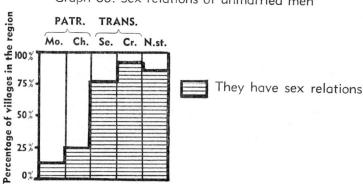

As can be seen, in 95 per cent and 80 per cent, respectively, of the villages of the patriarchal type, young men lived abstinently; in the type of abrupt transformation the figures were 30 per cent and 7

per cent, respectively; and in the type of new stabilization, 10 per cent.

(Methodological note: Since the premarital love life of the young men was one of the test questions for classification with the patriarchal type or the type of new stabilization, this graph has the following additional meaning: Of the Moslem villages belonging to the patriarchal type, 95 per cent follow the demand of sexual abstinency for young men; of the Christian patriarchal villages, 80 per cent. Of the villages belonging to the new stabilization type, 90 per cent follow the demand of premarital affairs.)

In this graph, one sees the same unbroken rising line as in the regional graph. In the graph according to types, one can see several important details which are not apparent in the regional graph. The type graph reveals two areas with a significant difference of levels. In both patriarchal variants, the level of premarital relations is very low, while in the total non-patriarchal area the level is raised by almost 50 per cent. Here is plainly and clearly what we presumed, but was not clearly apparent in the regional graphs, namely the gap between a patriarchal regime and one in which patriarchal life had collapsed abruptly. The difference in the height of the columns between these two areas is not apparent in the regional graph. This difference betrays the great change in theory and practice of love life and sex morals during the rapid dissolution of the subsistence economy and of the patriarchal regime.

The second example is taken from the chapter "Husband and Wife" and presents the husband's consultation of his wife. How different this graph is from the regional Graph 41 on page 274.

The curve in Graph 64 is much simpler and straighter than that in

Graph 64. Does the husband consult his wife?

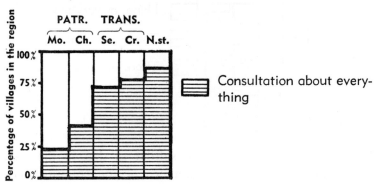

Consultation about everything

the regional graph. Here the deviation from the main direction, which occurred in the regional curve, has disappeared because the circumstance on which the deviation had been based was of no importance for the central problem. Here, more clearly than previously, is revealed how, parallel with the introduction of the money economy, the equality of the wife's and husband's positions developed. The leveling of the nonpatriarchal area, i.e. the smallness of the difference between the two parallel types of abrupt transformation, shows that the consulting of wife by her husband, which had its beginning with small holdings and individual property developed, was never given up.

(Methodological note: In the example the husband's consultation of his wife, one can observe the interrelationship of all manifestations of one family type. In the previous graph, one could object to the type method in that it pointed out obvious, and therefore unimportant, results; for the result [the abstinence of young men in a patriarchal environment] was known in advance because the villages had been selected according to this characteristic. This is why the usefulness of the type method is more apparent regarding the question of the husband's consulting his wife. If the inner structural connection among all characteristics of one type were not so strong, it would not offer such a clear statistical result and such a plain graph about conditions which had not served as indicators for the classification into types of family life.)

In the following graph, the question of marriage chances of girls from the chapter "Marriage" is presented:

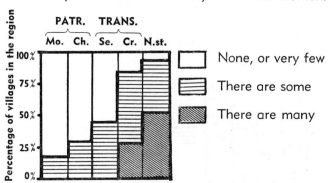

Graph 65. Are there many unmarried women?

The rising line of this graph is similar to that in the regional Graph 27 on page 175. The difference of the columns between

Serbian and Croatian villages is the same in both graphs. It is note-worthy that, with regard to this question, there is no great difference in column height between the patriarchal area and that of abrupt transformation in the Serbian variant. In contrast, there is a remark-ably large difference between the Serbian and the Croatian variants. The "jump" in the development occurs in the midst of the abrupt transformation area. While the Serbian villages, on the question of marriage chances of girls, reflect patriarchal conditions, the Croatian villages tend toward the type of the new stabilization. This graph supports our assumption that in the regional graph the major differ-ences between the Serbian and Croatian regions are not based on regional characteristics; the economic development of the Croatian villages was fundamentally different from the mode or the level of development of the Serbian and other Orthodox villages in formerly Turkish territory.

(Methodological note: Since the question about the marriage chances of girls determined classification within the patriarchal type or the type of the new stabilization, this graph has the following additional significance: 88 and 80 percent, respectively, of the patri-archal villages corresponded to the proposed requirement of favor-able marriage chances; 93 percent of the villages of the new stabiliza-tion corresponded to the demand of unfavorable marriage chances.)

A last example is a graph concerning the size of the family from the chapter "Patriarchal Regime." It explores whether, in the vil-lages, zadrugas, transitional forms, or small families were the rule.

Graph 66. Who as a rule is included in a household?

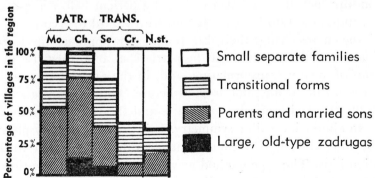

Comparing Graph 66 with regional Graph 1 on page 38, several differences as well as some conforming characteristics become ob-vious. In the type graph, the peak of the curve is not at the most ancient variant—the Moslem variant of the patriarchal type—but at the Christian variant. Thus, in comparing villages of equal development, one finds fewer living in zadrugas in the Moslem than in the Christian group. This confirms our supposition that Islam was a certain impediment in the development of the zadruga. The type graph shows another peculiarity, namely two peaks of the disintegration of the zadruga. The second peak is in the midst of the area of abrupt transformation. This again confirms our supposition that the money economy penetrating the Serbian villages (particularly in Serbia itself) did not destroy the zadruga as rapidly and irrevocably as in Croatia. The first waves of money economy which came to Serbia brought many advantages to the peasants; in Croatia, the new economy was linked with the agricultural crisis of the seventies and other unfavorable circumstances, thus it first of all brought misery and starvation.

Many relationships and conditions changed irrevocably, such as the break-up of zadrugas; birth control; the custom of the dowry; the diminishing distance between husband and wife; freedom of the younger members of the family, especially the young men; greater sexual liberty; and the peripheral problem of illiteracy.

The simple lines of the type graphs show plainly that the economic changes were responsible for the major differences in family relationships in various settings to a greater extent than traditional regional differences.

### Transitory Changes

Regional graphs concerning another series of phenomena and relationships look like the fever charts of a patient before and after a crisis. Inquiring into family relations with regard to accord and discord, the curves change their direction as they approach the Littoral region. From the low level of the patriarchal area, they rise in the regions of abrupt transformation, and, in the areas of the new stabilization, sink to the same level as before. The curves rise and fall with the regularity of a law of nature and the resulting semicircles have an almost incredible symmetry. Is it the evolutionary phase or the regional-traditional element that plays the decisive role in these relationships? The type method may help to solve this question.

When studying family conflicts within a regional framework, we cannot know with certainty what part is played by the regional peculiarity—the traditional proneness to fighting and feuding in every area—and what part is played by the time factor, the "infection"

444

spreading from the penetrating money economy. It becomes possible to dig deeper in the process of the "illness" and the nature of the "infection" only when new conditions are created for further research. The type method is like a laboratory or clinical method. It is similar to the practice of a physician doing research on some new epidemic, who sends his patients to the hospital for observation in order to separate the effects of the virus from the specific influence of the environment. In the following examples, the curves of the regional tables show a recurrent direction and suggest a spiral development.

The first example of disturbed relations is ill-treatment of women from the chapter "Husband and Wife." Regional Graph 39 on page 258 shows a curve with a strikingly high point in Serbia, declining in the Littoral villages to a level almost as low as that of the Albanian villages. Graph 67 is arranged according to types.

Graph 67. Do husbands beat their wives?

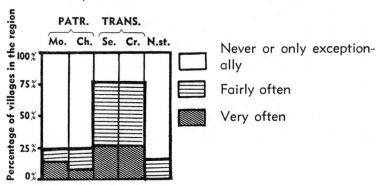

Graph 67 shows an impressive simplicity. Each of the three phases emerges as a complete unit. There is no difference between the variants—the graph could have been divided into three instead of five sections. As in the regional graph, the steep ascent and descent of the curve shows the stark difference between the patriarchal and the newly stabilized environment on the one hand, and those in abrupt transformation on the other. But there is one significant difference between the two graphs. In the graph by the types, the Serbian and Croatian variants of the abrupt transformation type are identical; there is no peak in the Serbian section, which means that in both Serbian and Croatian villages in the process of stormy economic change, women are subjected to the same rough treatment. Besides,

445

the graph shows that in all Serbian villages, regardless of phase, ill-treatment of women is common. Women are beaten in Serbia (including the other villages which were subsumed in that variant) in the transformational villages as well as the patriarchal villages and those in in-between stages. If this were not so, the curve could not have reached the outstanding height it did in the regional graph. This confirms our supposition that the frequency of ill-treatment of women in Serbia is not the result of abrupt transformation, but is rooted in old custom.

In the second example, ill-treatment of women is shown from two points of view: One outline indicates the frequency of women being beaten by their men; the other demonstrates public opinion of such treatment. (Compare with Graph 40 on page 269.)

Graph 68. The disciplinary right of the husband

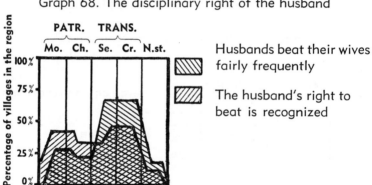

Husbands beat their wives fairly frequently

The husband's right to beat is recognized

On Graph 68, as on the regional one, it is evident that in the phase of abrupt transformation men beat their wives in spite of the fact that public opinion was opposed to it. Practice lags behind ideology. In the patriarchal setting, to the contrary, the practice favored women more than the theory.

This graph too shows the complete uniformity of the areas of abrupt transformation. The graph by types differs from graph by region also by a bolder relief, which means that the gap between practice and theory to the disadvantage of women is characteristic for villages of the abrupt-transformation type.

The third example shows the changes that have taken place in the ill-treatment of women.

On Graph 69, the relief is deeper than in the regional Graph 42 on page 283. The area of abrupt transformation is divided between the

446

Graph 69. Changes in the ill-treatment of wives

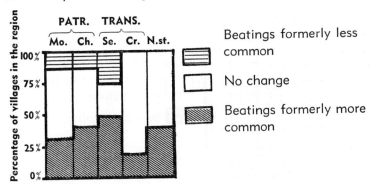

Serbian and the Croatian variants, and significant differences appear. In the Serbian variant, the changes are particularly marked in both directions. In the Croatian variant, too, the village conditions show more distinctly than in the regional graph. The white area predominates here, indicating a certain balance. During the period tested by our interviewers, family life in the Croatian villages did not change much, which proves that during that period the strongest jolts of the "earthquake" had already passed. Family relations had partly stabilized on a new basis. The custom of wife beating was conserved to a certain extent, although it no longer had the moral support of the public. There was no longer an acute struggle for position, but an old habit had been partly preserved.

The next example is borrowed from the chapter "Mother and Mother-in-law" and investigates whether the young husband is more on the side of his mother or of his wife in a conflict between the two. We remember that in the patriarchal setting the bond between the married son and his mother was stronger than in a later phase. In the earlier phase he tended to support his mother's authority, whereas in the later one a stronger bond with his wife is created in connection with their struggle for economic emancipation.

A comparison of Graph 70 with its regional equivalent, Graph 14 on page 442, reveals the flatness of the regional graph relief as contrasted to the steep type graph curves, which make interpretation easier. The area of abrupt transformation is divided, the situations in Serbia and Croatia were very different since Serbian zadrugas were not transformed as abruptly as in Croatia. In Serbia, invading money economy raised the living standard of the peasants, thus preventing a break within the zadruga and also preventing an alliance of the young couple in a struggle against the father of the house. The traditionally

Graph 70. Does the son take the mother's or the wife's side?

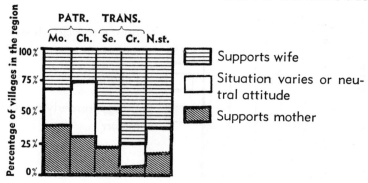

low position of the Serbian wife contributed to the young peasant's attachment to his parents rather than to her—in a conflict he was, therefore, frequently on the side of his mother. But in the Croatian variant the mother has completely lost her influence on the married son (and frequently forms an alliance with her husband). Our supposition of a "struggle of generations" in the transformation-type Croatian villages is thus strengthened.

The next graph (Graph 71), showing the relation between mother and daughter-in-law, also has a deep relief. As demonstrated in the chapter "Mother and Mother-in-law," peaceful or hostile relations between the two women run parallel with maintained or dwindled authority. Respect for the mother-in-law corresponded with the good relationship between the two women, especially in the first two phases of family development.

This graph displays a much simpler curve than regional Graph 13

Graph 71. Good and poor relations between mother and daughter-in-law

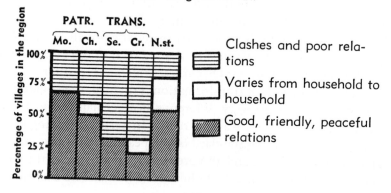

on page 107. The bulk of the conflict sector in the transformation area is uniform and undivided between the two variants. The Bosnian deviation from the main curve, which showed in the regional graph (for reasons irrelevant to the main problem), have disappeared here. The curve in this type chart resembles an ideal curve of disturbed equilibrium, such as we may see in a fever chart. Its steep lines show the great difference of the three types of family life.

The results of these reexaminations by the type method confirm our original supposition about the course which some phenomena of family life take, particularly conflicts. This method shows that we are actually confronted with a spiral-like development—the situation on a higher plane of progress reverts to the point of an earlier period. The symmetrical arrangement of the semicircular curves in the type graphs shows that family conflicts, particularly in the Croatian and Serbian villages, must be looked upon primarily as an equilibrium disturbance caused by an abrupt introduction of a money economy. The traditional predisposition of the individual region is of much smaller importance.

(The type method also shows that it was correct to evaluate the economic progress of the Littoral as of more importance than the seemingly conservative family relations; that it was correct to classify the Littoral areas as representative of historical progress and to place them at the end of the historical scale.)

### Conflicts and Consolidation

Is it possible to give definite answers to the questions raised in the beginning of this chapter? Are the conflicts in the family primarily dependent on the process of transformation or on regional peculiarities? Did the peaceful family life in the Littoral have a prognostic meaning?

One thing is certain. The stormy transformation of the economy had a parallel course with discord in the family. The sudden influx of money economy seems to a great extent responsible for violence and unfriendly relations in the family.

In favor of the theory that the time element is most important is that the regional curves rise in certain regions to a typical high and descend with almost incredible regularity in the Littoral when relations with regard to concord and discord are investigated. Since the falling of the curve begins in Serbian and Croatian villages the thought can be excluded that this is caused by the regional features of the Littoral; responsibility must lie in characteristics of the evolu-

tionary phases. Also, the fact that the variants of our types of transformation (Serbian and Croatian, Moslem and Christian) are level
on the type charts supports this theory. From features of the new
stabilization found in many Slavonic villages, we can conclude that
under similar economic conditions similar family relations are developing in spite of different regional traditions.

The type method gives this theory additional support. On the type
charts, the nature of the disturbed equilibrium becomes obvious.
These charts all look like fever charts; the low level of the curve
suggests organic balance, and the high, a disturbed balance. The low
level at the end suggests that the "normal" state is reached again and
the balance regained. According to these charts, the regional element
seems less significant than the evolutionary stage for every village.
When investigating the peaceful or feuding aspects of relationships,
the regional peculiarities seem to fade into the background.

The analogy of a fever disease, however, does not quite fit: A
complete cure of our "seriously sick" could not be established anywhere. The group of the "sick who had been discharged as cured" was
not entirely significant in appraising the course of the disease in
others, because this group had consisted of light cases to start with,
individuals who had become sick under different conditions, and had
been "immunized" before. Analogies with a group of "slightly diseased" do not lend themselves to prognoses; prognoses should be
based on the observation of the typically sick who had returned to
complete health and psychological equilibrium. Such a return to
health has not been observed here, however.

In Croatia, it was determined, for instance, that tension within the
family decreased as economic conditions became more stabilized; but
a condition of real equilibrium had not been found. Nowhere was
there a case where the sector of the new, uninhibited individualism
had been narrowed down to a point where conflicts were reduced
again to a low standard of individual cases.

While we can be certain that the conflicts in the family are dependent mainly on the phase of development of the single region, we
cannot be certain that in the future the patriarchal regions will go
the way of the "modern" ones. We cannot know whether the patriarchal regions will come into a similar state of unbalance as the
regions in stormy abrupt transformation. And still less can we foresee
whether the family in the regions of stormy transformation will
reach a state of new stabilization. Since it will never be possible to
duplicate the development of the Littoral, with its centuries of

gradual and advantageous influence of a money economy and the slow adjustment of people to it, it is most unlikely that similar results could develop in any other area. Although it seemed possible that with the consolidation of the economy the conflicts would decline and the wounds would be healed, we could not foresee whether relations would become as friendly and peaceful as in the Littoral. When relationships are once thrown out of balance, they can never again become like those which had never been disturbed. People who have fought are not the same as before. Traces remain—scars, bitter memories, and changed reactions.

When I entered the results of the survey into the tables and graphs during the first days of World War II, I assumed that in the regions of stormy changes the adjustment to money economy would become more complete, that the economic depression would be surmounted, and that family relations would become more peaceful. But when in the course of historical events the capitalistic economy was discontinued in Yugoslavia, the assumptions and the attempts at prognoses were overthrown. It was no longer possible to check their validity.

After the Second World War—to be sure—the subsistence economy continued to disintegrate at an accelerated tempo, together with industrialization and urbanization. Yet this planned economy cannot be considered the continuation of the money and market economy of the capitalistic kind. The evolutionary lines were broken, new waves and impulses of the economy were not immediately linked with the previous ones. The question whether the equilibrium of the family in the villages of abrupt transformation could be restored had there not been revolutionary changes remains open forever.

Only if the new situation were investigated, if the villages which I surveyed before the war were surveyed again, could answers be found to the questions I raised in the beginning of the survey. The answers might be of still greater scientific interest and more significance than if there had not been such fundamental postwar changes, although the answers could not be the precise answers to the old questions. Yet it could probably be resolved whether, and how much, the unrestricted individualism accompanying the onslaught of money economy is the decisive reason for discord in the family. Or else, does every revolutionary change, even one with a collective tendency, throw family relations out of balance, encourage struggles against authority and for positions, and diminish consideration for the weaker members of the family.

451

# Dissolution or Transformation of the Family

IN THE time of this survey, many pessimistic forecasts were made concerning the development of family relations, since the family in many parts of the country offered a picture of disintegration or collapse. But, in subsequent years, experience showed that the observers had underestimated the family's power of regeneration, something which had happened frequently before in times of crisis and upheaval. The pessimistic outlook was not justified.

The impression of serious illness given by the family of the thirties was partly deceptive. During the Second World War, it became evident that the family had been shaken only on the surface. In the days of ordeal, during bombardment, persecution, flight, exile, and concentration camps, the real greatness of family ties came to the fore. It was almost exclusively those who could rely on the help of parents, husband, wife, brothers, or children who escaped torture and death in the camps. Only the closest relations never gave up the struggle for a single person and had enough persistence to plan their rescue.

In this period, too, the love of children for their parents, which was thought to have weakened, showed itself clearly. In these periods of disaster, teenagers, up to then carefree children, frequently undertook to save their parents and their younger brothers and sisters. Though this generation—at least the city children—had grown up without any ideal of family life, the close ties of the family revealed themselves at that historic moment as still real.

As in an experiment, the tendency to preserve family life became evident among the survivors of German concentration camps. Thousands of young people were the only surviving members of their families. Many of them had been taken to camps (especially from Poland) as children and were liberated only five or six years later. Many had only a slight memory of their parents and home. When they had recovered physically after the liberation, the desire arose for marriage. They were not looking for sexual affairs; they had decided simply to found families, and they carried through this desire in spite of all impediments. In the UNRRA rehabilitation camps in Italy and Austria it was very difficult for young men to find wives, since many more girls than boys had died. The over-

as the only thing which could awaken
athy in which they were living.
ged completely. Only then did they begin
terest in their surroundings and in their
he terrible apathy into which they had
tly gave way. When a child was born to
ental equilibrium. Their passionate desire
eared spontaneously, as had their wish to
bies they showed extreme tenderness, and
nd spoil them in such a measure that they
rmal development of the children. All these
ically without conditioning, since many of
dly remembered home life or parental af-

was the physical and mental disposition of
arriages. Two or three years after the end of
usands of these children in the displaced per-
ny, Austria, and Italy. Though their parents,
ved bodily or mental injuries from their stay
bs, the babies were models of vigorous health
despite the fact that their parents spoiled them
y, where people are so fond of children, these
babies were constantly stopped in the streets because they surpassed
the Italian children in beauty. Their health and their grace surprised every observer. This also shows the power of regeneration of
the family—or perhaps of the human race.

Another postwar experience reflects the unexpected strengthening
of family ties and interest in the family. After the war, in the United
States a surprising change in attitude toward family life became apparent. Marriage figures rose suddenly, while the average marriage
age dropped by several years; marriages at twenty for the boys and
still younger for the girls became very frequent. The birth rate rose
considerably and soon became higher than in the South European
countries, with maximal birth rate figures as in Italy. Today in the
United States there are more than ten million children which continually cause a certain embarrassment to the statisticians who failed
to foresee them. Nobody, however, could have expected the radical
change in attitude of the young couples who started to plan big families and consistently carried their plans through. Only a few years
earlier much American writing in social psychology gave the impression that the modern family was undergoing a chronic decline, and

suggested that competent specialists were needed to introduce social measures to prevent further disintegration. Later development showed that here too the diagnosis was exaggerated, and that pessimism was not justified.

Other wartime experiences show the power of the need to live in families. During the war it became evident that it is nearly impossible to compel people to live basically differently than in small groups like families. In every refugee, prison, or embarkation camp, little stoves, pots and pans, straw or a blanket, appeared as if out of thin air. People showed that they would rather do their own inadequate cooking and sleep squatting in the cold, than stand at community kettle or sleep in a mass dormitory. People who were in solitary confinement in prisons and camps revealed that complete loneliness is one of the heaviest strains for a human being. Both living in barracks and living in isolation met with the same desperate resistance.

In the light of anthropological research, it is quite certain that, because the family may be shaken up, this does not mean that it is disintegrating. The family is with man and man has been part of it since he became "man." No extinct and no living tribe or nation has been without the family. As the age of man is considered about one million years, it seems quite improbable that a few decades of historic perturbation could uproot the oldest institution on earth.

The power of resistance of the family and its capacity for regeneration have shown themselves many times in history. The family has survived great migrations, tyrannies and revolutions, fatalistic and rationalistic, individualistic and collectivist turns of the pendulum and has never been essentially weakened, except for short periods. Nor can it be assumed that the family will disintegrate in the future. The family is too deeply rooted in human nature: It bridges the contradictions which result from the twin nature of man—as an individual and as a collective being—better than any other human institution. Not even the family, however, can overcome this contradiction completely.

# Appendices

## The Method Used

The method which I used in this investigation proved to be much more useful than I anticipated. In the beginning I had certain doubts, and only after many attempts and much checking was I convinced that the apparent weak points were not serious weaknesses and that the method was appropriate for exploring the collected material. I shall begin with a review of those points which caused me worry at the beginning.

1. I was afraid that the indirect method of questioning about intimate matters would not yield significant material; that my interviewers would receive irrelevant or untrue answers. This fear, however, was without foundation, for European villages are what may be called transparent. Since all villagers were born and raised in their village, they have known each other from early childhood, they also know about the parents and ancestry of the others as well as their own family. The houses of the peasants are often built in such a manner that every dispute can be heard in the entire neighborhood; in a zadruga, so many people live together that secrets cannot be kept.

While it would hardly have been possible to find a sufficient number of peasants who would give true information about their personal experience, we had no trouble in collecting reliable answers on general conditions. Peasants who would not always reveal their personal conflicts, fights for position inside the family, marital and extramarital relations, gave true reports about neighbors, relatives, and other villagers. My interviewers who had lived in the villages for years or were born there had a much better chance to learn about local conditions than either I or any newcomer in the village. (Reports from reliable witnesses are often more valuable than our own observations, as people will change their behavior if they feel watched by strangers.)

2. In the beginning, I hesitated to take villages rather than individuals or families as units for statistical treatment. However as I could not focus on close and distant objects at the same time, I chose a distant point of observation which opened up the desired vista: as I wanted to compare regions with each other I had to take villages as entities for the right perspective. (I had planned to supplement this study by an investigation of individuals and individual families; but this plan was made impossible by the outbreak of the war and could not be carried out later because the prewar conditions no longer existed.)

3. Another unknown element was the reliability of the interviewers.

Most of them I did not know and could not train. It was probably a stroke of luck that most of them were as conscientious, as they were shown to be by five test questions. The figures about legitimate and illegitimate births, the number of children in the families, percentages of men and women, and the number of illiterates which I received from the Office of Statistics, exactly checked with the data I had received from the interviewers. Minor mistakes which some might have made cancelled each other out.

4. I had been afraid that the statistical use of a relatively small sampling —305 villages in all—would not permit definite results. There was also the danger that the villages might not prove representative, as I had not selected villages but had simply chosen gifted teachers as interviewers. It was probably another stroke of luck that my apprehensions here also proved groundless. The results revealed that the statistical method yielded meaningful data which lent themselves to interpretation, in spite of the relatively small sample. The fact that the villages were typical and representative, could be seen in a comparison with the official figures of my test questions. I received from the Office of Statistics figures on communities, districts, and banovinas which checked with my own figures on the villages.

5. The questionnaire proved to be particularly suitable for encouraging the interviewers to concentrate on the problems raised and lead them to active inquiry. The questionnaire was less appropriate for the statistical treatment of the material because it asked for free formulations of answers. With this method, it is never easy to assign the answers to categories and deal with them statistically. However the advantage of the method of open answers was considerable for the study as a whole. Had I formulated the questionnaire with the main objective of receiving precise answers for statistical purposes, I could never have collected so much significant material nor would I have received so many original interpretations and initiative for further research on the part of my interviewers.

6. For a long time I was not satisfied with the regional classification of the material; I wanted to group the villages according to more generally valid, as for instance economical, standpoints. But after trying out several possibilities, such as distance from cities and traffic lines, standard of living, I realized that it was impossible to find precise indications that would distinguish the villages according to economic standpoints. Also I would have had to eliminate a large part of the material, as only a fraction of the villages belonged to clearly defined categories, as for instance sheep-raising mountain villages, pure agricultural villages, or fishing villages. All attempts to work over the statistical material without regard to region resulted in meaningless or meager information. The regional traits proved to be of fundamental importance in Yugoslavia. The dominant importance of the historical-political element of the country can probably

be explained by the fact that, until sixty or seventy years ago, all regions were at the same economic level of a subsistence economy, while the historical-political influences as well as the culture contacts were as different as one could imagine. Therefore I had to decide in favor of the regional principle for grouping the villages.

7. Another question presented itself: Were we justified in regarding the various regions as symbols of a step-by-step development? It seemed daring to adopt a working hypothesis which would allow one to draw conclusions from regions (measurements of space) to epochs (measurements of time). It was an uncertain undertaking to regard the patriarchal regions as an early stage, the regions of abrupt transformation as the present, and the Littoral region as a future development. In the course of the inquiry, it turned out, however, that this hypothesis and the grouping of regions according to it made possible many important conclusions and that the Littoral region had been given its proper place as representing the area of historical progress, in spite of some conservative trends and customs which in the beginning made me doubt my judgment. The grouping of the Littoral at the opposite end of the graph from the patriarchal region permitted me to recognize the retrogressive direction of some development trends indicating the transitory character of discord in the family.

8. One advantage of the method, which showed itself from the start, was the graphical presentation of the statistical tables. These line charts were most helpful, although from a technical point of view there may be room for objections. This simple technique, however, allows orientation at a glance, easy interpretations of the answers, and the comparison of the curves. Only the graphical presentation made it possible to grasp the situation in the whole Yugoslav region without a tiresome and time-consuming study of figures. The graphs helped greatly in the interpretation of the answers as they made possible a quick orientation of tendencies and trends in the entire country. Therefore the graphs stimulated me to undertake the labor and pain of counting the answers for all questions without machine for statistical treatment. They also give the reader the opportunity to follow easily what the figures have to disclose.

9. The method of grouping the villages according to evolutionary types also confirmed my interpretations of the straight curves which signified some of the relationships within the family. They were not the results of chance, nor were they dependent on regional peculiarities, but they were conditioned by the replacement of a subsistence economy or rather the penetration of a money economy, which remained a lasting factor. I also found a confirmation of my interpretation of retrogressive curves: The symmetry of the lines forming a half-circle, and especially the consistent level of the Serbian and Croatian variants, showed that the invading money economy was one of the main reasons for disturbances in the equilibrium of the family.

457

The applied method, built on unsure ground with foundations that seemed too weak to stand the strain of a test, proved to have a much larger load-carrying capacity than I could have hoped for. The methods and the techniques made possible most of the insights about regional characteristics, culture contact, phases of development, and the nature— and particularly the disturbances—of family relationships.

## Research Projects

Among the problems which emerged during the course of this investigation and which might stimulate further research, the following seem most important:

1. What relationship is there between the aggressiveness of people in their wider circles and their behavior within their family? Our South Slav material indicates two contradictory possibilities: Either the aggressiveness which dominates the wider circle of society increases aggressive attitudes within the family, or the aggressiveness in the one circle results in the opposite attitude in the other. The first alternative showed up in some South Slav regions of the first Yugoslav era, when a certain pattern of violence infiltrated from the state into the family, including aggressive tendencies, recklessness, and a belief that might made right. The second alternative was mentioned in connection with zadruga life during guerilla fighting against the Turks. As long as people had a chance to "work out" their aggressiveness in war and guerilla warfare, as bandits, pioneers, or freedom fighters, they apparently submitted easily to a strict family order. When, however, the chances for personal belligerent initiative disappeared, an unwillingness developed to submit to the demands of the family, and aggressiveness within the family grew tremendously. It would be important to explore whether, under all circumstances, man needs an area for his aggressiveness, so that he of necessity seeks a safety valve within the family if he has no chance to discharge his aggressiveness in his wider circles because of the demands of complete adjustment to the community.

2. Is the balance in the family shaken only by those social and economic changes which strengthen the individualistic traits, such as the penetration of the money economy into an area of subsistence economy? Or do all the great socio-economical changes—including those that strengthen the collective trend, such as revolutionary upheavals in Eastern Europe— result in a shaking up of the family, in increasing conflicts? How does the stormy technological process affect the family and does it by itself result in the fights for position and the aggravating of conflicts in the family?

3. Can regeneration or consolidation of family life be found, and under what conditions does it occur, if at all? Are there societies where the

family, once disrupted, becomes stable again? Are there generations which enjoy a more peaceful family life than their parents, and whose members recall discord and fighting within the family as a mark of rough customs of the past which stand in contrast to the humane and civilized customs of the present? Or do family relations, once thrown out of equilibrium, remain in an unbalanced state for long periods of time, so that several generations grow up in an atmosphere of roughness, fighting, and violence?

## List of My Interviewers

Brana Aksentijević, A. Altman, Ljubica Antunović, Vukosava Arandjelović, Ante Artić, Miladin Arsić, Jelka Augustinović, Sulejman Azabagić, Vlatka Babić, Petar Belanović, Dragica Benčak, Radmila Benković, Šefik Berbić, Paula Benić, Slobodan Blagojević, Radovan Boljanović, Mirko Bolfek, Stjepan Bosanac, Matija Bosanac, Ilija Bosanac, Petar Bobinac, Milenko Borić, Vukosava Božić, Toman Brajević, Anka Bunjevac, Stevan Carević, Ivan Cerovac, Viktor Cvitan, Ivan Čače, Bogdanka Čiplić, Nikica Čugelj, Ljeposava Deljanin, Vlaho Depolo, Božidar Dimitrijević, Ljubinka Dobrić, Margareta Dorčić, Ibrahim Dogladović, Esad Doko, Ladislav Dorčić, Dimitrije Donović, Petar Dragila, Zagorka Dragović, Uroš Drenović, Konstantin Djaković, Aleksandar Djordjević, Konstantin Djukić, Blažo Djuričić, Marija Erbežnik, Slavica Filipčić, Dorica Fiolić, Zlata Franić, Ivka Frank, Zvonko Frank, Šemsudin Gavran-Kapetanović, Metodije Garević, Mitar Gažević, Milanko Gogić, Josip Golac, Vukica Grbić, Ilija Grbić, Pero Grbić, Dragutin Grgičević, Josip Grotić, Dragutin Grohovac, Nikola Grospić, Jelena Grünwald, Djuro Guberinić, Izet Hadžimehmedović, Alija Hadžialijagić, Dragan Horvatin, Darinka Host, Mesud Hotić, Ante Hrovat, Ivan Jagodić, Ilija Janković, Dušan Jandrić, Stojimir Janković, Katarina Jerković, Milan Jevtović, Ignacije Jež, Radosav Jovančević, Milica Jovanović, Radivoje Jovanović, Mićun Jovanović, Zvezda Jovanović, N. Josipović, Trpko Kalajdžić, Ivan Kadić, Djordje Kalezić, Ante Kancijan, Eugenije Kartalović, Emil Kavgić, Tomislav Kalauz, Darinka Kehler, Predrag Kilaković, Marija Klarić, Božo Kolega, Andrija Kolembus, Grga Karlovčan, Ivan Kostelić, Olga Kostelac, Radomir Kostić, Petar Košutić, Petar Kovačević, Alija Krajišnik, Dragutin Krčelić, Eduard Kolano, Branko Kršnjavi, Miloš Knežević, Ljubomir Krneta, Franjo Klasan, Aleksandar Križanić, Vukajlo Kukalj, Vinko Lalić, Ljubica Lanović, Danica Lendjel, N. Levi, Tomo Lopičić, Miralem Ljubović, Derviša Ljubović, Marija Madjarić, Pante Mališić, Mijo Mandić, Spaso Marković, Borislav Manelić, Lazar Maksimović, Nada Marusić, Petar Matas, Katica Mažuran, Jefta Mendababa, Stjepan Merdžo, Milenko Mičević, Zlata Miholjević, Milislav Mijušković, Krsto Miljanić, Aleksandar Milih, Ante Miletić, Zarije Milačić, Mita Mitić, Ante Mioč, Esad Mekulović, Siniša Mihajlović, Milorad Milošević, Andjelija Miličević,

Dimitrije Momčilović, Branimir Molk, Katica Mogić, Ananije Mraković, Kosta Mudrić, Nikola Mugoša, Hasan Mujezinovič, Temeljko Najdović, Deva Nedžib, Osman Nijazi, Vojo Nikolić, Daut Nuredim, Radovan Nikolić, Stojan Obradović, Ahmet Omerhodžić, Jahija Osmanović, Ivanka Ožeg, Dorica Pajur, Safet Pašić, Muhamed Patković, Tomanija Pavlović, Katica Pavković, štefa Pazman, Stanko Paunović, Radovan Pejić, Vladimir Pejović, Stjepan Perčević, Zora Pešun, Mihajlo Petrovi, Miodrag Petrović, Radivoj Plavšić, Ante Plemić, Vera Polak-Tolnauer, Mijo Posavec, Djuro Potkonjak, Petar Prodanović, Ivan Pukanić, Tomislav Pureta, Jovan Radaković, Aleksandar Radulović, Hakija Raljević, Breza Rančić, Ivan Rauš, Ružica Rip, Slavica Roić, Nevenka Roca, Živadin Savatić, Ibrahim Sefić, Radivoj Sečujski, Ivan Semeraj, Vilko Simčić, Milan Savić, Nikola Simić, Josipa Smolčić, Rudolf Srnak, Mila Srdanov, Dragan Smolčić, Boško Svilokos, Svetozar Stojanović, štefa Stanešić, Slobodan Stanković, Mirko Stojanović, Djordje Subosin, Hedvig Spinčić, Mirko Stojnić, Ivo Sunarić, Danica Šanjeg, Stjepan Šeremet, Jurja Šafarić, Ljuba Šikić, Matko Šebelić, Mijuško Šibanić, Ruža Šimunčić, Vera Šoić, N. štol, Ivan Štefotić, Radmila Šubakić, Šaćir Tanović, Branko Terzić, Katarina Terzin, Anka Tomašević, Vjenceslav Tomljenović, Jovanka Tomašić, Anka Tomašević, Josip Tomljinović, Drago Tvrdeić, Anka Toljanić, Lenka Trivanović, Dr. Vinko Uravić, Eduard Vajnaht, Mara Veselić, Vlado Veselić, Dimitrije Vasiljević, Špiro Vidović, Mirko Vojvodić, Veljko Vučević, Zora Vučević, Miloš Vučević, Dušan Vrhovac, Petar Zdravković, Ruža Zebec, Hasan Zupčevič, Franjo Žagar, Salih Žilić, Alojzija Živković.

Quite a few of my collaborators are not listed (56). Many of the young village teachers feared persecution and, preferring to remain anonymous, did not disclose their names.

## List of Surveyed Villages

MACEDONIA, SANJAK

Village of Kozjak, district Prespanski; Resan, district Prespanski; Carev Dvor, district Prespanski; Podmočani, district Prespanski; Bač, district Morihovski; Srednji Egri, district Morihovski; Brod, district Morihovski; Dunje, district Prilep; Korošište, district Struga; Vevčani, district Struga; Bomovo, district Gornjodebarski; Silame, district Gornjopološki; Selokući, district Gornjodebarski; Broščica, district Debarski; Velešte, district Struga; Megorci, district Djevdjelija; Huma, district Djevdjelija; Pirova, district Dojranski; Drenovci, district Prilepski; Bogomila, district Veles; Busiljci, district Veles; Dorfulija, district Ovčepoljski; Donji Djudjanci, district Ovčepoljski; Gorobinci, district Ovčepoljski; Pavlešanci, district Ovčepoljski; Brežica, district Skopjanski; Buneš, district Kratovski; Nemanjica, district Ovčepoljski; Gredište, district Žegligovski; Gotovuša, district Nerodimski; Dubravica, district Kriva Palanka; Zubovče, district

Žegligovski; Rudjince, district Žegligovski; Peunovo, district Gornjopološki; Meteja-Kumanovo, district Žegligovski; Orizare, district Kočanski;
Nevoljan, district Vučitrnski; Brnjica, district Sjenica; Biljaša, district
Preševski; Potrk, district Bijelo Polje; Skudrinje, district Galički; Koko-
šinje, district Žegligovski; Židovići, district Plevlja; Kučin, district Mile-
ševski; Duf, district Gornjopološki; Dolac, district Beranski.

## BOSNIA AND HERZEGOVINA

Village of Čičevo, district Trebinje; Medjurječje, district Čajniče;
Mioče, district Višegrad; Ugljevik, district Bijeljina; Janja, district Bijel-
jina; Dvorovi, district Bijeljina; Brka, district Brčko; Seona, district
Tuzla; Plane, district Tuzla; Ivančići, district Sarajevo; Tvrtski Lukavec,
district Tuzla; Ljubače, district Tuzla; Gornja Vogošća, district Sarajevo;
Odžak, district Bugojno; Odžak-Pavice, district Bugojno; Počitelj, district
Stolac; Gorovići, district Sarajevo; Boranjska, district Sarajevo; surround-
ings of Foča, district Foča, Brčigovo, district Rogatica; Cavarine, district
Rogatica; Dovlići, district Sarajevo; Osinja, district Derventa; Mala
Sočanica, district Derventa; Lišnja, district Prnjavor; Hum, district Bu-
gojno; Muslimanska Jasenica, district Bosanska Krupa; Lastve, district
Bosanski Petrovac; Kozice, district Sanski Most; Donji Žabar, district
Brčko; surroundings of Mostar, district Mostar; Orahovo Zagredje, dis-
trict Travnik, Mošanj, district Travnik; Tasovčići, district Stolac; Velika
Kladuša, district Cazin; Otočak, district Derventa; Peći, district Bosansko
Grahovo; Bačvani, district Bosanski Novi; Uvac, district Višegrad; Gornji
Zovik, district Brčko; Kotorsko, district Doboj; Kostajnica, district Doboj;
Karaula, district Travnik; Pećigrad, district Cazin; Gerzovo, district
Mrkonjićgrad; Brštanica, district Stolac; Smailbegovići, district Visoko;
Baraći, district Mrkonjićgrad; Sljivno, district Banja Luka; Dobrnja,
district Tuzla; Pritoka, district Bihać; Kralje, district Bihać; Prusac,
district Jajce; Tobut, district Tuzla; Prekavice, district Banjaluka; Gornje
Hrasno, district Stolac; Donji Vakuf, district Jajce; surroundings of
Derventa, district Derventa; Ljuša, district Jajce; Klokotnica, district
Doboj; Liješće, district Derventa.

## SERBIA, MONTENEGRO, VOYVODINA

Village of Bufce, district Jablanički; Mlačište, district Vlasotinački;
Dobrović, district Vlasotinački; Konjarnik, district Dobrički; Semče, district Niški; Prosek, district Niški; Šarlince, district Dobrički; Milušinci,
district Banjski; Dugopolje, district Banjski; Bukovče, district Begički;
Lipnica, district Gružanjski; Goračići, district Dragačevski; Caparić, district Azbukovački; Rebelj, district Valjevski; Dučić, district Kolubarski;
Ceremošnja, district Zviški; Silbaš, district Bačka Palanka; Parcani, district Kosmajski; Rogača, district Kosmajski; Rakova Bara, district Zviški;
Margita, district Vršac; Koračica, district Mladenovac; Močioci, district

461

Ariljski; Radenka, district Zviški; Srpski Miletić, district Odžak; Neresnica, district Zviški; Koritnik, district Moravički; Velika Mostanica, district Posavski; Sremčica, district Posavski; Doroslovo, district Apatin; Trepča, district Andrijevica; Martinovići, district Andrijevica; Kočani, district Nikšić; Žabljak, district Šavnik; Sotonići, district Bar; Drušići, district Cetinje.

### CROATIA, SLAVONIA, DALMATIA

Village of Šatrinci, district Irig; Bačinci, district Šid; Morovići, district Šid; Petrovci, district Vukovar; surroundings of Županja, district Županja; Donji Vidovec, district Prelog; Vinkovačko Novo Selo, district Vinkovci; Jarmina, district Vinkovci; Vrbica, district Djakovo; Sotin, district Vukovar; Bistrina, district Valpovo; Čačinci, district Našice; Jelisavec, district Našice; Srpska Kapela, district Bjelovar; Vinica, district Vojnić; Požeške Sesvete, district Slavonska Požega; Lovčić, district Slavonski Brod; Donji Meljani, district Podravska Slatina; Bujavica, district Pakrac; Smrtić, district Nova Gradiška; Ravna Gora, district Vrbovsko; Špišić-Bukovica, district Virovitica; Trojeglava, district Daruvar; Skenderovac, district Pakrac; Dapčevica, district Grubišno Polje; Brezovac, district Novska; Mečenčani, district Kostajnica; Novigrad Podravski, district Koprivnica; Diniski, district Rab; Lovinac, district Gračac; Štefanje, district Čazma; Bunić, district Korenica; Rastovača, district Korenica; Lupoglav, district Dugoselo; Imbriovec, district Koprivnica; Pag, district Rab; Brdovec, district Zagreb; Čukovec, district Ludbreg, Kremena, district Metković; Druškovec, district Ivanec; Kalje, district Jastrebarsko; surroundings of Kutina, district Kutina; Tounj, district Ogulin; Lasinja, district Vrginmost; Sračinec-Svibove, district Varaždin; Dumače, district Petrinja; Radovan, district Varaždin; Vodostaj, district Karlovac; Lovrečen, district Varaždin; Divoselo, district Gospić; Sveti Rok, district Gračac; Kuriloved, district Velika Gorica; Mraclin, district Velika Gorica; Manja Vas, district Samobor; Goričan, district Prelog; Popovača, district Kutina; Cernik Čavle, district Sušak; Topusko, district Vrginmost; Vinica, district Vojnić; Bijelići, district Vrginmost; Sop, district Dugoselo; Popovac, district Garešnica; Hrašćina, district Zlatar; Rakovica, district Slunj; Knežević-Kosa, district Vojnić; Podrute, district Novi Marof; Apatovac, district Križevci; Rude, district Samobor; Sveta Helena, district Zelina; Zabok, district Krapina; Stupnica, district Dvor na Uni; Križišće, district Sušak; Dobroselo, district Donji Lapac; Crnac, district Donji Miholjac; Maja, district Glina; Komarevo, district Petrinja; Noršić, district Samobor; Plešće, district Čabar; Velika Graduša, district Petrinja; Vorkafić Selo, district Vrginmost; Bednja, district Ivance; Završje, district Varaždin; Bedekovčina, district Zlatar; Lički Novi, district Gospić; Vrbnik, district Knin; Vodice, district Šibenik; Lopar, district Rab; Dubrava, district Šibenik; Zaton, district Biograd na Moru; Vrbnik, district Krk; Siverić, district Knin; Raba, district Metković; Pristeg-Deranje, district Benkovac; Kaštel-Novi, district Split; Kastva, district Kastav; Vidonje, district Metković; Vrana, district Benkovac; Orlić, district Knin; Prapatnica, district Makarska; Maranovići, district Mljet; Kukuljica, district Preko; Župa, district Imotski; Supetarska Draga, district Rab; Bribir, district Novi; Malinska Poljica, district Krk; Žrnovo, district Korčula; Hosti, district Kastav.

This list is not complete, since I could reconstruct only partly the net of my inquiry. Most of the original material was lost during the enemy occupation.

# INDEX

The letter t preceding a page reference indicates tabular material; the letter g preceding a page reference indicates a graph.